Canada In The Fifties

From the Archives
of Maclean's

Introduction by
Pierre Berton

VIKING

VIKING

Published by the Penguin Group

Penguin Books Canada Ltd, 10 Alcorn Avenue, Toronto, Ontario, Canada M4V 3B2
Penguin Books Ltd, 27 Wrights Lane, London W8 5TZ, England
Penguin Putnam Inc., 375 Hudson Street, New York, New York 10014, U.S.A.
Penguin Books Australia Ltd, Ringwood, Victoria, Australia
Penguin Books (NZ) Ltd, cnr Rosedale and Airborne Roads, Albany,
Auckland 1310, New Zealand

Penguin Books Ltd, Registered Offices: Harmondsworth, Middlesex, England

First published 1999

1   3   5   7   9   10   8   6   4   2

Copyright © Maclean Hunter Publishing Limited, 1999

Printed and bound in Canada on acid-free paper ∞

CANADIAN CATALOGUING IN PUBLICATION DATA

Canada in the fifties: from the archives of Maclean's

ISBN 0-679-88295-X
1. Canada – History – 1945-1963.* 2. Canada – Social life and customs – 1945-
3. Nineteen fifties.   I. Benedict, Michael, 1947-

FC615.C36 1999   971.063'3   C99-931237-5
F1034.2.C287 1999

Visit Penguin Canada's Website at **www.penguin.ca**

Contents

Part Two: The More Things Change,
The More They Remain the Same

Part Three: Profiles in Fame

Part Four: Making News

Foreword
Maclean's in the Fifties

by
Pierre Berton

THE PIECES COLLECTED IN THIS BOOK have, for me, the bitter-sweet flavour of nostalgia. For most of the Fifties I was a member of the editorial staff of *Maclean's*, writing articles—more than 100 by my count—and editing thousands of others at a time when the magazine was undergoing a revolution.

The staff of young journalists that Arthur Irwin had assembled in the years immediately following the war was then beginning to mature. That maturity—Irwin's gift to the country—was making itself felt under the genial authority of Irwin's successor, Ralph Allen. What a cocky lot we were!—all of us young, all energetic, all convinced we were the best. We could not compete with our American rivals on their turf, but we could run circles around them on our own. Our mission, as Irwin had repeatedly told us, was "to interpret Canada to Canadians." No foreign publication could do that.

To be successful, every magazine, whether it be *Vogue* or *The New Yorker*, must understand its audience. At *Maclean's* we wrote exclusively for Canadians, producing for the scholars of the future a kind of social history of the era—and a rough profile of the nation itself.

One morning a week we assembled to exchange ideas for future issues and to shoot down others, with no holds barred. We screamed and shouted as we defended our positions and no one took offence because we all liked and respected one another. Once we had reached some sort of consensus we went out together and drank our lunch.

The creaky Maclean-Hunter presses forced us to operate on a six-week deadline. To stick to that and still stay contemporary—to cover major trends in Canadian society, past, present and future without the immediacy of the front page—was a challenge. But it forced us to take a longer and more thoughtful view than that of the daily press. Our task, Arthur Irwin had said, was "to make the obvious significant."

When Marilyn Bell became the first swimmer to triumph over the chill waters of Lake Ontario, her feat produced reams of newspaper copy; but nothing so thoughtful as June Callwood's brilliant account. The magazine's Ottawa correspondent, Blair Fraser, was able to scoop the newspapers time and time again, especially with his revelations about Mackenzie King. The drug LSD was to become front-page news, but not until Sid Katz travelled to Saskatchewan and, in a remarkable personal account, described its effects on him.

The Fifties was a period when the magazine enjoyed a prestige greater than at any time before. It was almost a medium in itself. It not only reflected the news, but it also made news, and it stood behind what it did. It opened doors for its people. David MacDonald remembers heading for Washington and being told by Bruce Hutchison, "You'll have to see Mike,"—meaning Mike Mansfield, the Senate majority leader. MacDonald went to the Senate, gave the page his card on which he'd scribbled, "Bruce Hutchison sent me." In 30 seconds, Mansfield was off the floor, asking "Where's the man from Bruce Hutchison?"

In those days, *Maclean's* was the place to be if you were a writer. Every budding journalist wanted to see his byline in the magazine, even though the pay was modest and the editorial assessments brutal. Articles for the magazine weren't published until the editors were satisfied that the author had done his best. They had to be written over and over again before the editors were satisfied. That led to the complaint that all pieces sounded alike. No doubt some did. But we were all learning our jobs—editors as well as free-lancers. Unwittingly the magazine was operating as an informal school of writing. We learned as we earned. The results have paid off. If you look at some of the bylines on today's bestsellers you will find many of the graduates of the *Maclean's* school.

We learned from each other and from our peers—not only from the recognized journalists, but also from the novelists who appeared in the magazine—Morley Callaghan, Hugh MacLennan, W.O. Mitchell, Thomas Raddall. The great Bruce Hutchison travelled coast to coast for *Maclean's*; so did the great Yousuf Karsh. Duncan MacPherson illustrated the work of our resident humorist, Robert Thomas Allen, before the *Toronto Star* lured him away.

Young women straight out of university joined the staff as stenographers, got their training by osmosis and went on to become historians, like Christina McCall, or editors, like Barbara Moon, later of *Saturday Night*, or Janice Tyrwhitt, later of *The Reader's Digest*. Robert Collins, who has several books to his credit, started as an intern. Scott Young, Lionel Shapiro, the Montreal novelist and foreign correspondent, Trent Frayne, all became household names as a result of their work for *Maclean's*. One young freelancer, Fred Bodsworth, submitted a dozen articles for the magazine before he made a sale. Later, he joined the staff and went on to write four successful novels, including his classic work, *The Last of the Curlews*.

The pieces in this book, all written nearly half a century ago, stand the test of time. Each tells us something about the century as it was then and also about the times themselves—the golden decade that preceded the Crazy Sixties. It was the era of the great Canadian economic boom, but it was also the start of a burgeoning literary boom—one that brought about the remarkable renaissance we are experiencing now on the eve of the millennium. That didn't happen by accident. One of the reasons why the literary community has been so active in the Nineties is that the seeds of its growth were sown in the Fifties. And much of the credit for that, I submit, belongs to Canada's National Magazine.

Preface

THE 1950S WAS TRULY A TIME when the past met the future. As the decade began, milk was not only delivered to one's home—but done so by horse-drawn cart. People lived in the lighthouses they operated while others were beginning to live in trailers. But post-war automation was poised to revolutionize all jobs, eliminate many of them, and create new work in its wake. The emphasis in public education throughout the decade, as it is again now, was on learning rather than on self-fulfilment.

Looking back, these articles demonstrate vividly the similarities and connections with contemporary events. The Dionne quints remained news-makers in the 1950s, along with debates over Canadian culture, the CBC and gambling. In business, the 1950s department store wars and accompanying battle plans to woo teenage spending resonate in today's commercial world. Celebrities, like Paul Anka and William Shatner who are profiled in this collection, join us with this not-so-bygone era.

Maclean's appeared bi-weekly throughout the 1950s and often generated headlines and controversy. Blair Fraser revealed Mackenzie King as a spiritu-alist, McKenzie Porter revealed that Intrepid, the superspy of the Second World War, was Canada's own William Stephenson, and the personality of Soviet defector Igor Gouzenko was simply revealed, by Fraser again. And more than a decade before the effects of the drug became widely known, Sid-ney Katz provided a vivid but horrifying account of the nightmares that could accompany LSD based on his personal experience.

The archives of *Maclean's* are full of surprises, and the 1950s are no excep-tion. Among the pearls, the whimsical encounter between Bruce Hutchison, that venerable interpreter of momentous occasions, and then reigning sex symbol Zsa Zsa Gabor. Another is Blair Fraser's touching profile of diplomat turned external affairs minister Lester Pearson, five years before Pearson fulfills Fraser's prophecy that he would become Liberal party leader—and prime minister.

The retrospective in these pages also underlines the twists history can take. In 1953, Fred Bodsworth profiled Boy Rocket Scientist Jerry Bull, then 24. Bull later became a central figure in Middle East intrigues and, in 1990 at age 62, Israeli secret agents killed him with two bullets to his head in front of his Brussels home.

THE ARTICLES IN THIS COLLECTION were shortened, but otherwise received little editing. Researcher Michael MacLean assiduously helped track down many of the writers to learn what happened to them and the subjects they wrote about. In this endeavour, he received valuable and generous assistance from Pierre Berton, Sidney Katz, Dorothy Sangster and David North, a former *Maclean's* Senior Editor who has written an in-house history of the magazine. Associate photo editor Kristine Ryall sought photographs from archives across the country. Special thanks go also to editorial administrator Sean McCluskey, who smoothed the transition from withered 1950s magazine pages to a contemporary book.

MICHAEL BENEDICT
EDITORIAL DIRECTOR, NEW VENTURES

Canada In The Fifties

From the Archives
of Maclean's

Part One

A Simpler Time

I Flew in the Avro, Our New Jet Fighter

by Ronald A. Keith

The first reporter to fly in Avro Canada's CF-100 twin-jet fighter tells you what it's like at 10 miles per minute in the perilous atmosphere, and gives you a chilling preview of war in the new air age.

THE BLACK AIRPLANE WITH THE needle nose rose like a rocket over Hamilton. Four miles above the city, the pilot rolled the twin-jet gently over and set course for Toronto, 40 miles away. We were there, right over the heart of the city, three minutes and 40 seconds later. That works out to almost 650 miles an hour, or better than 10 miles a minute.

I was flying in the rear cockpit of the CF-100, Canada's newest and best fighting plane, with test pilot Bill Waterton, who works for A.V. Roe (Canada) Ltd., of Malton, near Toronto, the designers and builders. The Avro CF-100 has been selected by the Department of National Defense, for which it was specially designed and built with plenty of range to cover our northern frontiers, as Canada's new frontline fighter.

If war should come the CF-100, together with the F-86 Sabre, a single-jet, U.S.-designed fighter being built in Montreal by Canadair Ltd., would take the place in the RCAF once filled by the famous piston-driven Spitfire.

Not only does the CF-100 replace the Spitfire and the later British jet, the Vampire, but it hurls Canadian airmen into a weird new world, high above the clouds, where airplanes travel as fast as sound and the final enemies are not the human foes, hostile pilots squatting under glass domes, but the air itself. For at these speeds and these heights the air becomes a killer, as strange and terrifying as any faceless demon out of science fiction. The air can freeze and choke and fry the men who fly in it. Up in that high world lurk mysteries so vast that their natures, much less the means of conquering them, are still hidden by the bland blue of space.

The CF-100 isn't in mass production yet. In fact, there are only two of them. But the RCAF has ordered 100 for earliest delivery. These, together with an order for the same number of Sabres make up a $200-million fighter-plane order recently placed. It's too early to estimate the cost-per-plane of the CF-100, since the prototypes must for the time being bear the huge book cost of the designing and testing of what appears to be a long vicious line.

Two Rolls-Royce Avon jet turbine engines, developing 6,000 pounds of thrust each, make the CF-100 in the words of its designers, "the most powerful fighter in the world today." It will later be powered with Canadian-designed Orendas, built by Avro. These will deliver about 6,500 pounds of thrust each.

The full facts of its performance, together with the details of its armament, are on the secret list but it can fly from Gander, Nfld., to Shannon, Ireland, almost 2,000 miles, without refueling.

I was the first reporter to fly in the CF-100. The only other civilian passenger test pilot Waterton had carried was Defense Minister Brooke Claxton, who made the trip from Toronto to Montreal recently in the record time of 30 minutes, 10 seconds.

I had been tugging alternately at the sleeves of Avro and the Defense Department for weeks for permission to fly in the new jet and the green light came suddenly on a sunny afternoon with a phone call. "Waterton here," said the 34-year-old Canadian pilot, who came to Malton by way of Camrose, Alta., the RAF and a British aircraft company. "I thought we might have a go at it today."

The big warplane had been wheeled out of the flight hangar by the time I arrived at Malton. The black of its flush-riveted highly polished hide is relieved only by a white lightning streak on its flanks, the rondels and the call letters of the RCAF. It's painted black for night work.

While Waterton was getting ready, I looked over the aircraft and talked to technicians who were giving their baby a preflight check. The CF-100 is bigger than the Spitfire. Its wing span is 52 feet and it is 52-feet, six-inches long. The Spitfire is only 29-feet, 11-inches long and 36-feet, 10-inches wide. Fully loaded, the twin-jet weighs 13 tons, almost as heavy as the familiar Dakota, or DC-3 transport.

The CF-100 has two seats—the pilot up front and the navigator in the rear. A navigator is essential because the plane will be used on long-range patrol work.

The wide straddle of its tricycle landing gear makes it look ungainly on the ground but, as Waterton told me, and as I was soon to see for myself, it's anything but sluggish when air-borne with its wheels tucked into its belly. The new plane responds instantly to finger-tip pressure on the power-operated controls.

While I strapped on a seat parachute the mechanics filled the belly of the

Test pilot Bill Waterton climbs up to the cockpit of the Avro CF-100.

jet with lead ballast to take the place of the guns and ammunition which will come later in the plane's career. The technicians explained that ours was no flip, but a test flight with a purpose.

Earlier tests had revealed a trembling of the airframe at certain speeds. There was a theory that this might be caused by the wheel-bay doors being sucked open slightly by the mighty force of the airstream. The job of watching the belly of the aircraft while we scooted along at 10 miles a minute would be done by a remote-controlled periscope camera trained on the suspected area. The films later revealed the doors did creep open and the designers went to work immediately on a correction.

By the time Bill Waterton joined us, preparations were almost complete for the test flight. Bill, who fought in the Battle of Britain, talks slower and flies faster than any pilot I have met. When Group-Captain E.M. Donaldson of the RAF set a new world air speed record in 1946 with a Meteor traveling 616 mph, Bill was his No. 2 pilot. By the way, the world speed record is now held by a U.S.-built Sabre jet—670 mph.

Waterton's flair for aerial showmanship attracted the Gloster people of England who make the Meteor. He was sent on the road demonstrating the Meteor to foreign buyers. He has been out of the service for nearly four years but retains his RAF handlebar maustache. He is currently on loan to Avro Canada.

Bill led the way up the 10-foot ladder into the front cockpit and I followed with the seat-pack of my chute banging against my legs. The rear cockpit where I sat, and which will be the navigator's "office" when the CF-100 goes to work, is simply furnished in contrast to the myriad dials, buttons, levers and gadgets of the pilot's department. There was a radio switch panel: an oxygen-flow indicator, and a plug for the dangling end of the earphone cord. Lashed to the sill was a steel tomahawk. This was for hacking your way out of the cockpit if necessary.

The most fascinating item of furniture was the seat itself. It was virtually an aluminum armchair with a parachute for seat cushion. I was fastened to this chair by a criss-cross of strong straps which went over my shoulders and thighs, holding me securely in place.

Waterton, who has logged 3,500 hours in 71 types of aircraft and has never had to jump, explained what to do in case we had to bail out on this flight. Getting out of a jet is difficult, so difficult that, without special equipment, the odds are against you getting out at all. If you go over the side, for instance, you hit a 600 mph slipstream harder than a brick wall. There is also a very good chance of being sliced in two by the tail assembly.

So when it comes time to say goodbye to a jet in flight you first release a catch which jettisons the cockpit dome, then pull down a canvas screen which protects your face. When you pull hard on the handle of this protective screen an explosive charge catapults you clear of the plane.

If everything works well to this point you are riding an aluminum armchair through the thin cold air high above the earth—at 10 miles up for instance, the air is so cold, about 67 degrees below, that you are in danger of freezing to death if you don't stifle from lack of oxygen. The next manoeuvre is to release the straps which bind you to your seat and fall free and fast, as fast as possible since you have no auxiliary oxygen supply, for some eight miles to a more friendly altitude. Here it is safe to open the chute and drift down the rest of the way in comparative comfort.

At the end of the runway Waterton set the brakes and pulled shut the perspex bubble which encased us like a couple of Buck Rogers characters. He nudged the throttles forward and the turbines screamed like banshees as they whirled faster. The big aircraft trembled to be going under the urgency of six tons of fiery thrust in its guts.

Waterton unlocked the brakes and we began to roll. Jet flight is like being shot out of a cannon. There is none of the gradual buildup of speed you get with conventional planes, the feeling that the aircraft is clawing its way into the sky with propeller talons.

I was slammed down in my seat as we gained speed. Less than halfway down the mile-long runway we were doing 100 mph and I didn't realize we were air-borne until I felt the thud of the wheels nestling into place. By the time we passed the boundary fence we were doing 200, straight and level. Then Waterton pulled back on the stick and I was lying on my back as the CF-100, pointing almost straight up, slashed through the sky.

We were flying level two miles up in less than a minute, and for the first time I had a chance to sort out my impressions of flight in this hottest airplane in the Canadian sky today. I've flown a great deal, as a pilot and as an aviation writer, but I have never had the feeling of literally flying into the future—a somehow terrifying future—that I had as we cruised smoothly, almost noiselessly, through the clear blue sky under our glassy bulb.

There is little noise, the shriek of the blasting engines is left far behind by the speed of the plane. There is only a steady dynamo-like hum of fierce power; the hiss of the airstream. There was little sensation of motion.

Even the earth we had left seemed remote and unreal under our wings as Waterton took us up to five miles. The sun glistened on the ebony hide of the jet and glanced off the fleecy peaks of cumulus that became, under the spell of jet flight, valleys and castles in a land that never was. At one point Waterton did a magnificent loop that took us through the sky in a great circle that began a mile above the earth and ended four miles up in the clouds.

Jet-borne air passengers of the future have a delightful experience awaiting them. But the aircraft I was riding in is not for fun. It is for war. And for the fighting pilot, jets are full of perils as powerful and mysterious as the forces harnessed by the jet engines themselves.

The military pilot must learn to fly, to fight and to survive in a strange world 10 miles or more above the earth. Learning to cope with every emergency of combat in the sub-stratosphere is something like getting set for life on another planet.

Present equipment, including the explosive seat, is adequate up to 50,000 feet, but combat jets will go higher. Thus, before long, the high-flying combat pilot must be equipped like superman to contend with such foes as cold, oxygen starvation, decompression sickness or the "bends" (nitrogen bubbles in the blood), and the explosive bursting of the pressurized cockpit in case of a mechanical failure or a hit on the transparent dome. Furthermore, the blood will literally boil at body temperature above 60,000 feet.

The oxygen at the 12-mile level is so scarce that a man thrust into that atmosphere without his own private air bubble (the pressure cockpit) would lose consciousness in seconds. The pressure cockpit begins to lose its life-giving efficiency as altitude increases, so that an oxygen mask has to be used. Even with a mask, at extreme height a normal flow of pure oxygen is not enough. It has to be forced into the pilot's lungs under pressure. This pressure breathing is a reverse process, which means the upper-air explorer has to learn to breathe all over again, relaxing to let the oxygen flow in, then exhaling forcibly. An elastic corset may be used to help the breathing-out effort.

The pilot is safe from these high-level gremlins as long as he can ride securely in the pressurized cockpit where the air is kept warm and healthful. For low-level jet flying, the cockpit has to have a refrigeration unit too, because the slipstream friction at great speeds heats the cockpit to oven temperature.

If there is combat at these speeds and these levels, it may be assumed that where old-style pilots aimed their guns at engines and gas tanks the jet-combat pilots will shoot for the perspex canopies without which men cannot live in the high world of the future. The pilot who does not get out and down quickly is sure to die. The aero-medical experts are talking now of a rocket belt that will propel pilots swiftly to the earth.

Our landing in the CF-100 at Toronto was smooth and not fast, about 100 mph, much the same as the landing speed of a Spitfire. Waterton told me when we were down that although we had hit 10 miles a minute he had kept the new jet under wraps, using only about 75 per cent of the push burning in the Avons. Even on his record-breaking flight to Montreal with Defense Minister Claxton he had not opened the CF-100 full out.

They are proud of the CF-100 in the Avro organization. Everyone from the men sweeping hangar floors to Walter Deisher, the general manager, was jubilant when the RCAF chose it as its standard patrol fighter. However, they aren't as pleased about the name the RCAF selected to put on the new jet. They're calling it the Canuck. The feeling around Avro is that while this is all highly patriotic it is a highly unoriginal name for a revolutionary aircraft. Besides, the name is associated with the Fleet Canuck trainer, a good but necessarily slow flivver-type plane.

Some alternative names have been offered to Brooke Claxton, who made the final selection. Some were: Tornak, from the Eskimo god of destruction, Iroquois, Thunderbird and Nighthawk. Other names offered by Canadians who would like to see more glamour in the name of the new fighter have been Rapier and Buccaneer.

But wherever it flies or fights it will, by its name, be unmistakably

Canadian. And by its very nature it will belong to the rising fleet of strange deadly aircraft which are flashing through the barriers of sound into the future with men born of the earth, far away, crouched under their glass-clear shells.

THE AVRO CANADA CF-100 *Canuck became operational in 1953 and served for 10 years in* NORAD *and* NATO *squadrons. Nearly 700 were built. Its successor, the legendary Avro Arrow, was cancelled by Prime Minister John Diefenbaker in 1959 before production could begin. The move shocked the nation and continues to inspire debate.*

BILL WATERTON *returned to England in 1951 where he continued to work as a test pilot, before becoming air correspondent for the* Daily Express, *in 1954. He wrote two books about flying, then returned to Canada in 1959 and now lives near Owen Sound, Ont.*

RONALD KEITH *was the longtime editor of* Canadian Aviation *magazine before he joined Canadian Pacific Airlines as its public relations director in 1952. Keith, who also wrote a biography of the airline's founder, Grant McConachie, died in Vancouver of a heart attack at age 71 in 1985.*

Goodbye, Barney, A Tribute to a Horse That Delivers the Milk

by McKenzie Porter

MARCH 1, 1951

WHEN THE FIRST-GRADE school children of today grow up, the only place they'll be able to see a horse earning its own living will be on the race course, a sward jealously restricted to descendants of the Anglo-Arabian thoroughbred.

By then specimens of the Percheron, Suffolk Punch, Clydesdale, Cleveland Bay, Justin Morgan and other purebred draft animals, perfected by man during a thousand years of equine eugenics, will doubtless be on show in zoos alongside their only known relatives, the zebra, the quagga and the ass.

Humble halfbreeds like Barney, who hauls a milk wagon for Borden's Dairy in midtown Toronto, will all have vanished to those green pastures which, if there is any justice, are reserved for the noblest of animals in heaven. Barney has been jogging his jingling load around the streets for five years now but has done nothing to excite any unusual admiration in his owners' breasts. They treat him well, but whether he dreams of better days nobody knows and nobody cares.

It is true Barney can distinguish between red and green traffic lights, judge distances accurately when cutting around parked cars, pick out from several thousand houses those of 268 customers and during his master's holidays show strange milkmen around the route with never a mistake.

But, like any other dairyman, Borden's expects these qualities in a milk horse. Barney would have to sell the tickets, collect the money and keep the books himself to ensure his ultimate survival against the ruthless encroachments of the machine.

The tractor is fast ousting the horse from the farm, and the truck is chasing him from the city. In the past 10 years, Canada's horse population has nose-dived from nearly three million to fewer than two million. The RCMP has forsaken the horse for cars, motorbikes and aircraft. Even the cowboys are turning speculative eyes on the ubiquitous Jeep. Thousands of unemployed Canadian horses will be shipped this year to Belgium where they are relished as steaks and roasts.

It is getting harder every day to find men who can handle horses. Old-fashioned blacksmiths are almost as rare as centaurs. City veterinarians know the horse only in theory and make most of their money off dogs and cats. Stables used to pay carters to take horse manure away. Now market gardeners, especially mushroom growers, pay high prices to collect it.

Ever since man learned to make fire, and suddenly discovered he could enslave stronger animals, the horse has humped and heaved his loads. The horse's contribution to civilization has been matched by no other quadruped. The era of the horse in bondage, which archaeologists believe has lasted a million years, is coming to an end, right now, with the speed of a thunderbolt. It is a poignant moment in history.

That's why we present Barney today. A year from now it might be too late.

Barney has kept his job to date because it is one at which the superiority of the internal combustion engine still remains in faint doubt. Although it costs Borden's $2 a week more to work Barney than it does to run a truck on the same route, Barney's advantage lies in his brain.

It is a small brain, smaller in proportion to his size than a dog's, a pig's or a cat's. But still big enough to give him a slight edge on the truck. Nobody has yet invented a truck which will follow a milkman up the street to save him walking back and forth, drive itself while the milkman sorts his tickets and cash, haul itself clear of deep snowdrifts, or make any better time than Barney does on his particular circuit.

Barney has another card up his feathers (those long hairs on his fetlocks).

He enables Borden's, a benevolent firm, to keep in employment many old and faithful milkmen who are just as nervous of steering wheel, clutch and brakes as up-and-coming bottle jockeys are of Barney's hoofs, teeth and psychological quirks.

A few months ago, however, delegates to the Ontario Milk Distributors' Association Convention in Toronto deplored the continued existence of Barney and his brethren in city streets as anachronisms and traffic snarlers. Borden's is fast coming around to this view. Since the end of the war, it has cut down its string of horses from 350 to 100—now divided between its midtown dairy on Spadina Crescent, where Barney works, and an uptown dairy in the north.

Borden's has found, like many other dairies, that gasoline pays better than horse sense on hilly routes which used to require a pair of horses, or on routes far from the stable. Even one-horse beats like Barney's, however, are now facing extinction. English truck designers are putting out a handy, rugged little vehicle which, a year or so from now, will sound Barney's death knell.

In the meantime, Barney faces the *Gotterdammerung* of his breed with quiet dignity. Barney, a big brown horse with three white feet and one black, works eight hours a day, five days a week. He's off every Sunday, since Sabbath deliveries have been stopped, and one other day, according to his own condition and the availability of six spare horses among his 30 stablemates. On his working days, Barney draws a ton of milk around 18 miles of backwaters in a district of old-fashioned students' rooming houses just north of the University of Toronto on Bloor Street West.

He wears out a set of rubber shoes each week in summer and a set of steel shoes each month in winter. His pay is 20 pounds of hay and three gallons of oats a day, supplemented by carrots to keep his blood in good order, occasional potatoes to fatten him, linseed oil and molasses for energy and a hot bran mash as a combined treat and laxative on Saturday nights.

Not even sex appeal lightens his monotonous routine—he was gelded as a youngster. Stallions are apt to get ideas about mares in city streets, with spectacular consequences. Jack Mumford, Borden's "vet," says sadly: "The milk horse's life is very humdrum."

But Barney makes the best of it. He has learned to unlatch the door of a baker's van and steal himself the odd loaf of bread. He once drank half a bottle of whisky proffered by two festive soldiers on Christmas Eve and never so much as showed the whites of his eyes. His driver was once horrified to learn from a crowd of bighearted high-school girls that Barney had consumed six ice-cream cones, four bags of candy and two big chocolate bars. Although horses are supposed to loathe the taste of flesh, Barney has accepted hot dogs, hamburgers and steak pies. He once ate a whole onion, probably in mistake for an apple, but he rejects dill pickles.

Like all other horses he's covered entirely in hair and walks on the single toe of each foot. His ancestors had five toes but through lack of use, two withered up the leg to become Barney's splint bones and two vanished. In common with his species Barney's fundamental characteristic is still excitability to motion. The wolf had fangs, the bull horns, the boar tusks and the lion had claws for protection. But Barney's family had nothing and

Barney, (right) visits with a friend during a break.

became fleet. There are some who believe, although it has never been proved, that a horse's eyes magnify every image to about eight times its actual size. If this is true Barney's readiness to "get on his horse" is understandable. When you think of some of the sights around Toronto he must live in a fearsome world.

Barney came into that world under bleak and uninspiring circumstances. His father and mother knew none of true wooing's lingering sweetness. They were united in an Ontario farmyard with cold mathematical consideration for their proportions and the utility and cash value of their projected progeny.

A milk wagon is lighter than a brewer's dray and heavier than a baker's van. Borden's needs a horse midway between the powerful slow walker and the speedy trotter. Barney's dad, therefore, was a Clydesdale from Lanarkshire, Scotland, standing 17 hands and weighing nearly 2,000 lbs. (A hand is the vertical height of a man's clenched fist: four inches.) His mother was a trim buggy mare standing 15 hands and weighing around 1,000 lbs. The result was Barney, standing 16 hands and weighing 1,500 lbs.

You can see he has little or no thoroughbred blood by his convex Roman nose. A concave or dishpan nose shows descent from the Godolphin Arabian, the Darley Arabian and the Byerly Turk, desert stallions introduced to English mares in the 17th century to reinforce Arab blood imported effectively during the Crusades. Every modern race horse, all over the world, stems through the stud books from these three sires.

Barney is known as "a coarse horse." Walter Midgeley, his driver, who's had a dozen horses in his 30 years with Borden's, describes him as "an average horse but a little bit independent." When he was bought by Borden's at a country sale and brought into the city he was blasé about the noise, traffic, lights and paved streets. It takes a month to break some horses to city streets. Barney was settled after four days. But he took a dislike to his first driver and went on strike. He refused to leave his stall for three days. Only Midgeley could get him out. The two have been together, with only one short break, ever since. Says Midgeley, "When you get used to a horse you stick to him. It saves a lot of time and trouble."

Barney refuses to be put upon. Sent out as one of a pair, to school a horse new to the city, he found his pupil bone lazy. Finally Barney, who had been taking all the load, gave his partner a good deep bite in the neck. The young horse began to pull his weight immediately.

Next, however, the new horse shied at a manhole cover while they were following the milkman up the street. (Inexperienced horses always mistake manhole covers for holes.) He dragged Barney and the wagon across the car tracks. Much ringing of streetcar bells and blowing of horns didn't help any. When Barney recovered control, the wagon was on the opposite side of the street facing in the other direction. Barney coaxed his pupil into a trot, made a U-turn at a convenient intersection after waiting for the lights, and brought the wagon back to its route.

On cruel winter mornings, sympathetic housewives sometimes invite 65-year-old Midgeley in for a quick coffee. Barney resents these interruptions and starts nickering impatiently. Midgeley gulps his coffee for, as he says, "The milkman's biggest nightmare is 'Will my horse be there when I get back?'"

Once in summer when Midgeley was gone unusually long collecting money, Barney pulled into the shade of a drive, lay down and went to sleep, and caused a housewife to run into the street calling: "Come quick! Your horse has died on me!"

Barney has only really disgraced himself twice. Accustomed to getting an apple every day from a minister, Barney was disappointed one morning when his benefactor failed to appear. He waited until Midgeley was up at a house then heaved his wagon across a lawn, over a flower bed, through a hedge, into a drive and started nuzzling the minister's back door. That cost Borden's money.

Last Christmas, Barney and Midgeley were held up at an intersection by Eaton's Santa Claus parade. When Barney saw the grotesque effigies advancing upon him—probably magnified eight times—he reared, brought his feet down on a car fender, and spoiled Midgeley's chances of his year's "safe driving medal."

One year in a horse's life is equal to three in a human's. By our standards Barney, who is actually nine, is really 27 and it's only natural that he should be getting set in his habits. Unfortunately he got so set in one habit that every day he performed an essential function in the same place. This is common with horses. Borden's was eventually telephoned by a furious householder who inferred in much stronger language that the atmosphere surrounding his front door suggested a stable.

Barney lives in a stable two floors above Borden's modern garage on College Street, several hundred yards from the dairy. He ascends unassisted and unattended four long padded ramps to rows of clean, whitewashed, well-ventilated stalls. Leaving at 6 a.m. and returning at 3:30 p.m., Barney halts automatically outside the harness room door where Ernie Prudames, the stable foreman, and Walter Midgeley put on or take off his trappings. Although Midgeley always releases him from the stall first thing in the morning and ties him up last thing at night to preserve mutual confidence, Barney finds his way alone around several turns to the harness room and stops for a drink en route at the big white bathtub trough.

After hooking up in the garage at the bottom of the ramps Midgeley drives Barney each morning to the dairy where the horse waits in a long queue of wagons to take his turn at the loading platform. During this line-up Midgeley can get away for a cup of coffee if he wants, because Barney usually follows the wagon in front until it's his turn at the platform, where Midgeley meets him.

One subzero morning, however, Barney failed to keep the rendezvous. He was nowhere in the line-up. Midgeley ran back to the stables thinking Barney had gone on strike. The foreman dispatched another driver in a truck to Midgeley's route to see if Barney had gone ahead alone. But Barney couldn't be found. At last an agitated garage proprietor rushed up to the dairy with the report that a horse had manoeuvred his van around behind dozens of cars inside his establishment and was warming himself at the big radiator.

But Barney is usually co-operative. Midgeley only uses two commands: "git up" and "whoa." If he wants Barney to trot he merely knocks on the side of the van with his knuckles. Barney has brought Midgeley safe home through freezing rain and dense fog when the driver could barely see as far as the horse's ears.

Barney's an orthodox eater which makes him easy to care for. He's content with one meal at 5 a.m. before work, a nosebag in the street and a supper at 5 p.m. In resting, Barney's habits are also conventional. He can relax completely on his feet. Only once or twice each night does he lie down and close his eyes in sleep. Then it is only for an hour or so. Horses don't sleep standing up. If they do "drop off" while on all fours they immediately fall down.

Borden's horses are so well kept that many go on working until their 20th year. Charlie, a big blue roan with a dash of Percheron, has, according to Ernie Prudames, "worked for 16 years and never been sick, lame or lazy." Several 20-year-old mares retired by Borden's have been sold to farmers and later thrown two or three good foals.

But, as he is only nine, it is doubtful whether Barney will live out his useful life in harness. He is not heavy enough to become one of a plow team, though he could serve as "third horse" for lighter work on a farm. The tractor, however, is damning his chances of this sort of retirement every day. There is just a glimmer of hope that when Borden's becomes completely mechanized Barney will be sold to a less progressive dairy. Even then the possibilities of him reaching a ripe old age will be remote.

It seems a certainty that one of these days Barney will have to be humanely destroyed. If it is any consolation to the hundreds of city animal lovers who will miss him he will then turn up for the last time as meat for their pet dogs.

BORDEN'S LAST *horse-powered deliveries were made in the mid 1950s; the last such deliveries in Toronto were made in 1960, when Jack Richards, a driver for Findlay's Dairy, retired.*

After writing for Maclean's *between 1948 and 1962,* McKENZIE PORTER *was a columnist at the* Toronto Telegram *and the* Toronto Sun, *retiring in 1990. He lives in Toronto.*

Ben Kravitz's Conquest of the New World

by Ken
Johnstone

APRIL 15, 1954

AT MONTREAL'S METCALFE and Burnside Streets, directly behind the Sheraton Mount Royal Hotel, there's a place called Bens De Luxe Delicatessen-Restaurant where more than 8,000 customers daily come to pack themselves into a 150-chair capacity space, pausing an average of precisely 12 minutes to consume a smoked beef brisket sandwich on rye with a dill pickle on the side and, of course, a cup of coffee.

Other sandwiches are served there, and soft drinks. You can order pastrami, salami, corned beef, liverwurst or smoked whitefish, or you can have a steak. But 80 per cent of the customers—who range from elegant socialites in evening clothes and silk toppers to ragged bums, from businessmen breaking away from a smoke-filled convention room to ladies of pleasure resting their weary feet, from blasé college boys and their chattering co-eds to starry-eyed tourists seeking a glimpse of sports or theatrical personalities whose autographs adorn the restaurant's walls—will end up by ordering a hot smoked-beef sandwich, dill on the side and coffee.

The sandwich will cost them 30 cents, the dill will cost a dime and the coffee another dime. Between two slices of round rye bread baked especially to Bens' specifications, the dark red smoked meat, slice upon slice, almost half an inch thick, protrudes from the sandwich, and its tantalizing aroma is akin in quality to its taste which some people say is akin to nothing less than ambrosia in a kosher form.

Paul Whiteman has called Bens [Bens does not have—and has never had—an apostrophe] "the place where I fall off my diet." Veteran vaudevillians Benny Field and Blossom Seeley called it their "other home." Burl Ives threatened to compose a song in celebration of Bens, and Charles Laughton has passed his august English approval. A restaurant owner in Miami offered to buy Bens' smoked-meat recipe on a royalty basis. A magician playing a date in Hong Kong wrote to tell Ben that the Chinese owner of the establishment where he was playing had been in Montreal and thought that Bens smoked meat was superb. A skiing party from Boston, passing through Montreal on the way to the Laurentians, wrote in advance to order large quantities of sandwiches to be picked up between trains. Sally Rand sent an eyebrow-raising Christmas card. A Kirkland Lake, Ont., businessman wrote an urgent letter confessing that he had boasted so vigorously of his expert knowledge of smoked meat that he had become committed to throwing a party to prove his point; he needed an immediate shipment from Bens. Outside a large San Diego, Calif., restaurant there is a sign, "Bens— 3,018 miles northeast."

All this has had singularly little effect on the proprietor of Bens, a 71-year-old slight, grey-haired, long-faced man in white coat and apron who greets his customers at the door or wanders almost aimlessly from table to table, mopping up spilled coffee here, removing a dish there, filling a water glass, lending a hand to hard-pressed waiters whose job it is to keep the customers fed, satisfied and moving. When Ben Kravitz came to Canada 55 years ago, he was happy and grateful that at last he had found a country where he could work as long and as hard as he wanted to without anyone stopping him. His only grievance today is that his wife, his three sons, his son-in-law and the 100 employees who call him Pop seem to be in a gigantic conspiracy to prevent their beloved boss from continuing to put in the hours and do the kind of work which has given him his deepest satisfaction. Already they have cut down his 20-hour work day to a mere 17, and if they had their way they'd reduce it still further. Because for all the success that has come his way in recent years, Ben still has a heart like a balloon, has never learned to say no to a panhandler and is essentially the same person as the boy of 16 who earned $2 a week at his first job in Montreal.

The story of Ben Kravitz, his wife, Fanny, daughter, Gertrude, and sons Solly, Al and Irving is one that has a remarkable parallel with the story of New Canadians today. For it is more than the story of a successful restaurant owner. It is the story of how a penniless immigrant family licked the New World through extraordinary courage, sagacity and humanity; of how the family became both commercially successful and fine citizens.

The Europe of Ben's youth was a hostile and unhealthy world for Jews without position or influence. Like the DPs of today, Ben ran away from it, dreaming vaguely of the opportunities and tolerance to be found in North America. And like so many DPs today, he found the North America of his dreams to be a bewildering and sometimes hostile place. In Montreal, the latent antagonism between English and French often finds its outlet at the expense of the Jew. And in Montreal, a newcomer from Europe must learn not one but two new languages if he is to survive. Ben brought with him two priceless assets: an unquenchable energy and a great sympathy for human beings. They served him well.

Ben Kravitz was born near Kovno, Lithuania, in 1883. He was the last of seven children born to poor parents, and prospects for him were dismal. The only hope on his horizon was the fact that relatives on his mother's side, the Joseph family, had gone to America. Settling in Montreal, they had prospered and in letters to his mother they urged that Ben should try his luck in the New World. They offered to send a steamship ticket for him to Hamburg. Ben would have to find his own way to Hamburg.

Ben set out from home, a big husky lad of 16, with all his worldly possessions in a sack on his back and a sizeable consignment of Lithuanian beer sent hopefully ahead, care of the steamship at Hamburg. He ran the Lithuanian-Polish border at night and the rifle bullet which was sent winging after him by an alert border guard went through the flesh of his heel without breaking a bone. He limped through Poland and scuttled safely across the German border without incident, finally reaching Hamburg to find both the ship and the beer awaiting him. He picked up his ticket and $15 in cash that accompanied it and on shipboard he engaged in a brisk traffic with fellow steerage passengers, doling out the beer at 50 *pfennigs* a cup. With the proceeds, and some spirited bartering in blankets and clothes, Ben ran up his capital of $15 to $110 by the time he reached Montreal and he was immediately able to refund the cost of his steamship ticket to his cousins.

One of the cousins had a butcher shop and Ben got his first job there. In addition to the $2 a week he got his board, and he felt pretty good about it. "It didn't matter what they paid you," he remembers. "The big thing was that you had a job." Ben set to work immediately trying to learn English and French, and when he felt that he could make himself understood, he got a job in another Joseph enterprise, bottling ginger ale and beer at $3 a week. Paying board of $2 a week he found that he could still save money. But his biggest financial windfall was in the winter when he worked shoveling snow for the tramways company which paid the fabulous rate of $2.50 a day, with a night rate of $1.75. Ben worked both day and night, and took a loaf of bread with him for food, washing it down with melted snow.

After four years in Canada, Ben had a modest little fortune of more than $200 when he met Fanny Schwartz, who had been in Canada about a year. Like Ben, she had fled her country. Born in Odessa, where the pogrom was a popular Cossack sport, she had seen other Jewish people cruelly beaten and had hidden once in a pile of garbage to escape a similar fate. Her father had been desperate to get her out of the country before worse happened to her, and failing to obtain either passport or visa he had bundled her off with 100 rubles. She, too, ran the border into Poland at night, crawling through a muddy ditch to escape the guards. Making her way into Germany, she was arrested for walking through a field of grain but was released with a scolding by a sympathetic policeman. Finally, she got to Antwerp and eventually reached Montreal, where her stepmother had second cousins.

Fanny rested at her stepmother's relatives for three days before she went out looking for work. She found a job right away. It was in a men's clothing factory pulling bastings out of suits. Her first week's pay was 75 cents.

The boss's family took a liking to Fanny and invited her to move in with them. One night there was a fire at the house and among the neighbors who appeared to help with the rescue work was a handsome young man by the name of Ben Kravitz. Fanny was overawed by his remarkable command of the English language and he was smitten with the comely little round-faced girl from Odessa. He shyly suggested taking her out for a five-cent sundae. One sundae stretched into another and then to the nickelodeon and long walks, until one day Ben just up and asked her to marry him.

They walked home from the wedding, two bright and eager youngsters. Ben had bought a basket of apples at the market, for they made the room smell nice. They set up housekeeping in the dining room of Fanny's former employer and they paid $6 a month and had the use of the kitchen. The honeymoon was brief. Ben was back at work next morning, a serious married man with new responsibilities.

The ambitious Fanny wanted a home of their own. Ben was still working at the bottling factory earning a steady $6.50 a week, making syrup for the ginger ale and washing bottles, and six months after they married, they rented a four-room house at $10 a month, and took in three boarders at $3 each a week.

Their first boy, Sol, was born there in 1905. By this time, Ben had decided to branch out for himself and he bought a horse and a delivery wagon. He was able to average as high as $10 a week delivering cloth to textile factories in the St. Lawrence district, carrying them up five and six flights of stairs with the ease and careless strength of youth. He was big, and strong as a horse, and he worked like one, night and day. But one day he came from a delivery to find the horse and rig and load of goods vanished. He finally located the horse and rig near the docks, but the goods had been stolen. Ben made good every penny of the theft to his customers, but it wiped out his saving of seven years, close to $500.

It was at this point that Fanny decided to open a small shop on St. Lawrence Blvd. She bought a modest stock of canned goods, fruits, candies and biscuits. Ben made a counter of boards and erected a partition in the long narrow store that gave the family a room in the back. Business was poor at the start and then Ben had the bright idea which was to make the family fortune.

He had noticed that when factory girls dropped into the store they often asked for sandwiches. He remembered his youth back in Lithuania when the farmers used to pickle and smoke beef briskets that acquired a new tang and succulence in the treatment. He decided to try to prepare meat this way and to serve it in sandwiches. He bought the meat and put it in brine, then went out in the back yard and smoked it over hickory bark. Before long, his first smoked beef brisket was ready for customers.

But if the brisket was ready, the customers were not. The meat looked black and dirty from the smoking and they were not tempted. Vainly, Ben and Fanny begged them to try the sandwiches, at five cents each, or even a free sample. But this was not the kind of sandwich they knew or trusted. They ordered cake. But Ben and Fanny persisted and finally, one factory girl gingerly tried a sandwich after Ben's patient pleading. She liked it and she told other girls about it. They tried the sandwiches and were won over to the exotic fare. The business slowly began to improve.

Ben meanwhile continued his backbreaking schedule, working long hours back in the factory, making deliveries at night and then coming home late to prepare the meat and the pickles. Finally, his schedule caught up to him and he doubled over one day, helpless with pain. He was hurried to the hospital with perforated ulcers. The 190-pound Ben came out of the hospital weighing 120 and went back to the factory the same day. The family needed the money. Irving was born in 1915. Fanny rented a room at a midwife's for the occasion and stayed there a week.

Back on the job, she knew that the store which had soaked up all their money was their only salvation. She slaved away there, keeping it open until the last night owl had called and then, catching a brief snatch of sleep in the back room, she was ready for the first early-bird customer in the morning. Sol manfully did his share and Al, at five, had his regular chores. By 1916, business was good enough to encourage Fanny to seek more space. She negotiated the sale of their location for $700, enough cash to close a deal for a larger store with a $40 monthly rent but with three big rooms for living quarters in the back and a large basement. It was just half a block away from the old store and the customers faithfully followed the aroma of hot smoked meat.

By the time Gertrude arrived in 1917, there was plenty of room for the family and Bens was becoming well-known throughout the garment district. The demands of the business were sufficient to require Ben's attention full

time now, and he gave up his factory job. They kept the store open seven days
a week, 24 hours a day and they did a thriving business day and night.

In 1929, with the arrival of the Depression and the wholesale blight
of the needle-trade business that supplied the bulk of Bens' customers, the
family decided on its greatest gamble to date. With business falling off, the
family decided to move from the needle-trade district into the bright-lights
area where there was activity at all hours. Ben rented a little grocery store in
the parlor of an old house on the northwest corner of Burnside and Metcalfe
and the family spent six weeks converting it into the new Bens Delicatessen
Sandwich Shop. This was the gamble that paid off in the present prosperity
and international renown of Bens.

Here, smack in the centre of the hotel and tourist district just on the
fringe of the night club and theatre bright lights, two short blocks from
Montreal's heart of Peel and Ste-Catherine Streets, the legend of Bens really
began to grow. Celebrities of the theatre world discovered the place and their

Bens at 2 a.m., 1954. Note the line-up at the back for tables.

fans followed them. Along with Paul Whiteman, Benny Field and Blossom
Seeley, Red Skelton openly plugged the place in his vaudeville appearances
at Montreal theatres. George McManus ran an outrageous plug in his
comic strip, Bringing Up Father, when he depicted a billboard announcing,
"You want to be strong? Eat at Bens." Sir Anthony Jenkinson in his book,
Where Seldom a Gun Is Heard, devoted a page to quotes from Bens' whimsical
signs: "Imported sturgeon needs no urgin'," "Mary had a little lamb, What
will you have?" "Use less sugar, Stir like hell. We don't mind the noise." Even
Walter Winchell discovered Bens. Members of New York's Metropolitan
Opera making a Montreal appearance staged an impromptu concert at Bens.
It became the place to go after the last night club had closed its doors or for
a quick bite between shows or a morning coffee and sandwich before starting
the new day's performance.

However, all this did not happen overnight. There were long years of
hard slogging, uncertainty and setbacks for the whole family before Bens
became finally established. Ben did not wish to see his children end their
careers with an apron behind a counter. Sol had ambitions to become a clothing designer and got a job as a cutter in a clothing shop. Al wanted to be a
musician and studied the violin. Irving took a college course. But they all
helped in the store in their spare time.

Al was making brilliant progress with the violin, playing in the Montreal
Symphony Orchestra. But in 1929 he broke the little finger of his left hand
in a basketball game and it remained permanently stiff. Sol found there was a
large and apparently unbridgeable gap between the job of a cutter and that of
a clothes designer and in 1933 he came into the store. When Irving finished
college with an accounting degree he told his father that he too felt he could
be useful full time in the store. Ben said, "Remember, son, I'm not asking you
to come in. I'd like something better for you, though we need you." In 1935,
Irving came. And Gertrude became the store's cashier until 1941 when marriage presented another career to her. Her husband, Herb Polaski, joined the
firm in 1951.

At the beginning of the new venture, the burden fell chiefly on Ben,
Fanny and second son Al. Among them they never left the store for five minutes. They cured their meat and made their pickles in the basement. They

bought a house a few doors away and when Fanny and Al went home to snatch a few hours' sleep at night, Ben ran the store alone. It was in the worst days of the Depression, but Al was puzzled that they were not doing better with their sales. Then, one morning he opened the Montreal *Herald* and saw a big three-column picture of Ben, taken at dawn, handing out sandwiches to a long line of destitute men. "It was only leftovers," his father lamely explained.

Al knew his father well enough to realize that protest was useless and Fanny loyally supported her husband. The line-up continued through the Depression, and Ben continued to make up sandwiches and dole them out. As times improved, the line-up gradually disappeared but Ben continued to be a soft touch for a hard-luck story, or a man with imagination. One expert panhandler captured Ben Kravitz's imagination with his flowery and erudite speech. He was in tatters and Ben protested, "Such an educated man cannot be dressed like that." He took the panhandler home and rigged him out in his own best suit. But two days later the panhandler reappeared in his old filthy clothes, but looking happy.

"What happened to you?" Ben asked, bewildered.

"Who can beg in those clothes?" the panhandler answered, and dismissed the subject. Ben meekly fed him and listened in awe to his flow of words.

Isaac Ruvinoff, a talented professor of dancing, was suddenly bankrupted through a fire and Ben met him on the street shortly afterward and asked him to eat at the store. That was nearly 20 years ago and Ruvinoff is still Ben's mealtime guest, complaining loudly and bitterly if the service falls below his rigorous standards.

The boys began to worry every time Ben disappeared from sight. He went for a short walk one winter evening in a smart new overcoat, came back in a ragged torn topcoat. He had swapped coats with a derelict on Dominion Square. "He needed it worse than I did," Ben explained.

But Ben makes a sharp distinction between those who can't work and those who won't work and dishwashing has always been his penalty for the latter when they tried to beat him for the meal check. "Sometimes during the Depression years, it seemed we had more dishwashers than customers in the place," Al remembers.

A shabbily dressed girl came into the shop one evening and ordered a bowl of soup with bread. Ben watched how carefully she stretched out the bread with the soup and he sent over a steak and dessert to her. She objected, "I didn't order this."

"It's okay," Ben explained, "we always make it on the house for the thousandth customer each week." The girl took one long look at Ben's homely smiling face and then burst into tears. She didn't even have the money for the soup. She was broke and out of work. Ben got her a job with a clothing firm whose owner was a regular customer.

The biggest improvement in the firm's finances took place when they persuaded Ben to abandon the cash desk to Gertrude. He had collected rubber cheques amounting to hundreds of dollars. One day, Al saw from a distance of five yards a girl offer Ben a decidedly peculiar-looking $10 bill. He knew better than to interfere but when the girl left the store with her change Al turned up the bill. It was Mexican.

"You accepted this?" he asked his father reproachfully.

"I didn't have my glasses," his father offered. "Besides, she was such a nice girl, and she probably needed the money very badly."

In spite of Ben's quixotic attitude toward money the business grew steadily. In the early Thirties, long before the era of Pacifique Plante, who as city morality director in the late Forties closed down Montreal's flourishing vice rackets, the district had its share of bordellos, and smoked-meat sandwiches were popular with waiting clients. This catering service later developed along more legitimate lines into an important part of Bens' operations. Conventions and sales conferences are frequently graced by Bens' smoked-meat sandwiches and dill pickles.

As the business gradually grew, Ben continued to punish himself with long hours, working each day from five in the morning until past midnight. They were able to afford a maid by now and one day Ben came quietly home and asked the maid, "Would you please call the doctor?"

The maid called the doctor on the phone.

"Ben himself asked for me?" the startled doctor queried. She confirmed it. "He must be bad. I'm sending an ambulance right away," the doctor said hastily.

Ben was hurried to the hospital where Fanny was recovering from a broken ankle. She was to leave that day but the doctor told her gravely, "You had better come downstairs. Ben is here and he's pretty sick."

It was perforated ulcers again, complicated by a ruptured appendix and peritonitis. The doctor doubted that Ben would survive the operation and Fanny looked upon her grey-faced husband with sinking heart.

Ben came out of the operation, life feebly flickering. He seemed to have lost the will to live. On the second day following the ordeal the doctor spoke to him sternly. "Ben," he said, "they need you at the store." It was only then that Ben began to rally.

The doctor estimated it would be six months before Ben could move about and he questioned that he would ever be able to work again. But after three weeks of steady progress Ben began to fret, and lose weight. So the doctor sent him back to the store. In his familiar white coat and apron again, Ben quickly recovered. It was then that the family determined he would never again assume the load that had nearly finished him twice.

By now, all three boys were active in the business and it was decided to enlarge and remodel the premises which were hopelessly overcrowded most of the day. They doubled the capacity by purchasing the entire building. Yet it was not enough and a few years later, in 1949, they made their biggest gamble of all by purchasing a building diagonally across the street, tearing it down and erecting a modern three-story building at a cost of $300,000. The top two floors were turned into office space and 3,000 square feet on the ground floor made a new Bens De Luxe Delicatessen and Sandwich Shop. The old Bens was retained; it is destined to be demolished in the city's plan for the widening of Burnside Street. Meanwhile, it handles the overflow from the new Bens, which has already proved inadequate to handle rush-hour crowds.

Faced with the realization that their wildest dreams had still failed to come up to the demands of an apparently endless reservoir of patrons, Ben and his family are now in the process of contracting for a new building to be erected alongside the new Bens De Luxe Delicatessen. It will double the present floor space to 6,000 square feet, doubling the seating capacity from 150 to 300 persons and give them a million-dollar structure.

During the war years, when both help and supplies were hard to get Ben abandoned his seven-day week and 24-hour schedule in favor of a six-day week and a 22-hour day. In the family vote for the shorter week his was the only dissenting opinion and Fanny claims that on Sunday, when the store is closed, Ben looks 10 years older as he wanders distractedly around the house with nothing to do. He still wears his white coat though, even on Sunday, and over her protest that callers will think he is the butler. The only event that makes him happy on Sunday is when there is something to do at the store, something to fix or repair. Yet he has always been notably inept at repairs. Whenever he disappears into the basement with a monkey wrench to fix a leaky pipe Fanny waits patiently for his despairing cry "Fanny, quick, call a plumber!"

While the family has persuaded Ben to cut down his own working day down to a bare 17 hours, from 5 a.m. to 10 p.m., on Nov. 3, last year Irving caught his father guiltily slipping out of his apron at 7 p.m., and he asked, "Leaving so early?"

His father apologized, "It's our 49th wedding anniversary."

Last year, the boys prevailed upon Ben and Fanny to take their first holiday in almost 50 years. They engaged rooms at a smart New York City hotel, made train reservations and packed them off for a well-earned rest. Two days later, Ben was back at the store at 5 a.m. "It was lonesome down there," he explained. The boys stopped trying.

Yet more than simple dedication to work is responsible for the remarkable growth and success of Bens. With it goes a thorough knowledge of the food business, from the purchasing of the best quality of foods to the most efficient handling of large numbers of people. In this knowledge the whole family shares. Ben himself still goes to the market at the proper season to buy cucumbers, tomatoes and peppers, and farmers vie with each other for his business, for he pays the best price and expects the best products. He pays cash deposits for his orders and asks for no receipts, speaking a French that the boys swear only the farmers can understand. He also selects the choice beef briskets that go into the smoked meat; he supervises the curing and smoking of the meat according to his own formula, as he does with the dill pickles that are only slightly less famous than the smoked-meat sandwiches.

Quick service is the key to the amazing daily volume of customers that pass through the store. At rush hours there is always a line-up but people do not mind waiting if they know that the wait is a short one and that they will be served promptly once they have been seated. The atmosphere of Bens is deliberately calculated to discourage long dawdling over coffee. While full-course meals are available, they are not featured. The lighting is bright to the point of glaring and waiters pounce on you the moment you are seated. The volume of business per square foot of space is carefully calculated; within two years the volume in the new Bens exceeded the per square foot volume in the old Bens, though there is a greater feeling of elbow room in the new building. In the kitchen and in the supply rooms, the most modern and efficient equipment is installed. Ben boasts he has the only air-conditioned garbage-disposal room in the country.

The family's loyalty and affection for their senior member verges on fanaticism and they cheerfully attribute practically every favorable feature of the store's operation to Ben. But Fanny herself has played a major role in the growth of Bens and it was her word that was final in the lighting and color scheme of the new building, just as it was Fanny who watched and checked every move of architect, engineer and contractor. The boys tell how she stood by with a supply of assorted nails, bolts, nuts and screws to furnish the workmen and prevent them from using this excuse for going off the job. From the first day that they had to hire extra help, Ben proved himself constitutionally incapable of firing anyone and it was the forthright Fanny who assumed this task.

Ben consistently refuses to admit he is slowing down but sometimes he takes little cat-naps during his 17-hour day. The boys are familiar with the pattern. He brews himself a cup of tea with lemon, leans an elbow on the counter and pretends to be deep in contemplation. A guilty start and a quick look around always finds the boys looking in another direction. Thus they support his gentle fiction.

Ben's hearing is not as acute as it once was. Recently, Irving advertised for a waiter. The next morning a customer came in, spoke to Irving, and Irving called to Ben, who was behind the counter. Ben heard, "Pop, will you get him a coat?"

Ben came from behind the counter and motioned for the man to follow him. Together they went down the stairs to the basement and Ben produced a broom. "Sweep the floor," he ordered. The man dutifully began to sweep the floor and Ben nodded his approval, reached in a locker for a coat. Suddenly the man stopped sweeping and threw down the broom. "What the hell does a guy have to do in this joint to buy a Coke?" he demanded.

BEN KRAVITZ *died in 1956, aged 73, and Fanny at 81 in 1968.*

Bens ultimately moved into a larger space in a building next door and the deli is still run by family members—Jean Kravitz, a daughter-in-law, and several grandchildren. And it remains a major attraction for tourists and locals. Smoked beef on rye continues to be the most popular sandwich; it sells for $3.95, a dill pickle costs $1.50 and coffee $1.00.

KEN JOHNSTONE *was assistant editor of* Maclean's, *from November, 1955 to September, 1956.*

What It's Like to Live in a Lighthouse

by David
MacDonald

AUGUST 1, 1954

IT WAS THE VERY DEVIL of a winter's night in 1952. As Margaret Tucker, the wife of the lightkeeper on Gannet Rock, N.B., dried the supper dishes and watched her three small children playing on the kitchen floor, a cacophony of noises assailed her ears. Outside the wind shrieked as it churned up the Bay of Fundy. Sleet rattled windows and beat a tattoo on the wooden shingles of the lighthouse towering up against the side of her box-like concrete home. Her husband, Frank, was up in the lighthouse lantern where a gigantic beacon winked its warning across black waters. Hard by, a foghorn moaned dismally. But the only sound that troubled Margaret Tucker was a persistent pounding at the back door. Gannet is an island—a mere cluster of rocks—and the pounding was the sea around it, wanting in.

Suddenly, battered by a huge wave, the door flew open. A torrent of brine rushed into the kitchen, washed back like a breaker on a beach and—happily—slammed the door shut again. An inch of water covered the floor as the pounding began anew.

"Come," said Mrs. Tucker, lifting one child and shooing the others ahead of her, "we'll play in the living room till this blows over." And so, calmly, they did. Today, after seven years of life in a lighthouse, Margaret Tucker, a dark attractive woman of 30, concedes that it differs mightily from life in her old home town, cosmopolitan Montreal.

Gannet Rock is half an acre of nothing thrusting up abruptly from the

Bay of Fundy's depths, eight miles south of Grand Manan Island. Its rocks, rounded by eons of rubbing by the sea, were once a nesting place for gannets. But these birds have since gone, evidently convinced that so rugged an isle is not for them. There isn't a blade of grass on it, for there's not a trace of soil. It is ringed, instead, by seaweed and surf. Often, in angry moments, the sea sweeps over the entire island, casting spray a hundred feet in the air to the top of the lighthouse tower. The tower, like the Tuckers' home adjoining it, is anchored to the rocks by heavy steel cables.

In this unlikely setting Frank and Margaret Tucker have spent most of their married life, tending a light. They have a three-week vacation ashore but remain all the rest of the year on the rock, unable to roam more than few paces in any direction from their doorstep.

They belong to a widely scattered community of almost 700 men, women and children who live in lighthouses on remote islands or frowning headlands around the Bay of Fundy. Gannet Rock happens to be the most isolated of them all.

Except in summer, when the odd tourist journeys out to the island to have a close-up look at their light—a 1,000-watt bulb encased in a barrel-like lens—the Tuckers have no visitors except a supply ship which may or may not call twice a month, depending on the weather. They rely on the ship for everything from round steak and clothing to nose drops and drinking water. Three of their four children have known no other home but the lighthouse. When the fourth, eight-year-old Frank Jr., moved ashore to Grand Manan to go to school, he stared at a house and asked, "Where's the light?" He had trouble adjusting himself to schoolmates, too, for while the Tucker children see whales, seals, ships and storms from their home, they don't see other kids.

Their nearest neighbors are other lightkeepers—Ottawa Benson, 14 miles to the west on Machias Seal Island, and Harvey Benson, at Southwest Head, on Grand Manan. To them, the outside world is a voice on the radio and the truest word for their life is lonely. Even the light in their window means "Keep away."

Gannet Rock has been blinking its warning each night, sundown to sunrise, since Christmas Day of 1831. Built by Saint John, N.B., merchants who wearied of losing ships and cargoes to the treacherous shoals that surround it, it's now part of the federal Department of Transport's vast network of light stations, fog alarms, sentry ships and bobbing buoys that steer shipping safely around Canada's jagged coastline.

This network is at its thickest in the Bay of Fundy, one of the most ornery bodies of water anywhere. An arm of the Atlantic Ocean reaching up to separate Nova Scotia from New Brunswick, it has all the moody quirks that cause seamen to shudder: frequent, sudden and violent storms, murky fogs, swift-running tides, lurking reefs and shoals and a ragged rocky shore. Fundy's floor is littered with the bones of ships and men, its victims of more than 200 years.

The Gannet Rock, N.B., lighthouse, in splendid isolation.

In earlier times, sailing on the Bay of Fundy was a dangerous operation. The lighthouses and their keepers have changed this so much that Sir James Bisset, retired captain of the *Queen Elizabeth*, has said, "The Bay of Fundy is as safe for navigation today as any body of water in the world." Three years ago, a life-saving crew that operated out of Grand Manan for 50 years was disbanded. There just wasn't enough business.

Even among Fundy's lightkeepers, inured to isolation, Gannet Rock is regarded as a seagirt Siberia. Margaret Tucker knows the feeling. Until she met Frank, an RCAF radio instructor, and married him in Montreal in 1943, she had never seen a lighthouse—"except on postcards." To her, a foghorn was the sound on a radio commercial for soap. They spent three days of their honeymoon at a light station on Big Duck Island, near Grand Manan, where Frank had been an assistant keeper before the war.

"At night," she remembers, "we could see the light from Gannet Rock. I used to feel sorry for the poor people who had to live way out there—practically nowhere."

Four years later, after Frank had tried vainly to make a go of radio repairing on Grand Manan, he got a lightkeeper's job. Soon a government boat put them ashore at their new home—Gannet. Margaret Tucker gazed up at the light tower, boldly striped in black and white and reminding her somehow of a prison convict; and at Gannet Rock itself, hemmed on all sides by the sea. Her reaction was immediate, vocal and typical of a city-bred girl of 23. She said, "Gawd, no!"

It was eight months before she got ashore again—to have her second baby, Linda, now six. And after that another 14 months crept by before she and Frank went ashore together for a holiday in Montreal. Since then she has come to terms with Gannet Rock.

"I used to hate every square inch of it," she says, "and if we were transferred ashore I'd still pack pretty fast. But you can get used to anything—even loneliness. Sure, sometimes we get bored—who doesn't—but most of the time we're too busy. I've got a family to look after and Frank has the light."

At first glance, looking after the light would seem to be the easier job. Frank, a boyish-looking man of 35 with a crooked grin and an overgrown crewcut, has to see that his beacon is lit at dusk—a flick of the button and it begins flashing automatically—and turned off at sunrise. Comes fog, another button sets his foghorn to blaring through the mist. The diesel generators that power the light and the great boilers that belch compressed air into the foghorn must be kept in good order, for their failure could cost lives. Once a year the tower and Frank's dwelling need painting and repairing.

Because someone has to be on watch 24 hours a day, in case fog rolls in or the light goes out, Tucker has two assistants to spell him—his father, Cecil, a grizzled one-time fisherman, and young Harvey Greenlaw, from Grand Manan.

In physical terms their job amounts to semi-retirement. The toughest task is simply being there. On Gannet Rock there's nowhere to go and the sights to be seen there—playful porpoises cavorting, whales spouting, gulls diving at immense schools of herring, lightning dancing on the water and the ever-changing mood of the sea—soon become commonplace. It has none of the diversions of larger, less barren islands where lightkeepers can pick wild berries and dulse in their spare time, cultivate gardens, dig clams, collect gulls' eggs, gather queer-shaped pieces of driftwood for sale to tourists, or take their children swimming on the beaches. The opportunities for boredom are overwhelming.

"If there isn't any work to do," Frank says, "we damned well make some." With time hanging heavy on their hands, lightkeepers have been known to polish the lenses of their lights each day for 10 days in a row, or to scrape, paint and repaint one door a dozen times. Hobbies, too, help to chase tedium. Some lightkeepers carve model ships or make novelties from seashells. Others study astronomy or whittle lobster pegs while their wives knit, hook rugs or crochet doilies that inevitably grow into tablecloths. One keeper spent years inventing perpetual motion machines that didn't work.

Frank Tucker's hobby is amateur radio. At night, when the light has been lit and the children are asleep, he puts in hours searching the radio band for familiar call letters, and talks to hams in England, Australia and South America. When they're on watch through the night, the men of Gannet Rock read, listen to all-night disk jockeys on neighboring New England radio stations, drink black coffee, play solitaire or write letters.

Writing is an old pastime on Gannet Rock. Eighty years ago, an assistant keeper who was bored to the bicuspids wrote a note. It said he was lonely and would like to get a letter. He put it into a bottle and tossed it into the waves. The bottle drifted ashore at Seal Cove, on Grand Manan, where it was found by a young girl. She sent him a note in reply. Two years later they were married.

In 1906, helper Charles Moran wrote a history of Gannet Rock, sealed it in a rum keg and cast it adrift. It landed in the Saint John *Telegraph*. Prefaced by "As I had a few leisure moments," it told, among other things, of how the first keeper, a Mr. Wilson, and his assistant ventured out from the rock in a dory in 1837 and were both drowned in a storm.

A year after Moran wrote his history, Gannet Rock witnessed one of Fundy's worst shipwrecks. On a dark rainy night the freighter *Hestia*, out of Glasgow, rammed into the Old Proprietor Ledges nearby. Thirty-three people were lost. The only survivors were six men who stuck with the ship and were rescued by a life-saving crew from Seal Cove.

While Gannet Rock is an extremely solid chunk of real estate, it's easy to forget this when the waves come crashing over it. About 10 years ago a new keeper went to the island with his wife. "Nice peaceful place," he told her. "You'll like it."

At last report he was still munching these words. Thirty solid days of storms, capped by a roaring hurricane that flooded their kitchen, sent them packing.

The Tuckers have had to bail out their kitchen several times. It's a disturbing experience but other threats trouble them more than the sea. One is fire. Until diesel generators were put on the island last year, they nervously fed kerosene to the beacon in their wooden lighthouse. "A fire here would be a big success," says Frank. "There's nowhere to run but into the sea."

The sea and the rocks make it unhealthy for the Tucker children to stray outside their home. Sometimes in winter they stay indoors for five and six weeks at a time. Only in summer, when storms are fewer, do they get out regularly to play in a small walled quadrangle beside the house.

"Lighthouse families always seem to be close together," Margaret Tucker says quietly. "Not just physically either. We *feel* close, like a family should. Our house is more than just a place to eat and sleep. It's the centre of our lives. Some of my happiest moments have been here, in winter, when it's blowing hard outside and we're all cooped up together."

The isolation that knits a family together also, paradoxically, breaks it up, as it did last fall when the Tuckers stood on the rocks and waved goodbye to eight-year-old Frank, their eldest son, who was bound for his grandmother's home on Grand Manan and school. "We hated to see him go," Frank says, "but what could we do? He has to get an education and—almost as important—learn to get along with other kids."

Though most lighthouse families are isolated geographically, they keep in touch with the outside world. Mail, magazines and newspapers come to Gannet Rock with the supply ship. The Tuckers have a radio and Margaret, like mainland housewives, suffers daily with soap-opera heroines. A radio-telephone linking them with the New Brunswick mainland and other lighthouses is meant for official business only. But it's nobody's secret that on the odd night when one lonely lightkeeper calls another for an unofficial chat nobody hangs up.

Mrs. Tucker uses it also to order groceries from Harvey Benson, a Grand Manan lightkeeper who, in turn, relays her shopping list to a grocer. Here arises another problem that would tax any housewife. Since the supply ship comes only twice a month, she has to plan all meals more than two weeks ahead. If she forgets something, they go without. "I forgot salt once," Margaret recalls, laughing, "so Frank boiled down sea water. I'll never forget salt again."

Supplies for Gannet Rock and neighboring Machias Seal Island are ferried out by Weldon Ingalls, a 37-year-old Seal Cove lobster fisherman. Though his trips, paid for by the Department of Transport, are tentatively scheduled for the first and 15th of the month, storms may delay him as much as two weeks. Ingalls needs calm water to land at Gannet and even then it can be hazardous. A few years back, a fishing boat brought Mrs. Tucker's grandmother to the island for a visit. She stepped cautiously into a dory, thence to shore. Then, in rapid order, her trunk was lost overboard and a sudden wave sat her down. She hasn't been back since.

Worse than being unable to land on an isolated island is being unable to get off it in a hurry. Last spring Allison Benson, an assistant on Machias Seal Island, acquired a cranky appendix, indicating a hasty trip to hospital. But storms came up. It was three days before they let up and Allison, by then a stretcher case, could be taken to the mainland. He was operated on just in time, the doctor said. When seas are rough, broken arms and nagging toothaches become major ordeals. On each of the three occasions when Margaret Tucker has gone ashore to have babies she has played it safe by leaving two months early.

Occasionally when Weldon Ingalls brings supplies to Gannet Rock he takes one of Tucker's assistants ashore for a month. For every three months they spend on the island they're entitled to one off. Frank, who earns about $3,500 a year tending Gannet light, takes his family to Montreal for a radical change of scenery on his annual vacation.

In mid-December Ingalls goes into the woods, fells a spruce tree and takes it out to Gannet Rock. "That's when we feel loneliest," says Margaret Tucker. "It's Christmas and we'd love to be somewhere with people, to go walking in the snow and see some bright lights—the kind they have on Ste-Catherine Street."

When winter melts into spring the Tuckers see no bursting buds or green grass. To them spring is warmer weather, more fog and the sight of brightly painted lobster boats and great flights of birds winging back from the south. Many of the birds get no farther than Gannet. "They get in the beam," says Frank Tucker, "and fly right at the lantern. Some mornings, spring or fall, we find 200 to 300 birds lying dead around the tower." Once, before Tucker's time, a black duck flew at the lantern. It crashed through plate glass—three eighths of an inch thick—and lived to fly off again.

So powerful is the Gannet Rock beacon that when it flashes to the west on a clear night it lights up the home of Ottawa Benson on Machias Seal Island. Benson is a slight balding man of 46 whose face is creased and browned from years of squinting seaward. He is a great-grandson of Walter B. McLaughlin, a legendary figure among lightkeepers. Old W.B. kept the light at Southwest Head, on Grand Manan, and like many a lightkeeper he found that to keep from mental dry rot it was best to keep busy. This he did by reading everything from grammar textbooks to tomes on canon law. Though his formal education had ended abruptly in the fifth grade, he taught himself Greek. At night he pored over the *Iliad* by lantern light. He came to be regarded as one of the best-read men in New Brunswick, and one of the most patriotic. When a son was born to him on July 1, 1867—the first Dominion Day—he named him Ottawa.

Ottawa Benson, a grandson of the 1867 Ottawa, became a lightkeeper in 1944, neither for tradition's sake nor because he eschews society. "I was a lobster fisherman," he explains frankly, "and business was bad." Ever since then he has been living on Machias Seal, a small crescent-shaped island off the coast of Maine. While not so bald as Gannet Rock, it's a bleak mound of rock and grass against which the wind whistles eerily when it blows off the water.

"It may be a bit lonely at times," he says, "but it's steadier work than fishing and I'm my own boss."

Unlike the Gannet lighthouse, which is painted with perpendicular black and white stripes, Benson's tower on Machias Seal is entirely white. There are other differences. Gannet light shows a half-second flash, an eclipse of two seconds, another half-second flash, then 12 seconds of darkness. Machias Seal merely flashes every three seconds. Similarly, the two stations have distinct fog signals, varying in the length of their throaty blasts and the silence between them.

These differences are all part of the language of the sea. Lights and foghorns aren't merely warnings; they're also landmarks, each with a set of characteristics as obvious as Bing Crosby's ears. Passing within sight of Gannet light at night, a skipper can identify it, and thus check his position, by timing flashes and eclipses for one minute. He can also check his position by timing the blasts of a foghorn. Two lights on the east coast may have the same flashing signal. But not two in any one area. It's assumed that a skipper off Grand Manan knows that he is not off, say, Cape Breton.

Ten miles across the water from Machias Seal, at the southern end of Grand Manan, Southwest Head light squats on the edge of a jagged 500-foot cliff, scalloped with surf. Here, where Walter B. McLaughlin read Homer in another day, Harvey Benson, who is not related to Ottawa, now tends the light.

Benson, a stocky red-faced man who has been a lightkeeper for 25 of his 41 years, speaks with the New England drawl of Grand Manan, as distinctive as its famous smoked herring. ("What with mah choahs, the TV and the doag bahkin' every moanin', a man don't hahdly git any sleep.")

During the first four years of the Second World War, Benson and his wife, Thelma, had Machias Seal Island all to themselves. Usually they worked in shifts but once Harvey stayed on the job five days and nights in a row. Often their relief ship came only once a month and they were reduced to skimpy rations. But there was a cloak-and-dagger element to their work. Every evening they received coded radio messages telling them whether to light their lamp that night. With German U-boats skulking around the Bay of Fundy convoy lanes, beacons were sometimes blacked out.

From an office in Saint John's grimy old Customs Building, Frank McKinnon, the department's superintendent of lights for the Bay of Fundy district, keeps in close touch with 158 lightkeepers spotted along the 1,000 miles of coastline in his district. Daily by radio, phone or radio-telephone, they report to him on weather condition and request supplies, help or—in some cases—transfers.

He also handles job applications. At present there is a waiting list for most lights, Gannet and Machias Seal excepted. "When times get a little tough and jobs are scarce," McKinnon says, "a lot of people decide they want to keep a light. We look them over pretty carefully. It's a vital job and our men have to be dependable." Applicants who merely want to get away from nagging wives, escape the H-bomb or recuperate from nervous breakdowns are politely turned down.

At Saint John, the transport department has two elderly ships, the *Dollard* and the *Franklin*. Nautical trouble shooters, they freight supplies to lighthouses, set out buoys and round up strays that have been cut loose by storms. Once a month, one of them steams down to the mouth of the Bay of Fundy, hauling provisions to the Lurcher lightship. Stubby, barnacle-studded, this sea-going lighthouse rides at anchor year after year, 18 miles off Yarmouth, N.S. Her lights, atop both masts, gleam through the night like a cat's eyes, warning ships away from the treacherous Lurcher shoals.

Another stop for the supply ship is Bon Portage Island, off the southwest coast of Nova Scotia. It's the home of Canada's best-known lighthouse dwellers, Morrill Richardson and his wife, Evelyn, an ex-schoolmarm turned author. The Richardsons had been living in happy obscurity on Bon Portage for 16 years when Evelyn decided—with no previous literary experience—to write a book about it. Her book, *We Keep a Light*, won the Governor General's Award for creative non-fiction in 1945 and became a Canadian best-seller.

In it Mrs. Richardson described their old oil-burning beacon and the antique foghorn they had to crank by hand whenever ships came near. Soon after, coincidence or not, the Department of Transport installed an electric light and an automatic fog-alarm on Bon Portage.

Morrill Richardson is still tending his light and Evelyn is still writing. Last year she produced her first novel, *Desired Haven*, which won the $1,000 Ryerson fiction award.

Though they are isolated, lack many of the comforts of modern living and must work hard at filling in long lonely hours, most lighthouse dwellers are happy tending their lights. Records show that those who don't like it don't stick at it; those who remain grow deeply rooted to their rocks and their islands and the sea around them. But they have a hard time convincing outsiders—city folks who feed on entertainment—that they aren't slightly mad. Recently Cecil Tucker, the elderly assistant keeper at Gannet Rock, was coming ashore for a holiday when he got to talking about strange sights.

About a year ago, he said, he and his son Frank were keeping watch around 3 a.m. when they saw a round greenish glow that hovered over the water, then shot ahead. In fits and starts it circled the island.

"Flying saucers," he explained gravely.

Had they reported them?

Mr. Tucker snorted eloquently. "What's the use?" he said. "People'd only say we'd been living too long in a lighthouse."

THE TUCKERS *were the last family to live on Gannet Rock, and they left in 1955 after eight years. Individuals continued to live on the island until it was "destaffed" on May 1, 1996. (The lighthouse is now maintained automatically by the Coast Guard.) There are now 52 manned lighthouses in Canada: 27 in British Columbia, 24 in Newfoundland and one in the Bay of Fundy.*

FRANK TUCKER *died in 1987 at 68. Margaret remarried, and now lives in New Glasgow, N.S.*

DAVID MACDONALD *joined* Maclean's *as an assistant editor in 1952, shortly after placing second in the magazine's annual short story competition. He left in 1957 and worked at* The Globe and Mail, Star Weekly *and* Reader's Digest *before becoming a full-time freelance writer in 1985. He lives in Kingston, Ont.*

How Marilyn Bell Swam Lake Ontario

by June Callwood

NOVEMBER 1, 1954

THE DAY THAT 16-YEAR-OLD Marilyn Bell swam across Lake Ontario was a cold, sunny 9th of September. The small, tousle-haired Toronto schoolgirl swam 40 miles from a log retaining wall in Youngstown, N.Y., to a slimy concrete breakwater off Sunnyside, Toronto, and thereby collected for herself whatever immortality awaits pioneer marathon swimmers, plus approximately $50,000 in contracts, prizes and gifts from Canadians who were moved by her courage.

While the lustre of her achievement cannot suffer, the swim will be best remembered, by those who watched it firsthand, for the petulance and undignified bickering of the officials and for the weird newspaper war it provoked between the *Toronto Star* and the *Toronto Telegram*. No other human-interest event in Canada since radio covered the 1936 Moose River, N.S., mine disaster has stirred a reading and listening public so deeply and no other event has had such a bizarre and hectic setting for its drama.

At one point, with the girl's heavy, aching arms flogging the water between them, and her brain almost unconscious with exhaustion, a Canadian National Exhibition official and Marilyn's trainer engaged in a sharp, shouted debate over the most advantageous spot for her to land. At another point, *Star* and *Telegram* reporters pushed and connived for possession of the stretcher and ambulance that would carry the pale, shaking swimmer from the dock. Every now and then, rarely and wonderfully, someone showed real concern for Marilyn Bell.

The swim had been planned by the Canadian National Exhibition sports committee as a crowd-drawing spectacle to demonstrate the prowess of Florence Chadwick, a 34-year-old American considered by many to be the world's greatest woman swimmer. The CNE paid Miss Chadwick a $2,500 advance of the $10,000 she was to collect if she succeeded in swimming the lake. Two Canadian swimmers, Winnie Roach Leuszler, 28, who had swum the English Channel three years before, and Marilyn Bell, 16, dived into the lake behind Miss Chadwick to demonstrate something or other to themselves and their friends. Neither expected any reward if she failed, but Mrs. Leuszler had hopes that a large hat would be passed among CNE spectators if she succeeded. Marilyn Bell, who was the first woman to complete a 25-mile swim eight weeks before off Atlantic City, expected nothing.

The expenses of both Canadian swimmers, including a $700-a-day boat rental, were being paid by the *Toronto Star*. Marilyn's coach, Gus Ryder, had offered the *Telegram* an opportunity to sponsor his swimmer at the same time as the *Star*, but the paper refused.

Around four o'clock in the afternoon of the day it happened Toronto suddenly seemed to awake to the fact that Marilyn was the only swimmer left in the lake. Half-hour bulletins on two Toronto radio stations, CKEY and CKFH, relaying broadcasts from boats beside the swimmer, whipped the city into a frenzy of excitement. The highly vaunted Flo Chadwick had been pulled out of the water, sick and retching, at 4:30 in the morning; strong, heavily built Winnie Leuszler had quit in agony from cramps 10 hours after her start. But a five-foot-one, 119-pound child was still swimming 17 hours after entering the water at Youngstown.

Offices began to empty and a traffic jam formed between downtown Toronto and the grandstand that the CNE had built overlooking the lake. Radios everywhere were tuned to those stations which offered live coverage. Toronto's two publicly owned CBC stations, which had remained aloof from the swim, began to pirate news bulletins. Marilyn Bell's Grade 12 classmates at Loretto College School, who had been fretting through History, Latin, Geometry and French, had already been dismissed in the middle of Chemistry so they could buy flowers and take them down to the lakefront to meet Marilyn.

Down at the lakefront, several thousand people were gathering on the plank seats of the grandstand. Most were in summer clothes, with their arms crossed over their chests to keep off the cold wind from the lake. Far out on the grey water was a smudge that some people thought was a group of boats. A newsboy cried: "Read all about it—Marilyn only an hour away!" Pink flares, sent up by the CNE, cracked high in the sky to guide the swimmer in. A pink *Telegram* fluttered in the stiffening wind. "2 miles to go!" screamed the headline.

Beside one of the grandstands was a floating wooden dock and a small square of lawn fenced off and guarded by policemen. Inside, reporters, cameramen and CNE officials were milling around in a swelling excited babble of conversation.

Rumors of the brewing newspaper battle kept *Telegram* reporters at the lakefront anxious. Marilyn was, they knew, accompanied by *Star* boats, and it seemed likely that an attempt would be made when she landed to keep her away from the *Telegram*. One story had it that a *Star* launch would pick her out of the water as soon as she touched shore and take her to a hiding place. The *Telegram* hired an ambulance to stand by and planned to have stretcher-bearers hustle her from the water when she touched the CNE jetty. They would take her to a *Telegram* hiding place. In the meantime the *Telegram* printed 3,000 extras, with the headline MARILYN MAKES IT! hidden in *Star* trucks around the CNE grounds.

A loudspeaker blared "Marilyn Bell has been pushed west by the strong wind . . . for every 100 yards north she swims, the waves push her 200 west but she's still in the water!"

George Duthie, CNE sports director, pushed through reporters as he climbed out of a motorboat. "I've just seen her," he said gloomily. "She's in bad shape. She'll never make it."

Seven miles out in the lake, across choppy water, being blown almost parallel to the shore, Marilyn was ready to quit for the fourth time. She was treading water, swimming two strokes and stopping to tread water again. She could sometimes see the grey shoreline past the heaving waves and for hours it hadn't been getting any closer.

By now she had been in the water 18 hours. Florence Chadwick's contract with the CNE had permitted her to pick her own time to make the swim. This meant that she also picked Marilyn's starting time and Winnie Leuszler's.

Both Canadians had envisioned the swim as a race and they wanted to start at the same time as Chadwick and touch Canada ahead of her. Miss Chadwick announced at nine o'clock Wednesday night that she would start at 10:30. Marilyn Bell, who hadn't slept all day, promptly climbed into the loose black silk-and-nylon suit distance swimmers always wear, low under the arms and high over the legs to reduce friction. Jack Russell, a professional boatman who was to operate the outboard motor on the lifeboat that would guide Marilyn, gave her a lucky four-leaf clover and she wrapped it in wax paper, put it on top of her blond, boyishly cut hair and pulled a white rubber shower cap over it. She was ready.

At eleven o'clock, Chadwick, escorted by a detachment of U.S. soldiers, had emerged from a Coast Guard building, walked sternly through reporters and Youngstown citizens who had collected in a drenching rain and slipped feet first into the water. She began swimming immediately, a strong, beautiful stroke that invoked cheers. Marilyn watched her as a spotlight followed her in the black water, then she slipped off her robe, kissed her parents goodbye, walked to the edge of the Coast Guard lawn and dived off the retaining wall. It was 11:07.

Marilyn started off rapidly, like a sprint swimmer. Her simple purpose was to get ahead of Chadwick, and stay there. For a while the searchlights shone on the two women who were joined a few minutes later by Winnie Leuszler, and then they were lost in the blackness of the night.

This was the part of the swim Marilyn had dreaded most, swimming in darkness for the first time in her life. Ahead of her she could see only the flashlight held in her tender by Ryder, her trainer and the outstanding swimming coach in the country. She had said earlier: "If I feel an eel on me, I'll scream!" but when the first eel, a little one eight inches long, struck her stomach and hung there she kept calm and punched if off with her fist. In the next few hours three more clamped to her thigh and she beat them off without any hysteria. Ahead of her, beyond the falling and climbing water was the white pencil line of a CNE searchlight that burned all night as a guide to the swimmers.

What Gus Ryder later called the crisis came around four in the morning, at almost the same time that Chadwick quit swimming. Marilyn, exhausted from fighting 12-foot-high waves, stopped swimming and looked pleadingly at Ryder, "I'm cold, I'm numb," she called in her light child's voice.

"Marilyn," Ryder shouted back, "you've swum all night and that's really great. If you can do that you can do the rest. In another hour the sun will come up and it will be really nice." He fastened a paper cup into a ring at the end of a six-foot stick, poured corn syrup into the cup and passed it to the girl. She stood in the water, treading lightly to keep afloat. She sipped the nourishing drink and tried not to cry. Ryder didn't offer to take her out of the water and after a moment she let the paper cup float away in the darkness and started swimming again.

When dawn came Marilyn was 14 miles into the lake. Ten feet away from her was the 24-foot lifeboat, *Mipepa*, steered by Jack Russell and carrying Ryder, a *Star* reporter-photographer named George Bryant, and a 13-year-old boy, Peter Willinsky, whose father owned the boat. Some distance away, and well behind the *Mipepa*, was the yacht, *Mona IV*, with Marilyn's parents and *Star* reporters and photographers aboard.

As the sky lightened, everyone in the lifeboat was shocked by Marilyn's appearance. Her normally pretty and gay face was haggard, the muscles around her mouth slack and her eyes glassy. She said later, "My arms were tired, my legs ached, my stomach hurt in one big awful pain and I couldn't get my breath. I wanted to quit. When it gets to your stomach, marathoners say, you're through." For more than an hour she had been swimming with her arms alone, dragging her legs motionless in the water behind her.

Bryant noticed that she was crying and found himself crying too. "If it had been my decision," he later told friends, "I'd have got her out of there right then."

Ryder passed Marilyn more corn syrup, but her hand was shaking so much the cup spilled into the water. Next he passed her some liniment he had scooped out of a jar and dropped in a paper cup. Under his direction, she rolled over on her back and rubbed her legs with the liniment. She continued to cry.

"Swim over here, Marilyn," Ryder called. "We'll take you out."

The girl began to swim and Ryder watched her closely, noticing that her legs were moving again. "Pull away, Jack," he ordered. Russell moved the throttle and the boat moved away from Marilyn. She kept on swimming, still crying.

"That's a bad sign," Ryder told Bryant. "If she keeps on crying, I'll have to take her out." After a while she stopped crying and as the sun began to climb she was swimming strongly.

The nautical phase of the battle between the *Toronto Star* and the *Toronto Telegram* began a few hours later. As dawn broke, *Star* and *Telegram* boats crossed paths as they attempted to find the ferry boat that Chadwick had hired to follow her. They could find no trace of it. Four hours after Chadwick had been pulled from the water, both newspapers discovered her at the National Yacht Club in Toronto. After that it was Marilyn's swim, with Leuszler not a serious contender. At eight in the morning the *Telegram* contingent aboard the CNE press boat *Ja-Su* decided to get their first close-up pictures of Marilyn in the water. They found the schoolgirl swimming strongly beside the *Mipepa* with Russell at the helm. Flanking the *Mipepa* snugly were two *Star* yachts.

The *Ja-Su*, carrying four *Telegram* reporters and photographers, was crowded to the rear by Marilyn's escort. A dinghy was lowered with the photographers and rowed to within camera distance of the swimmer. Later, when the *Telegram*'s second boat, with two reporters and a photographer aboard, found the flotilla, tempers grew shorter. The *Telegram* sought to wriggle between the *Star* boats and there was talk of ramming. A woman threw a pop bottle, missing a newsreel photographer by inches. A *Star* boat and the *Ja-Su* lightly collided. The *Star* later explained that its boats had been trying to protect Marilyn Bell from "eager fools in powerboats" who were jeopardizing her safety.

The water temperature, which can be a bitter 50 degrees even on a late summer day, kept between 60 degrees and 70 degrees, the only break the lake gave Marilyn that day. Though her navigators were unaware of it at first, currents were pushing her west of Toronto. Toward noon the waves began to quiet.

At 10:30 a.m. Ryder noticed Marilyn tiring again. He scribbled on a blackboard the news he'd been saving for such a crucial moment: FLO IS OUT. He held the board so she could read it. Marilyn, delighted to learn she had outlasted the world's greatest woman swimmer, swam with renewed vigor. When she faltered again, toward noon, Ryder wrote some more notes in chalk: SWIM FOR ME and DON'T LET THE CRIPPLED KIDS DOWN. Marilyn stared at the notes, put her face in the water and began swimming again. Her stomach was a steady pain and her legs ached. Ryder refers to his chalked notes to Marilyn as "blackboard psychology."

In Toronto, CNE President Robert Saunders announced that since Florence Chadwick was out of the water, forfeiting $7,500, any swimmer who finished would get "a substantial amount of money." Around four o'clock in the afternoon the *Star* boats heard the news on their radios that Winnie Leuszler was out of the water and that Saunders had announced Marilyn would get $7,500—the balance of the Chadwick fee—if she finished.

It seemed doubtful, to everyone but Ryder, that she could finish. She had been in the water for 17 hours and she hadn't slept in 31 hours. The Toronto Harbor Commission, concerned that she might drown before anyone could reach her, dropped two dinghies into the water with lifeguards at the oars and they began to row beside her, watching her steadily. As she swam, relaxing her arm when it was in the air and pulling it hard through the water, relaxing the other and pulling, relax and pull and kick, kick, kick, kick, she began to fall asleep. During the Atlantic City swim she had hummed "O Canada" and "The Happy Wanderer" to break the monotony; this swim she hadn't felt like humming at all. The voices in the boat began to seem far away.

"Marilyn! Marilyn!" shrieked Ryder. She opened her eyes and read the blackboard he was holding: $7,500 IF YOU FINISH. Her heavy bloodshot eyes read the figure as $750. "I'll split it with you, Gus." she called.

Earlier it had struck Ryder and Bryant that Marilyn needed extra encouragement. They located Marilyn's best friend, a tow-headed girl named Joan Cooke. One of the *Star* boats hurried to Toronto, picked up Joan and manoeuvred a few hundred yards from the *Mipepa*. There was no small boat to take Joan across, so she stripped off her shoes, jacket and watch and dived into the water wearing a blouse and knee-length slacks. Ryder and Bryant pulled her into the *Mipepa* and she stood in the boat, shivering in her wet clothes and yelling, "Atta girl, Marilyn." Bryant remembered his duty to his newspaper and took a picture of Joan as she was hauled into the boat. It was the last picture he took that day as the anguish of rooting Marilyn home blotted out everything else. He neglected entirely to keep a notebook. He and Ryder and Russell stayed awake 21 hours in an open boat and forgot their own weariness to such a degree that it occurred to none of them to open the gallon thermos of coffee someone had provided. They ate nothing.

The summoning of Joan Cooke turned out to be fine strategy. Toward

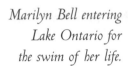

Marilyn Bell entering Lake Ontario for the swim of her life.

five o'clock Marilyn began to falter again, clawing the water with no strength. Her legs no longer hurt—they had no feeling at all—but the pain in her stomach was steady. Ryder asked Joan to jump in and swim beside Marilyn.

"I can't swim in slacks and a blouse," she protested.

"Take them off," suggested Ryder.

Joan looked around at the 20 large and small boats fanned out behind the *Mipepa*—most of them were festooned with photographers, their collars turned up and their hands gripping cameras. "They won't take a picture of you," Bryant assured her. She pulled off her clothes and dived into the water in her panties and brassiere.

The splash of the dive woke Marilyn, who had been dozing again. She looked at her friend and laughed. "Don't touch her, Joan, you'll disqualify her," screamed Ryder. Joan nodded and called briskly to Marilyn, "Come on, let's go." She began swimming quickly and expertly. Marilyn's stroke picked up and a tiny flutter of white water behind her showed that her feet were kicking. Joan stayed in the water a few minutes more, then climbed back into the *Mipepa* and wrapped herself in blankets.

At five o'clock, Ryder pointed to the Toronto skyline and wrote on the blackboard, WE ARE TAKING YOU STRAIGHT IN. In spite of this, Marilyn's stroke slowed from the 64 strokes per minute she maintained at her best to 50 strokes a minute. She stopped twice in two minutes, staring dazedly at the boats collecting from Toronto and Hamilton. The wind grew stiffer and colder and the waves pushed her west of the pink flares popping over the Exhibition.

Two seaplanes dipped overhead and roared away: *The Star* had hired two planes to carry photographers and reporters with walkie-talkie sets and the *Telegram* had one plane. Newsmen covering the swim were beginning to realize they hadn't slept for two days and a night and they watched the child in the water with wonder.

To people listening in their homes and cars, the radio coverage seemed a phenomenon in itself. "She's swimming now," the hoarse voice of the announcer would say. "Now she's stopped and Gus Ryder is holding up the blackboard. It reads 'One and a half miles to go' but we estimate it is closer to four. Probably trying to encourage the girl who . . ." Officials of CBLT, Toronto's television station, dallied with the notion of sending their mobile unit to the lakefront to photograph Marilyn's arrival but decided against it. The unit was needed to cover a scheduled prom symphony concert that night.

As the afternoon wore out, Ryder huddled in his jacket. Bryant stood beside the blanketed Joan Cooke. The two lifeguards, one clad only in his bathing suit, pulled steadily at their oars. All of them unceasingly watched the rise and fall of the white arms in the water, the bathing cap that turned and became a grey face gulping air and then became a bathing cap again. Once, when she faltered, Ryder wrote on the blackboard: IF YOU QUIT, I QUIT.

Behind them now was the queerest collection of ships Toronto's harbor had ever seen: sleek yachts, shabby motorboats, sailboats, the monstrous tug *Ned Hanlan* belching smoke, a motorboat carrying several adults and two starry-eyed boys of four and five, and another with several men in business suits, a woman and a year-old baby girl dressed in pink. On the fringe were kayaks and rowboats.

An air-force officer on the *Ned Hanlan* came away from the boat's radio and yelled into a megaphone to Ryder, "She's been offered another $6,000." Ryder prepared a new sign for his blackboard: NOW $15,000. Marilyn, close to unconsciousness again, didn't notice.

People in the boats could now distinguish trucks moving along the highway on the shore and each separate building of the Sunnyside amusement area, west of the Exhibition grounds. Some newspaper and newsreel photographers crossed from smaller boats to the more comfortable Harbor Commission launch.

"I don't think those *Star* guys are going to let her land at the Ex," one of the *Telegram* photographers said excitedly. "She's swimming straight for Sunnyside!"

"We'll get her all right," replied Allan Lamport, a member of the CNE Sports Committee. He yelled to Ryder a moment later: "Isn't it just as close to take her to the Ex? We've got a crowd waiting there for you."

"We can't get in there," Ryder hollered back, "She's going against the waves." The sun was gone by now and the moon was a cold oval in the sky.

"Poor girl," said Harbor Commissioner W.H. Bosley gently. "I hope this isn't going to hurt her."

"Gus, you're headed for the widest part of the bay!" cried Lamport.

Ryder leaned over the end of the *Mipepa*. "Swim for the yellow building, Marilyn, the yellow building, Marilyn!" Marilyn opened her eyes, found the building and plodded on with her mechanical stroke. She had two miles more to go.

"No, no," shouted Lamport.

"Keep quiet," retorted Ryder fiercely, "we're running this."

Another motorboat, containing Robert Saunders, president of the CNE; George Duthie, sports director; and Hiram MacCallum, general manager, pulled up beside the Star yacht.

"Have her swim to the Ex," Duthie yelled. "We've got a pot of earth there she's to touch."

"She'll land wherever she can," a *Star* reporter shouted back.

"Is this a *Toronto Star* swim?" asked Saunders indignantly.

"The CNE had nothing at all to do with this swim," answered the *Star* men. When CNE officials moved closer, Syd Bell, Marilyn's father, screamed, "You get out of here!" The officials retired a distance away.

At that moment, at 6:35 p.m., Marilyn stopped swimming and stood up, treading water.

"Come on, keep going," shouted Ryder.

"I'm tired," Marilyn wailed.

"Come on!" cried Joan Cooke. "Fifteen minutes more!"

"I can't go any farther."

"Come on," shouted Bryant, "only a little more!"

"I can't move!" Marilyn said, crying.

Her father called across the water: "Take her out, Gus."

Ryder, not hearing, shouted, "Fifteen minutes more, Marilyn. Come on!"

Like an obedient child, Marilyn put her face in the water and started swimming. At that point her conscious mind blanked out and she had the feeling she was far away, floating bodiless and light. In the distance, voices were whispering, "the yellow building, the yellow building," and her stomach ached dully.

Once again she stopped and Ryder passed her the last of the eight pounds of corn syrup and the package of uncooked pablum he had brought.

"Do you want to come out?" he asked when he saw her face.

"Which way do I go?" she muttered vaguely and started to swim again. She became aware of a feeling that if she stopped once more she would be finished. She never paused again.

"Gus has a mad on for the Ex, you can see that," commented Lamport furiously as he watched Ryder lead the girl toward Sunnyside. The Exhibition grounds, black with people, were a mile to the right. It was dusk and the buildings, the boats, the sky and the water were varying shade of blue. It became so cold that men in the boats shivered and it was hard to hold a pencil. The strange fleet showed running lights, like fireflies. The moon was brighter.

At 7:50 p.m., Ryder's hoarse voice could be heard shouting "Come on, Marilyn, ten minutes more!"

"If she touches the breakwater, that's sufficient," Bosley observed in the Harbor Commission launch. The shore was only 450 feet past the concrete breakwater.

A voice on the *Star* boat called to Ryder: "When your boat touches the sea wall, bring her right here. Don't let her get up, just touch!"

Ryder turned on his flashlight. The darkness along the shore ahead turned out to be thousands of people, screaming unintelligibly. A launch owner pushed on his horn and the fleet unleashed a cacophony of horns, whistles and sirens. Every man began to shout, and some to cry. The *Mipepa* pulled aside and let Marilyn go in to the breakwater alone. She touched it with her left hand and stopped. It was six minutes after eight. She had been in the water 20 hours and 59 minutes. The lake is 32 miles across, but she had swum 40 miles or more fighting the currents.

Marilyn Bell can't remember touching the breakwater. When the lifeguards tried to pull her into one of their dinghies she was furious. "Let me go!" she cried. She thought they were trying to take her out of the water before she had finished the swim. "I'm all right," she said firmly and pushed herself a few yards into the lake again. Ryder's boat came beside her and she became aware of the shouting thousands and saw rockets bursting in the sky.

"Are these people crazy or am I?" she whispered as Bryant and Ryder, weakened too after 21 hours on constant watch, laboriously pulled her into the *Mipepa*. She was taken to the *Star* boat where her parents hugged her and she was put to bed.

Telegram reporters sorrowfully watched the *Star* boat swallow the biggest news story of the year. The crowds around the Exhibition's lakefront grandstand continued to wait for the heroine, cheering the Harbor Commission launch hysterically when it docked. Through the din came the sound of Loretto students screaming, "One, two, three, four . . . Who are we for? . . . Marilyn, Marilyn, . . . Rah, rah, rah!" The voice on the public-address system abruptly explained, "We regret that Marilyn Bell's condition does not permit her to receive her admirers."

Marilyn, lying in a bunk on the *Star* boat was sipping cocoa when she was struck by the notion that her legs were paralysed. "I can't walk!" she cried anxiously. "I can't feel my legs."

"Sure you can, honey," her mother assured her. The girl was not convinced so her mother put an arm around her and walked her around the cabin. Marilyn sank back in the bunk greatly relieved.

At the Toronto Lifesavers' Station dock, an ambulance hired by the *Star* waited to take her to the Royal York Hotel suite and a *Star*-hired doctor and nurse. A line of parked taxis had been ordered for *Star* reporters. It was, however, the worst-kept secret of the day.

The *Telegram* knew every detail of the *Star* scheme—including the room number of the hotel suite. Every available editorial employee was called to help separate Marilyn Bell from the *Star*. In case of a slip-up, one group waited at the National Yacht Club, another large group at the Lifesavers' dock near downtown Toronto and four more groups at the four entrances of the Royal York; and, as a precaution, a small delegation was at the King Edward Hotel and another at Marilyn's home.

The offence started with a *Telegram*-hired ambulance, which arrived ahead of the *Star*-hired ambulance at the Lifesavers' Station. The stretcher-bearers unloaded their stretcher and prepared to wait for the swimmer. The *Telegram* had rented a large bedroom in the Royal York Hotel for her.

Star men spotted the *Telegram* ambulance standing empty at the curb with the keys still in the ignition and quietly drove it a few blocks away, removing both the keys and the cap of the distributor. Two more ambulances replaced it at the curb, one hired by the *Star* and the other a mystery to both papers. The Lifesavers' jetty then held three stretchers, each complete with a pair of stretcher-bearers screaming at one another, "This is the official stretcher!"

Marilyn's father asked Ed Hopkins, an official of the Harbor Commission, to clear the jetty of everyone but "friends, relatives and the *Star*." *Telegram* men resisted the order and 12 police constables from No. 1 precinct were called. The jetty was cleared, but only for an instant. *Telegram* photographers infiltrated back behind barrels and posts and waited for Marilyn.

The swimmer herself, catching the spirit of the occasion, suggested to a *Star* man: "Would you like me to put a blanket over my head so they can't get pictures?" It was a tempting offer, but he refused. She walked off wearing a two-piece sweat suit and climbed on the waiting *Star* stretcher, which someone finally had identified. As she was loaded into the ambulance, the *Telegram*'s Dorothy Howarth climbed in beside her, assisted courteously by a somewhat dazed *Star* man. He realized his error immediately and snarled, "Get outa there, you!" Dorothy backed out.

Joan Cooke climbed in beside the stretcher and squeezed the swimmer's shoulders. "That was wonderful, Marilyn," she said. "Congratulations."

"For what?" asked Marilyn blankly.

"For the swim," said Joan. "For finishing the swim."

"I did?" cried Marilyn incredulously. "I finished?" It hadn't occurred to anyone that the girl didn't know.

The Star ambulance eventually arrived at the Royal York Hotel's freight elevator, and Marilyn was carried aboard. The elevator descended to the basement, where a hundred waiters, bus boys, chambermaids, porters, cooks and waitresses clapped and shouted as her stretcher was taken across the basement to a waiting passenger elevator. The corridors of the fourth floor were filled with *Telegram* and *Globe and Mail* reporters and photographers and the *Star* pushed the stretcher through the mob with difficulty.

Eventually the door of room 469, part of a three-room suite, closed behind her and she climbed into bed. The doctor who examined her, Dr. F.R. Griffin, remarked to the reporters in the hall that he expected Marilyn had lost 20 pounds during the swim.

Actually Marilyn's health, the subject of much gloomy conjecture that night, was so superb that Griffin was baffled. Her heart, pulse and respiration were normal. Except for bloodshot eyes and a rubbery feeling in her legs, she appeared to have suffered no harm at all. In fact, she had gained a pound.

IN THE TWO YEARS following her Lake crossing, Marilyn Bell swam the English Channel and Juan de Fuca Strait—each time receiving a ticker-tape parade in Toronto. She then retired from long-distance swimming, married and moved to New Jersey. In the Seventies, she became a school teacher, but took early retirement in 1991 because of back pain resulting from scoliosis, which prevents her from swimming. She and her husband now live on Sugarloaf Key, in southern Florida.

JUNE CALLWOOD is an award-winning journalist and author who contributed her first article to Maclean's *in 1947. Callwood, who lives in Toronto with her husband, fellow writer Trent Frayne, has written more than 15 books on a wide variety of topics.*

Simpson's vs. Eaton's: The Big Battle of the Big Stores

by Fred
Bodsworth

FEBRUARY 1, 1955

WHEN SIMPSONS-SEARS LIMITED opened one of its plush new stores on the outskirts of Hamilton last November, the downtown Hamilton store of the T. Eaton Co. sent a huge bouquet of white mums with good-luck wishes. Then Eaton's, having observed business protocol, quietly began to do everything in its power to prevent those good-luck wishes from coming true.

For Hamilton had temporarily become the focal point of the nation's hottest merchandising battle—the coast-to-coast Eaton's-Simpson's struggle for the biggest slice of Canada's billion-dollar-a-year department-store sales. Eaton's has had the biggest slice by far, with annual sales probably double those of Simpson's. But two and a half years ago, after some 80 years during which Simpson's didn't seriously challenge Eaton's lead, the Robert Simpson Company joined forces with the powerful Sears Roebuck Company of the United States, set up the new Simpsons-Sears and began a program of swift and aggressive mail-order and store expansion with the apparent aim of toppling Eaton's from its long-held spot on the top of the department-store heap.

Simpson's is still a long way behind, but it is challenging the Eaton's colossus as it was never challenged before. The merchandising war is reaching into virtually every Canadian home from the Eskimo tents of Aklavik to the mansions of Westmount, for there are few Canadians indeed who do not at some time or other buy something displayed in an Eaton's or Simpson's catalogue or store. And with each side striving to outdo the other with service and bargains, most Canadians stand to gain.

The Hamilton battle last November was a miniature of the nationwide struggle. Hamilton had been an Eaton's stronghold for many years. Its six-floor downtown store had been the city's biggest—in size, sales volume and prestige. But the long-standing Eaton's supremacy was threatened when the dazzling new Simpsons-Sears store opened at the city's eastern outskirts. Eaton's, on its six floors, has 190,000 square feet of selling space; Simpsons-Sears on two floors has 220,000 feet. But perhaps more important for today's shoppers—Simpsons-Sears is surrounded by a floodlit, 17-acre parking lot, large enough to accommodate 1,500 cars—more parking space than on all of Hamilton's downtown streets.

Eaton's had been planning for the Simpsons-Sears opening almost as long and as carefully as Simpsons-Sears itself. Early last fall when it became known the new Simpsons-Sears would be open six full days a week, Eaton's, which had always closed Saturday afternoons, began to stay open all day Saturday. Long before Simpsons-Sears was completed, Eaton's and other downtown stores started advertising the slogan: "It's Fun to Shop Downtown—Where the Shops Are Tops." And Eaton's meanwhile was saving up bargains for a blitz to coincide with the Simpsons-Sears opening in mid-November.

The opening was scheduled for Wednesday, Nov. 17. On the preceding Saturday, Eaton's launched a sale which it called a "Pre-Christmas Shopping Festival" and heralded it with four pages of advertising in the Hamilton *Spectator*. It followed that with two pages of ads each night for the next week. It splurged with its best bargains the night before the Simpsons-Sears opening and hedged them with a "no telephone or mail order" restriction to lure customers downtown from the equally attractive bargains Simpsons-Sears was offering to mark its suburban opening.

Simpsons-Sears slashed its $334 automatic washer to $288, a $46 saving. Eaton's offered a $319 automatic washer for $219, a flat $100 cut.

One of Simpsons-Sears' best bargains was on women's woolen sweaters normally priced up to $10.95. It cut these to $4.98. Next day, Eaton's featured the same sweaters—for $4.98 too. Simpsons-Sears had 59-cent nylons on its first day, Eaton's had 59-cent nylons the next day. Simpsons-Sears, for one day only, sold $7 nylon window curtains for $4.49. Two days later Eaton's were featuring slightly smaller curtains of the same quality for $3.98.

Simpsons-Sears reduced a line of women's winter coats, which normally sold anywhere from $40 to $50, to $29.90. Eaton's cut the same coats to $29.88, and when these sold out a similar line was offered for $27.

Hamilton hadn't had such a week of bargains in years, and each store did a roaring business. But Eaton's didn't lure many shoppers from the Simpsons-Sears opening. As has happened everywhere that a new Simpsons-Sears store has opened, crowds began gathering long before the opening ceremony. Fifty police toiled to untangle traffic jams that extended like spokes of a wheel in every direction. When the doors of the store were thrown open, a crowd of 7,000 swept in.

"It was havoc," said L.E. Coffman, former manager of a Sears Roebuck store in Omaha, Neb., now manager of the new Simpsons-Sears at Hamilton. "We sold out our main brand of refrigerator the first day—105 of them. And that first day we sold 12,000 pairs of nylon hose, practically every one we had."

The shopping crowd saw a store that differs radically inside and out from those of its downtown rivals. It's framed with ornamental shrubbery and has covered outdoor walkways so that the exterior resembles a luxury hotel. Its two floors sprawl across three acres. There are no conventional boxed-in display windows; instead picture windows dropping almost to ground level open directly to the main floor, in effect turning the store into one vast display window.

Inside, tables of merchandise are arranged for self-selection. There are few conventional store counters. The floors of many departments are covered with $15-a-yard broadloom. To promote what Simpsons-Sears calls "family shopping," there is a service station and auto-accessory shop attached to the store where pop can browse or get a grease job for the car, and there are TV sets through the store where mother can leave the children while she shops.

Hamilton's bright new Simpsons-Sears store is just one of seven the company has already built across Canada. For the Eaton's-Simpson's battle is not a short-term price war but a long-term, multi-million-dollar merchandising struggle geared to the biggest department-store building race of Canada's history. And prices and new stores are only two of its phases. It is also providing Canadians with a broader selection of goods in lines as divergent as suede windbreakers, geiger counters and automobile insurance—in both mail-order catalogues and retail stores. It is speeding deliveries and providing easier credit-buying terms. It is bringing new industries to Canada. And it is bringing lower prices based on streamlined manufacturing methods rather than here-today-gone-tomorrow price wars.

How do the two sides stack up?

Before Sears Roebuck came in, dramatically changing the picture, it was a simple two-team line-up—the T. Eaton Company versus Robert Simpson Company. Eaton's had a coast-to-coast chain of more than 50 department stores and a mammoth mail-order business, the biggest in the Commonwealth. Simpson's was a modest chain of five stores (Toronto, Montreal, London, Halifax and Regina), with a mail-order business reputedly about half that of Eaton's. Both were big, between them commanding close to three-quarters of Canada's total department-store trade, but Simpson's was a distant second to Eaton's.

Then, late in 1952, Simpson's and Sears Roebuck tossed $20 million each into a kitty to set up Simpsons-Sears, the new company to be half owned by each of its parent companies. The original Robert Simpson Company still operates its five department stores, but the former Simpson's mail-order business went to Simpsons-Sears in the deal. For its part, Sears Roebuck contributed the world-wide connections and buying power that have made its U.S. chain of 700 stores the biggest name in department stores. The newcomer, Simpsons-Sears, in addition to reorganizing Simpson's mail order with the mass-selling techniques pioneered by Sears Roebuck, also launched the big store-building program which, to begin with, will put about 15 Sears-type stores in Canadian cities.

But Eaton's, with almost five times as many stores doing business as Simpson's and Simpsons-Sears combined, is still far in the lead. And there is no doubt Eaton's cash registers jingle louder and oftener than those of the opposition.

The dollar value of the business Eaton's does is one of Canada's most closely guarded business secrets. Eaton's is a family-owned company with no public stock, so it does not have to reveal business figures except in confidence to the government. But the Dominion Bureau of Statistics publishes each year the total business by all Canadian department stores—around $1 billion. Since many stores publicly announce their figures, it is possible by elimination to arrive at a total sales figure that must be Eaton's. By this means it is estimated that Eaton's stores and mail-order offices sell between $450 million and $500 million worth of goods a year.

Simpson's at the time of the Sears Roebuck merger was doing around $200 million worth of business a year. With seven new Simpsons-Sears stores opened in 1954 and the mail order offering a much wider range of merchandise, Simpson's and Simpsons-Sears between them last year probably hit $250 million. "They are closing the gap," said Ed Nelson, secretary of the Canadian Retail Federation, "but Eaton's still has a comfortable lead."

The merchandising war got under way in August, 1952, within a few days after the Simpson's and Sears tie-up was announced, and five months before it was actually to take effect. And the opening round was over credit terms. Simpson's Toronto store pulled a surprise out of the Sears Roebuck bag of tricks and on a wide range of items cut the required down payment to a straight $10 instead of the customary 10 per cent. The offer was for August only, it advertised, and applied to many high-priced articles like furniture, cameras, rugs, radios, TV sets, electrical appliances, boats and motors—$200 and $300 items on which down payments had been $20 and $30. This gimmick—"a $10 bill gets you anything in the store"—was a trick Sears Roebuck had been using effectively in the United States for years. It also indicated that Sears Roebuck ideas and methods as well as Sears Roebuck dollars were going to invade Canada.

To experienced retailers, this Simpson's move had two significant implications:

1. It was aimed straight at Eaton's because it covered only "hardlines" (furniture, appliances etc.) which were an Eaton's specialty but in which Simpson's had not previously been strongly interested;

2. It meant that Simpson's planned a real fight, because competing in the credit field is costly and hazardous. Credit sales tie up money in partly paid goods and increase the cost of doing business. "When stores start trying to outdo each other on easy-credit terms," another Toronto merchant said, "it is almost certainly a sign they are squaring off for a long hard fight."

Eaton's reply to the Simpson's offer came the very next day when the company advertised a no-down-payment plan for the duration of its August sale. Then in January, 1953, when the first big Simpsons-Sears catalogue also appeared, it was accompanied by another coup in credit selling. The catalogue announced that on a wide range of home appliances priced at $200 and more, a down payment of only $10 would be required—instead of the customary 10 per cent. Appliances priced below $200 could be bought for only $5 down. This time Eaton's didn't nibble at the bait. It left this line of credit to Simpson's and continued to demand 10 per cent down on all credit purchases.

In addition to competing for customers with easy credit, the two firms are now engaged in a store- and warehouse-building race to accommodate the customers they now serve or expect to get. Between them they have spent in the past couple of years or will spend soon about $75 million on new buildings.

Simpsons-Sears has pioneered a new department-store trend for Canada—locating stores on suburban wasteland far from downtown areas. Morgan Reid, a young Simpsons-Sears executive who has played an important role in planning the expansion of the new Canadian firm, said: "People are moving into the suburbs, so we are moving out there after them. The automobile has become the biggest factor molding shopping habits and the modern store must make adequate provision for automobile parking."

There is more to building in the suburbs than parking however. Property values are lower and, perhaps most important, it permits outward instead of upward expansion. "Cooping people in an elevator like cattle in a car is a poor way to promote sales," said one Simpsons-Sears executive.

"You've locked them in a box where they can't see the goods you want them to see. Escalators are better. At least they take your purchaser to every floor. But the single-story or two-floor store is best of all. No selling time is lost while you go through the costly business of lifting your customers to shopping areas."

Eaton's downtown Toronto flagship store, 1954, site of the Eaton Centre today.

But for a majority of Canadians, Eaton's and Simpsons-Sears are not city or suburban stores at all, but the familiar names on the fat slick mail-order catalogues that are awaited eagerly twice each year in practically every Canadian rural and small-town home. In many thousands of those homes, Canada's two big mail-order catalogues form the main, often the only, link with the outside business world. They and the Bible are the three books you are sure to find in every farmhouse.

They set the styles for almost half of Canada. They are the inspiration for thousands of children's letters to Santa Claus ("and please bring daddy the electric fence on page 472 cause the black heifer is getting in the fall wheat"). The women's lingerie pages torn from catalogues are the only pin-ups known to thousands of boys who have never heard of Marilyn Monroe.

During the past two years these catalogues have become probably the main battleground in the Eaton's–Simpson's rivalry. "The battle of the big books" is grim and closely fought. Mail-order sales represent about half the total business for each side, so the stakes are large. And the risks are high, for once a catalogue is issued, the issuer is committed to its prices for months until the next catalogue appears. A price higher than the competitor's cannot be adjusted as is possible in newspaper advertising.

The first Simpsons-Sears catalogue appeared in January, 1953, after several months of feverish preparation by a staff augmented with a number of Sears Roebuck mail-order veterans. And it was immediately obvious that the new company was going to give Eaton's a run for its money in mail order as well as retail stores. For the first time Simpson's, now Simpsons-Sears, had a catalogue thicker and brighter than Eaton's (556 pages against Eaton's 552). When the next catalogues appeared, Eaton's hit back with a bigger, more colorful 676-page book. But Simpsons-Sears had just started. It jumped to 708 pages and now held a 32-page lead. By this winter's catalogue, Eaton's was still catching up and Simpsons-Sears' lead had dropped to eight pages.

Under Sears Roebuck influence, Simpsons-Sears has been breaking with the old Canadian catalogue tradition and injecting a good deal of razzle dazzle into its book. The catalogue sparkles with gadgets, gimmicks and guarantees. You can buy a geiger counter with instructions on how to find uranium, or a plumbing system, an astronomer's telescope, "sizeless" nylons, car insurance, an electric alarm that wakes up Junior the second he begins bed-wetting.

Today's mail-order customers are more conscious of style and fit than they used to be, so both catalogues bulge with charts and measuring advice. Eaton's has a half-page chart to order a man's suit; Simpsons-Sears helps women find out if they are petite, shapely, classic or tall in nylon-stocking sizes. Eaton's provides a diagram telling women how to wear a brassiere for the utmost "support and flattery."

With the stiffening of competition, the basic mail-order appeals of the two companies have not changed. Simpsons-Sears still makes its main pitch to suburban and small-town residents; Eaton's catalogue is aimed principally at the laboring man and farmer. So the Eaton's customer has 56 different brands, shapes and colors of men's long underwear to choose from; Simpsons-Sears has 35. Eaton's has four pages of men's work shirts, Simpsons-Sears has two. Eaton's has four styles of snowshoes for trappers and lumberjacks, Simpsons-Sears has none. Eaton's still has a full page of harnesses and harness supplies for the farmer, but only one saddle for the riding fan; Simpsons-Sears has four fancy saddles for the suburban dude ranch but not a stitch of harness for a work horse.

Eaton's wasn't sorry to see one traditional mail-order service for farm customers copied by Simpsons-Sears. It was the selling by mail of live baby chicks and turkeys, often a nuisance because Eaton's had to assume responsibility every time cold weather or a railroad delay caused the chicks to die. Eaton's stuck with this business for years simply as a service to its thousands of farm customers. Simpsons-Sears now offers baby chicks and turkeys with the same live-delivery guarantee.

Each firm publishes six catalogues a year—two main ones for winter and summer and four supplementary editions. The small editions are spaced between the two main issues so prices can be reduced on items from the preceding catalogue that are selling slowly, and so that new styles can be tested to determine what treatment they merit in the next big catalogue.

Officials of both sides staunchly declare they wouldn't think of spying on one another's catalogue prices ahead of publication, yet both surround their catalogue-production divisions with a security system as tight as the

Iron Curtain. "If the other people got possession of advance proofs of our catalogue they could crucify us, practically put us out of business," said J.H. Thomson, Simpsons-Sears catalogue manager. "They could beat us on every price and we couldn't do a thing about it for six months."

To prevent this, catalogue-production employees are carefully screened, and trained never to discuss their jobs outside. Copy on the way to printers is watched closely so it cannot go astray. And the whole operation is so decentralized in both firms that most individuals have access only to information relating to limited departments. Only a few key men know the whole picture. If a man engaged in catalogue production has to be dismissed, the firing is almost certain to be postponed until the catalogue is off the press so that he cannot retaliate by taking information to "the other people."

At the end of the war, Eaton's had a catalogue circulation of about one million and Simpson's was somewhat less. But last February Simpsons-Sears, when floating a bond issue, announced its catalogue circulation to be more than 1.5 million. Other retailers believe that each firm is now distributing close to two million copies of each edition of its catalogue.

Average catalogue postage is 28 cents, but with the two companies trying to outdo each other circulating into remote areas they are spending many times more than that to get some catalogues to their destination. The big books of both are now sent to Aklavik in the Arctic by air at a cost of almost $7 a book.

When Simpsons-Sears began doing business there were some indignant accusations that the new company was only an "import house" and a "Yank invasion" of Canadian business. Eaton's was careful to keep its name from being linked with these back-stabbing accusations, but it launched its own subtle attack against the U.S. connections of its competitor. Soon after the Sears deal was announced, Eaton's began to boast of its long all-Canadian background in a demonstration of patriotism skilfully designed to contrast with the newly acquired U.S. roots of Simpsons-Sears. Instead of calling itself simply "Eaton's" in its ads and on its delivery trucks, it suddenly blossomed forth as "Eaton's of Canada." Symbolic maps of Canada, and Union Jacks to draw attention to its British-made goods, were spotted through the Eaton's catalogue. While the Simpsons-Sears catalogue overlooked the fact that many of its "hard line" items were Sears Roebuck brands imported from the United States, Eaton's catalogue was playing up Canadian and English-made goods wherever it could, stressing that its woolens come "from Britain's finest mills" and that its furniture is the product of "finest Canadian craftsmanship." Even Eaton's budgie birds are "from Canadian talking strains."

Meanwhile at Toronto, the birthplace and modern headquarters of both firms, the nation's biggest individual Eaton's and Simpson's stores face each other across narrow Queen Street, eyeing each other's movements like belligerent eagles on neighboring crags. Like newspapers, they are always striving to scoop each other. The day Marilyn Bell swam across Lake Ontario last September, Eaton's window-display staff worked late and secretly behind drawn curtains setting up a special window to honor the teenager who had suddenly become Toronto's sweetheart. Then they crossed the street hopefully to see if they had scooped "the other people." It was a draw. The Simpson's display staff was just putting the finishing touches on their Marilyn Bell window.

Every shopping day a surging stream of shoppers flows back and forth across the street between the competing stores. What the shoppers do not know is that among them often are Eaton's or Simpson's spies furtively crossing the street to spy out the opposition's newest bargains or merchandising methods. In the trade they are called "comparison shoppers," but no cloak-and-dagger undercover agent has had greater claim to the title "spy." Because of their comparison shoppers it has become virtually impossible for one store to have an exclusive bargain more than a few hours—the other store's comparison shoppers spot it, rush back home with the word and the bargain is quickly duplicated in the second store.

The identity of comparison shoppers is kept secret in their own stores as well as outside, for their duties include spying on their own staff as well as the opposition. A Simpson's comparison shopper recently bought at Eaton's a dress she deliberately selected as requiring alteration before it would fit. Then she bought a dress at her own store that required the same amount of alteration. Her own store, Simpson's, wanted one day longer to make the alteration. Next day the department manager was curtly informed that Eaton's was giving faster alteration service and that his service must speed up or else.

Both stores refuse to discuss their comparison-shopping staffs or methods, hardly admitting that such staffs even exist. But one thing is certain—the battle of the big stores has only begun.

THE HUDSON'S BAY CO. *acquired Simpson's in 1978; in 1991 the two companies merged and the Simpson's name disappeared, although Sears Canada still exists and continues with catalogue sales. (Eaton's dropped its catalogue in 1976.) In 1997, after a long decline in market share, and in the face of increased post-free-trade competition from American companies, Eaton's sought bankruptcy protection and closed 21 of the chain's 85 stores.*

FRED BODSWORTH, *who lives in Toronto, was an assistant editor at Maclean's from 1947 to 1955 and wrote approximately 100 articles for the magazine. He has written five books, including the acclaimed novel* Last of the Curlews.

Just Look at the Old Ice-Cream Parlor Now!

by
Trent Frayne

July 7, 1956

It's a good bet that almost every Canadian past the age of 40 has a nostalgic memory of the old-fashioned ice-cream parlor, a reigning social institution in the dewy youth of the century. It was there that scrubbed swains held hands under wire-legged tables with blushing maidens while they stared calflike at each other over tall enchanting glasses. It was there that young lovers walked of a summer evening in the early days of the horseless carriage. It was the invariable destination after a band concert in the park, a boat ride in July or a five-cent movie. It was there that the young blades assembled after a dashing game of croquet or a rousing set of tennis, and it had such grace and dignity that its tables were never barnacled with blobs of chewing gum.

The ice-cream parlor was the shrine of the age—where juvenile virtue was rewarded with peaks of strawberry, chocolate and vanilla, capped with cherries and whipped cream. But, alas, it has gone the way of the Model-T and the frilly pantaloon.

Yet just as the Tin Lizzy and the frills have been replaced by peach-colored convertibles and sleek nylon, so has the old ice-cream parlor been superseded by a modern counterpart: the sprawling drive-in, with more asphalt than a service station, a 20-foot illuminated sign shaped like an ice-cream cone, a bevy of car-hop waitresses dressed almost entirely in skin, and huge chains of roadside outlets like the Howard Johnson restaurants in the United States that serve 28 (count 'em) 28 flavors.

In Canada, the new kind of ice-cream parlor has reached its apex in the unlikely little town of Stoney Creek, Ont., a historic fruit-growing community in the Niagara Peninsula. The busiest place in town, day and night, is a low, rambling, red-brick-and-stone collection of additions and more additions called the Stoney Creek Dairy. But it is not a dairy at all—it is the old ice-cream parlor in modern dress. Here, on a hot and humid holiday, six uniformed young men with crewcuts are employed to direct cars that roll, often bumper-to-bumper, into the dairy's black-topped parking lot from all over the peninsula. They come principally from Hamilton, which is just a few miles west, but they also come from Buffalo, 50 miles south, and from Toronto, 40-odd miles east. On such a day 12,000 people will pour through the little town of 3,451 residents and will buy 1,200 gallons of ice cream, 400 pounds of bananas, 600 quarts of milk, 10 gallons of sundae syrups, 35 pounds of nuts and 4,000 cherries. Of the 1,200 gallons of ice cream, a good 500 will be in bulk, generally half-gallon cartons for home freezers.

"People figure we're exaggerating when we quote them these figures," remarks the dairy's owner, a plain, blunt, 49-year-old ex-farmer named George Dawson. "Well, we just let 'em look for themselves."

It's an arresting sight. The cars line up side by side in long rows as they're directed into a parking lot that can accommodate 400 cars. Fathers climb out from behind the wheels and line up in winding queues before wide windows of block glass from which, at night, diffused colored lights glow. They give their orders to high-school girls in white nylon uniforms, as many as 45 of them working over long rows of ice-cream containers in a wide spotless booth on the parking-lot side of the dairy. Then the customers carry aluminum trays back to their cars, carefully balancing double-decker cones or lavish sundaes.

The parking lot is spotted with sections for outdoor tables under multi-colored umbrellas, green lawns with garden chairs and spare young trees nodding gently in the summer breeze. Dawson planted every tree on the property and under them sportshirted customers sit staring across the apple, peach and cherry orchards at the broad outline of the Niagara Escarpment against which Stoney Creek nestles.

This is the ice-cream parlor as it looks today. In an age when there's an automobile to every six Canadians, it's within reach of every motorist, just as its counterpart early in the century was within reach of every walking customer. The evolution of the ice-cream parlor into big-volume outlets like George Dawson's at Stoney Creek is a story as engaging in its own way as the story of the evolution of the very automobile that now takes its Sunday thousands to Dawson's door.

Right after the First World War, costs began to climb—rents, labor, ingredients and the cost of such standard equipment as long-stemmed glasses, elaborate mirrors behind the counters and even the sani-onyx tabletops that resembled marble and were veined in numerous colors. Inevitably, the price of ice cream went higher and the days of the 10-cent banana split and the five-cent strawberry sundae were gone forever. Zooming overhead produced a competitor that helped topple the ice-cream parlor that mother used to know: the dairy bar.

In the middle Twenties, the dairy bar, a forerunner to mass-production outlets like Dawson's rambling affair, was a small, high-volume, low-cost operation that did away with almost everything that was sacred about the ice-cream parlor. Sani-onyx tables and wire chairs were replaced by counters and stools. The elegant long-stemmed glassware that required careful handling was replaced by cheap, disposable paper disks that fitted into aluminum containers. The ice-cream-parlor waitress who used to stroll leisurely to a table of customers with paper napkins, glasses of water and a tastefully turned-out menu was replaced in the dairy bar by one girl standing behind a counter. Behind her on the wall was a single, large-printed menu. On the counter was a pile of self-serve paper napkins—they were later placed in aluminum dispensers—and the glass of water was eliminated. The counter girl could handle five times the volume of business of her ice-cream-parlor counterpart, in half the time.

The advent of soda fountains in drugstores in the late Twenties also took a whack at the ice-cream parlor. One executive of the National Dairy Council, Jack Lawrence, recalls that in 1925 there was not a single drugstore selling ice cream from London to Windsor, 120 miles to the southwest. Lawrence was then manager of the ice-cream department of the old Walkerside Dairy in Walkerville, Ont. (now a part of Windsor). His firm installed 85 soda fountains in the last five years of the 1920s. Most ice-cream manufacturers underwrote the cost of the fountains for dealers, installing them for only a little down and collecting the remainder of the money in regular payments.

The early Thirties brought another blow to the ice-cream parlor. This was the invention of the double-decker ice-cream cone which, actually, was an optical illusion served up in wholesale lots in the dairy bars and drugstores. People *thought* they were getting two dips of ice cream, but what they were really getting was a delicious flavoring of air. Food and drug standards did not govern ice-cream manufacture then as they do today, so it was possible to inject compressed air into a normal mixture of ice cream and blow it up to twice its size. The trade called this "over-run," meaning less ice cream than met the eye. Today a gallon of ice cream must contain a minimum of 1.9 pounds of food solids.

Ice-cream parlors, already staggering under the growing competition, received a blow that prevented any kind of recovery during the Second World War when the industry as a whole was placed on a *status quo* basis by the federal Department of Agriculture. The ice-cream industry was restricted early in 1942 to the same ice-cream volume in gallons that it had produced during the year ending March 31, 1941. This restriction, aimed at conserving sugar, was not lifted by the department until April 1, 1947.

But if the parlor is no more, ice cream has never known the popularity it enjoys today. In 1955, Canadians ate 32,672,000 gallons of the stuff—a per-capita consumption of 16.07 pints, second in the world only to the warmer United States. The fact that ice cream was declared a food by the Department of National Health and Welfare in 1947 has encouraged people to use it as a dessert, and the development of home freezers has enabled them to buy it in bulk and store it for future use. And that means increased business for producers like Dawson. His Stoney Creek Dairy can turn out as many as 22 varieties of ice cream and find a steady market for them now that customers can store their purchases at home.

The publicized fact that ice cream has a low caloric content has also stimulated its sales, according to Walter Fetterly, the recent secretary-treasurer of the Ontario Association of Ice Cream Manufacturers. One quarter brick of ice cream contains 210 calories, as compared with an ordinary serving of apple pie which contains 370 calories, a two-inch slice of chocolate layer cake which has 350, a piece of lemon meringue pie which has 280, or a half-cup serving of rice pudding, which has 250.

These facts have helped swell George Dawson's business but they can hardly explain why he serves 12,000 people on a busy Sunday. Indeed, no one is precisely sure why four times the population of Stoney Creek beats a path through the quiet little town, but almost everyone agrees it's a combination of things. For one, the town's historical background is a drawing card. Stoney Creek was a bloody battlefield during the War of 1812 and a concrete spire commemorates a British victory there.

One hot August afternoon, 18 sight-seeing buses rolled up to the Stoney Creek Dairy while 979 beribboned women climbed down for 979 dishes

Enjoying ice-cream sundaes and banana splits at Stoney Creek Dairy.

of ice cream. They were delegates to a Toronto convention of Associated Countrywomen of the World, representing 25 countries, and intent on viewing the landmarks from Queenston Heights to Stoney Creek.

But a towering war memorial alone can't be responsible for the mass invasions that Stoney Creek residents have come to regard as commonplace. Burton Corman, a fruit-farmer who has been reeve or deputy reeve for 35 years, says Dawson's dairy provides at least three good reasons.

"George doesn't scrimp; you get measure for your money," he says. "The girls behind the counter are spotless; they can smile and they make you feel they're glad you came."

Bank manager Walter Scott feels Dawson's location is a major factor in its success. The dairy is close by two main roads leading from Hamilton. Sunday drivers need only turn off one, stop at the dairy for a refresher and then swing back to Hamilton on the second road for a brief and inexpensive family outing.

Twenty-one-year-old Arleen Gulliver, daughter of Tom Gulliver, one of the town's three policemen, has worked as a part-time waitress at the dairy for five years. Dawson, she says, seldom is caught napping. A few years ago, when the dairy lacked the facilities it has now, there were long line-ups at the front entrance. One afternoon while she was on duty, Arleen recalls, people began dropping out of line and turning back to their cars. Dawson dashed up.

"Tell everybody who looks impatient that if they haven't their orders in three minutes, they can have 'em free," he told Arleen.

People smiled and many of them stayed on, just to time him. Dawson went behind the counter himself, worked on orders and actually did serve most of the orders within three minutes.

Arleen's father, Tom Gulliver, the cop, says Dawson succeeded because he was never afraid of hard work. "I worked for him in a little two-man milk business back in the early Thirties," he recalls. "He'd be at it 18 hours a day, seven days a week, buying raw milk from the farmers, bottling it, delivering it and then spending half the night in a door-to-door canvass for more customers. He coaxed me to go into partnership with him, but I couldn't see it. I never dreamed it'd be such a business. Now, he's got another gimmick— every Easter Sunday he gives a rose to the first 2,000 women customers. They flock to the place. George never lets up."

Dawson is an unostentatious man who looks a good 10 years younger than his 49 years. He has brown, slightly wavy hair, blue eyes and a preoccupied expression. He dresses plainly, wears a grey fedora indoors and out and rarely puts on a topcoat, even in the winter. Half a block from his business, Dawson has built a $25,000 stone house with a basement recreation room large enough to accommodate a regulation-size bowling alley—which it does.

Born on a farm in Lincoln County, south of Stoney Creek, Dawson curiously enough has no particular recollection of a special fondness for the product that was to make him a reasonably wealthy man. "I suppose I liked ice cream all right," he says in his solemn way, "because most kids do. But I can't remember any particular ice-cream parlor, or spending any money I made on sundaes."

Until 1946 George gave no thought to ice cream; his ambition all those years was to own a dairy farm as his father had done before him. By 1929 he'd saved $5,000 and was able to buy a dairy farm near Smithville, southeast of Hamilton, and began supplying Borden's dairy with raw milk, as his father had done.

"I tried bottling milk myself, too," he recalls, "and landed a few customers. I took a two-quart call from Borden's, and when they heard about it they cut me off. I was left with nothing but the 26 customers I'd drummed up on my own."

Twenty-five years ago, door-to-door calling was possible because there were no government pasteurization laws and raw milk could be bottled and sold. It was delivered at 13 cents a quart (or eight quarts for a dollar). A milk war between the big companies forced the price down to 12 cents. Dawson and his wife, the former Gwen Ducker, of Toronto, worked 18 hours a day but they couldn't make a go of it and lost the farm. For three years Dawson worked in a Hamilton coal company, then returned to the milk business. He rented a tiny house and garage for $18 a month, and set about building what was to become the Stoney Creek Dairy on the vacant lot next door. He did all the work himself. Again he bought milk from nearby farmers, bottled it and in three months had 200 customers.

He needed money to expand the business and turned to a neighbor, an old gentleman named Oliver Nash. Dawson asked for $3,000. Nash fixed him with a silent stare. After an eternity, as Dawson recalls it, Nash replied. "All right, George," he said. "Just give me a note."

Dawson kept working and his milk routes kept growing. In 1946 he put in a counter, tables and chairs, hoping he'd attract people to buy ice cream who would then become acquainted with his milk business. He bought the ice cream wholesale from Silverwood Dairies. When *that* business began to catch on, he realized he couldn't make a sensible profit unless he made his own ice cream.

So he went to see Walter Scott, the bank manager, and convinced him that a loan of $20,000 was a good risk and was not excessive. He installed his own ice-cream-making equipment. During the first winter he closed the ice-cream section. In 1947 there was sufficient business to warrant staying open during the day in winter. The next year the ice-cream bar was kept open in the evenings until nine, and since then it's been open until midnight the year around. In zero weather people drive out to the dairy, hustle their orders out on an aluminum tray stamped "Stolen from the Stoney Creek Dairy" and sit in their cars, the heaters whirring, as they eat a Dawson sundae.

Dawson figures he loses $2,000 worth of trays and glassware a year to souvenir hunters, and has found that stamping his trays "stolen from" hasn't deterred brash visitors. When it failed to have any effect, he philosophically continued to stamp the trays, reasoning it was at least good advertising. Recently he had reasonable proof he was right. He was driving home from a dairymen's convention in Atlantic City and stopped at Buffalo for a snack. When the waitress took his order she stood looking at him thoughtfully.

"I know you," she said, her face brightening. "You're the man at that ice-cream place at Stoney . . . at Stoney Creek. I've got one of your trays."

As the town's reeve, Burton Corman, observed, Dawson does not stint on the size of the cone or sundae he serves, nor does he stint in its quality. He buys cream, eggs and milk from the district's farmers one day and, because of his large turnover, is able to serve these fresh products in his ice cream the next. Fifty-four farmers within a 20-mile radius of Stoney Creek are called on daily by Dawson's milk trucks, which bring all milk they can supply to the dairy for pasteurizing and processing. "Our idea mainly is to provide the kind of sundae you can eat and still want more," he says.

Dawson's biggest seller is his banana-split sundae and he is a dreamer if he thinks an ordinary mortal can cope with one and want to take on another. This overwhelming confection contains three large scoops of ice cream, two vanilla flanking one strawberry. Crushed pineapple is heaped on one vanilla scoop, and crushed-strawberry syrup on the other. Whipped cream, topped by a dash of rainbow coconut and crowned with a cherry, smothers the middle strawberry scoop. Two long slices of a quartered banana complete the 30-cent dish.

Ice-cream cones are served in every conceivable flavor, two huge scoops on a cone for a dime, or one big one for a nickel. Flavors include the inevitable vanilla—it constitutes 55.09 per cent of all the ice cream sold in Canada—chocolate and strawberry, the next most widely consumed in this country. In addition there are maple, orange, fruit, buttered pecan, chocolate-ripple, black raspberry, banana, butterscotch-ripple, coffee, grape, pineapple, peppermint-chip and lemon-and-lime.

On special days, such as Christmas, Dawson brews up a confection called plum-pudding ice cream, which includes figs, prunes, raisins, currants, chopped nuts and rum flavoring. His Hallowe'en special features pineapple, orange and chocolate in judicious mixture.

His "superduper" starts out with an innocuous ladle of pineapple syrup in the bottom of a tall glass. But then it starts to get serious. A scoop of vanilla ice cream is plopped into the syrup. Then a heaping of whole walnuts. Then a mound of strawberry ice cream. Then a ladle of strawberry syrup and another heaping of vanilla ice cream. A quartered banana is propped, points down, into the four corners of the glass, and whipped cream is piled on top. Chopped coconut is sprinkled on the whipped cream and a cherry tops the whole awesome challenge. The price of this sundae, which protrudes a full three inches above the top of the tall glass, is 45 cents, and anybody who can eat two of them should consult his physician.

For such delicacies, and others like them, the caravans keep pouring through Stoney Creek. The one curious note about the evolution of the ice-cream parlor is that with all the changes—in volume, in refrigeration and in numbers of customers—there has really been no basic change at all. Forty-five years ago it was the fashion to stroll to the park for a band concert or to take your best girl to a movie and then top off an inexpensive day with a sundae at the ice-cream parlor. Today, for 50 miles around Stoney Creek at least, it's the fashion to take the family for a drive—and top off an inexpensive day with a sundae at George Dawson's ice-cream supermarket.

Essentially, under its flashy exterior, the new ice-cream parlor is pretty much like the old. It's just that it's done up in asphalt.

GEORGE DAWSON *sold Stoney Creek Dairy to his sons Greg and Charles in 1972. The elder Dawson died in 1986 at age 79 of heart failure. The ice-cream parlor remains, and the dairy distributes its own brand regionally as well as Ben & Jerry's.*

TRENT FRAYNE *wrote his first piece for* Maclean's *in 1941 and has contributed hundreds to the magazine since then. He is the winner of numerous awards and has written 14 books. He lives in Toronto with his wife, fellow writer June Callwood.*

Branksome Hall's Ungentle Formula for Raising Young Ladies

by
Shirley E. Mair

MARCH 2, 1957

IN THE LONG AND CONSTANTLY changing struggle between the so-called traditional and so-called progressive educationalists, there is at least one beacon that never seems to change—a brisk, tiny, determined woman named Edith Read, who has stuck to her own convictions and remained a serene individualist. After 51 years she finds herself praised and condemned by progressives and traditionalists alike. But it's an indisputable fact that in a day when private schools are closing down through lack of funds her own institution, Branksome Hall in Toronto, is turning away applicants. Dr. Read has built Branksome to its present proportions almost entirely by her own efforts, and on it she has firmly imprinted the stamp of her own character.

At 77, she is one of Canada's oldest career women. She went to Branksome in 1906 to teach mathematics, taking with her one year's teaching experience, a tennis racquet and three university degrees, along with her natural asset, ash-blond hair. After 51 years (47 of them as principal) she has lost the tennis racquet and her hair has turned white. She has a fourth degree, an honorary LL.D. from Dalhousie University in Halifax. And from Branksome she has graduated more than 5,000 girls, most of whom remember her as a short, wiry, volatile woman bent on developing hard-working and discriminating girls.

Her graduates include the Conservative member of parliament for

York-Humber, Margaret Aitken, and Frances Dafoe, who won the world championship for figure skating in pairs with Norris Bowden in 1954 and 1955, and with Bowden placed second in the 1956 Olympics. Also among Miss Read's alumnae are a handful of doctors and lawyers, two girls' summer-camp directors, hundreds of nurses, social workers, housewives and an occasional gay divorcee.

When she stands before her fifth-form Scripture class, Miss Read is in strict mathematical terms only five-feet, three-inches tall. But somehow she gives the ridiculous impression that she is taller than the tallest guard on Branksome's basketball team. And she still has an energy that exhausts her students. Rising at 7 a.m., she literally runs through the succession of electric bells that mark off events of the school day. Long after the senior girls' lights-out has rung, she strides from her office in the school's main building to her private residence on the border of the school's property. She has never missed a school day through illness in her career. "I haven't time to be sick," she snaps.

To begin a typical day's work recently, Miss Read presided over a morning prayer meeting of 500 teenage girls. Twenty minutes after she had dismissed the girls from prayers she was in Toronto's City Hall obtaining a building permit for a combination laboratory-library from the metropolitan planning board. After a quick lunch she arranged for temperature control in a swimming pool and interviewed two applicants for a teacher's position. Later she inspected the latest style of women's millinery on display at a department store and still later announced to a dinner gathering of 100 girls that the new fur cloches were unflattering. "They hide the healthy faces of young, attractive women," she declared forthrightly.

Aided by a tongue that would be more in keeping with the tone of a board meeting than of an afternoon tea, she vigorously challenges and champions many facets of Canadian education. At present she is crusading against progressive educationalists who place self-expression ahead of discipline. "Send the product of progressive education to me," she suggested recently, "and I'll straighten the brat out with little difficulty." Paradoxically, Miss Read used at least some theories of progressive educationalists long before such theories joined filtered cigarettes and sports cars as popular conversational subjects. "You can't point out the right road for a student and then refuse to give her enough freedom to travel along it," she says.

In the last 50 years, she has fought against two extremes in education and has been considered unorthodox by both. In 1907, she shocked Victorian educationalists by allowing her students to play the hot, sweaty, unfeminine game of basketball in huge billowing bloomers, to leave school grounds unchaperoned by a teacher, and even to laugh lustily. "Now, I'm frowned upon if I don't allow them to chew up the carpets," she says. "People say I'm stunting their self-expression."

Her library doesn't contain a single book on child and teenage psychology, but it does include 200 Bibles, fingerprinted by her young students. The Bible is her textbook. Above everything she believes that a student must be honest, have a strong faith in God and develop each talent to the maximum.

These beliefs were already well fixed in her when she arrived at Branksome three years after it was founded in 1903 by Miss Margaret Scott, once head of Ontario's Model School. Its first humble years were financed by Miss Scott, whose academic mind couldn't comprehend the intricacies of high finance. Miss Read bought Branksome in 1910 when its first principal retired. It was then a one-building school housing 80 students. Miss Read has in 47 years built it into an 11-building institution scattered across 13 financially fertile acres of Toronto real estate.

The phrase "private school" usually conjures up a serene picture of ivy-clad stone buildings, rolling lawns, quiet paths and green sports fields, far from soot, traffic, worldly temptations and high taxes—a place for scholarly meditation, midnight feasts, mail from home and unaltered routine. Branksome, as if deliberately trying to be an exception to the rule, is a heterogeneous collection of Victorian brick residences and squat modern classrooms with play fields situated wherever there is enough room to build a cement tennis court or dig a high-jump pit. Its buildings are stacked as close to one another as most city dwellings.

Instead of the shady paths characteristic of country schools, Branksome's grounds are bisected by one of Toronto's busiest thoroughfares. The Clifton Road Extension, built in 1950 to ease Toronto's perennial traffic problem, created a traffic problem for the school. Before the completion of the road,

Miss Read saw that unless a traffic light were installed her students would be hotfooting it between speeding autos to get from one class to another. She applied at a Toronto City Council meeting for a signal. Her application was turned down. The day the road opened she put on a brilliant red coat and, waving a hand-painted stop sign, stepped determinedly into the morning rush-hour traffic. After the traffic had screeched to a halt, she beckoned her girls across the highway. A few days later she gleefully watched workmen begin putting in the traffic signals. "I don't know why City Hall fights me," she said. "I win nine times out of ten."

Branksome offers education from kindergarten to college. It is divided into junior and senior schools corresponding to the public and high schools in Ontario. Since the principal doesn't believe every girl is suited to go to college she provides courses in domestic and secretarial science and a history-of-art course for the artistically inclined. Extracurricular activities include drama and choral groups, individual music lessons and participation in the school's radio station. The station broadcasts from one of the school's common rooms and is heard in the senior gymnasium. "I am not interested in graduating students with the highest academic standards in Canada," Miss

Headmistress Edith Read with some of her Branksome Hall charges, 1957.

Read says, "but each girl does have an individual talent. It is Branksome's job to uncover that talent and develop it."

This conviction was handed down to Miss Read by her father, Dr. H.H. Read, a Halifax physician. Most well-to-do Victorian fathers encouraged their daughters to take the grand tour of Europe and when at home to concentrate on social pursuits, but Dr. Read encouraged his daughter to fit herself for a career. She majored in mathematics and science and graduated from Dalhousie in 1900 with her B.A. and from Radcliffe College in Cambridge, Mass., in 1901 with the same degree.

In 1902, she returned to Dalhousie to receive her MA And while Miss Read's school chums daintily wielded croquet mallets, she developed a smashing tennis serve and learned to ski. She still waxes her skis every year as a gesture to the past, although she doesn't actually perform with her girls at Branksome's 50-acre ski farm, 25 miles north of Toronto. She does, however, toboggan in winter, and when junior students bring out skipping ropes in early spring their principal can't resist playfully jumping through the rope as she passes them on her round of school business. Her enthusiasm for sports led her to re-arrange school hours so girls can be dismissed at 2:30 p.m. Branksome has seven basketball courts, five tennis courts, a baseball diamond, track fields, two gymnasiums, volleyball and badminton courts, archery targets, bowling alleys and a pool 60 feet by 30.

Although the sports fields take up more of the school property than the classrooms, Miss Read severely disenchants a student who puts tennis ahead of algebra. Those who neglect their studies are summoned to her office to give an accounting. The headmistress often interrupts every sentence with, "I've never heard of such a thing!" The truth is that she has heard all the excuses innumerable times and the fact that she can put on a display of horrified disbelief while the girl stutters and mumbles over her story is a tribute to Miss Read's sense of drama. It also reduces the number of interviews.

Miss Read often worries about her girls' "too serious natures." "They are constant worriers; it's typical of their generation. They have complexes and phobias galore," she reports, "and they believe an Aspirin tablet can cure any ill." During one school term she became so alarmed at the number of headache tablets disappearing from the school's infirmary that she charged 25 cents for each pill. "Perhaps the large bill for headache cures will draw this stupid habit to the attention of parents," she said.

While parents might wonder at the high cost of Aspirin, they might be equally puzzled by the initial amount spent on the school uniform. A student must own a kilt and tie in the Hunting Stewart tartan, a tie pin, at least three pairs of green knee socks and bloomers, an equal number of beige long-sleeved blouses, a green blazer, running shoes and oxfords. All items are purchased from the school's supply shop except the shoes. The cost of the outfit is higher than for most Canadian girls' schools, which dress their pupils in the more conventional tunic or middy and short skirt, but the unique and colorful uniform is part of Branksome's Scottish tradition.

Branksome was named after the ancestral home of its first principal, Miss Margaret Scott. One of her fellow clansmen, Sir Walter Scott, had referred to the castle in his ballad-poem, "The Lay of the Last Minstrel," as "Branxholm Hall." Miss Read has liberally supplied the school with Scottish property effects. Bagpipers play at all official school functions, sports cheers are in Gaelic and at an occasional formal Scottish dinner party a girl must prove her loyalty by eating haggis. The students are divided into 11 clans for sports.

Although three Ontario girls' private schools have closed down in the last five years through lack of funds and students, Miss Read has trouble limiting her enrollment to 600. She believes Branksome cannot give individual attention to more than that number and her prime concern is to avoid assembly-line education.

But even with a capacity enrollment she has financial worries. The Ontario government does not assist private or independent schools and they must rely on tuition fees and the gifts of alumnae and friends. Current fees at Branksome run from $175 for kindergarten, $200 for grades one to four, $250 for grades five to eight, $300 for senior school to $1,200 for resident pupils. Branksome is held as an educational trust and operated by a board of governors. Unlike a privately owned school, where profit can be pocketed by the owners, Branksome's profits return to the school treasury.

The setting up of the trust cost Miss Read legal ownership of Branksome but she still retains full control of its operation. Surveying her 13 school acres she remarks, "I've been rather fortunate in real estate." Some years ago J.K. Tory, then director of the Sun Life Assurance Co., said to the lieutenant-governor of Ontario, W.D. Ross, "She beats the Dutch; if she were a man you and I would be her office boys."

Last year, she turned down a million-dollar offer for a six-acre portion of the school and rejected another plan that would give her an entire city block and money for any buildings she wished to construct in return for the school's present property. "This is Branksome," she told real-estate agents. "It's priceless!"

Branksome was purchased building by building; after completing one deal Miss Read celebrated by dismissing classes so students could see a bull-dozer clearing trees and shrubs on the new land for a track field. "I wouldn't have been surprised if she were running the bulldozer herself," one of her pupils said. She will put on a wig and school uniform to imitate her girls and become the butt of their laughter when she performs in a school play; but minutes later she can command dignity simply by walking into a class while it is in session. The attention and respect she receives would make some parents blush with envy. Students rise when she enters a room, see that she has a comfortable chair, clear a path for her down a crowded corridor and address her by her name before starting any conversation. She hears her name over and over again during the course of a day. "Miss Read, may I have permission . . ." "Miss Read, you have a visitor . . ." "Miss Read . . ."

But to Miss Read, instilling respect in her students is only part of her non-academic job of giving the girls a well-rounded school life and adequate preparation for womanhood.

Her program includes sending her housegirls to as many cultural activities as studies will permit. This is a boon for out-of-town students who come from smaller communities that don't have the plays and symphonies Toronto does. By scanning the newspapers Miss Read determines which events are suitable for her students. Amazed at the number of girls who signed up to hear one pianist, she decided to go along to find out what the attraction was. It wasn't until she was in her seat that she learned that Oscar Peterson was a jazz pianist; Miss Read disapproves of jazz. She left the audience and stalked up and down the foyer until his performance was over. The girls were permitted to remain, however.

Unlike James Hilton's fictional Mr. Chips, who mellowed into a hazy memory in the minds of his students, Miss Read remains in sharp focus for her girls. Rev. C.W. Sowby, principal of Upper Canada College, a boys' school in Toronto, once remarked to her, "Canadian girls owe you an unpayable debt and so do the men that married them."

EDITH READ *retired in 1958, but remained in her house on campus, attending morning prayer and special events, until her death at 83, in 1963. Branksome now has some 850 girls who in 1999-2000 will pay tuition of $13,250, or $27,450 for boarders.*

SHIRLEY MAIR *started at* Maclean's *as a receptionist in June, 1957, upon her graduation from Toronto's Ryerson Institute of Technology's journalism school. Mair was an assistant editor when she left the magazine for* Chatelaine *in 1963. Shortly thereafter, she left journalism to help her husband run the family nursery and gardening business in Richmond Hill, Ont., where she still lives.*

The Queen's Visit

by June
Callwood

December 7, 1957

ELIZABETH, QUEEN OF CANADA, stepped off a plane in Ottawa on October 12 around tea time of a bright cool Indian summer day and departed well past midnight from a floodlit airport near New York City nine and a half days later. In the intervening 225 hours and 20 minutes of her visit to North America, she slept about 54 hours—or an average of nearly six in every 24—and spent the rest attending some 50 separate functions, few of which she could have enjoyed. She changed her clothes 27 times and made 16 speeches. Her husband, Prince Philip, zealously establishing himself as an amateur scientist, dealt six times with separate matters, one of them duck shooting but almost all the others related to his hobby. They shook approximately 10,000 hands, at the rate of up to 20 a minute, heard God Save the Queen played with consistent excellence 21 times and were seen by about five million people along parade routes and by about 56 million more viewers who followed their progress by television.

Specters and old prejudices lowered over the graceful receiving lines, the innocuous speeches, the brisk inspections of guards of honor. The Queen's role in Canada, it appeared to some observers, hinged on calculated pageantry, just enough to warm the pride of Canadians who revere tradition and stateliness above state but not so much as to antagonize those who consider royalty a blindingly off-color bauble in an age of lean fear. For Virginians marking the 350th anniversary of the first English colony in the New World, near Williamsburg, Va., she had the tightrope task of complimenting, without a trace of sarcasm, sons of the successful rebels who routed England's armies. In Washington, it was hoped she would warm the atmosphere of distrust that has long chilled the House of Representatives toward all who speak with a British accent. In New York City, she was expected to be a girlish gay tourist properly delighted by the towering skyline and eddies of ticker tape.

This was a woman, only 31 years old and frequently so tense with anxiety that she moved like a rigid mechanical doll, who did nothing wrong. At a time when criticism of the moat of snobbery that surrounds Buckingham Palace had reached a furor unprecedented in her lifetime, she kept a valiant dignity. Throughout her North American tour it was noted that she could not relax enough to be warmly charming, as her mother can, but neither did she choose haughtiness. While inexperience still paralyzes many of her public appearances, Elizabeth seemed to the people who saw her most often to be unmistakably lonely, which won her sympathy; consecrated to something greater than herself, which made her awesome; and touched with shy humor, which made her delightful.

The Queen had moments when, unwittingly, she was absurd. During her surprise visit to a supermarket outside Washington ("A surprise," someone commented wryly, "to everyone but the State Department, the White House and assorted embassies"), Elizabeth examined a shopping cart with a small child secured in a folding seat. "How nice that you can bring your children along," she remarked kindly, innocently unaware that most suburban shoppers, on a no-servant budget, simply have no alternative.

Elizabeth also was the central figure in several stunning tableaux that only high majesty could make memorable. One of the most moving occurred at the British Embassy in Washington, when officials of the Commonwealth embassies were invited to have coffee and liqueurs following a state dinner given by the Queen and Philip for President and Mrs. Eisenhower. The diplomats were ushered into a shimmering Fiberglas tent, constructed on the embassy lawn to protect some 3,000 guests at the previous afternoon's Commonwealth reception. The grass floor had been covered with soft green rugs, wall to wall, the supporting poles were ringed with flowers, and fragile satin sofas furnished it. There was easy conversation in this extraordinary billowy-ceilinged drawing room until a pipe major appeared at the top of the steps leading from the embassy building. He was followed, with stately slowness, by two pipers playing Over the Seas to Skye. For a heavy moment the archway behind them was empty, and then the Queen arrived, glossy with satin and glittering white fire from her diamonds, on the arm of President Eisenhower. They stood motionless, brave and splendid images. One guest, a man normally given to skepticism, realized he had stopped breathing. The Queen and President released the drama by moving, becoming people again.

Elizabeth had this same effect on the 200,000 people who watched her exit from the House of Commons in Ottawa after reading the Speech from the Throne. She was driven away, dazzling in the pure warm sunlight, in an open carriage with footmen at her back. Before and behind her rode red-coated Mounties, pennants fluttering from their lances, on coal-black horses. She was wearing her jeweled coronation gown and a crown of diamonds; her husband, in an army uniform, sat tall beside her. The procession gave the effect of being both real and unreal, straight out of a big-budget production of *Cinderella* and straight out of the spine that helps keep Englishmen proud.

The Queen turned hearts over again at Arlington Cemetery outside Washington, where she placed a wreath on the tomb of the soldier "known only to God" and another wreath at the foot of the Canadian Cross, which honors Americans who died with the Canadian forces in 1914 to 1918. The day was dull and drizzling, with a brooding quality that suited the occasion. The bugler sounded a silvery Taps when the first wreath was laid and Last Post and Reveille for the second. Elizabeth's small face was grave and there was genuine mourning in her movements. She gave an unexpected sense of new grief to what usually is as unremarkable an event on a dignitary's agenda as laying a cornerstone.

Reporters and photographers who covered the entire tour, considered by all the most punishing assignment journalism has to offer, could not avoid comparing the Canadian reception, which was only lukewarm, with the United States reception, which was a blazing triumph. In Ottawa, excursion trains from Montreal and Toronto arrived unfilled and the crowds that lined the route of her arrival were patchy. In Washington an estimated one million people stood in the rain to watch her drive past on the day she arrived; three days later, when she and Philip drove 55 miles into Virginia to visit a private estate where they could look at horses, there were people waiting to see them almost every foot of the way.

There were other ungainly contrasts, possibly more meaningful than crowd counts, which might be a direct reflection of the disparity in population. In the United States, Elizabeth and Philip were given so many gifts that their transportation became a serious problem. President Eisenhower, in spite of the pressure of the rounds of golf and Sputnik, had found time to paint them a portrait of their son and also presented them with historical documents valued at half a million dollars. They were given silver spurs and riding crops by Virginians, a fine porcelain statue of Philip playing polo, a mutation mink coat valued at $15,000, toys for their children, silver replicas of a communion service used in 1661, a gold-plated model of the Empire State Building with a ruby on its tower, and an assortment of valuable volumes and paintings.

Canada's principal gift was a minor painting. In addition, the days preceding their arrival in Canada were marked by inhospitable bickering about the cost of the visit, particularly the half a million dollars spent by the CBC. A Canadian Institute of Public Opinion poll conducted in August had found only four out of every 10 Canadians pleased with the news that Elizabeth would open parliament.

It is possible that no event in Canada's history has received coverage as extensive as that given the visit of Elizabeth and Philip. More than 1,000 reporters, photographers and technicians were accredited in Ottawa (about 350 of these from the CBC); 1,300 were accredited in Washington and 1,000 in New York. It was estimated that 60 million people in the United States—one in every three Americans—either saw the Queen on television or heard her on the radio; 12 million Canadians—or three in every four—either saw or heard her. It was the first time Canadians had been linked coast to coast by television. (Vancouver's Grey Cup game and the British Empire Games didn't reach the Maritimes.)

"Ottawa isn't equipped to handle a journalist project of this scope," announced Andrew Ross, of the Department of External Affairs, at a press briefing held before the Queen's arrival in Ottawa. "No one ever conceived," continued Ross, "of an event that would be covered by a thousand people when the Senate Chamber was built." He then outlined a system of preferential treatment and pooling that was to keep every succeeding press briefing in an uproar. At events that could be covered by only a few people, wire services would get first priority, in order of nationality. Canada was first, then Commonwealth outside Canada and then United States. Daily newspapers would come next, with a draw from a hat to determine which individual

The Queen, wearing her coronation gown, and Prince Philip enter the Senate to open Parliament, Oct. 14, 1957.

would attend, with the understanding that the winner would later "pool"—that is, share—his information with the losers. Magazines were last.

Just outside the newsroom, the CBC was rehearsing its televised coverage of the Queen's arrival. Monitor screens showed shoppers idling along the sidewalks, people boarding streetcars, empty front lawns. The commentators' voices provided a curious contrast. "The excitement is gathering," one was exclaiming, as the camera picked up a woman carrying groceries. "It doesn't seem possible but the crowds are getting bigger . . . You can almost feel through this stone wall the sense of excitement." Cameras showed placid traffic but the voice hustled along. "Youngsters are sitting on their fathers' shoulders and in some cases on their mothers' . . ." A CBC producer admitted that most of the spontaneous-sounding commentary was carefully scripted in advance.

Ross was concluding his press briefing inside. "About protocol now," he announced. "It isn't a rigid rule any longer to avoid initiating conversation with the Queen. Call her 'Your Majesty' first and after that 'Ma'am.' With Philip, it is 'Royal Highness' and then 'Sir.' Her Majesty has no objection to women wearing black when presented to her but she does prefer the wearing of gloves when she is meeting a great many people. I think that's understandable."

A handout, printed by a new photographic process that enabled the newsroom staff to have 1,000 copies ready in five minutes, announced that the Queen would be wearing an afternoon dress in shades of red, topped by a velvet coat. A fashion writer waved her hands in furious circles. "I could scream!" she wailed. "That woman has no imagination. I'll bet she's wearing black open-toed shoes as well, suede."

The Queen's daytime clothes, it was to develop later would, indeed, rarely be of any distinctive style that would not have been suitable 20 years ago and will not be suitable 20 years from now. As with her public personality, Her Majesty plays it safe and freezes. It was to strike some observers that Elizabeth seldom has a sense of her own attractiveness, such as her sister enjoys. She prefers to wear inconsequential clothes that require less confidence.

The CBC was still rehearsing. The screen showed a bus, flying a small Union Jack. One woman climbed out and stood irresolutely. "The giant murmur is growing," the practicing commentator was saying, "but even through the sound this crowd is making . . ."

The Queen was scheduled to step off the British Overseas Airways Corporation DC-7C at 4:30 p.m. This would give the *Toronto Star*, which had sent 42 men to Ottawa, and the *Toronto Telegram*, which sent 16, only time for a last-edition bulletin.

The 15-minute ceremony of welcome at the RCAF Station Uplands, outside Ottawa, had been planned with the precision of a military campaign. Officers lectured their staffs weeks ahead with pointers and diagrams and delegated authority with clipped commands. An actual four-engine plane was towed into position for rehearsals and RCAF officers pinned labels to their jackets reading "The Queen" and "Mrs. Diefenbaker" and gracefully shook hands with one another. Four men spent a full day practicing to unroll a red carpet from an immaculate white spool.

The effort may have been justified; the arrival of the Queen at Ottawa was faultless. She was to emerge from planes three times more and from a train once during the tour, but the Canadian arrival was the smoothest. A 21-gun salute boomed in the distance, the band played God Save the Queen and the color guard moved with stately slowness, as through syrup. The Queen was solemn as she was welcomed by the Diefenbakers. Philip was debonair. The former prime minister, Louis St. Laurent, watched from a third-row seat in the grandstand, his face non-committal. Fashion writers were making notes. The Queen was wearing black open-toed shoes, suede.

Five hundred and thirteen of the accredited press attended the Queen's first formal duty, a reception at Government House. She and Philip stood in a white-walled room, with a red carpet, and shook hands with everyone in less than an hour. When everyone had been presented, Elizabeth and Philip walked alone into the room where the guests were having cocktails. Spying a newspaperwoman he hadn't seen since the 1951 royal tour, Philip put an arm around her, kissed her on the cheek and asked considerately about her grandchildren. Elizabeth was so solidly ringed with the surging curious that on one occasion, as she stepped backward, she bumped into one. It was, of course, a *Toronto Star* man, George Bryant.

Upstairs in some of the 60 rooms of Government House, official residence of Canada's governors general, servants were unpacking the two tons of luggage brought by the royal party. The Queen's ball gowns were the bulkiest item, packed in crate-like boxes labeled simply "THE QUEEN" and shipped bolt upright.

The next morning, Sunday, the Queen and Philip laid a wreath at Ottawa's cenotaph and attended church at Christ Church Cathedral. Their first afternoon in Canada was kept free of formal engagements, partly because it was well known that the Queen was very nervous about her first live television broadcast, which was to be delivered that night. The royal couple, it was announced, would picnic, or enjoy a drive in the Gatineau Hills or a walk. Reporters sensed a rare opportunity for an exclusive.

The *Toronto Star* posted radio-equipped cars around the gates of Government House and the *Telegram*, getting a tip on the probable picnic site, dispatched a photographer and a reporter, Dorothy Howarth, one of the country's outstanding newspaperwomen. Another photographer sneaked into the Government House grounds and hid himself in some bushes. His three-hour vigil was rewarded. Elizabeth and Philip decided to walk in the gardens, where she took color films to show their children. They came upon a totem pole near the photographer and, seized with a sudden exuberance, skipped around it hand in hand. The delighted photographer, later discovered and ejected by the Mounties, sold his pictures to *Paris Match*, a French magazine noted for the enterprise of its photographers. (One *Paris Match* photographer, barred from leaving a ship with exclusive pictures of Grace Kelly on her way to her wedding, wrapped his negatives in plastic, put his passport in his teeth, jumped overboard and swam across the harbor to shore.)

Elizabeth was dreading the television show but it seemed vital, in view of the storm over her formal filmed television appearances in Britain. When she is afraid, she hides deeper within herself and presents an inflexible exterior. Her demeanor was calm when a CBC producer, Michael Hind-Smith, arrived at Government House late that afternoon. He was not fooled and launched a conversation about trivia. "The biggest problem," he commented later, "was to get her relaxed."

Her speech, most observers felt, was charming. She seemed assured, she smiled shyly and had a few comments that connoisseurs of her addresses said were of rare thoughtfulness. Speaking of the next day's opening-of-Parliament ceremonies, she said, "There are long periods when life seems a small dull round, a petty business with no point and then suddenly we are caught up in some great event." Her French accent, when she switched to that language, was better than flawless—it was unstudied.

When the program was over, Her Majesty breathed a deep sigh of relief, grinned gaily at her husband and Philip poured a Scotch and soda for himself and Hind-Smith. "I think," he said, "that we both need this."

There was pandemonium in the newsroom when Andrew Ross, of the External Affairs Department, that day announced that there would be room for only 60 standees in the press gallery of the Senate the next day, 16 invitations to the state reception the same evening and room for one state dinner peeker, who would be concealed behind a potted palm, and 12 reception peekers, who could stand in a pantry and look through curtains.

"Will the potted palm peeker pool?" someone asked, deadpan.

"Certainly," said Ross, equally seriously.

The Queen and Philip received the committee of the Privy Council and about 100 diplomats the next morning, Monday. Talk centred on the full bag of ducks the Duke had shot at dawn. After lunch they drove to the House of Commons, where the Queen read the Speech from the Throne in a bath of spotlights that brought the temperature of the room to 93 and measured 500 on photographers' light meters, an amount of light comparable to that used in a television studio. The strong lights, needed for a National Film Board documentary of the visit, blew all the fuses in the House of Commons just five minutes before Her Majesty arrived. For four minutes and five seconds there was total power failure. CBC technicians wept when power was restored with 55 seconds to go.

The state dinner, attended by more than 100 and served by 35 butlers and footmen, featured turtle soup and duckling. It was the first time the Queen ate turtle soup and duckling during the tour, but not the last. She also left North America with the imprint of ham firmly on her palate; in two days in the United States she was served ham four times.

At the state reception, Mrs. Davie Fulton, wife of the Minister of Justice, was making conversation with the Queen. It presented a problem that was to trouble close to a thousand people during the tour, since the subject matter had to be interesting without being either trite or controversial.

Mrs. Fulton chose the sturdy middle ground of children and explained to Her Majesty that her three children had been disappointed when watching the Queen drive by because she hadn't worn a crown.

The Queen was sympathetic. "I know," she replied warmly. "It is very important for a queen to look like a queen. After my coronation I saw some children who are relatives of mine, they've known me all their lives. They were gaping at me as though I was a stranger and I couldn't understand it—until I suddenly realized I was wearing a crown."

The next day, Tuesday, was busy. The royal couple paid a courtesy call to Hull City Hall, set off an explosion in loose clean earth that inaugurated a $31 million highway, to be known as The Queensway, which will be a link in the Trans-Canada Highway, planted a tree, shook hands with 1,342 people at a government reception and dined quietly with the Diefenbakers. In addition, Philip received Canadian members of a study conference he had called last year to examine industrial problems in the Commonwealth. Afterward he made a radio broadcast, describing the study conference.

The handshaking at the reception lasted a steady hour and 20 minutes. Aides cautioned the guests, who formed a line that snaked all through the Chateau Laurier Hotel lobby and moved imperceptibly, "Please don't shake hands too hard." The couple asked their usual quick questions ("What are these medals?" "Who are you with?"), this time of every fifth or sixth person. They paused longer when 10 Indian chiefs in mufti came through the line. The Indians had explained to reporters that they would not wear feathers because headdresses are considered formal dress and the royal invitations had stipulated informal attire.

Philip touched a button worn by Six Nations Chief Clifford Styres. "What's this?" he asked. "Twenty-five years with the post office," explained Styres proudly.

Elizabeth heard full-bodied cheering for the first time when she visited Lansdowne Park the next morning on her way to the airport. The stadium was packed with 15,000 school children, who screamed with almost hysterical joy when they saw her. She stayed 15 minutes and left to board an airplane, the RCAF's handsome C-5, for her flight to Williamsburg. She left Canada at 11:30 in the morning.

Three hours later her plane landed at Patrick Henry Airport, named for the rebel who wanted liberty from English rule, or death. In the next eight hours, the Queen was to give four speeches and visit nine separate locations. Clearly stipulated on the agenda was one rest stop—ten minutes for her and five for Philip.

It was for everyone the most punishing day of the trip. The entire area of Williamsburg is a museum, restored by John D. Rockefeller at a cost of $61 million to resemble a 17th-century village. The state of Virginia spent another $25 million so the area could celebrate in lavish style an eight-month festival marking the 350th anniversary of the first English settlement at Jamestown. It was to crown this festival that Elizabeth and Philip were first invited to North America. Buckingham Palace showed a dull interest at first but when Suez shredded Anglo-American trust, the trip was essential. Protocol demanded the inclusion of Washington as well, Canada clamored not to be ignored and the Queen had always wanted to see New York City. The tour was arranged to touch all bases.

That evening in Williamsburg, as exhausted reporters were digesting the news that they would have to be up by five the next morning in order to catch the press plane to Washington, talk turned to Elizabeth's husband. He had been from the first an enigma, a man of sharp wit that often hurt, high intelligence and periods of gregarious charm. He gives some people a feeling that he keeps fury capped behind a handsome smile; he sometimes demonstrates arrogance, with no excuse save the insufficient one that he is clever.

Philip had been demonstrating some nagging habits that repetition couldn't fail to impress. He tended to lag behind the Queen, seemingly absorbed in small conversations, so that she had to wait. He did this before 10,000 people at the Ottawa cenotaph ceremony and again outside a tiny old church in Jamestown that day.

His scorn of reporters and photographers was steadily becoming more icy.

On the press reception line at Ottawa, Lucien Côté, supervisor of outside broadcasts for the French network of the CBC, was fumbling for something courteous to say to Philip. He asked politely, "How was the trip?"

Philip stared. "You've flown in an airplane?"

"Yes, certainly," replied Côté.

"Then you know how it is," said Philip, turning away.

It was at the press reception in Washington, where she shook 1,000 more hands, that the Queen inserted a sentence in her speech. Except for a one-word ad lib in Williamsburg, inserting "even" before a mention of George III, which caused a chuckle, she never deviated from her typewritten texts. "I am told that . . . this is one of the largest press corps in the world," she read. She lifted her head, "As I look around I don't find that hard to believe." The crowd laughed and the Queen flushed with delight. A few days later, according to a man who was present, the Queen chided one of her speech writers gently about "the platitudes you have me say" and gleefully reminded him that her ad lib had drawn the biggest laugh she had ever known.

Elizabeth was making news with the fashion writers by wearing sheath evening dresses at night as she had in Paris. Inez Robb, of Scripps-Howard, saw one and wrote, "At the risk of royal displeasure, I can only say that if any other woman had appeared in it, I would have expected her to sing St. Louis Blues."

Sunday afternoon in Washington, as the previous Sunday in Ottawa, was set aside for comparative privacy. Elizabeth and Philip, 16 policemen on motorcycles, three state police cars and a press bus drove into the Virginia hunt country to visit a private estate owned by multi-millionaire Paul Mellon.

New York rained 200 tons of confetti and streamers on Elizabeth and Philip. Only General Douglas MacArthur, in recent years, has received more. Placards in shop windows read "WELCOME LIZ AND PHIL!" The couple saw some of New York's most impressive sights. Crossing from Staten Island in a ferryboat, they saw the skyline rise up rootless out of a mist, saw the green and grave Statue of Liberty with the toy ship Mayflower II bobbing at her feet, drove up Fifth Avenue in bubble-topped limousines, strolled through the airy United Nations building and felt wonder at the top of the Empire State building.

They ate lunch with 1,500 and dinner with 4,000. Since the Waldorf-Astoria Hotel couldn't accommodate all the dinner guests in one room, a closed-circuit television setup was arranged so that those in smaller dining rooms could watch the head table and hear the speeches. The Queen, naturally, knew of this arrangement but she obviously did not understand either

(a) that the camera would be on her while she was eating, or (b) that a zoomar lens on a camera can fill the screen with the face of a person 400 yards away. The result was an odd and interesting insight to Elizabeth's personality.

Reporters who had been watching the Queen incessantly for almost 10 days saw a stranger. She laughed gaily, but was so taut that she thrummed her fingers on the table frantically while she laughed. She talked with her mouth full. She fussed with her tiara, patted her too-tight curls, adjusted the shoulder straps of her gown more than 10 times. She scratched her face and grabbed back an almost-empty wine glass that a waiter began to take away.

Driving to the airport well after one in the morning, she and Philip saw the lacey lights of New York recede, heavy bridges etched in spangles in the darkness, streaks of reflected light to show that a river was beside them. As their car and escorting motorcycles passed beneath bridges, lonely policemen looked down. A guard had been mounted for hours, to ensure that no one drop anything in the path of the royal visitors. Women in dressing gowns, with topcoats thrown over their shoulders, left apartment houses to watch the Queen pass and people walking dogs stopped and stared.

Wearing a multi-colored ball gown, a dazzling tiara and an ermine coat, Elizabeth climbed the steps to the airplane. The band, chilled through by the east wind blowing across the runways, bravely played Auld Lang Syne. Elizabeth waved and disappeared into the plane. At 1:50 a.m. she was airborne and headed for England.

Canadians waited until she was home before they demanded the cost of entertaining her. Best guess: $600,000 for the three and a half days. But Elizabeth must have had a deep sense of satisfaction: throughout a touchy nine and a half days she had not made a mistake.

The Brave New World of Trailer Living

by Christina McCall

JANUARY 4, 1958

ALONG THE FRONTIERS OF THE FIFTIES, at every major construction project from the Trans-Canada pipeline, to the uranium sites and the St. Lawrence Seaway, thousands of chrome-and-aluminum caravans are herded together—in neat suburban rows. In these gaudy two-toned trailers lives a new race of gypsy-like pioneers that has sprung up as a result of improved highways, prosperous times and housing shortages. There are now 60,000 trailerites in Canada and almost three million in North America. If grouped together in one colony, the continent's trailer dwellers would form a city bigger than Montreal and Toronto combined.

These modern frontiersmen can stand in their living rooms on bulkhead-to-bulkhead broadloom carpeting, pull back floor-length chintz drapes and gaze through picture windows into the wilderness beyond. Their houses on wheels bear little resemblance to the "tin-can-tourist" or "rolling coop" trailers of the Thirties. They don't even have the same name. Trailers have become "mobile homes."

After years of disrepute as one of the ugliest of community eyesores, the trailer is beginning to gain a measure of respectability as a possible remedy for the traditional evils of the boomtown with its makeshift shacks,

dangerous overcrowding and rent gouging. Trailerites are no longer automatically derided as parasitic and prolific nomads parked behind gas stations in homemade square boxes on wheels.

But trailer owners are still plagued by problems in spite of improvements
in standards of trailer living and wide recognition of a need for mobile housing
in new communities. Habitable trailer parks are scarce. Insurance rates are high
and many municipalities have anti-trailer legislation. Still, the number of mobile
homes manufactured in Canada per year since 1950 has increased from 20 to
4,000. Including American imports, 10,000 trailers were sold in Canada in 1957.

For their owners, the daily frustrations of irritating job conditions and
tool-borrowing neighbors can be remedied with relative ease. They simply bundle blanket-wrapped knickknacks into the bathtub, jam pillows in the kitchen
cupboards, unhook the service lines and they're ready to roll to what they hope
will be pleasanter surroundings, higher-paying jobs, different neighbors, more
temperate climates. Today's mobile home has most of the conveniences of an
up-to-date suburban home. For $10,000 (the price of one uglier-than-average
strawberry-box bungalow) you can buy the most luxurious of trailers—a
double-decker, with air conditioning, two bathrooms, a dishwasher, built-in hi-
fi, a bar and a fireplace—and park it in a sun-soaked California oceanside playground in February and a cool northern Ontario pine forest in July.

In the face of such unabashed romanticism, trailer haters, usually people
who have tried and abandoned the way of life, are quick to point out that
the biggest trailer is still smaller than the tiniest bungalow, and that in
a bedroom not much larger than a normal bathroom, claustrophobia is
inescapable.

In their attempt to make trailers homelike, manufacturers have thought
up dozens of ways to beat one of the biggest problems trailer dwellers have
to face—lack of space. Originally they borrowed many ideas from ship-
builders. Now, architects are using in houses the same space-saving gimmicks found in trailers. Storage cupboards line the hall and bedrooms;
appliances are scaled to fit into cramped areas. A typical mobile home, in
the most popular size (40 feet by 10 feet), sleeps six people. Including all
furnishings, from the shower curtain to the door chime and the Venetian
blinds, it costs about $6,000.

The oak-paneled living room has windows on three sides, with floor-to-ceiling pull drapes. Furniture consists of a hide-away-bed sofa, a matching armchair, two end tables and a lamp. The purchaser can choose the decorating scheme. Current tastes run to lipstick-red with metallic-thread chesterfields and wrought-iron legs on everything. Most trailer owners in receiving areas have television sets; a TV hookup aerial is a standard service line in trailer parks.

Anything else squeezed in depends on the individual family. The hi-fi craze has hit the trailer population, too, and people are building their own sets, using the kitchen-living room divider as a bombast for the speaker. Trailer kitchens are as trim as a submarine's galley, with 10-cubic-foot refrigerators, double sinks, eye-level ovens, apartment-size gas ranges, exhaust fans and lots of cupboards. There's a 20-gallon hot-water tank concealed under the sink. A dividing shelf with a flat top for work space usually separates the living room from the kitchen, and some trailers have bamboo screens to completely conceal the kitchen. A four-chair dinette suite fits into this area but a few models have drop-leaf tables and folding chairs that can be stored in a cupboard.

The master bedroom, crammed with built-in drawers and overhead cupboards with sliding doors, is located in mid-trailer. In it, a double bed is flanked with night tables and a mirrored dressing table huddles against the wall. The bathroom, next door, has pink or turquoise fixtures, a full-length tub, glassed-in shower, toilet and mirrored washbasin. Another, smaller bedroom at the rear, usually equipped with bunk beds, provides sleeping space for children. Toys or dirty laundry can be stuffed out of the way into storage drawers under the beds.

Heat is provided by a thermostat-controlled, centrally located oil heater and a winter's fuel bill, even in the far north, is rarely more than $90. The fact that mobile homes can stand up to severe Arctic blizzards is a surprise to many people who think of them as summer-only propositions. There is a large trailer colony at Tok, Alaska, where temperatures drop to 65 below zero. The H.F. McGinness Co., of Peterborough, Ont., has built trailers on sleighs for use by the Canadian and U.S. governments in Arctic defense projects.

A complete housecleaning only takes about two hours, so trailer wives have more time to spend with their children. But what to do with the kids on a rainy day is a thorny problem. Recent models have sliding doors between rooms so one end of the trailer can be shut off and children can play on the hallway floor.

A Central Mortgage and Housing Corporation survey in 1955 showed that the average trailer dweller's income was just under $4,000, or $300 more than the national average. Some trailerites in uranium boom towns earn more than $10,000 a year. Most trailer owners are under 40 and, contrary to popular belief, there are rarely more than three people (usually a couple and one child) to each trailer. Three quarters of them are either skilled workers whose specialized jobs make it profitable to follow the booms, or married armed-service personnel whose frequent postings make permanent quarters impractical.

The rolling home is a familiar sight in Canada's pioneer communities, and more than half of the 60,000 mobile-home owners are drawn from the group of itinerant workers who move from one unpopulated job site to another—miners, engineers, construction, pipeline and hydro workers. Trailer settlements around Cornwall, Ont., are housing much of the Seaway labor overflow.

At Elliot Lake, Ont., the site of the largest uranium mines in the world, a whole new community has been built out of the wilderness. There are 1,500 mobile homes housing nearly 4,500 people. Trailers are being used for almost everything. Dentists pull teeth in them. The Bell Telephone has installed a mobile switchboard in one of them, capable of handling 500 phones. The Bank of Montreal cashes cheques in a mobile branch, and there's a beauty salon on wheels.

Construction-company owners and mining interests have realized the advantage of housing workers in mobile homes. Officials of Steep Rock Mines at Atikokan, Ont., have formed their own community of 100 company-owned trailers. They rent them to employees. The Ontario Hydro bought a fleet of trailers last year and they're being used as bunk-bed dormitories for hydro men working in the bush. Company officials say they just can't get skilled workers earning large salaries to stay in unpopulated areas without good accommodation.

The second biggest group of mobile-home owners are armed-service members, mostly men in the air force. Servicemen have difficulty finding suitable housing quarters for their families. At most military centres there aren't enough married quarters to go around, and rented housing often costs an exorbitant amount. At Camp Borden, P.E.I., before the establishment of a mobile-home park was approved by the township, landlords were charging $75 a month for condemned hen coops. At some air-force bases, such as Gander, Nfld., or the jet base at Cold Lake, Alta., married quarters or rented housing aren't available at all. The airman with a mobile home has the only possible means of keeping his family with him when he gets such a posting.

For a third group, retired people living on modest incomes, trailers can be the ideal accommodation. Some parks are luxurious playgrounds. At big parks in California, space rent goes as high as a $175 per month. Services include oceanside mooring for the trailerite's boat, telephone, television, a swimming pool, clubhouse and shopping centre.

In Canada, the trailer-park situation lags far behind that in the United States. At the few good parks in Canada, rent is about $35 a month and services include electricity, water and garbage collection. But many people are still living in shabby parks without adequate drainage, garbage disposal or proper sanitation, and municipalities, especially in Ontario, are reluctant to either build parks or to encourage the establishment of private ones. Their reluctance stems from ugly memories of the trailer camps that sprang up 10 years ago in urban areas where work was plentiful and houses scarce.

Canadian manufacturers are doing a brisk business in custom-built trailers acquired for a variety of unusual uses. In Montreal, there's a Roman Catholic chapel for cabbies in a converted trailer. Besides the altar, it has a lounge and snack bar and moves to a different location in the city every day. The Anglican Church has a similar Mission to Seamen trailer that parks on Toronto's waterfront. Trailers are also used as bookmobiles, Red Cross dispensaries, laboratories and as salesmen's display space for everything from chinaware to clothing.

Probably the world's most luxurious mobile home was built in the United States for the late King Abdul Aziz Ibn Saud of Saudi Arabia. It had a diamond-studded throne room, mahogany-paneled walls with an inlaid solid-gold crest in the royal bedroom, plus a small harem. The house trailer of the future promises to be almost as opulent. John Hays Hammond Jr., a Boston inventor, is already building 18-ton trailers with Plexiglas observation domes, sundecks, wall safes, movie screens and attachable 10,000-gallon swimming pools. Another project of Hammond's is a self-propelled helicopter mobile home.

In 1936, Roger Babson, a well-known American business prognosticator, created a fearful flurry with his prediction that within 50 years half the population of North America would be living on wheels. With trailers looking more and more like ranch bungalows and trailer parks beginning to resemble sections of suburbia, it's possible that his forecast may come true.

TODAY, *The Recreational Vehicle Dealers Association estimates there are one million trailers, motor homes or truck campers in Canada. They range in price from $5,000 for a tent trailer to $500,000 for the biggest (12.5 m), most luxurious motor home.*

CHRISTINA MCCALL (NEWMAN) *was on staff at* Maclean's *from 1956 to 1958, and again from 1971 to 1974. One of Canada's most respected non-fiction authors, her* Trudeau and Our Times *(Vol. 1), co-written with Stephen Clarkson, won a Governor General's Award in 1990.*

Flin Flon: The Town Where Everybody Plays

by
Trent Frayne

January 4, 1958

FLIN FLON IS A TOWN THAT teeters on lonely rocks 600 miles northwest of Winnipeg in the loop of longitude where summer days are almost nightless and winter ones mostly dim. It is a remote town that startled a good many Canadians last spring by producing a largely home-grown hockey team that won the junior championship of all Canada. The victory was the more remarkable because Manitoba's Flin Flon Bombers defeated the heavily favored Ottawa Canadiens, a team sponsored by the world's professional champion Montreal Canadiens and lovingly packed by them with some of this country's best young players.

While the defeat of the eastern Canadian champions may have astonished most of the hockey experts—it was the first time since 1948 that the western representative had won the national championship—only the most pessimistic fan in Flin Flon was more than mildly surprised. Nestled in the middle of a rocky nowhere, the 12,000 inhabitants of the area have made the pursuit of sports trophies a year-round avocation in relieving the monotony of their isolation, and they've grown accustomed to the pace.

Ultimate success on a national scale was a matter of time to most people in Flin Flon because they had seen one of their women's curling rinks win the western Canada championship in 1955, and their junior girls' basketball team win the Manitoba crown seven times in the last nine years, and the high-school girls win the Manitoba title six times in the last eight years. In hockey, the juniors won the Northern Saskatchewan league championship four times in the last five years, the midgets won the Manitoba championship three times in the last four years, and the juveniles won the Manitoba championship twice in the last three years.

On a local scale, there were sports of all sorts for all ages. Kids not old enough or big enough to catch a place among the 220 youngsters playing Little League baseball, or on the eight teams (four of boys and four of girls) in the 13-and-under softball leagues, played supervised games of volleyball and croquet and soccer on the town's six playgrounds. Fathers and even mothers coached the 18 hockey teams in the Tom Thumb and Pee Wee hockey leagues, and 400 people belonged to the nine-hole golf course incredibly fashioned out of solid rock, huge boulders and dense boggy muskeg. Five thousand people sprawled in the summer sun on a fantastically concocted artificial beach, and 1,600 curled in the town's three rinks.

Sometimes it's hard *not* to play something in Flin Flon. When Doug Dawson, the manager of the champion junior Bombers, moved there as a teenager 10 years ago, he was watching some high-school boys play hockey in the Flin Flon rink. A stranger standing beside him at one end of the rink asked him if he played hockey.

"Sure," said Dawson, "I played in Winnipeg."

"How long have you been here?" asked the man.

"Three days," said Dawson.

"Well then, why in thunderation aren't you out there playing now?" roared the man.

Flin Flon's battered old corrugated-tin rink has been standing since 1935, seven years after the town was first settled. The Hudson Bay Mining and Smelting Company, which now employs 3,000 men and thereby dominates the town, began to bring in hockey players in '35 to give diversion to the townspeople. Well-known Winnipeg hockey players Buddy Simpson, Ray Enright, Gordie Hayes, Cliff Workman and Buddy Hammond moved north to take jobs and play hockey. Wally Warnick and Slim Holdaway went there from Brandon, and Sid Abel, later a star centre for the Detroit Red

Wings and coach of the Chicago Black Hawks, joined the Bombers from Melville, Sask.

These were the original Bombers, a name that acquired hockey fame in the west in the old Saskatchewan Senior Hockey league. Buddy Simpson, now Conservative member of Parliament for the Churchill constituency, recalls that he received 42 cents an hour and worked in the mill 56 hours a week, which produced a weekly pay cheque of $23.52. He was married and unemployed in the mid-Thirties, as were most of the players who went to Flin Flon even before a road was through from The Pas, 100 miles south. Teams traveled by train on a spur line of the Canadian National Railways. The routes to Winnipeg or Regina or Saskatoon still wind so circuitously around the literally thousands of rock-bound lakes of northern Manitoba that the journey to any one of them requires at least 20 hours, including connecting-line stopovers.

Hockey teams have covered that route every winter since 1935. Eight years ago, the emphasis swung from senior to junior hockey, with last season being the most successful in the town's history. It reached its glorious culmination when three games of the Dominion junior final were played in the shabby old rink. This was a monumental undertaking, since the rink seats only 1,145 people and the Canadian Amateur Hockey Association asked for a guarantee of $4,500 a game when the Bombers made application for home games.

Ordinarily all seats are sold for 75 cents each for league games. To raise the required $4,500, the club boosted prices to $3 for reserved seats. The town was in a frenzy of excitement four days before the opening game. Every seat had been sold when it occurred to Pinkie Davie, the manager of the town's Community Club, which administers all children's activities, that there would be no room in the rink for the kids. He consulted Simpson, then an HBM&S company official. They organized a crew of workmen who set to work to knock one end out of the rink. When this was completed, long rows of two-by-four planks were set up at the open end of the rink to form temporary bleachers from which the kids of Flin Flon could see the Memorial Cup finals.

Meanwhile, the Ottawa Canadiens had arrived in Winnipeg on a Sunday and were practicing there before traveling to Flin Flon for the opening game on the following Wednesday. Thirty-six hours before game time, queues began to form outside the Flin Flon rink for the $1.50 standing-room accommodation. Finally game time arrived—but the Canadiens didn't. They didn't reach Flin Flon, in fact, until Thursday. There'd been a confusion about dates and venue, said their coach and manager, Sam Pollock; there'd been talk the series would start in Winnipeg.

That started the series off on a high note of acrimony. The mild-mannered Simpson said that Pollock ought to be thrown out of hockey for life. The stirred-up fans felt the same way. When the first game finally was played, two days late, the jammed crowd in the little rink hooted and hollered at Pollock as the Bombers won. In the second game the Bombers led 3-to-2 with two minutes to play, but the Canadiens piled in two goals in the last 90 seconds to win, 4 to 3. The third game played in Flin Flon was won by Canadiens, so that the teams entrained for Regina to complete the series with the the Canadiens leading, two games to one.

The giddy crescendo was reached when the Bombers won two of the next three games, forcing a seventh and deciding game on May 8. In Flin Flon that

The champion Bombers, after winning the 1957 Memorial Cup.
Six team members, including Teddy Hampson, Orland Kurtenbach and Jean Gauthier,
went on to play in the NHL.

night, a music festival was in progress in the Hapnot school auditorium. Rev. Douglas Rupp, the lean quietly composed pastor of the Northminster United Church and president of the Music Festival Association, interspersed his remarks between the music competitions with bulletins from Regina. At 10:30 p.m., the festival's imported adjudicator was delivering his critique when Rev. Rupp came bounding down the aisle. "We won! We won!" he cried, and shouts rent the auditorium while the adjudicator stared in amazement.

Outside, people began honking the horns of their automobiles and the din swelled and echoed across the rocky hills on which the town undulates. Bernice Barrett, a school teacher originally from Ontario, says she thought it was the end of the world. "I never had much interest in hockey before I came here," she says, "but this time you couldn't escape the charged atmosphere. It swept you up and carried you along. When they won, it set off a chain reaction, like the stroke of 12 on New Year's Eve."

Mixed with the normal exhilaration of the victory itself was irrepressible pride in the fact that eight players were born or raised in Flin Flon and had climbed up through pee wee, bantam, midget and juvenile ranks to the junior Bombers right in the tumbledown rink at the edge of town. That's a unique progression nowadays when professional clubs move accomplished young players to teams they sponsor and on which the players can be developed in the pro team's system and pattern. These days most junior hockey stars maintain contact with their families only with the co-operation of the postman. In Flin Flon, the fans had been watching Captain Teddy Hampson, who scored the winning goal in the deciding game, from the day his mother had registered him with Pinkie Davie at the Community Club.

Three other Bombers, Mel Pearson, Carl Forster and George Konik, were the sons of underground miners. Forster's father, in fact, was 5,000 feet underground the night his son was playing for the national championship. Ron Hutchison's dad was a boilermaker and Duane Rupp's father a laborer. Most of the people in Flin Flon could remember the winter Ken Willey had first played in the Tom Thumb league, and there weren't many people in town who didn't know that Mel Pearson's mother and Ken Willey's mother were sisters.

Most of the other players were the products of a week-long tryout camp held every mid-September in the Flin Flon rink. The Club advertises its school in small-town newspapers in Manitoba, and players who make the grade with coach Bobby Kirk, a former New York Rangers forward, are given jobs with HBM&S Co. If their work is satisfactory they qualify for advancement like any other employee. The players practice every morning and work at the plant every afternoon. They play a 55-game schedule, 30 at home, in a league that includes Saskatchewan's Estevan, Prince Albert, Regina, Melville and Saskatoon.

On road trips, the Bombers are ambassadors for Flin Flon; the club supplies each player with maroon flannel jackets and grey flannel trousers for off-the-ice wear and players are instructed never to appear in public without a white shirt and maroon knitted tie. They were wearing these natty clothes at a Memorial Cup victory dinner in Jubilee Hall as they returned in triumph from Regina when 380 Flin Flon citizens paid $5 a plate to honor them.

This was the climax of something more than a mere sports victory. "When our team won," philosophized Lou Parres, a consulting geologist who has lived in Flin Flon for 10 years, "it was a reflection of the determination and the *esprit de corps* of the people who live here. Those are qualities of our isolation. To most people in this country it was highly improbable that Flin Flon would win. The people in this town have come to know that the highly improbable is entirely possible. Look at the town itself."

Flin Flon *is* an improbable town. Its street lights are never turned off. Many of the houses have no cellars and are built on stilts. Most of the sidewalks are built on sewers, boxed in and insulated with sawdust. Every night the whole foundation of the town shakes slightly as dynamite charges are set off in the mines a mile below the surface through solid rock. In June, it's light enough to play golf at midnight, and in December it's necessary to turn on the lights of an automobile to navigate the winding climbing streets at four in the afternoon.

The lights are left burning because the city engineers discovered that when they were turned off in winter, the cold weather weakened the filament. Constant turning on and off burned out the lights. Since electricity is extremely cheap in a country of numerous lakes and rivers, it was found to be less expensive simply to keep the lights burning.

The company, which hits a payroll of about $12 million a year, with an average wage of $4,700, is the life blood of the community but in some respects it is a blight, too. Smelter smoke containing sulphuric-acid fumes pours endlessly from a tall spire of a chimney that dominates the town and is a landmark for airplanes 50 miles around. When the atmospheric pressure is low and the wind is right, the smoke floats across the town and it can burn out lawns and kill plants overnight. Consequently, practically no one has a lawn in Flin Flon.

On the other hand, the company created out of complete wilderness an unbelievable summer resort and golf course for the residents. The beach forms a horseshoe around one arm of Phantom Lake, a mile southeast of the town. The lake is bordered by 100 yards of soft fine sand which in turn has a 200-yard border of grass nestled under birch and poplar trees, far enough removed from the company's smoke stack to escape the deadly fumes. The beach was literally created. The company sent a fleet of trucks 16 miles north of Flin Flon to a sand pit and the trucks transported hundreds of thousands of yards of sand to the edge of the lake in early spring. The sand was dumped across deep stretches of ice and snow. When spring came and the ice melted, the sand settled at ground level, dried out in the sun and formed the beach. Tons of sand are transported every spring to the water's edge and the beach refurbished.

The nine-hole golf course is another phenomenon. It was fashioned out of rock and muskeg. The course, a couple of miles from the plant, now has greens of Washington bent grass, and fairways of Kentucky bluegrass. Howard McIntosh, the company spokesman, says that "as long as you use a commercial fertilizer in the proper proportion, you can grow grass on damned near anything," and Flin Flon's golf course is the living proof. It took three years to build, presented drainage problems as the engineers endeavored to follow ravines in the rock outcroppings to clear the muskeg, and turned up thousands of tons of stones and boulders which potential golfers helped clear in work parties armed with rakes and shovels and their bare hands.

The company provides things like the golf course and the summer resort, Howard McIntosh explained in a recent tour of the area, "to keep the people happy."

"We're pretty remote," he amplified. "There can be monotony. But if the people are happy, the work gets done."

It was a frontier town when the mine began to be developed in

December, 1927, with tent homes and saloons and gambling rooms and ladies of pleasure, a town whose main street oozed dirty water from its muskeg. Jack Freedman came soon after. A small voluble cigar-chewing man of 68, Freedman was a newsie on the CNR when the spur line first reached Flin Flon. Now, he owns a confectionery store and newsstand with a slanting floor on the main street called the Fall In because, as he explains, "you've got to practically do that to get in the joint." He has a large blackboard outside his premises on which he chalks daily homilies upbraiding the town council or censuring the mayor or applauding the hockey team. "Everybody kowtows to the company, including the council," explains Freedman. "I speak my mind."

To a visitor in Flin Flon, it seems that most people speak their minds. They're obviously aware of their isolation because when they speak of taking a trip they always use the word "out." Saul Nathanson, the manager of the Rex Theatre, one of the two movie houses in town, has left Flin Flon five times but he's always returned. "I've lived in Saskatoon, Edmonton, Lloydminster, Dawson Creek and Calgary, but I've always come back," he says. "You feel you're part of something here. For example, we all felt we were personally connected with the Bombers as they made their way toward the Memorial Cup. It really wasn't the Bombers; it was *us* showing the country what we can do."

FLIN FLON'S BOMBERS *continued to produce hockey talent—the Philadelphia Flyers Bobby Clarke is probably best-known—but 1957 was the only time they won a national championship. From that squad, Teddy Hampson was the first to break into the NHL, in 1959 with the Toronto Maple Leafs, and played professionally until his retirement in 1981. The next season, Orland Kurtenbach and Jean Gauthier also made it into the NHL— Kurtenbach joined the New York Rangers and played 13 seasons for four teams, while Gauthier broke in with the Montreal Canadiens and played for three other teams over the next decade. Mel Pearson, Ron Hutchison and George Konik also played in the NHL.*

Going Steady: Is It Ruining Our Teenagers?

by
Sidney Katz

JANUARY 3, 1959

IN THE AGE-LONG BATTLE between adolescents and their parents, the two factions are now embroiled in what is perhaps their most turbulent and acrimonious controversy.

The subject at issue is "going steady," a dating custom which made an immense leap in popularity just after the Second World War and has now reached epidemic proportions among our youth. "Going steady" means that a boy and girl—usually in the 12- to 17-year-old age group—form a relationship which can best be described as a form of premarital monogamy. As long as their pact lasts, they vow tacitly or in fact to be "faithful" to each other. They don't "cheat" by looking twice at, or going out with, another member of the opposite sex. If they live near each other, they walk to and from school together. They eat, study, play and go to dances and parties as a couple. They are, in matter of fact, as inseparable as a husband and wife and their union is regarded as inviolable by their contemporaries.

Going steady has kicked up a hullabaloo of astronomical proportions. In a recent *Canadian High News* poll, 82 per cent of parents were opposed to their daughters going steady. Anxious parents are constantly seeking advice on how to deal with problems related to going steady. Steady dating is frequently discussed at meetings of organizations interested in youth and millions of words on the subject, pro and con, have appeared in print in the last few years.

Many parents are alarmed—especially if they have a daughter—by the chance that "something might happen." They point to the inexorable law of nature that "biology plus propinquity equals intimacy." They are supported by a statement from a Roman Catholic theologian that "going steady is a proximate occasion of sin—a situation from which sin will almost inevitably result. It places too much strain on the moral fibre of the individual." Apart from the danger of an "accident," parents dread the possibility of their youngsters drifting into early marriage long before they are economically or socially prepared for it. An unprecedented number of teen-age weddings confirms the reality of this fear: since the outbreak of the Second World War, the proportion of teenage brides (no doubt partly under the influence of better economic conditions) has increased by one-third. Sociologists have completed several studies underlining the hazards of early marriages. A teenage bride and groom, these surveys show, are twice as likely to be divorced as a couple who are married in their twenties.

On another level, many parents object to going steady on the grounds that it has a stultifying effect on the social and intellectual growth of their offspring. One father told me, "It's a cut-and-dried, hidebound affair. It has no excitement or freshness to it. They don't have any fun. At the ripe old age of 15 they're like a stolid middle-aged married couple—the girl is bored and the boy is henpecked. It's a nauseating and silly business all around."

Teenagers who favor the institution of going steady react to these parental outbursts in puzzlement and anger. "Why do they get so hysterical over going steady?" an attractive 15-year-old brunette asked me. "Most of their views are ancient and idiotic—I get a good laugh out of them." Many girls go steady, I learned, "because everybody does it. If you don't, you're dead—an outcast." Having a steady automatically guarantees that you'll be going to all the parties and dances. "You don't have to spend your time before every affair suffering with the jitters." They prefer a steady beau because they don't have to get all dressed up "and make an impression on a new fellow every week." They find it comforting to know somebody well enough "to confide in." As for the sexual dangers, they say, "Parents are filthy-minded and suspicious, that's why they think that way. A smart girl doesn't let things go that far."

While not as wholeheartedly sold on the idea of having a permanent attachment, many of the boys I spoke to had kind words to say about going steady. A shy 15-year-old, who had been going with a girl for three months, told me, "If you phone a few girls and they refuse you, the girls talk and the word gets around and you're the laughing stock. This way I'm always sure of a date." A more sophisticated 16-year-old observed, "We've got a gang of about eight couples and the girls are always arranging parties. It's an easy and inexpensive way to have a social life. If you take out a new date every time, you have to go to expensive shows and dances. Who's got a million?" An added economic advantage is that the steady girl friend often pays half the entertainment bill.

Are the fears of parents about going steady justified? Are teenagers being unfairly pilloried because of a harmless dating custom? To get the answers to these and several other pertinent questions, I have spent the last several weeks interviewing teenagers, parents, teachers, youth leaders, clergymen, sociologists and psychiatrists. While nothing can be said which would be true of all teenagers everywhere, here are my main conclusions:

- The vogue of going steady is largely due to the teenagers' almost pathological desire to conform to current dating practices. While they boldly defy their parents, they're terrified of each other. They recoil at the thought of being singled out as different in any way. Conformity is one way of acquiring a feeling of personal security.

- Going steady is not providing a large proportion of teenagers with the security and satisfactions they hoped to get out of it. When *Canadian High News* polled steady couples in 10 cities, 53 per cent of the girls and 40 per cent of the boys reported, "My steady doesn't meet my requirements." But they would rather go steady than not. One girl, who had described her beau as "a fuddydud," asked me, "What do you want me to do—leave him and put myself on the shelf?"

- Many of the steady relationships are psychologically unhealthy for both the boy and girl concerned. Some psychiatrists speak of them as "neurotic clutchings." An example I encountered was the 16-year-old boy, dependent on his mother, who sought a substitute in his 15-year-old girl. She picked his clothes for him, decided what school courses he should take and became deeply involved in the frequent quarrels he had with his family and friends. It was weakening for the boy and the immature girl was trapped and betrayed by her maternal instincts. I found several other relationships where an insecure boy receives satisfaction by bullying and dominating his girl. A 16-year-old girl told me, "He even used to call me foul names in front of my friends. I was only 15 then; he was 17. I was afraid of him. I didn't have enough guts to walk out on him until a few months ago."

- I found that another emotionally unhealthy aspect of steady dating is the aftermath of a "divorce." It is the female who bears the brunt of the suffering. A pert blonde of 15 told me how she felt "alone, adrift and scorned. None of the boys would come near me for a few months." Parents told me of their daughters who cried for days after a breakup with a steady boy friend, and stopped eating and sleeping. A teacher told me of an excellent student who was jilted at Christmas time. Her marks steadily declined and she failed her year. "Divorced" couples often become enemies and avoid each other—even to the extent of refusing to go to the same parties.

- Sex play is an important part of almost every steady relationship. Whether the boy or girl kiss, neck, pet or "go all the way" can depend to some extent on the individuals involved, their family background and the area in which they live. I visited one low-income-bracket neighborhood where there are many broken homes. Youth leaders who worked in the district told me that "going steady" was synonymous with "sleeping together." In some of the new suburban areas, where there are no established traditions of behavior, some couples hang out in groups where a variety of sex activity, including intimacy, is the expected pattern of behavior. One of their favorite games was a "kissing contest"— the girl who could cause her boy's pulse rate to increase the most was declared the winner. The growing number of teenage, unwed mothers—despite the widespread use of contraceptives—indicates that many adolescents are "going all the way." One large urban social agency told me that the majority of the 2,000 married mothers they interviewed during 1957 were in their teens; over 100 of them were 14 years old or less. On the other hand, my overall impression is that the vast majority of steady couples stop short of sexual union.

- The custom of going steady is largely a female device—initiated (however subtly), encouraged and perpetuated by the girls. It is the female answer to the "wallflower" problem. Under any other system of dating, most girls wouldn't have as many dates. The boys go along with the system because it fills certain of their needs and has certain advantages. A woman youth leader observed, "On the whole, the girls seem to be smarter, and more aggressive—many girls hold the boy captive like a rabbit in a snare." Many girls complained to me about the growth of the matriarchal system and the lack of masculine aggressiveness among the fellows they knew. "You can lead most boys around by the nose," said one girl. "They never assert themselves. They don't want to be stronger and better than women any more."

- Parents, despite their general opposition, have completely failed to halt the going-steady habit. Viewed as a class they seem to have lost their grip on children in the 14- to 17-year-old age group. "Nothing works any more," said one father, sadly. The teenagers seem to have closed their ranks. Parents don't seem to be able to reach their children; children don't seem able to reach their parents. In one large-scale American survey, 76 per cent of adolescents complained that they couldn't discuss intimate matters with their parents.

• I found that many parents, when it comes to asserting authority, are paralyzed and immobilized. This condition is often due to real confusion in the parent's mind as to what's right and what's wrong. Part of the conflict can be traced to the torrent of psychological teaching during the past 40 years—much of it contradictory—emphasizing the importance of the individual adjusting to the group. A father who refused to allow his daughter to see her "steady" for the fifth night of the same week later had misgivings. "Do you think I'll hamper her development?" he asked. Much of the psychological talk has filtered down to the youngsters who sometimes use it opportunely. "What are you trying to do—make me dependent?" asked a 15-year-old boy who was told to be home from a party by midnight. Many parents, seduced by the current cult of popularity, have abdicated the traditional role of being wise and guiding elders to their offspring. They want their children to regard them as buddies and pals, rather than stuffed shirts and old fogies. Many teenagers seem to resent the intrusion: they prefer friends of their own age. Despite their defiance, they want and need authority.

Among the numerous groups I interviewed, anywhere from one-quarter to two-thirds of the youngsters had chosen a steady mate, whether their parents liked the idea or not. The custom generally starts when the girl is 13 or 14. Among girls, going steady seems to reach its peak somewhere between the 16th and 17th year. After that, many girls refuse to enter an alliance just for the sake of an assured date. They insist on liking to be with the person they're going out with.

Once a couple have started going steady, they will often go to extraordinary lengths to be together. In the three-minute interval between classes, a girl may rush the entire length of the school to catch a glimpse of her beau. In some high schools, teachers are assigned to a daily "pigeon hunt"—patrolling the corridors and routing out the "hall pigeons," couples who have arrived as early as 8:15 to moon and to mug. As a symbol of belonging to each other, couples sometimes affect similar dress and styles.

The keystone of the going-steady relationship is "faithfulness" and the cardinal sin is to "cheat." Cheating usually means dating others of the opposite sex or, sometimes, merely showing a personal interest in them. One girl spent an hour in the school nurse's office, crying because her boy friend had been making eyes at another girl. A boy roundly chastised his steady because she stopped to talk to a male classmate in the corridor a few times. A mother told me that her son was forced to give up dropping in on a girl in the neighborhood, whom he had known since childhood, because her regular date objected. At dances, steady couples generally dance every dance together. If the pattern is broken, hard feelings and fist fights are likely. A boy or girl who cheats or who switches steadies more than once or twice a year can become the object of scorn and contempt. I was told, "That's cheap—they would be acting as badly as those people in Hollywood you read about." One vivacious youngster who charmed a boy away from another girl was ostracized by her group for several weeks. Most boys, like one 15-year-old I spoke to, passively accept the system: "I wouldn't dream of going after a girl who was going steady no matter how much I wanted her."

Young love: going steady reached "epidemic" proportions in the 1950s.

After several months of going steady the relationship may assume all the sparkle and spontaneity of a couple who have just celebrated their silver wedding anniversary. Dress and manners sometimes tend to become casual. One 16-year-old girl often receives her boy friend clad in a shabby bathrobe, her face covered with cold cream and her hair up in curlers. In the middle of the evening she may wander off to take a bath, leaving him with members of her family. She bawls him out for getting low marks in physics or for going out with boys who are known to drink. One anti-going-steady youth told me, "You see them driving in a car, not talking to each other; she's looking out the window; he's concentrating on his driving. They remind me of my parents."

One good feature of this kind of unglamorized propinquity, in the opinion of some parents, is that it discourages sexual activity. "George is over at the house a lot," one father told me. "He knows the whole family well. He sees my girl under all kinds of circumstances. She's less likely to get into trouble than if she went out with a long succession of strange boys." On the other hand, from many interviews it is my impression that kissing, necking and heavy petting are characteristic of many if not most going-steady relationships. Several girls told me, "Sex is the chief problem between my boy friend and me." Others said, "It's up to the girl to stop it." Several boys told me how they exercised self-restraint: "If you like the kid, you don't want to get her into trouble."

I found that many parents were making the mistake of assuming that their children know more than they actually do. One youth leader is often approached by teenagers with elementary questions about sex, who preface their speech with, "I know I'm supposed to know all this but . . ." A father, who was cautioning his 15-year-old son about the dangers of becoming aroused was told, "It's not that serious. It's like a game. I see how far I can go and still keep control." A 13-year-old pregnant girl explained, "I like this boy and I just didn't know how to say 'no.'" A 16-year-old boy observed, "I've played around quite a bit, but I didn't know you could get a girl pregnant that way."

Recently, with a social worker, I reviewed several hundred cases of teenage pregnancy. Many of the couples had been seeing each other regularly, with little or no supervision. Most of the liaisons had taken place in parked cars, in homes where the girl was baby-sitting or at the homes of friends whose parents were out of town. The social worker observed, "Many parents place a burden on their children by trusting them too much." Another conclusion she came to was that many homes failed to emphasize acceptable standards of behavior and moral values. The result is that many adolescents feel no guilt about what they've done. Questioned about his knowledge of five teenage pregnancies in a suburban community, a 15-year-old boy replied, "What's all the fuss about? We're no worse than any other place." Later, he confessed that he was part of a gang that "went all the way." The gang set the standards; if you didn't adhere to them, you were "chicken."

One highly qualified social scientist affiliated with a large Canadian university believes that going steady is the forerunner of a social revolution in sex behavior. He sees no harm in premarital relationships for adolescents if the social taboos and fears of conception are banished. He predicts that at least one of these barriers will soon be removed with the discovery of a foolproof oral contraceptive. He says, "Perhaps the future pattern of mating will be for each child, once he or she has reached puberty, to experience a series of temporary 'pre-marital' marriages. Finally, when they are mature in their 20s, they will settle down with a single partner."

But this view, of course, is far from general. And parents can find further reassurance in the fact that the average period of going steady is fairly brief. It often ends with the school year. Sometimes it doesn't survive the football season: the girl may be dazzled by a star fullback and disenchanted when he's no longer a public idol. Teenagers give a variety of reasons for breaking up. One said, "He began to bore me. We used to talk on the phone an hour. Now a five-minute call is mostly made up of pauses. We've got nothing to say to each other." Another girl walked out when her boy friend insisted that it was her duty to allow him greater intimacies. Cheating, of course, is always sufficient grounds for a separation. When a boy ends an alliance it's sometimes because the girl has become too possessive. One lad rebelled when his partner insisted that he phone her every night; another when he was practically ordered to skip some of his basketball practices in order to spend more time dating.

Parents frequently ask the experts in psychology, "What can we do about going steady—especially when we disapprove of the other child?" Most psychologists would advise them to talk over the matter with the child in as calm and friendly a manner as possible. If it can be arranged—and this suggestion came from a bright 16-year-old girl—the discussion should take place during a period when the children are between steadies. The success of a heart-to-heart talk with a 15- or 16-year-old depends on how successful parents have been in maintaining contact with their children. Parents are advised to keep close ties with their youngsters around the period of puberty and after—11 to 14. That's the time when parents and children grow apart.

One course of action usually fails: forbidding the relationship. It leads to rebelliousness and builds an intense loyalty to the boy or girl. At any rate, judging by several of my interviews, the couple will continue to see each other clandestinely, at school, at a club or at a girl friend's home.

Several parents told me that they refrain from criticizing a boy they don't approve but encourage their daughter to invite him to the house. One father recalls, "This boy spent two or three evenings with us playing ping-pong, cards and watching TV. He wisecracked, he was ill-mannered and his conversation was limited. None of us said a word but my daughter stopped seeing him shortly after. She was able to evaluate him in the light of her own background and recognize that he didn't fit in."

For a more meaningful understanding of the custom of going steady, parents—no matter how modern they claim to be—have to realize that they and their children live in two different worlds. Several teenagers told me that they were shocked by their parents' suggestion that they go out with several boys. "It sounds like something immoral," they said.

What is the nature of this new world inhabited by our adolescents? There is an almost obsessive need for security. Our children want everything settled and arranged in advance; they want to take no risks. It is significant that when several thousand American teenagers were asked to name the main prerequisite of a happy marriage—and the results would probably be the same here—nine out of 10 replied, "Money." Children, evidently, have absorbed in concentrated form the adult emphasis on security as evidenced by our own advocacy of health insurance, pensions and guaranteed annual wages. The teenagers' premature conservatism and excessive desire to conform are also symptomatic of their search for security.

Another characteristic of the new world is a growing unwillingness to struggle and make sacrifices. Reared during a cycle of prosperity, many youngsters have been robbed of the opportunity to strive for what they want. They tend to lack initiative and be passive—an attitude summed up by the password of the Beat Generation, "No sweat!" Thus, when many modern teenagers reach the age when they're interested in girls, they discover that going steady snugly fits in with their deeply felt need for security, conformity and passivity.

Trained in psychology and social work, SIDNEY KATZ started his 15-year writing career at Maclean's in 1950, before joining the Toronto Star. In 1979, he left daily journalism to become adjunct professor of journalism at the University of Western Ontario for five years. He now lives in Toronto.

Part Two

The More Things Change, the More They Remain the Same

What it Means to Be a Canadian

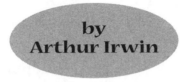

by
Arthur Irwin

FEBRUARY 1, 1950

Last June, Arthur Irwin, who retires as Editor of *Maclean's* with this issue, was asked to define the Canadian to an American audience at Buffalo, N.Y. The great interest aroused by his speech leads the editors to publish it here as his last staff contribution to the magazine.

I COME HERE TODAY as a Canadian to try to tell you something about my country and its people.

Who is this Canadian and what makes him act the way he does?

Few of you, I would suppose, have ever heard of Sir John A. Macdonald. Sir John was the first prime minister of the Canadian confederation. He was a lovable old cuss, and as adroit a politician as this hemisphere has produced. He was also a statesman who envisioned the rise of a nation on the northern half of this continent which should have dominion from sea to sea and from the river unto the ends of the earth.

On April 9, 1867, he wrote privately to a friend in India this letter:

"I have been in England since November. I have at last succeeded. I sail in four days for Canada with the Act uniting all of British North America in my pocket.

"A brilliant future would certainly await us were it not for those wretched Yankees, who hunger and thirst for Naboth's field. (Naboth, you will remember, was the owner of a Biblical vineyard which his neighbor coveted and took.)" When he wrote that letter Sir John undoubtedly was thinking of the tension which existed between Great Britain and the North during and after your Civil War and the fear in Canada that this tension might result in an American attack on Canada.

No doubt he remembered, as did all his generation of Canadians, that twice during the previous 82 years American forces actually had tried to capture Canada and that during one of those attempts an American army actually had occupied Montreal for more than six months.

We don't do it that way now—which indicates that perhaps both of us have learned something worth learning. As I passed through customs at the Peace Bridge last night I was reminded how different was the most recent reciprocal invasion of American territory by a Canadian force.

Believe it or not, when it came to organizing a joint American-Canadian Expedition to throw the Japanese out of Kiska, during the last war, it was discovered that under your customs regulations the Canadian troops couldn't get into Alaska without paying duty not only on their personal effects but on their weapons.

Such a situation demanded radical treatment and your then Secretary of State, Cordell Hull, found it. After noting that the Canadian forces were the first foreign troops since Lafayette "to stand beside our own armed forces in expelling the enemy from American soil," he calmly designated the entire Canadian contingent "distinguished foreign visitors," which meant that no one could collect duty from them.

"I come to protect you, not injure you," proclaimed your General Hull when he crossed into what is now Ontario with an army from Detroit in 1812: "The United States offers you peace, liberty and security; your choice lies between these and war, slavery and destruction. Choose then—and choose wisely."

The Canadian did choose and what he chose was to seek peace, liberty and security *in his own way* with results that only in recent years have begun to speak their inner meaning.

Let me illustrate. The scene is the Social and Humanitarian Affairs Committee of the United Nations at Lake Success, N.Y. The year: 1946. There's been a bitter argument about the policy to be followed in continuing relief to

Europe. Former Mayor Fiorello La Guardia of New York City, head of UNRRA, has been arguing vehemently for one position. He's been adamantly opposed by the U.S. government and by Britain. Britain and the United States, on the other hand, have failed completely to win support from some 40 other countries.

The battle has gone on for most of one day, far into the night and most of the next day, at times with vitriolic intensity. The Canadians, as suppliers of relief, are vitally concerned and have been involved in the wrangle but not in such a way as to be irretrievably entangled with any of the contending factions.

Finally, La Guardia makes a dramatic intervention. "We've got to bring this thing to a head," he says. "I will take sight unseen any resolution which the Canadian delegate will propose."

After a two-hour adjournment, the Canadian submitted a resolution which gave everybody something of what they wanted but nobody everything. It was at once adopted unanimously save for the Russian bloc. In itself this was a trifling incident, but something very like it has happened far too often to be accidental.

Why did La Guardia so trust the Canadians? Why did the other contending factions display a similar confidence? And how did it happen that the Canadian had the skill to resolve their difficulties?

Apparently something pretty fundamental has happened to the character and status of the Canadian since American armies knocked at his door and a Sir John Macdonald worried about more of the same to come. What is it?

To the outsider, of course, I admit we must be a bit puzzling. The King of England is King of Canada and yet he has no more political power in Canada than has Chicago's Col. Robert McCormick. We are an independent nation, yet we have an English governor general who doesn't govern.

When Canadian troops go into battle abroad, they fly a Canadian flag— but at home we have no national flag because we haven't been able to agree on one. The resources of two official languages have not provided us with one word to define The Canadian satisfactorily in both.

We belong to a world-circling Commonwealth which has no constitution and no common agreement to fight as a unit but had both the strength and the spirit to stand alone against Hitler when Europe fell.

At times our domestic dissensions seem to threaten to blow our state apart and yet we are probably one of the most stable countries in the world today. When recently an Ontario Presbyterian of Scottish extraction was succeeded as prime minister by a French Roman Catholic from Quebec, there was scarcely a ripple of change discernible in either the internal or foreign policies of our government.

I repeat then: who is this puzzling Canadian and how did he get that way?

I suppose you know that just a little less than half of the 13,300,000 we number are of Anglo-Saxon extraction. One third are French and the rest of other European stock.

We are sprung from many sources but the one thing we now have in common as a people is that we are Americans . . . North Americans . . . just as you are. Some of us were very early Americans. The French Canadian, for instance, has more American generations behind him than any other white stock north of the Rio Grande save the Spanish.

But two things distinguish us from other Americans.

One: We are the northern North American with all that implies in terms of influence of climate and terrain on character and a way of life.

Two: We are the unique American in that we alone among all the Americans of two continents have insisted on maintaining political connection with our parent stem in Europe.

Up and down the hemisphere all the way from Baffin Island to Patagonia, all other Americans at one time or another have cut the connection or had it cut for them . . . the Dutch, the Spanish, the Portuguese, the French, the midcontinent Anglo-Saxons who launched the U.S.A. Only the Canadian American refused to break his political continuity with history.

This is, of course, a simple and obvious fact but in my view, it is the first basic clue to the Canadian character. I don't think you can understand the Canadian unless you appreciate that he is really two separate persons in one.

In one aspect of his being he is a Geography Man, a man molded by the geography of North America, a man who has had to build a way of life suited to a stern and difficult land, in the face of great obstacles both physical and political.

In his other aspect he is a History Man, a man who has responded and still responds to the pull of history, a man driven by a deep intuitive response to the traditional values enshrined in his heritage overseas.

The Canadian, in short, is the northern North American in whom there has been and still is a constant conflict between history and geography.

And the resulting dualism in his life has had a profound effect on his character, his attitudes and his status and role in the world. You can see this dualism operating in the individual Canadian in the group and in the nation as a whole. I've seen a Canadian prime minister go to an imperial trade conference, for example, and do his utmost to throttle textile imports from England's Lancashire to safeguard the Canadian textile industry. That's the Geography Man acting on the basis of sheer self-interest.

The next day the same prime minister would get up on the platform and with a gesture worthy of a Roman senator wrap himself in the flag that flies over Lancashire. That's the History Man.

And the two men in one act with equal sincerity. Which must be a bit baffling to the outsider. Sometimes it's baffling to the Canadian himself.

Like you, the Canadian in meeting the challenge of his geography had first to unlock the keys to half a continent. You have only to look at your own map to see evidence of his footsteps in a wilderness. LaSalle, Marquette, St. Louis, Champlain, Cadillac, Detroit, Ford's River Rouge, Duluth . . . all these and many more are Canadian names, for it was the Canadian who first explored the great central interior of this continent from the Gulf of Mexico to Hudson Bay.

Like you, we had to thrust steel from ocean to ocean and being very few in a very large space we had to take some wild gambles. Our first transcontinental was built by a population of 4.5 million; yours by a population of 37 million.

As with you, our geography broke down European class distinctions and made us democrats. The first English governor who came to Ontario after your revolution wanted to build a new British state in the north on the basis of an established church and a hereditary aristocracy based on the ownership of land.

But it wouldn't work. You couldn't make a duke out of 10,000 acres of virgin Ontario bush. There was more than enough for everybody and no man had to serve under another. The land laughed at the aristocrat and sprouted a New World democracy. It is not an accident that today we have no titles, hereditary or otherwise, despite the fact we have a king.

To survive in a harsh and empty land we had to breed a tough and stable people. At times we've had to take long chances but basically we are more cautious than you. We've had to be. Our climate allows us less margin of error. On the average the Canadian farmer, I suppose, must be poorer than the American farmer by four or five weeks of warm weather a year.

Our frontier is the Arctic wilderness and the wilderness still presses close upon our cities. From our capital's Parliament buildings one looks upon the everlasting hills which, scarcely scarred by human hands, stretch unbroken to the empty northern sea. Nearly every Canadian at some time in his life has felt the shiver of awe and loneliness which comes to man when he stands alone in the face of untamed nature; and this is one reason why we are a sober and essentially religious people.

Your true Canadian loves this land and it has yielded him a competence which no nation, outside your own, has equalled.

All of us are familiar with the fabulous outburst of productive energy which has swept your country during the past 10 years. Some of you may not be aware that something very similar has happened north of the border. Between 1938 and 1948 our population increased 16 per cent, employment increased 40 per cent and the volume of goods and services produced by 75 per cent. This has meant an advance in our average standard of living of roughly 50 per cent. Your advance, I'm told, has been approximately the same.

Geography has done very well by the Canadian.

What then impelled the Canadian to remain a History Man and alone among all the Americans stubbornly to cling to his political root in the face of a century and three-quarters of rising isolationism in the whole American hemisphere?

The reasons for this go very deep and I'm not going to try to probe them fully here. One obvious cause was the dynamic expansionism of a United States which during much of the 19th century felt its Manifest Destiny was to embrace at least all of North America above the Rio Grande. And we didn't want it that way.

Our original French, defeated by one conqueror, feared engulfment by another. The Anglo-Saxon loyalists, who came to us after defeat in your revolutionary war, understandably were determined not to be twice defeated. So together they drew on the power of the Old World to maintain a balance in the New.

Other deep emotional and spiritual urges were also at work, but reasons aside, the tenacity with which this Canadian American insisted on maintaining the political link with Europe was extraordinary.

Even at a time when governing statesmen in England were talking about getting rid of "those wretched colonies . . . those millstones around our necks" and "looking forward without regret to Canada becoming an independent state," this dual personality which is the Canadian insisted on sticking to his original political base come hell and high water.

But—and here we reach the heart of the story—he insisted on sticking *on his own terms*. With remarkable results.

Three years before your Declaration of Independence, Governor Hutchison of Massachusetts told the Assembly of that state: "I know of no line that can be drawn between the supreme authority of Parliament (of Great Britain) and the total independence of the colonies."

The Canadian found that line. And in doing so he incubated a new political idea of major world significance. For out of the struggle within the Canadian between History and Geography came first the fact and then the concept of that unique world political system known as the British Commonwealth of Nations, a system built on the idea that nations can achieve freedom and independence without complete separateness from others.

It took you 10 years to write your Declaration of Independence and make it stick. It took us a century to make our declaration and we didn't write it— we lived it.

As with you, the Canadian, to survive in the American scene, had to adjust his life patterns, his political patterns, to his geography. He had to be free to run his own affairs in his own way. This meant that he had to insist on the right to tell a king on the other side of the water how the king's business on this side of the water should be run. But, unlike you, he couldn't or wouldn't give up his king. His sense of history's continuity ran too deep for that.

As with you, in the beginning there was violence. Rebellion, marching and countermarching, blood spilled, towns and villages put to the torch; there were trials and hangings; political prisoners from the Canadas were shipped in hulks to far-off Tasmania.

But in the end the Canadian got his way. Even as down through the centuries the king had become the servant of the people in Britain and the symbol of their oneness, so on this side of the water he became the servant of an American people and the symbol of their tie with an ancient root.

First, we secured the right to govern our internal affairs without interference. Then, because it was the only one which would work in Canadian geography, we had to devise a federal political system and graft it into the British system of parliamentary government.

Then, little by little, we got control over our external affairs. Slowly the concept emerged of a wholly autonomous nation freely associating with other nations for the preservation of a common way of life.

Slowly, the concept spread around the world as the other Dominions grew in the Canadian pattern. Slowly, the consequences of the Canadian's adjustment to the North American scene were projected back into the parent political structure and an empire was transformed into a commonwealth that was something new under the sun.

In a sense one might say that the Canadian won an American revolution but did it on the world stage. And in so doing he remained the Keeper of the Bridge between the Old World and the New during a century and three-quarters of American isolationism and sired one of the great political inventions of his or any other time.

That, in my view, is the larger significance of the word "Canadian." That is the background which has made the Canadian what he is and given him a status and influence in the world greater than either his numbers or his material power would seem to warrant.

Inevitably this experience has left its stamp on his character and personality. His are both the weaknesses and the strengths of a man who has lived with compromises. His has been the middle course between time and space, between history and geography, as I have tried to show you.

The nation he contrived was born of compromise between two races, two languages, two cultures. Inevitably he has had to learn that there are always two sides to a case. And by the same token, down through the decades there have always been two kinds of Canadians to look at a case.

In buttressing his state against external pressures he has had to learn the art of balancing power against power, the power of a United States against the power of a Great Britain.

In economics, the nature of his resources and his capacity to produce wealth in abundance greater than his need have made him a man of two markets, home and foreign. The man who draws nearly one-third of his stake from the world abroad knows that he cannot live unto himself alone.

Emotionally, he has been the man of two worlds, the Old and the New, drawing spiritual sustenance from one and finding inspiration in the challenge of the other. Culturally, his has been the task of trying to span the gap between the Latin and the Anglo-Saxon, between medievalism and modern materialism, Catholicism and Protestantism.

Inevitably such a man is a moderate, a Man of the Middle. He is a conservative but not a reactionary. He walks with tradition even as he marches with change. It is no accident that the only socialist government on the continent north of your southern border is in a Canadian province—no accident either that it is only mildly socialist.

Inevitably such a man is skilled in the art of bringing opposites together, in the art of finding basis for agreement between two contending extremes. This had to be true down through the generations or there would have been no Canada and no Canadian.

These, I suggest, are some of the reasons why on that day back in 1946 at Lake Success, La Guardia placed so much trust in his neighbor from the north and why that neighbor was able to resolve a dilemma.

These are some of the reasons why his status in the world is what it is.

Because of the vastness of his space he covets no other man's space, hence no man fears him.

Because you and he have learned to share a continent in peace, he has been conditioned to the struggle of man against nature rather than of man against man. And yet when he has to fight he goes all out and can be very tough.

On the world's political stage he is not big enough to be dangerous but he is big enough and so strategically situated that he has to be taken into account.

In an air age he sits astride the great circle routes between Eurasia and the Americas.

He is the X which marks the spot where the north-south axis of the Americas cuts the east-west axis of the world's major land masses. In an age in which the world's centre of power is shifting from the basin of the Atlantic to the basin of the Pacific, he has a door on both, not to mention his door on the Mediterranean of the Arctic.

Whether you look at him in relation to time or to space, destiny seems to have called this man to the role of The Man in the Middle. Some of us are beginning to wonder if one day he may not become the ham in the sandwich between the Russian colossus and the American leviathan—minced ham, that is.

But perhaps the most important aspect of his Man in the Middle role derives from his unconscious reconciliation of the seemingly opposite poles of nationalism and internationalism.

You have seen how the Canadian in resolving his history and geography conflict presented the world with the fact of the Commonwealth. Not so obvious, though, is the concept which is implicit in that structure . . . the concept of limited national sovereignty.

The Canadian has shown that a nation can be . . . can achieve independent identity . . . can capture freedom to live its own unique life . . . under a sovereignty not unlimited, but a sovereignty limited by organic association with other nations for a common purpose.

And that way lies the only tolerable solution to the great problem of our time . . . the problem of achieving order with freedom in a world made anarchic by the unlimited sovereignty of the modern nation state.

ARTHUR IRWIN *joined* Maclean's *in 1925, at the age of 27, and soon became the magazine's driving force. He was editor from 1945 until 1950, when he became Commissioner of the National Film Board. Later, he was high commissioner to Australia, ambassador to Brazil and Mexico, and publisher of the* Victoria Daily Times *before retiring in 1971. He celebrated his 100th birthday in 1998 in Victoria, where he lives with his wife, the poet P.K. Page.*

Everybody Boos the CBC

by
Pierre Berton

DECEMBER 1, 1950

OF ALL CONTENTIOUS CANADIAN institutions, past or present, public or private, powerful or puny, not even the city of Toronto has received the Niagara of vilification, imprecation, tirade and abuse which has drenched the corporate head of the CBC.

The Canadian Broadcasting Corporation has no exact counterpart anywhere, but it is a single aspect of its unique makeup which qualifies it for the title of Public Whipping Boy No. 1: Listeners to most radio networks occasionally feel like putting in their two cents' worth; listeners to the CBC see no reason why they shouldn't put in their $2.50 worth. If the recent talk about a $25 license fee for television is upheld by the forthcoming Massey Report, the name calling may well increase tenfold.

It is the license fee—plus the fact that we own the corporation lock, stock and studios—that gives us all the right to boo the CBC. The chorus grows loud each spring when the courts are choked with people who have neglected to pay the license fee. But A.D. ("Davey") Dunton, the slight young ex-newspaperman who is chairman of the CBC's Board of Governors, and who describes his job as "getting grief," says he likes the idea of the fee. This way, he points out, you know exactly what you're getting, for exactly what it costs. Besides, he says, the fee encourages everybody to criticize the CBC and that's good.

Certainly the criticism is vociferous. In recent years, the CBC has been publicly called bullheaded, autocratic, dictatorial, spineless, weak, pathetic, extravagant, cheap, high-handed, bumbling, nonsensical, dishonest, power crazy, idiotic and absurd.

It has been called a milch cow, a centaur and a dog-in-the-manger. Conductor Sir Thomas Beecham, an Englishman who doesn't pay the license fee, has described it as "the worst broadcasting system in the world." Members of all political parties have attacked it. In a single debate, M.J. Coldwell complained the corporation discriminated against the CCF, E.G. Hansell (Social Credit) complained it was too favorable to the CCF, and Liberal Walter Tucker kicked about a news broadcast. Opposition leader George Drew has gone on the CBC itself to attack the CBC.

The Canadian Association of Broadcasters, which represents the private stations, has mountains of statistics to show that in Canada hardly anybody listens to the CBC. Yet the most obscure CBC item can sometimes draw howls of protest.

Let a West Coast speaker make a sly reference to newsboys, say, and a dozen papers led by the *Vancouver Sun* roar with anger about "drivel" from "the limp-wristed characters on the CBC." Let a Winnipeg announcer say "crick" for "creek" and the Guelph Board of Education is up in arms. Let the CBC *Times* put Alexander Graham Bell's birthplace at Brampton instead of Brantford and the *Toronto Telegram* is out with an instant editorial of reproof.

As if all this weren't enough, the CBC subjects itself to a 10-minute period of self-immolation each Sunday night when speakers are asked to criticize the network's own programs on "Critically Speaking." Curiously, the big task is often to get people to be critical enough. In an effort to achieve this, the CBC once engaged Dick Diespecker, a former private station man turned radio columnist, to appear on the show. To everyone's chagrin, Diespecker was inordinately kind. Then he twisted the knife neatly at year's end in his Vancouver *Province* column by picking "Critically Speaking" as the year's most uncritical show.

The CBC bends backward to be fair to everyone, including its critics. The calm reasoned voice of the 10 o'clock news has been heard reporting the harsh things that Joel Aldred, an ex staff announcer, had to say about the corporation. Reports of House of Commons debates almost always mention speakers from all parties. The CBC recently canceled a "Court of Opinion" broadcast because all four speakers on the panel favored Canada sending a representative to the Vatican. If there had been a dissenting vote the show would have stayed on. "The CBC tries to be impeccably impartial, and you can't be that impartial without being dull," wrote Tommy Tweed last spring. The remark was part of a radio satire broadcast, of course, on the CBC.

Unlike the big U.S. networks, which try to please most of the people most of the time, the CBC's job is to please *all* of the people part of the time. Its lowest mass listening level comes between the hours of 6 p.m. and 8 p.m. when it broadcasts such minority-interest programs as the full weather report, the market summary and "International Commentary," a series of political talks. Yet each of these programs is of prime importance to certain groups of people. "If we dropped the weather broadcast, Niagara fruit growers would go crazy," says Ernest Bushnell, director-general of programs. The same is true of the fishery broadcasts in the Maritimes. "There's not a damn thing you can do to make the weather report palatable to the guy who's not interested in it," Bushnell says. "But if we don't give it to them, who's going to?"

These are some of the reasons why the CBC is attacked for putting on too much Greek tragedy on Wednesday nights and too many chicken recipes on Saturday nights; for carrying too much symphony and too much soap opera; for carrying too many British accents and too many Yankee twangs. The CBC cannot think only in terms of the "mass listening audience," which dictates communal network fare. It must think also of those people who do not belong to the mass but who also pay their $2.50.

Partly because of this, the corporation has had a strong influence on the Canadian mosaic. Close to 7,000 Canadians get cheques from it each year, ranging all the way from a $5 royalty on a Canadian poem to the record $20,000 that actor Bernie Braden earned in 1947. The CBC acts as a sort of superpatron of the arts, commissioning original poems, short stories, music and drama. In 18 weeks its French network broadcast 65 popular songs written by Canadian authors. Without the CBC, Winnipeg would have no symphony orchestra. Indeed, the corporation is the largest single contributor to symphonies in the country.

In Aklavik every morning, Eskimo children do physical jerks to CBC transcriptions. In Toronto, an interdenominational church was organized by a group of people who met originally to listen to the CBC's "Citizen's Forum." In the Maritimes, fishermen and farmers in remote spots no longer get scalpers' prices for their lobsters and strawberries—thanks to CBC market broadcasts. In the Arctic, a man held onto his girl friend and eventually married her thanks to the CBC's "Northern Messenger," the only regular winter mail service the people of the Far North receive. In Quebec, the CBC is changing the speech habits of the Canadien, who once called precise announcers *"fifis"* (sissies) and now complains if they slur their phrases in the Quebec manner.

Fifteen hundred farm groups gather faithfully each Monday to hear the CBC's "Farm Forum" and half a million school children hear the morning school broadcasts on weekdays. These school broadcasts have standardized the Shakespearean plays studied in most provinces and have caused the addition of two new courses—conservation and guidance—to the Ontario curriculum.

Canadians almost anywhere in the world can hear CBC programs. Three

*A CBC radio drama, with actor John Drainie (second from right),
and Andrew Allan (right) producing.*

Oblate missionaries listen regularly: one to the French network in Montreal, one to CBC short wave beamed to the Queen Charlotte Islands and a third to the International Service in Chile. An Italian street urchin recently wrote in for a CBC schedule explaining he was too poor to own a radio but had found a house in Rome where CBC programs came through an open window. A Brazilian wrote that after hearing the CBC he'd broken a sacred vow to visit the Holy Land and would come to Canada instead. In a recent poll taken of 6,000 listeners around the world by the International Shortwave Listening Club, the CBC ranked fourth in a field of 26, three places ahead of the Voice of America, whose budget is seven times larger.

Sometimes Canadian producers feel they are without honor in their own country. When Swedish-born Esse Ljungh produced a series of folk legends, he got 16 letters from CBC listeners, most of them derogatory. The series was also carried on a New York City station and produced 2,000 letters from Americans. Only one beefed.

CBC programs regularly win radio oscars from the Institute for Education by Radio, at Columbus, Ohio. Last year the CBC took more of these awards than any of the U.S. nets.

Recently, a group of U.S. radio people, including Norman Corwin, the gifted writer, listened to a recording of the CBC's two-hour production of "Hamlet." Canadian Mavor Moore, who was present, noted with dismay that Corwin grew gloomier and gloomier as the play progressed. It turned out, however, that Corwin wasn't upset by the production but by the fact that in the United States it wouldn't be commercially possible to produce a two-hour Shakespearean drama free of commercials.

U.S. radio is as different from its Canadian cousin as the Manhattan towers of Radio City are from the one-time young ladies' seminary that now houses the CBC's Toronto studios. There is little of the frantic atmosphere of sales and soap on this side of the line. Ernie Bushnell recalls walking into the office of his opposite number on a big American net. It was a perfect Bedlam. A playback machine was roaring out a recently transcribed program; a loudspeaker hooked to a rehearsal studio was blaring from another corner; and there seemed to be three radios as well—all tuned to different programs. Bushnell has one old-fashioned radio in his office to which he seldom listens. "Quite frankly I can't work with that damn thing on," he says.

"The American nets are interested primarily in making money," one CBC man said recently. "The CBC is interested in losing it."

The reason for this difference in concept—a difference which will almost certainly be carried over into television—can be traced directly to Canadian geography and history. A Canadian network must operate in six time zones and two languages and it must also service the sparsely populated districts which make up most of the country. Only a network prepared to lose money could do this.

Before the first Royal Commission into radio, Canadian stations were largely northern extensions of U.S. networks, primarily serving city areas. The occasional Canadian network show was handled by the Canadian National Railway and on one occasion listeners to a musical program were treated to a fine display of profanity by a CNR dispatcher who hooked into the network by mistake. As late as 1932, only two-fifths of the country outside of Toronto and Montreal could get regular programs and there were no French programs at all. The CBC, like the railways, defies geography to link the nation.

The present radio setup is the result of the recommendations of a Royal Commission under banker Sir John Aird, created by a Liberal government in 1929 and implemented with some modifications by a Conservative government in 1932. The Aird report urged total nationalization of radio, but a Parliamentary committee decided that private stations should be allowed to continue to serve local needs while a government-owned network should serve national needs. A board of governors, serving without salary, was appointed to sit in judgment on both, giving preference to national interests.

The initial result was Hector Charlesworth's Canadian Radio Broadcasting Commission. "If the politicians leave us alone we shall be all right," said Charlesworth. They didn't. Jean François Pouliot rose in the Commons at one point to suggest that Charlesworth's tongue should be torn from his mouth and wound seven times around his whiskers.

The CRBC was fettered with a civil-service atmosphere. Salaries were held up for weeks pending Treasury approval. When Charlesworth sent a $10 wreath to the funeral of the president of the Canadian Radio Manufacturers'

Association, an order-in-council was needed to approve the spending. The CRBC, as one MP put it, was "alone, yet not alone." Four years later, it was replaced by the CBC, which is divorced from direct government interference and has control over its own expenditures.

It is a curious legal animal. Mackenzie King once agreed with prominent Tory Gordon Graydon that it was "half and half partly a department of the government, partly a public corporation." Nonetheless, it has withstood the scrutiny of seven Parliamentary committees and two Gallup polls.

There have been a few attempts at political control. For example, General L.R. LaFleche, when he was Minister of National War Services, once successfully ordered a controlman in Montreal to pull the plug on a program he didn't like on the state of Maritime Insane Asylums. But these have been subtly resisted by the CBC itself.

The corporation started with 135 employees and six hours of network broadcasting a day. It now has 1,430 employees, operates its trans-Canada network 21½ hours day, its French network 16 hours a day and its Dominion network six hours a day. The value of its equipment has increased from $310,000 to $9 million.

Its new studios in Montreal's former Ford Hotel are the most modern on the continent. It operates 19 key stations, 17 relay stations and feeds its programs regularly to 86 private stations and, on special occasions, to 56 others. Private stations get CBC sustaining shows free and are paid a fee (which some of them think is too low) for carrying network commercial shows. The CBC gets $2.3 million from advertising but 80 per cent of its shows are free of commercials. And it broadcasts more than 14,000 hours of home-grown talent each year.

Last year, the CBC's over-all expenses totaled $8 million, of which close to $5.5 million came from license fees. Advertising revenue almost but not quite made up the difference, for the corporation showed an operating deficit of $243,000 for 1949. An estimated 2.9 million Canadian homes have radios, but only 2,192,400 set-owners bought licenses. Thus the corporation missed out on some $1,770,000 in unpaid fees or seven times its deficit.

Since the days of the Aird Commission, the principle of public radio has been under continual fire from private station owners. Two of the most blistering briefs submitted to that commission in 1929 were written by Ernie Bushnell himself, then a private station spokesman. Bushnell, a big blunt sandy-haired man who used to be tenor in a radio quartet, is now on the opposite side of the microphone, but others still fight the good fight.

The chief lobbyist for the private interests is James Allard, a smallish sandy-haired man who used to be a radio announcer and still speaks with the rich mellow tones of a cigarette commercial. Allard is president of the Canadian Association of Broadcasters, to which most private stations belong. He owns six radios but never tunes any of them into a publicly owned station.

Briefly, the CAB would like to see a separate regulatory body supplant the present CBC Board of Governors to control all broadcasting in Canada. This, the CAB hopes, would pave the way for the setting up of commercial radio networks and the withdrawal of the CBC from commercial broadcasting.

Mild Davey Dunton, who also owns six radios, feels that this arrangement would badly cripple Canadian-style broadcasting. He suggests that many stations would simply revert to the old position of being northern spouts for U.S. networks, that many private stations which now carry CBC programs would junk them for commercial U.S. shows, leaving gaps in the national network, and that the loss of present commercial revenue would injure CBC programs or else force an increase in the license fee.

Undoubtedly Canadian TV will be simpler and cheaper. The CBC is determined that, like radio, TV shall be primarily Canadian. Viewers will certainly see many U.S. telecasts. The CBC makes no secret of the fact that it would like to get the World Series and the heavyweight boxing championships, but the bulk of the offerings will have a Canadian flavor. For instance, Fergus Mutrie, the ex-farmer who directs the Toronto end of the TV setup, is trying to line up some puppet characters who will be original and distinctively Canadian.

But the program pattern will be quite different from radio. Few if any of the familiar radio shows will be transferred directly to TV. (One possible exception would be Wayne and Shuster, who have already appeared on TV programs in New York.) Many of radio's best-known actors and writers may not prove adaptable to the new medium which in other countries has drawn large slices of talent from vaudeville, night club and stage.

At first, viewers will probably see special events such as the Canadian National Exhibition, perhaps simple plays using a few sets and not more than six actors, variety programs and short operettas by the CBC Opera Company. It's doubtful if there'll be spot news broadcasts at first. One 15-minute news broadcast on TV costs as much as an hour-long drama show. On the other hand there will be many inexpensive how-to-do-it demonstrations using one or two people and simple props.

A TV network will come slowly to Canada. The first step will probably be to link Montreal and Toronto, later adding Ottawa, Windsor and Quebec City. Western and Maritime stations will develop independently, using locally produced shows supplemented by films of network programs.

In the meantime the CBC's three radio networks will continue to operate and probably to expand, doling out the curious brew of corn, culture and Canadianism which like so many other facets of life above the 49th parallel lies somewhere between the British and the American way of doing things. There is no reason to suspect that the ceaseless investigation of radio in Canada will stop after two Royal commissions and eight Parliamentary committees have said their piece about it.

As long as public radio exists in Canada, people will make complaints, suggestions, attacks and demands upon it.

And why shouldn't they? They're paying for it.

PIERRE BERTON *began writing for* Maclean's *in 1947, and was managing editor from 1953 to 1959. He is the author of many books, and continues to write from his Kleinburg, Ont., home.*

My Neighbors, the Dionne Quints

by
Bruce McLeod

DECEMBER 15, 1950

THE BUXOM MATRON WITH OHIO stenciled on the back of her white shirt slid off a stool at the soda bar of a North Bay, Ont., dime store. "How about driving down to Callander for a look at the quints?" she suggested to a slack-clad companion.

The second woman shook her head. "You can't see the Dionnes any more," she said. "I hear they're going to be nuns."

"OHIO" dabbed at her chins with a serviette. "I wouldn't be surprised," she nodded. "A friend told me that's why Mrs. Dionne went to see the Pope last year. And have you seen recent pictures of them? My goodness . . ."

A few feet away, two pleasant-looking teen-agers with chunky legs and high cheekbones examined a counter filled with costume jewelry. As the Americans strode toward an exit the girls politely stepped aside to let them pass. But neither "OHIO" nor her friend realized they had just brushed elbows with two of the famous five.

Indeed, with the possible exception of a few North Bay people, it is doubtful if anybody in the store recognized the youthful shoppers as Emilie and Yvonne Dionne.

Few persons, of course, expect to find the quints, whose bank account runs into a million, shopping unescorted in a crowded five-and-ten. Or anywhere else, for that matter. For reasons which Oliva Dionne, their farmer father, professes not to understand, the public usually associates movements of the quints with burly police guards, deep secrecy and special precautions. Actually, this is not always the case, though Dionne still fears crowds and seldom permits more than two or three of his daughters to appear publicly at one time.

Members of the North Bay detachment of the Ontario Provincial Police, who always disliked being nursemaids to the quints, are happy about Dionne's decision to let his daughters sally forth without a police guard. "Thank God," one of them remarked to me recently, "we're no longer assigned very often to the Petticoat Patrol."

Actually, it's surprising how many people wouldn't know a quint if they bumped into one. Not long ago I was in a North Bay grocery when three of them, accompanied by classmates from Villa Notre Dame, their private school, bustled up to a fruit counter. A woman nearby nudged her husband and whispered, "Look, triplets!"

She, like countless others, probably still thinks of the Dionne quintuplets as they were when they were five or six years old. She doesn't picture them as they are today: doesn't realize that Marie, Emilie, Yvonne, Cécile and Annette, now approaching 17, have, in fact, grown up. The fact that they have been seen so little in recent years, coupled with a declining interest in them generally, has left the public with some rather vague and antiquated notions.

When the quints traveled to New York City last October, they received a rousing welcome. But this has always been the case when they appeared in a group of five, dressed in identical clothes and preceded by a tremendous publicity blast. Many people think that the quints, attired in contrasting costumes and appearing in twos or threes, could walk down Fifth Avenue without turning anybody's head. As a matter of fact, after their hectic welcome at the New York station, they stopped off at church on their way to the convent at which they were to stay and none of the worshippers guessed their identity.

Unfortunately, the people who best remember the quints as they were 10 years ago sometimes take it for granted that the unhappy situations which developed in those bygone days still exist. Too many ill-informed people write the sisters off as stubborn, not-too-bright Canadiens who suffer from inferiority complexes because of the controversies and bitterness which swirled around them during their formative years.

Once the annual summer rush of holidayers gets under way, receptionists at the North Bay Chamber of Commerce Information Bureau can expect questions such as these: "Why don't the quints speak English?"—"Has Marie a bad eye?"—"Is it true that the Quints have false teeth?"—"Does Oliva Dionne set dogs on people who go on his property?"—"Is Mrs. Dionne really going to have triplets?"—"Will Poppa Dionne still sell his autograph?"—"Do the Quints have boyfriends?"

For the record here are the answers:

The famous five do speak English but with an accent and usually only when making guest appearances. The legend that they never speak English became popular after a Mother's Day broadcast in 1941 when the quints insisted on delivering their message in French. They received 4,000 indignant letters.

Marie wears glasses and has trouble with one eye but the story about false teeth is a myth. Their teeth are bad, however, and Dr. Allan Roy Dafoe

The Dionne quints with their father during their 1950 visit to New York City.

once told me that if Mrs. Dionne had given her permission, operations would have been performed when the girls were babies to correct malformations of their jaws.

Recent reports that Mrs. Dionne was expecting again and that X-rays had disclosed the birth was to be multiple (triplets) are indignantly denied by Mrs. Dionne.

Poppa Dionne keeps at least one large watchdog, but he insists it's friendly. This view is not endorsed, however, by a Toronto reporter who barged unannounced onto the Dionne property not long ago and was chased back into his car by a dog which he described "as big as a horse and eager to taste-test my leg."

As for boy friends, the quints haven't got to that stage yet, though dates may be arranged for them before long. When dates are arranged you can bet they'll be boys carefully chosen from French-speaking families.

Oliva Dionne is a stubborn and sometimes irascible man in most matters concerning his famous daughters, especially when he tries to reconcile the myths with which the public often surrounds the quints with the facts as he knows them.

When it was announced the girls would visit New York in October to attend a benefit dinner for the Alfred Smith Memorial Building, a New York department store offered to outfit Dionne's daughters with identical gowns. Oliva accepted, then indignantly rejected the proposal when New York newspapers suggested he couldn't afford to clothe his children. "Why don't people find out the truth?" he complained. "I wish they'd leave us alone."

But when the girls returned from New York, Oliva said he was grateful for the attention focused on them and the kindness shown to them. The quints visited young movie star Margaret O'Brien and the 17-month-old Collins quadruplets of Brooklyn. Oliva refused to comment on the suggestion that the trip was all part of a plan to recoup some of the public notice the girls had lost in recent years—along with advertising contracts, which had fallen to an all-time low.

These incidents provide an insight into the enigma that is Dionne. In one breath he invites people to know him better. In the next he rebuffs them with a demand to be left alone. He deplores publicity, yet is piqued if ignored. On occasion he can be most gracious; on others, exasperating, unreasoning and difficult.

I remember once while working for the North Bay *Nugget*, I called on Oliva and he greeted me very coolly. I mentioned this to Keith Munro, business manager for the quints, and he offered to investigate. It turned out that Poppa was peeved because the *Nugget*, quite by accident, had dropped him from its mailing list of free papers. When the paper was restored, he was all smiles again.

In the 16 years since the morning in May, 1934, when the quints were born I have enjoyed an unusual opportunity to watch their story unfold. I visited them frequently during their childhood and in 1944 I conducted the first press interview with them. Looking back over those years I cannot help but feel that the quints themselves were less bruised by the problems which beset them than most of the people around them.

Their biggest problem—survival—is far behind them. They are normal, healthy young girls who haven't required a doctor in two years. They are not good-looking but pleasant, unspoiled, reasonably intelligent girls with varying emotions and abilities. Far from being introverts, as predicted by some authorities, they are if anything extroverts inclined to show off. They love people and crowds and even at the age of three displayed all the footlight temperaments of born *prima donnas*.

One of Oliva's biggest beefs during the years the quints were supervised by the Ontario Government until 1942 was that they were "being made a show of." He needn't have worried. The quints loved it, sometimes wept if bad weather or illness canceled a showing.

Yvonne Leroux, the quints' first nurse and a woman who knew them best in those early days, once observed: "Each wanted to be leading lady. No matter which one we picked up first for the public to see, the others' faces dropped with grief."

Sometimes the quints still sulk if forced to share the limelight.

North Bay never got very het up about the quints. While many followed the quint story with interest, hundreds in the city have never seen them, couldn't be bothered traveling 11 miles to Dafoe Hospital even when the famous five were being shown. The late Alexander Woollcott, who made a short movie with the quints in 1939, noted this and remarked: "People in Niagara seldom go to see the Falls. When you have one of the wonders of the world in your own back yard it's only human to take it for granted."

But this annoys and puzzles Oliva Dionne, who feels North Bay should be grateful to his daughters for helping to augment the city's $4 million-a-year tourist industry. Most persons agree that the birth of the quintuplets gave the district's vacation business a tremendous shot in the arm, but many believe that, had it not been for action by the Ontario Government to prevent the babies being exploited, they would not have lived. They recall how, a few hours after the babies were born, Oliva signed them to a contract to appear at the Chicago World's Fair. People screamed that for $100 a week this farmer was selling his babies to a midway.

At the time, Dionne was a confused, desperate man. Poor, though never actually on relief as some people claimed, he was suddenly faced with the problem of feeding, clothing and caring for five new babies. A $3,000 mortgage on his farm was almost due. He consulted his parish priest, who recommended that Dionne sign the contract. Not even Dr. Dafoe objected; he was sure the babies were living on borrowed time. When he realized his error, Oliva acted to cancel the contract.

Dionne has always insisted that he and his wife could have raised their children without government interference, that Dafoe got credit he didn't deserve.

I remember visiting Dafoe one afternoon in 1941. It was on his 58th birthday. He had been away for medical treatment and when he came home he discovered that the forces which had always sought to turn the quints against him had finally succeeded. The quints refused to speak to him. The clash of personalities, religion, money, language; the constant bickering and jockeying for position—all were ended.

"Do you think," I asked him, "that there was a better way to have handled this business? Perhaps a greater understanding of the parents' point of view?"

He scratched his massive head. "Maybe," he shrugged. "I don't know. My job was to keep the babies alive. Sometimes when you rescue a man from drowning it's necessary to poke him on the jaw."

"But maybe if someone had taken the time to explain things to Oliva . . ."

"Impossible," Dafoe stabbed air with his pipe stem. "Dionne wouldn't believe anything he couldn't see. I tried to explain to him about germs—why diapers and bottles had to be sterilized. His babies were dying of dysentery and he wouldn't believe it because I couldn't actually show him the germs. How could anybody talk sense to a man like that?"

The day the "Little Doc" was ousted, Dionne ordered the metal plaque bearing Dafoe's name removed from the stone gates in front of the Dafoe Hospital. And Dafoe died without collecting the $15 which he billed Oliva for attending Mrs. Dionne at the birth of the quints. "He got enough out of it as it was," Oliva once told me.

Few tourists today visit the site of the quints' 18-room Georgian-style home on Highway 94. The wide stretches of pavement in front of the new residence are deserted most of the time. They make a fine practice ground for the quints who are learning to drive their father's new car. Even on a Sunday afternoon in midsummer, there are seldom more than half a dozen cars parked where once 7,000 cars a day stood bumper to bumper.

Two of the old souvenir booths—one still operated by Oliva—remain open for business. The building which was the Dafoe Hospital is used as the quints' private school and the log-sided nurses' residence is occupied by sisters of the teaching staff. The pavilion where the quints appeared daily stands deserted and neglected. Nobody looks in the wooden trough where childless couples and honeymooners used to buy stones as good-luck charms—"passion pebbles" one guard at the nursery used to call them.

The quints spend much of their leisure time on the so-called "back lot" behind the Dionne home. There they picnic, hunt, ski and skate and cut their own Christmas tree each winter. The grounds are surrounded by a high wire fence and flood-lit. The gate, which is always open, bears a "NO ADMITTANCE" sign. Many people who eye the yellow brick mansion with its red roof and bright red door think it looks more like a government institution than the kind of home you'd expect to find in the northern pines.

In Callander, two miles away, the quint boom is a fading memory. There are empty stores and rooms for rent in hotels and tourist camps. Gone are the promoters, hucksters and shysters who thronged the village streets. Madame Legros, who helped deliver three of the quints before Dr. Dafoe arrived, runs her small souvenir shop and still advertises "the original basket of the quints"—in spite of Oliva's claim that he gave her a substitute and Dafoe's statement that he burned the original basket.

Villagers sit in Reeve Len Wookey's Red Line Inn, sip their beer and talk about the days when 200,000 cars a month rolled past the taproom on the way to Dafoe Hospital. And the reeve, a retired opera singer who went to Callander at the height of the rush, shakes his shaggy mane of black hair and delivers ringing arguments in favor of a monument for the "Little Doe" (in a park directly across from the Red Line).

And the quints' future? It's anybody's guess. I wouldn't be surprised if they go abroad, perhaps to Europe, in the next year. Oliva Dionne says simply: "They will make their own decisions with no pressure from us. They are getting their religious and social life as well as we can give it to them. They have seen a lot more than we ever did at their age."

OLIVA DIONNE died in 1979, at age 78; his wife, Elzire, at 76 in 1986. Of the quints, Emilie died at age 20 during an epileptic seizure; Marie, who suffered from depression and alcoholism, died at 35 in 1970 of a blood clot in her brain. Yvonne, Annette and Cécile live together in St. Bruno, Que., near Montreal. In 1998, the three sisters—at the time living on a combined pension of $746 a month—demanded compensation from the Ontario government for their early exploitation. After public controversy, they received $4 million, the promise of an inquiry into Quintland and a personal apology from the premier.

BRUCE MCLEOD was an assistant editor at Maclean's from 1942 to 1944. After a distinguished cross-Canada radio and TV career, he retired to North Bay, Ont., where he is now working on a book about suicide around the world.

Is Bingo Bad For Your Town?

by Herbert Manning

AUGUST 6, 1955

THREE MONTHS AGO, when the Canadian parliamentary committee on criminal law sat down one day to consider the state of the nation's morals, it created something of a stir by asking 500 of Ottawa's best-known citizens to show that they weren't lawbreakers. The citizens were the members of three service clubs—Lions, Kinsmen and Richelieu—and one war veterans' organization—the Montgomery branch of the Canadian Legion. The law they were asked to consider was contained in sections 168 and 179 of the Canadian Criminal Code—the sections dealing with gaming houses and lotteries and vaguely, with bingo, a mild and apparently inoffensive pastime often indulged in by children. But in Ottawa, as in other Canadian cities, bingo is far from child's play. It's a $500,000-a-year business for the Lions, Kinsmen, Richelieu and Legion who stage 35 bingos a year in the city's two largest indoor arenas and attract more than 250,000 people to them.

The bingo played in Ottawa is not like the bingo played anywhere else in the world. It's called Monster, for one thing, and with good reason. One night's show in suburban Eastview brought out 25,000 people who gambled $44,000 to win $22,000 in prizes, including five new automobiles. In the past 12 years, the Lions Club—by offering stage-loads of prizes that would shame Cinderella's fairy godmother—has lured more than a million people to 169 bingos and grossed at least $2 million.

The popularity of bingo in the capital is something to inspire wonder and, in many quarters, alarm and dismay. Two years ago, one Ottawa clergy-man, Dr. Hugh M. Rae, provoked newspaper headlines when he said scathingly, "Ottawa is the Canadian centre for bingo." He was not overstating the case. Recently, a Toronto novelty-goods supplier, H.F. Dix, who sells bingo equipment to clubs and carnivals right across Canada, said, "Taken over the past 10 years, the Ottawa game is the biggest in the world."

Almost like burlesque, Ottawa's bingo is many things to many people—a boon and delight to some, a public danger and disgrace to others. It has been condemned by the leaders of almost every church in the city and a few outside. By special decree, Catholics in the city are forbidden to organize or support bingos. At a meeting of the Ottawa Presbytery of the United Church, Rev. T.W. Bird said the service clubs were corrupting the minds of growing children by running bingos, and at a Montreal–Ottawa conference of the church Dr. Rae—a persistent critic—said they were perverting the men-tality of the whole city. Yet at one bingo an elderly widow told me the game had kept her alive for 10 years by giving her an interest in life.

It has been condemned in the city's police courts, upheld in the Ontario Court of Appeal, banned by Mayor Charlotte Whitton and barred from the

Nearly 10,000 people jam the Ottawa Auditorium for a giant Lions Club bingo, 1955.

air by the CBC after one club staged a "radio bingo." It has also paid for social and medical benefits for thousands of needy Ottawa people from the cradle to the grave. It has built baby clinics, bought milk for undernourished kids, paid for their summer holidays and their musical education and sent them to college when they were old enough. It has built a recreation centre for the blind, helped arthritics and is now paying for a centre where people who have cancer can go for cobalt-bomb treatment. In the past 12 years, the Ottawa Lions, who started the bingo craze in 1942, have spent half a million dollars on welfare work in Ottawa, every dime of it from the club's big bingos.

Bingo is also the only public social activity in the capital—outside of eating and drinking—that has not only survived the onslaught of television but effectively fights back. During the past year, the overpowering attraction of TV programs has driven both professional baseball and professional hockey out of business in Ottawa. So far it hasn't made the slightest impression on bingo. In fact, on one big bingo night last March, the CBC, with a TV monopoly and thus no other competition in the district for its viewers, admitted reluctantly that its viewer ratings took a slight dip between 8 p.m. and 10:30 p.m.— the bingo hours. It did not attempt to explain why, but after 10:40 p.m., when the bingo multitudes began returning to their hearthstones— some of them with newly won TV sets—the ratings went back to normal.

Bingo is also the bane of theatre operators, who once petitioned Ottawa police to ban it because the monster games were hurting their business. That's the trouble with bingo in Ottawa. It's so big and popular and there's so much money involved that it sometimes has a hard time staying respectable. Crooks and racketeers have tried repeatedly to muscle in. Even the charitable organizations that run the games have to keep assuring the public—and the police—from time to time that all the money they make really goes to charity, as the law says it must. In the last two years, two automobiles offered as major prizes at bingo games have been "stolen" by crooks: once by forging winning numbers on a bingo card and the other time by planting a false checker (the man who checks the numbers on winning cards). On both these occasions the trickery was discovered in time and the cars were recovered. But Ottawa police have stated that at least six other top prizes at the big bingos have been won illegally.

The four clubs running bingo do their best to keep the game respectable. The Lions pay uniformed Pinkerton men to keep an eye on things at their games—but they don't tell the public how much they make from bingo or exactly how they spend it or how much is eaten up in operating expenses. When I asked officials of all four organizations for a breakdown of their bingo revenues and expenditures, they flatly refused to let me have it. What's more, they don't have to let the public in on such details, according to the law, although that doesn't stop the public, the police and—right now—a special committee of parliament from asking questions.

And so a simple pastime of county fairs and carnivals (it's also called lotto, keno and housie-housie) has become an important force for good or evil—depending on where you're sitting in our capital. In Ottawa, while the Lions, Kinsmen and Richelieu clubs support practically their whole welfare programs on the proceeds of bingo, other outfits such as Kiwanis and Rotary won't touch it. Last January, Roman Catholic Archbishop M.J. Lemieux banned bingo as a church activity in the Ottawa archdiocese. But thousands still pour across the river from Hull, Que.,—a predominantly Roman Catholic community—for every bingo.

The reason Ottawa is able to play any bingo at all lies in the peculiar phrasing of the Criminal Code. Under section 179 it's an indictable offense to "dispose of any goods, wares or merchandise by any game of chance or any games of mixed chance and skill in which the contestant pays money . . ." And under section 168 you can be sent to jail for two years for running any place in which a "fee is charged to or paid by the players for the privilege of playing or participating in a game or using gaming equipment." Both these pronouncements fit bingo to a T, but the Criminal Code leaves an escape hatch. This is clause 2b of section 168 which says that a place is not a common gaming house if it is used "occasionally by charitable or religious organizations for the purpose of playing games . . . if the proceeds from the games are to be used for a charitable or religious object."

The key to the whole question of bingo's legality is thus the word "occasionally." In 1946, the chairman of the Kinsmen Club's bazaar committee, William L. Parrott, was charged by Ottawa police with running a bingo and convicted in Magistrate's Court. But Parrott and the Kinsmen appealed and won. The appeal judges noted the word "occasionally" and it has protected the service clubs in Ottawa ever since. As long as they keep their games "occasional"—a club would not operate on the same night every week, for instance, or announce a whole season's schedule in advance—and as long as they use the money for charity, they can play all the bingo they want. Both the Anglican Church and the United Church have petitioned Parliament to repeal this section of the Criminal Code and make bingo illegal.

Meanwhile, at least once a week during the autumn, winter and spring—and sometimes every night in the week during the Christmas season—anywhere from 6,000 to 9,000 people crowd into the Ottawa Coliseum or the Auditorium for bingo. The big reason for bingo's popularity is probably the fact it's so simple that almost anyone can play it without instruction. And then there are the prizes. I listened to two members of one club discuss seriously the feasibility of putting up six new cars as prizes in one night. Three years ago, the Richelieu Social Club gave away five cars in two hours, plus another $10,000 in prizes. That was the biggest bingo ever held anywhere. Twenty-five thousand people came by car, bus, tram and on foot. It was the biggest traffic jam in Ottawa history, with 10,000 cars packed into the small community. Ottawa sent a dozen uniformed police to help the 13 Eastview cops, but traffic was still a mess. The bingo multitudes sat on wooden planks stretched across 6,000 cinder blocks and balanced cards on their knees. When it was all over the Richelieu Club had taken in $44,000, which was carted away by two Brink's Express trucks working in a relay. The club reported a profit of $22,000 and spent it all on a children's health clinic just two blocks from where the bingo was played. "If it had rained, we'd have lost our shirts," Raoul Landriault, who was club president at the time, said recently. The shrewd Richelieus carried $15,000 rain insurance, just in case, and paid $1,500 for it.

The Lions Club had set the pace for the Eastview Richelieu a couple of years earlier with a "radio bingo" for which they sold 18,000 bingo sheets. Instead of going to the Auditorium, the Coliseum or a schoolyard, the players simply went to a nearby newsstand, bought as many sheets as they wanted, went home and tuned in to the bingo program on radio—and the game was on. If they got a "bingo"—filled a row on a sheet—they telephoned radio station CFRA in Ottawa, where a battery of telephone girls was waiting. Then the next day the winning players submitted their bingo sheets for checking.

It was tedious and unwieldy and it provoked a storm of protest from the churches. The CBC's Board of Governors listened to the protests and promptly wrote a new bylaw: "No station shall broadcast any program involving a lottery or similar scheme in which a contestant pays tiny sums of money to become eligible for a prize." This was "not a proper use of public air channels," the governors announced. That ended Ottawa's radio bingos.

But the inventive service clubs are constantly hatching new schemes to drag out another thousand bingo fans—such gimmicks as "mystery prizes," brass bands, fully decorated Christmas trees loaded with gifts, and all-expense honeymoon trips. Next fall, they plan to stage Grey Cup bingos, with all-expense trips to Vancouver to see the first Canadian football final played there, plus Grey Cup tickets. Secondary winners will get TV sets to see the game. "We have a big investment in bingo—$10,000 a night in prizes alone," Martin Glatt, president-elect of the Kinsmen Club, said recently. "We have to run it like a business. We can't afford to stand still."

A few weeks ago, I went to a monster bingo put on by the Lions Club in the Ottawa Auditorium. Seven thousand people were there, about 40 per cent of them from Ottawa, the rest from neighboring communities. The Gatineau Bus Co. runs special buses from Aylmer, Wakefield, Gatineau, Buckingham—30 miles away—and other towns in Quebec. The bus waits while they play, and then takes them home again.

The bingo starts at eight o'clock, but some of the Lions had been in the Auditorium since afternoon decorating the 90-foot stage and putting the prizes in place. It takes about 100 service-club members to run a monster bingo, and they're drilled like a professional football team. Only three are permitted on the stage: the caller who announces into a microphone the number of the ball he plucks from the cage, the head checker who keeps a master board of the numbers called and another checker who keeps track of the prizes. Ten others are in the "money room," counting and parceling change as it pours in.

The atmosphere was as tense as that at a Stanley Cup hockey game, but there was one startling difference—in the whole cavernous place there wasn't a sound except the monotone voice of caller Wes Brown, an office manager in the Ottawa Hydro Electric Commission: "Under the B . . . number five . . . Under the O . . . sixty-two . . ." At last another voice somewhere in the upper reaches of the Auditorium called, "Bingo!" A checker hustled over, called back the numbers to the stage and another game started. Like clockwork, winners were found for clock radios, a portable typewriter ($79.50), two power lawn mowers ($94 each), a television set ($224), a clothes dryer ($250), an electric power-tool set ($300), a Chevrolet sedan ($2,390) and other prizes totaling about $9,000.

Few of the bingo players in Ottawa are new to the game; most are women and most are over 50. Eric Kinney, an insurance executive who has helped the Lions Club run its bingos for 10 years, told me that 75 per cent of the players go to every bingo, no matter who runs it or where it's held. In one row of 220 players in Ottawa's Auditorium, I counted 174 elderly women.

Some are like Mrs. Margaret Thibeault, a widow who has no children and lives alone in her midtown home. "I like to be in the crowd and see the people. It's so exciting," she said elatedly. "There's always a chance I may win something, too."

The queen of Ottawa bingos is Mrs. Victoria Lacroix, a pleasant buxom woman who went to the city's first big bingo staged by the Lions 13 years ago and hasn't missed a game since. She says she's attended 750 and spent $2,200 at them. But she's won a car and numerous other prizes. "It's the only place I go, you know," she said. "I don't know what I'd do if it weren't for bingo."

Besides making a lot of older women happy, however, bingo has caused one legal headache after another. In spite of the vigilance of the service clubs, who realize the game must be honest if it's going to survive, it has been an inviting playground for crooks and cheats. And it has been a source of endless confusion to the Ottawa police. "How are you going to tell the police to clamp down on gambling," one senior inspector asked recently, "when they know that the best people in town are running the biggest gambling games, and it's all right with the law? And how are you going to teach people that gambling and lotteries are illegal when you can't even make bingo illegal?"

For a brief eventful period two years ago crooks had a heyday with Ottawa's bingo and almost drove it out of business. It started when two men who turned out to be from Detroit won a new automobile and $200 as a consolation prize at a bingo staged by the Kinsmen. The next day, the man who won the car tried to sell it at a used-car lot. The dealer suspected it might be stolen and reported it to the police. At police headquarters it was discovered that the man was the car winner—and also that he was using a fictitious name and a false address in Ottawa. So was the man who won the consolation award. Police started checking back and found that the names and addresses given by six major winners at earlier bingos were false. Three were women. One address was a cemetery and one of the names was on a tombstone.

Police finally decided that all were probably members of the same ring and worked their racket through a phony checker. The Kinsmen haven't enough members to stage a bingo by themselves and often use friends or business acquaintances to help. Thus, by misrepresenting himself as a visiting Kinsman, the police reasoned, a member of the gang was able to volunteer as a checker. Then, when the game for a major prize came up, he would simply take down on a slip of paper the numbers called off by the caller, a confederate would shout, "Bingo!" and the false checker would call back the numbers to the stage, not from the player's sheet but from his own slip of paper. Thus one of the crooks would win a car.

But nobody could prove that it actually happened that way. The police confiscated the car and the two Detroit men were simply ordered out of the country.

It began to show official Ottawa, however, that bingo was a sucker game in more ways than one, and when still another and different fraud was worked on the bingo public, Mayor Charlotte Whitton stepped in. This happened when a car winner was called down to have his card checked and suddenly changed his mind and bolted. It turned out the card was forged. The player had started with an empty card and simply punched in the numbers called with a rubber stamping gadget.

Mayor Whitton promptly banned bingo. For the first time in 11 years, the Lions, Kinsmen, Richelieu and Legion got together to protect their common interests. They called H.F. Dix, a bingo-supply dealer in Toronto, to

Ottawa and asked him to find a foolproof bingo that would satisfy the mayor. Dix promptly tightened up the whole bingo operation. He pointed out that, for every card or sheet sold at a bingo, there is an identical master card or sheet which is kept by the master checker on the stage. Thus when a player shouts, "Bingo!" the checker in the crowd calls the number of the player's card to the stage, where the duplicate master card is brought out. This is checked against the numbers called. In this way it is impossible for a phony checker to "call back" a card that doesn't exist or to forge a card for which there is no master card.

But even in its cleaned-up condition Ottawa's bingo is by no means out of trouble. In addition to pressure from church groups who feel it's morally wrong and pressure from the police who think that so much easy money is an inducement to crime, there is pressure from the public for more and bigger and costlier prizes. "Ottawa's on the way to pricing itself out of bingo," novelty-dealer Dix said. "They've gone crazy with prizes. One car isn't enough now; you have to give away two or the players aren't interested."

In its latest financial statement, the Montgomery branch of the Canadian Legion said it made only $1,619 on seven bingos during 1954. Emmett Collins, a vice-president, said, "Prizes cost a lot; on some bingos we lost money."

Not long ago in an office in downtown Ottawa I talked to Wes Brown, a thin, pleasant, middle-aged man who is a former president of the Ottawa Lions Club. He started Ottawa's monster bingos. At that time the Lions were trying to finance their war effort and were having a hard time raising money. With another Lion named Roy Baker, they rented the Auditorium for $250 (now it's $1,000), put up $1,000 in prizes and cleared $440. Ottawa's bingo grew from there. Other service clubs came in, bigger prizes brought bigger crowds and bigger problems.

"We built a health centre for $50,000," Brown told me, "and a cerebral palsy centre for $21,000; we're sending kids to school and university with scholarships, our cobalt-bomb building will cost us $79,000 and the federal government will provide the bomb. A few years ago, one youth won a car at one of our bingos and sold it. He's going to university with the money. We bought an artificial arm the other day for an Ottawa civil servant so he could get a better job—a raise in pay from $100 to $175 a month. Perhaps we can't always keep out crooks and cheats. But when I look at those things, I feel proud about bingo in Ottawa."

BINGO REMAINS BIG *in the nation's capital. Ottawa has 12 bingo halls, some offering games from 10 a.m. until 4 a.m. The Criminal Code still requires that the proceeds go to charity or to a provincial government. In 1996, Statistics Canada estimated that 12 per cent of Canadian households had at least one bingo player, and that average household spending on the game was $677.*

HERBERT MANNING, *who began his journalism career at the Win-nipeg* Tribune, *was an editor at* Maclean's *from August, 1954 to January, 1959, when he left to join the* Toronto Star. *He later worked as a radio host in Montreal and died sometime in the 1960s.*

Will a Machine Ever Take Your Job?

by Norman DePoe

OCTOBER 1, 1955

EVEN THE MOST CASUAL OF newspaper readers has recently become aware that something new—and big—is going on in North American industry. It's already being described as the Second Industrial Revolution. The difference is that the first one used machines to *do* things—to cut, to spin, to weave, to shape, to lift—but always for a human operator. Now, the engineers have taught machines to think for themselves, and eliminated the human hand on the levers.

These self-operating self-regulating machines, which can pour out goods better, faster and cheaper than ever before, are the tools of a new industrial way of life called automation, whose implications are frightening or roseate, depending which way you see it. This new technology, hailed as the gimmick that will liberate man at last from labor, and denounced as the final triumph of the soulless machine over human endeavor, will make radical changes in nearly every basic condition of our daily lives. The question is, what will those changes be? Will they spell paradise or chaos—unlimited leisure or nation-wide unemployment?

The process behind this suddenly fashionable catchword—automation—is already making dramatic and sweeping changes in factory production. It has invaded scores of "non-mechanical" white-collar jobs. It has a hand in mailing out the Family Allowance cheques received by hundreds of thousands of Canadians every month. Thousands more of us, though we may not call it by name, already use automation to heat our homes or dry Monday's wash. Automatic oven controls cook dinners for thousands of Canadian housewives. Many of the meal's ingredients may be ready-to-use products prepared in the first place by other automatic machines.

To Norbert Wiener, the American mathematical wizard whose book *Cybernetics and Society* is the most popular text on automation, this continuing drive to perfect almost self-sufficient machines and invent new ones is an open invitation to an "abrupt and final cessation of the demand for the type of factory labor performing purely repetitive tasks." And eventually, he predicts, we'll be deep in unemployment on a scale that will make the Depression of the 1930s seem like a pleasant joke.

This apocalyptic view is emphatically not shared by people like Benjamin Fairless, former chairman of the board of United States Steel. This giant company, which has moved into automation as fast as developments warranted it, sees the changeover as a kind of revolution, admittedly. But Fairless told a business audience in Johnstown, Pa., recently that fears of mass unemployment were "just plain silly."

What is the process that can produce such flat contradictions? How does it work? Most of all, what is it going to do to us—and how soon?

The ideal automated factory of the future—still a long way off for most industries—would be a place where raw materials (ordered by machines as needed) were delivered at one end, passed rapidly through a series of operations (all carried out by automatic self-regulating machines), and emerged at the other end as neatly packaged finished products. Inside the plant, there might be a dozen or so engineers, doing little but studying control panels and servicing machines which, by flashing a light or buzzing a buzzer, indicated they had broken down.

Science fiction? A pipe dream? More than 10 years ago, during the Second World War, American scientists ran the giant Oak Ridge, Tenn., atomic installation from a single central control room. It was linked to 10 miles or so of control panels requiring, on the average, only 20 human operators to the *mile*.

Or take a modern oil refinery, which comes within a hair's breadth of the automation ideal. The raw material—crude oil—arrives by automated pipeline. Its passage through the plant is regulated by pre-set controls, which can be adjusted to determine what the end products will be, and which maintain the right operating conditions at each stage in refining. Finally, the finished gasoline and other products are drawn off automatically to tank storage, to tank cars—or to another automated pipeline that will take them hundreds of miles without human help to a distribution point.

McKinnon Industries, of St. Catharines, Ont., moved this year into the forefront of automation with a new assembly line to turn out V-8 engines for General Motors of Canada in Oshawa, Ont. All of the basic work on the engine blocks—more than 800 separate operations—is accomplished with only 27 men. In a few months, when further automatic controls are installed, the number will be cut to 21.

Even a breakdown doesn't stir up much human activity. Special circuits in each control panel report trouble instantly to a central unit, and the whole line is electronically stopped until the bottleneck is cleared. Then the same impersonal switches and relays speed things back up to normal again. The line will turn out 70 fully machined blocks an hour—with the expenditure of less than a third of a man-hour of human labor on each.

But what about the men who tend the machines of automation—what's their reaction to this revolution they're shepherding? Like the theorists, some see it as a boon, others as a curse. "It's a completely different job, and a lot better," says Robert Handley, a well-muscled 27-year-old St. Catharines, Ont., man who, after six and a half years as a machinist, is now a toolsetter, electronic style. "For one thing, you're not just running one machine all the time, doing the same thing over and over." To run machines that utterly dwarf him, Handley had to absorb training in electricity and what he calls "efficient operations"—in effect, the theory of mass production. Today, he has more responsibility and makes more money (the average operator's bi-monthly basic pay envelope is five to 10 dollars heavier than those of conventional machinists).

To Handley, the future seems bright: "I guess I'll stay here for good."

But Gordon Lambert, a husky heavyweight worker in the foundry where the blocks are originally cast, isn't so sure. "Now," he says, "all I do is push a button on an automatic machine and take out the finished product. They've taken most of the skill right out of the job." The machine has also knocked

Lambert's salary down. Formerly, a skilled coremaker like Lambert, working under a system of incentive bonuses, could average $2.02 an hour. Now, mainly because the machine is independent of human skill—but partly because the union, as a matter of policy, demanded abolition of the incentive system—the job pays a flat $1.85.

Lambert, in his capacity as an official of Local 199 of the United Automobile Workers, says the union is dubious about other aspects of automation as well. There's a general feeling that without production planning the machines will turn out a year's requirements faster, resulting in longer layoffs. And such hard-won union demands as seniority rules appear to offer less protection to long-service employees than formerly.

Digital computers, or electronic brains, obviously give real promise of fulfilling the dream of the completely automatic factory. They can replace clerks as well as laborers, and they are already outshining routine human effort in offices as well as in factories all over North America. General Electric uses a giant Univac calculator to make up the weekly payroll for the 12,000 employees in its plant at Louisville, Ky. The brain does the entire job. It adds bonuses earned, makes income tax and medical-plan deductions, figures overtime—all the things a payroll clerk has to do to a pay cheque in mid-twentieth century. It distributes all totals among the cost accounts of the company's various departments. Then it writes out a cheque for everyone concerned, prints a payroll register, and reports ready for the next job. The whole complex process takes less than six hours.

You'll find evidence of a similar set of operations in the neatly punched holes that decorate one corner of Canadian Family Allowance cheques. But that's only one type of electronic brainwork. The Prudential Life Insurance Company has a computer that will bill policy holders for premiums, figure agents' commissions, calculate dividends, and work out all the statistics on which premium rates are based. Officials estimate that the brain will take over the work of 200 human employees in one department alone.

Several firms make electronic systems that displace not only elevator operators, but also the starters who used to control traffic. Computers have replaced clerks to register and allot train and plane reservations. One company recently demonstrated a robot toll collector for bridges. It will make change, count the number of cars going through and balance the cash at the end of the day. If any mere human being thinks he can drive past this electronic watchdog without paying, the machine slyly takes a photograph of his rear license plate and passes it along to the local constabulary.

From these examples, it's evident that automation may turn up almost anywhere. In most cases, the only possible limiting factor is economic: the employer or manufacturer must determine whether a routine operation can be repeated often enough to cover the original cost of the machine.

In spite of such things as automatic corn huskers and cotton pickers, farming is generally considered immune from complete labor displacement because of the relatively short season and the widely varied tasks that must be done. Complete automation is unlikely, too, in several small service occupations and in the manufacture of specialty products in limited quantities.

The mere thought of introducing total automation into industry without thorough planning first being done has drawn cries of alarm from North American labor leaders. CIO president Walter Reuther, testifying before a congressional committee this year, demanded that the U.S. government do some planning immediately, before the country drifted "aimlessly into dislocations and disruptions, mass unemployment and catastrophic depression."

In Canada, a similar demand was made last June in the House of Commons by Colin Cameron, the CCF member for Nanaimo. Citing the example of a new $17 million pulp-and-paper mill in his own riding which employed 100, he called on the Department of Labor to make a full-scale survey of automation's growth and impact. Social Crediters agreed with him that the new system held disturbing possibilities.

The debate, which was inconclusive, also brought out the other side of the argument—that automation can only lead to a higher standard of living. William Hamilton, a Montreal Conservative, even had a brush with Mr. Speaker when he described critics of the new age as "barnacles on the backside of progress."

Outside the House, the optimistic view was summed up in the same month by J.R. White, president of Imperial Oil. "Automation," he claimed, "does not destroy jobs. Instead, it creates them."

Both sides in the running controversy can buttress their arguments with figures. Labor leaders point to the U.S. steel industry, which is turning out as much steel this year as it did in 1953—and doing it with 70,000 fewer men. In the auto industry, though cars are being turned out at a record rate, the American membership of the UAW has not risen appreciably in five years.

Electronic brains have also moved in on the baking industry, with taped formulas for turning out bread, cake, or pretzels—including bending them. In addition, thousands of housewives are using ready-mix baking products which are blended and packaged by automated equipment. The whole development is tolling a louder and louder knell for the old-fashioned baker.

Multiply cases like these by scores, and the alarm expressed by union leaders over the dangers of advancing into an automated age without adequate industrial planning is understandable. Some big businessmen, on the other hand, quote figures that tell a different story. E.H. Walker, president of McKinnon Industries, points out that his company increased its employee roster from 710 in 1929 to 5,416 last spring—and that over the same period, more and more machinery, some of it automated, has been used. R.M. Robinson, general manager of Canadian General Electric's electronics division, says that in spite of such developments as printed circuits and automatic soldering, staffs in CGE's electronics plants have doubled over the past five years. And in office accounting, where machines have made their most dramatic advance, U.S. figures show 71 per cent more people at work in 1950 than there were in 1940.

All the experts agree that this is one of the major shifts caused by automation: there may be a shrinking demand for unskilled workers but there are new—and more highly paid—opportunities for men with a technical and scientific education. But will the new demand for technicians and draftsmen balance the shrinkage in unskilled labor? In any one industry, the answer seems to be "No." Will the growth of small subsidiary service organizations that don't need automation mop up the people displaced? To that one you'll find as many opinions as there are experts.

Some prognosticators have gone so far as to paint a future in which there is ever-increasing productivity and prosperity for those with jobs, while the new machines squeeze a few more people out of the golden circle every year.

Every worker displaced, they point out, is also a consumer removed from the market that automation needs.

Labor unions, on the other hand, have already made up their minds: they welcome anything that makes labor less laborious but, they insist, there must be the most careful planning in introducing the new technology to industry so that dislocations are kept to the minimum. Ted Silvey, educational director of the CIO, told a conference this summer that his organization "has definitely taken the position that automation is a blessing." He added: "We must plan to use it so that it blesses mankind." The unions see no reason why industry should not continue along the same road it has followed ever since machines first began to extend human output. Union plans are to take their slice of the new productivity in the form of better pay and security (the guaranteed annual wage is a current example) and in more leisure through shorter hours.

The central dilemma of automation can be summed up in a single anecdote, possibly apocryphal. Walter Reuther, the story goes, was touring one of Ford's new automated plants with a company executive. Looking at the machines, the executive remarked, "You're going to have quite a time getting them to join your union."

"Yes," Reuther is supposed to have replied, "and you're going to have quite a time trying to sell them cars."

The legendary broadcast journalist **NORMAN DEPOE** *was CBC-TV's chief Ottawa correspondent in the 1960s; in all he spent 29 years with the Corporation. Born in Portland, Ore., he came to Canada at age six and died at 62 of heart failure in 1980.*

The Myth That's Muffling Canada's Voice

by
Lionel Shapiro

OCTOBER 29, 1955

One of the most versatile and widely recognized writers Canada has produced, Montreal's Lionel Shapiro took up the craft on second thought. He graduated with honors from McGill University in 1929, intent on becoming a psychologist. A summer job as a sports writer on the *Montreal Gazette* changed his mind. In the 26 years since, Shapiro has been a drama critic, a Broadway columnist, a White House correspondent, a war correspondent, a foreign correspondent; he's written a successful stage play which was produced by the Old Vic in Bristol, five television plays produced in New York City and London, a batch of short stories, song lyrics, movie scripts and four books, three of them novels with a total circulation of more than two million copies.

The Sixth of June, his latest novel, is a Book-of-the-Month selection and has been sold to Hollywood for a sum in six figures. Its reception by the critics, while mixed in part, has been heavily favorable. "Not since Hemingway's *A Farewell To Arms* has there been a war-love story as good," declared the *Baltimore Sun*. "This might well become a minor classic of our times." The *Chicago Tribune* observed, "It has style, pace, story and glamor." "It is magnificent journalism-in-depth," said the stately *New York Times*.

> Today, Shapiro lives a commuter's life. His home is in Montreal, he works in New York, spends some time in Hollywood and each year tours Europe. At 46, he's still a bachelor: "I can't stand noise," he explains.

A LONG TIME AGO, I decided that a writer born, bred and educated in Canada is not necessarily less skilful, less perceptive or less readable than a writer born in the United States, Britain, France, India or China. I decided that a Canadian has not only an equal chance but also an equal right to jump out into the world forum and make a reputation and a livelihood as a writer.

This required a simply terrible snobbishness on my part. More than snobbishness. Pure gall. For although Canadian bankers, soldiers, doctors, actors, engineers and explorers could be, and are, acknowledged world leaders in their fields, I was brought up to believe a Canadian has no writing tradition to build upon, that he is a mouse in the world of creative writing—not only a mouse but a mouse in diapers—that there is no distinctive Canadian literature in the English language, that someday, somehow, a great Canadian novel will be written and this will be the signal for Canadian literature to begin its growth. Until then, the legend went, the lad born in Niagara Falls, N.Y., has a chance of becoming a Hemingway but the lad born in Niagara Falls, Ont., had better walk in the dark of the moon until a Canadian Shakespeare materializes and hastens the dawn.

Thanks to my incurable snobbishness, I ignored these fables, foibles and unreasoning fears. I elbowed them out of the way. And, to my astonishment, it has worked.

Since 1947, I have written three novels. They have been published (and translated where applicable) in Canada, United States, Britain, France, Belgium, Spain, Italy, Switzerland, Holland, Denmark, Norway, Sweden, Germany, Mexico and the Argentine. The total circulation of these books in all editions is as yet incomplete but it certainly runs well in excess of two million copies. All five television plays I have written have been produced by NBC in New York and two of them by the BBC in London. The one stage play I attempted was produced by the Old Vic Company in Bristol and was received with profound respect and even enthusiasm by critics from such newspapers as the *Manchester Guardian* and the august *Times* of London. The latest novel, *The Sixth of June*, recently published, was bought by Twentieth Century-Fox, and is being translated for world-wide distribution.

The purpose of this listing is not to recount a success story; it is, rather, to sketch the outlines of a tragedy in the development of Canadian creative writing and to trace a formula of native Canadian provincialism which has deterred and deflected Canadians in all creative fields from the free pursuit of their ambitions. The best examples come to my mind in the field of writing. Having traveled extensively most of my adult life, my acquaintance with Canadian writers is much restricted; yet I can name a dozen Canadians who can outwrite me left, right and centre, whose intelligence is broader and

Second World War correspondent Lionel Shapiro was a successful playwright, Broadway columnist, movie and TV scriptwriter and novelist. His The Sixth of June *won the 1955 Governor General's Award*

deeper and quicker, who would be coddled and acclaimed in any other country of the world, and who have gained scant recognition, no popularity and piddling circulation in Canada or, for that matter, anywhere else. They are people who have been discouraged by the legends and the foibles and by the very formidable roadblocks erected by Canadians themselves against the free passage and development of Canadian artistic creation.

If this article, which is bitter in the writing and probably in the reading, encourages one or two Canadians to ignore the local handicaps, it will have been handsomely worthwhile. A Canadian literary tradition must necessarily be born inside Canada, but I venture to predict it will become a tradition in the outside world first and belatedly in Canada.

The handicaps that beset a Canadian intent on a writing career are formidable. They embrace both shadow and substance, and the shadow is probably a more powerful deterrent than the substance.

Prof. F.M. Salter of the University of Alberta, speaking last May in Toronto to the Humanities Association of Canada, deplored Canadian literature as "academic and rootless." He went on to urge all interested in literature to dig out the traditions of folk poetry and folklore "on which any healthy literature must depend." He said, "The best in the arts springs direct from the people. If we are ever to create a distinctive Canadian literature we must anchor ourselves to the Canadian way of life."

At the risk of being unfair to Salter (the above is merely an excerpt from a newspaper report of his speech), I must confess that his thesis infuriates me, if only because this is a prime example of the psychological handicap writers of my generation have been weaned on. Well-meaning, sincere people like Salter have been echoing and re-echoing their discouraging plaint across all the days of my years: rootless . . . no distinctive Canadian literature . . . rootless . . . rootless. The wail is in tremulous harmony with the strange noises made by some politicians who claim we can't be a nation until we carve the Union Jack out of the flag.

Canadian literature rootless? What language do we speak—Esperanto? And what are we—goat-herding Ki-kuyu? I for one am gratefully happy with the roots of our literature which, among others, are Milton, Chaucer, Shakespeare and Donne. Furthermore, I do not fully comprehend what is meant by "a distinctive Canadian literature." If enough Canadians apply their Canadian minds to the world around them, and the seats of their Canadian pants to the seats of their Canadian chairs, we can have a burgeoning Canadian literature.

Indeed, we have a pretty good flowering of Canadian literature right now. Try to bemoan the state of Canadian writing in any literary gathering in New York or London or Paris and you will be challenged with a flood of names: Robertson Davies, Morley Callaghan, Hugh MacLennan, Thomas Costain (who lives in the United States but is widely regarded as vigorously Canadian), Mazo de la Roche, Lawrence Earl, Gwethalyn Graham, Roger Lemelin and half a dozen other Canadians writing in the French language. These are writers of various types and schools, and readers will differ violently on their merit or lack of merit, but bundle them up and they are a formidable lot. My point is that only in Canada is Canadian writing derided, decried and indeed dismissed as nonexistent.

Perhaps the principal area of dispute lies in the question: what is a Canadian novel? That is a blood brother to the question: what is a distinctive Canadian literature?

There is a group of people, based mostly in Toronto, with tentacles reaching deep into radio, television, publishing and the book pages of principal newspapers, that I like to call the Inner Coterie of Canadian Authors. Many of these self-appointed arbiters of Canadian culture are connected with the Canadian Authors Association, whatever that is. This group would seem to believe that a Canadian novel must restrict itself to Canadian characters, locales, situations and problems. My own definition of a Canadian novel is one written by a Canadian, or more exactly, one written by a product of Canadian education and upbringing.

I have scant sympathy with the provincialism that holds that a novel must be about a hut in northern Saskatchewan or incest in the Maritimes or the clash of our two great cultures to qualify as Canadian literature. This is the essence of timidity, the root of a terrible inferiority complex. One might as well dismiss *Julius Caesar* and *Romeo and Juliet* as Italian plays, and *For Whom the Bell Tolls* as a Spanish novel. Are our newspapers less Canadian because they print a preponderance of world news on their front pages and deal with world problems on their editorial pages? Is Mike Pearson less Canadian because he doesn't restrict his speeches to wheat, the St. Lawrence Seaway and Canada's air space? Is a writer less Canadian because he refuses to believe that British and American novelists have a monopoly on universal problems and big canvases? And bestsellers? And, Heaven forbid, enough popularity to attract offers from Hollywood?

Just as there is a distinctive Canadian policy on the world stage of foreign affairs and a distinctive Canadian position in the world of finance and commerce, there can be, I believe, a distinctive Canadian niche in English-language literature. The three novels I have written, though they deal mostly with non-Canadians, could not easily have been written by anyone except a Canadian. All three books deal with the impact upon Britain and Europe of a great and historic development: the uneasy accession of the United States to world leadership and responsibility. Who can look at all sides of this momentous event better, more compassionately than a Canadian? Who else in the world has a more immediate comprehension of, and intimacy with, both sides of the Atlantic? This, in my view, is a clear and unchallenged Canadian literary function, even though the characters in the three books are mostly Americans, British and west Europeans.

A man writes what he knows best and feels deepest. I happen to have been a foreign correspondent most of my adult life. Does this make me or my books less Canadian? John P. Marquand remarks in his review of *The Sixth of June*, my most recent novel, "For once, the English and the Americans in a wartime novel are equally convincing." This is a Canadian literary function.

Of course, I would like to see great powerful novels written by Canadians about our own country, her problems and her folklore, displayed in bookstalls all over the world. I am sure this generation will see Canadian Joyce Carys and Canadian Robert Penn Warrens emerge. But let's not insist on putting the cart before the horse. First we must expand our cadre of crack professionals. We must encourage Canadian novelists to get out on the world stage. We must convince them that they are not condemned to garrets and to the whims of the Inner Coterie of Canadian Authors, that they have both roots and opportunity, that the psychological handicaps can be blown asunder with a single deep breath of courage.

At this point I must become even more personal than I have been heretofore, simply because my most expert witnesses on the subject are pages out of my own experience.

In early 1944, I was in England, awaiting the assignment to D-Day. I decided to spend the time writing a book, my first. The title chosen was *They Left the Back Door Open*, because it was a report on the conquest of Sicily and the storming of the Bay of Salerno by the U.S.-British Fifth Army. The manuscript was completed in March of that year and I mailed it to a major Canadian publishing house in Toronto.

No one except a writer can know the excitement bound up in sending his or her first book to a publisher. It is heaven and hell, dreams and feverish torture. Especially torture, and especially the waiting, waiting, waiting. As it turned out, I didn't have to wait too long. One fine spring day the millennium arrived in the form of a cable from the editor-in-chief of the publishing house: ". . . Splendid . . . accepted . . . publishing quickly as possible." Glory be!

One deliriously happy month later, a letter arrived from the same publishing house. It was a most sympathetic letter. They were deeply sorry to disappoint me but, it turned out, they had decided to publish a major American author's report on the Mediterranean campaign and, as the subject matter was more or less similar, well . . . crash!

Only a writer can measure the disappointment, and only I can know how valuable a lesson I learned from it. My London bureau manager, a grand Englishman who was never caught without an umbrella, bundled up a carbon copy of my manuscript and sent it to a major British publishing house. One week later, the publisher took me to lunch, told me it was the finest book he had read on the Mediterranean campaign and handed me a cheque for the British equivalent of $400 as an advance royalty. The fact that another Canadian publishing house subsequently accepted the manuscript couldn't erase that first disappointment nor could it obscure that first lesson: if you think you're as good a writer as the next man, get out into the world, lad, out into the world. Canada will eventually come charging up from the rear.

Small wonder then that when I returned from the war in 1946 with a burning ambition to write a first novel, I offered my first two chapters and a story outline to LeBaron Barker, Doubleday's executive editor in New York.

He was blissfully ignorant of the fiction that Canadian writing is rootless and he promptly produced a contract and a substantial advance royalty cheque. The novel turned out to be *The Sealed Verdict*. It sold about 25,000 hard-cover copies in the United States, Canada and Britain, over 150,000 book-club copies, some 600,000 paperbacks, was translated for publication in France, Denmark, Italy, Spain and Norway, was made into a movie by Paramount, serialized by *Cosmopolitan* magazine and attracted a wealth of superlative reviews all over the world. *The Saturday Review of Literature* listed my name at the top of their gallery of the best first novelists of 1947.

Had I made the grade in my own country? Not by a long shot. The Inner Coterie of Canadian Authors, based mostly in Toronto, sniffed like a consti-pated owl. Wrote the critic of the Toronto *Globe and Mail*: "This is a sideline view of Allied Military Government in action in which the author theatrically stacks the cards with all the ornateness of a soap opera and melodramatically telegraphs the outcome. The six chapters of *Sealed Verdict* are labeled in the pre-scribed Monday through Saturday formula of radio's washboard weepers. How-ever, *Sealed Verdict* has already been purchased by Paramount Pictures, serialized in *Cosmopolitan* and will undoubtedly be a lending library success . . ."

Well, the years roll on. I write a second novel, *Torch For a Dark Journey*, which has a fine critical reception in the United States and Europe but is largely ignored in Canada. And now a third novel, *The Sixth of June*, pops out of the typewriter. It seems sure of success with the public and critics alike. It is the August selection of the Book-of-the-Month Club, an immediate best-seller from Gander to California. The movies have bought it (how low!) and foreign publishers are outbidding one another crazily. And all the time I kept wondering: did I make the grade in Canada?

It seems I not only made the grade but am suddenly too bloody good. A curious strain ran through the principal reviews: "If there be fault here," writes the *Globe and Mail*, "it may be resentment in a few minds that the novel is too slick, too well plotted, too credible, too ably and smoothly con-trolled . . ." The *Montreal Star* wrote: "It is not Shapiro's fault that his novels have such surface gloss and appear to be written with so shrewd an eye on the market that one tends to dismiss them as all surface. They are better than that: the craftsmanship is sure . . ."

In 1952, I wrote a drama for the stage; again I had an experience that may prove of some value to Canadian dramatists who feel they must make good locally before moving out on the world stage. The play, *The Bridge*, was selected for production by the famed Old Vic Company. Its critical reception by England's first-string critics was widely reported in Canada. The *Manchester Guardian* wrote the morning after a wonderful first night: "Henry Sherek has found a new dramatist and the Bristol Old Vic Company presented his first play tonight at the Theatre Royal—*The Bridge* by Lionel Shapiro. There has not been as good a theatrical examination since Sartre's *Les Mains Sales* of the conflict between personal and political loyalties in a world divided by beliefs hardened into hatreds . . . Mr. Shapiro is a fortunate beginner. He seems to have no trouble with construction, every scene ending with a theatrical crackle. He not only deserved success tonight but had it thrust upon him by the excellence of the Bristol Old Vic players."

A few weeks later, I flew into London and consulted my agent. The news was good. Amsterdam and Copenhagen had purchased the play for production. Offers were flowing in from England's famed repertory companies. "Anything from Canada?" I asked. The answer was no, not even an inquiry.

Let's turn to television, which is both a wonderful market and experience for the developing writer. In early 1952, I did my first TV script, an hour-long drama called *The 23rd Mission*. It was immediately accepted by NBC's *Television Playhouse* and scored so well that the CBC was finally cajoled into buying a year's option for Canadian production. The following year, I had the pleasure of seeing it done in London by BBC's superb television company and the critical reaction was far beyond my rosiest expectations. The *Daily Express* critic called it "one of the neatest and most touching short plays of the season." The *Sunday Times* was extravagant indeed. Its critic, Maurice Wiggin, wrote: "It may seem farfetched to call a television producer a poet, but the best of them do a poet's work. To be simply a technician is manifestly not enough. There are about half a dozen men who deploy both technical skill and creative imagination: when they collaborate with good writers, they make possible a stay against confusion. Most of them work in the drama department. Lionel Shapiro is a good writer, and a writer who believes in goodness, which is much less common and much more important . . . *The 23rd Mission* was written especially for Armistice Day, a rash and even reckless venture, which succeeded, so far as I was concerned, perfectly . . ."

The point of this story is that, a year later, when I arrived back in Canada, a CBC executive explained to me in a plaintive voice that the play had not been televised because no CBC producer cared for it sufficiently. There apparently is a grand panjandrum of drama in the CBC who was enjoying a purple mood that season and specialized in the bizarre, the supernatural and in lecherous Orientals. I concede him the right to like whatever he pleases, but he must concede me the point that when one man controls TV playwriting in Canada it accentuates a terrible weakness in the system of government-owned TV.

This bleak and angry chronicle rises not out of a spirit of recrimination but in pursuit of high purpose. I have no need for mumbling over past disappointments for I am not blind to the fact that I am probably the luckiest three-novel writer alive—lucky in the terrible game of jackpot lottery which every writer must play in this day of high pressure and mass media, lucky in the tangle of circumstances that sent me abroad at a time when I was young enough to shake off the sense of timidity which paralyzes the creative arts in Canada.

The purpose of this article is to emphasize that the most important thing in the life of a writer is what happens in those quiet contemplative hours when he or she is alone with a typewriter and a blank sheet of paper. It doesn't matter whether the writer is sitting in New York or Tunbridge Wells or Regina; what does matter is the magic of creation and this flows from the trifling of God that is in all of us.

In all of my journeyings into the far corners of the earth I have yet to meet a person who doesn't think it is a grand thing to have been born and brought up a Canadian. There is no reason why this shouldn't apply to Canadians who work in the creative fields. Sometimes pride can be a form of courage and too much modesty only a form of cowardice.

LIONEL SHAPIRO *was Maclean's chief foreign correspondent for nearly 20 years. The Sixth of June won the 1955 Governor General's Award for fiction; it was his last novel. He died of cancer in 1958, at age 50, in Montreal.*

The Scramble for the Teenage Dollar

by John Clare

SEPTEMBER 14, 1957

FOR YEARS, TEENAGERS HAVE BEEN regarded with loving perplexity and occasional alarm by nervous outsiders. Statisticians have run them through computing machines; sociologists, amateur and professional, have run them down, and some observers, who seem to think of a pair of blue jeans as being roughly the equivalent of an SS uniform, show an inclination to run for the nearest exit.

But now teenagers have been discovered by a group of friends who think they are "earl," "ivy," "cool" and even "the most." To put it simply, these new friends think teenagers are "Joe Lovely." For the word has got out that young people are loaded, and while they are not throwing their money around like junior Jim Bradys, they aren't stuffing it into any abandoned tea cosies either.

Once they were regarded as a modest but steady market for such commodities as soda pop and bikes. Some stores set up junior councils to act as advisers and work as clerks with the idea that they and their friends would keep coming to the shop when they grew up to be serious shoppers. That time has come ahead of schedule on the crest of a boom and a wave of war babies who will hit the teens and the market place with rising authority over the next 10 years.

Teenage spending in Canada has already reached $100 million a year, according to a survey conducted among a 150,000 high-school students in Toronto, Montreal and Edmonton. The survey was sponsored by *Canadian*

High News, a weekly newspaper for students, with a circulation of about 30,000. To many observers of the growing teenage market, this spending figure is low, even though it is confined, as is the scope of this article, to high-school students and excludes those young people who have left school at the legal age and gone to work. In the United States, a more comprehensive survey indicated that teenagers in that country are spending $9 billion a year and will be spending $14 billion by 1965 if business stays brisk. Merchants who sell in this market feel that the Canadian figure could be doubled or tripled and still legitimately represent the teenage contribution to the economy as consumers. As in the United States, their spending is expected to increase greatly, probably to twice the present amount, between 1951 and 1971.

Canada in 1955 had 1.6 million young people between the ages of 15 and 19; in 1960 the figure will be 1.5 million, but by 1965 it will be up to 1.9 million. The rise, fall, and rise again in the rate follows the family pattern of the war years, with many marriages in the early years, the departure of thousands of men overseas in the middle years, and their return home by 1945 to add to their families.

The slow flowering of the love affair between business and the teenagers has some of the classic lineaments of the theatrical situation in which a storekeeper discovers the pest he was about to throw out on the street is really an eccentric millionaire. For all their strange talk and outlandish clothes, teenagers are as welcome as a couple of Grey Cup tickets these days.

Canadian business has, for the most part, been slower to make a special pitch to the new customers than merchants in the United States. But businessmen are constantly being nudged by communiqués such as the one issued by J.K. Edmonds, an economist writing in *The Financial Post*, who said: "The businessman who wants a bonanza in 1965 should start planning now to appeal to the hi-fi rather than the high chair set." And Eugene Gilbert, who runs a marketing service for U.S. advertisers and calls himself the George Gallup of the teenagers, recently said: "The advertiser who touches a responsive chord in youth can generally count on the parents to finally succumb to the purchase of the product. Since youth is graced with unparalleled resiliency and buoyancy, parents generally have little resistance or protection against youth's bombardments. Thus, with the parents rendered helpless, it becomes evident that youth is the market!"

In addition to sounding like a general planning to soften up an invasion beachhead, Gilbert has put his finger on a wide and as yet unmeasured area of buying influence that reaches far beyond the teenagers' own expenditures. Jim McEwen, a Toronto car dealer, provided a glimpse of this new power wielded by the young when he told of a man and his wife who came to his showroom to pick out a car. The selection of the model was made and the deal appeared completed. But wait. "Now," said the wife. "That's all we can do until Judy sees it." Judy was their 17-year-old daughter, and they wouldn't think of buying a car until she had a chance to offer her opinion on the color scheme.

Judy may wield more influence than most teenagers in most families; her power is felt in the buying of food, clothing and many major family items. Part of this influence may stem from the changing pattern of family life which permits the discussion of family purchases. Some of it may come from the fact that some parents dislike saying "No"—because they have to rule negatively on cigarettes, liquor, late hours and other disciplinary matters, they welcome a chance to give their children their way in such matters as the choice of colors for the family car.

What kind of merchandise do teenagers buy with their own money? Clothes are the biggest single item in their budgets, but when it comes to a major purchase like a winter coat their parents will put up the money. A quarter of all teenagers have a typewriter, and it may be significant that their favorite is a make that beams a special appeal to high-school students, suggesting they will get better marks if they work on a keyboard. Almost 80 per cent of them, the *High News* survey found, own watches and the rest are going to get one as soon as they can.

Almost 70 per cent have a bank account and most teenagers have a regular system of saving. Sixty per cent have cameras.

They drink three bottles of pop a week, eat two candy bars (boys prefer Oh Henry; girls Sweet Marie), buy one record at about 90 cents for a 45-rpm disc and up to 98 cents for a 78. If they live in Western Canada or the Maritimes, their pop tunes will cost them a little more.

The girls own four to 10 sweaters each (one girl whose father was in the business had 27 cashmere sweaters) while boys own an average of two to four. Teenagers are big users of cosmetics such as lipsticks. One shampoo company reported a jump in sales when they changed their advertising theme to one they hoped would appeal to teenagers. "We used a Hollywood pitch, urging them to make their hair as lovely as the stars, and it's increased our sales. We always knew that young girls wash their hair more than anyone, probably because their hair is oilier when it's young, but this increase has been fantastic," said the agency representative who handled the advertising campaign.

Maybe it's because no one in his right mind throws snowballs at Santa Claus, but merchants as a group think these young people are smart shoppers. A woman might come into a shoe store and say she wants "something in white." Half an hour and 20 boxes later she may still not have narrowed the choice between a Cuban or a spike heel and she may be talking wistfully about black patent pumps. But teenagers have usually pre-shopped their purchases. They know—from observing what the gang is wearing, from reading their favorite fashion magazine (for girls *Seventeen* is an authority on clothes), or from watching the clothes being shown on television or in the movies— exactly what they want. All the clerk has to do is provide the right size. They usually know the color they must have.

One clerk described their crisp no-nonsense shopping technique this way: "They know what the kids are wearing, and that's what they want. You're wasting your time to try and sell them on anything else. They're like finicky rich people when they shop, and I guess that isn't far from the truth. After all, they have everything—a place to stay, meals, schooling—and the money they bring here to spend is their own. They aren't going to throw it away."

"We have more trouble with the parents than we have with the kids," said one shoe clerk. "Fathers seem to be the worst. They worry whether the shoes will wear well and if the heels aren't too high to be comfortable." Mothers, who seem to remember more clearly what it was like to be young, are much easier to get along with, he said.

Most teenagers would prefer to shop by themselves unless they are buying a big item like a winter coat; then they'll ask one of their parents to come along as an adviser. They will bring friends along if they are picking up a pair of nylons but rarely do they want them around if they are buying a dress or some larger item. Boys seem to like no one around except the clerk when they are making a purchase.

Eaton's thought they were well aware of the vagaries of the teenage shopper until they stocked a short coat they called a band box. They thought it would appeal to boys who rode bikes because of the freedom of action it gave their legs, but the boys showed no interest. So the store moved the buttons to the left side and sent some of the coats to the girls' department. They drew another blank. But, they discovered, girls were going to the boys' department to buy the male model. Anxious to save them a trip, the store moved the boys' coats with the buttons on the right side to the girls department. Sales picked up, but not in the girls' shop. They continued to slip into the boys' department to buy the male version.

Merchants with goods to sell to teenagers have made other discoveries about their customers. They have found out, for instance, that they don't like to be talked down to. They want to be treated like young adults— which they are, for they enter that world, economically at least, at an early age these days. One Canadian soft-drink company, under the mistaken impression that teenagers talk that way all the time, mounted a series of advertisements in which the message was in jive talk. The product was groovy and it was cool in more than the usual ways. They won't say whether or not the campaign was a success, but they have a new advertising manager, a new sales manager and they have changed advertising agencies. Their ads are once more beamed to young people, but they are told, in the same tone of voice that is used to persuade adults, that the product is refreshing and delicious.

What makes an item a fad or a flop with teenagers? Merchants and promoters wish they knew, and often when they think they have the answer this discriminating and sometimes fickle teenage market just refuses to react. A fad like the Elvis Presley industry, which drew an estimated $20 million from teen-agers' pockets in the United States and Canada last year, is fairly easy to plot. A star gets a name with the youngsters and then, under agile and shrewd management, proceeds to cash in on it by selling not only such obvious items as records but unlikely merchandise like lipsticks or pictures of

Elvis that glow in the dark for an hour after the fans have climbed into bed. These will sell for $2.

Fads imported from the United States usually arrive a little bit late, which should, but doesn't, make matters simple for Canadian storekeepers. Not all the fads take. For instance, white jeans for girls were big in the United States a couple of years ago, but made no impression on Canadian youngsters. A Canadian manufacturer who made hats in school colors, copying a U.S. fad, found himself with a brightly colored flop on his hands.

White bucks (buckskin shoes) have been popular for school and informal wear by both boys and girls for some years. They had their birth as a fad in eastern U.S. universities a decade ago, about the time saddle shoes were getting a foothold at girls' schools like Bryn Mawr. When the high-school students adopted them for their own, one manufacturer assumed they would insist on them being dirty, so he sold them ready-soiled. The Ivy League tradition of elegance had called for soiled bucks. But high-school crowds insist that their white bucks be white, so he had to tidy them up before he could sell them.

Pat Boone, incidentally, who wears them himself, has probably done as much for white bucks as Prince Philip did for cigars when he broke with tradition and lit one at the state dinner at the Louvre during the royal visit last spring. Naturally, manufacturers are only too anxious to have movie and television stars wear their product before the cameras even if it doesn't get a plug.

But sometimes a manufacturer or designer will get his ideas from television or the movies rather than plant his creation with them. Calypso blouses were inspired by the West Indian musical invasion and the popularity of such singers as Harry Belafonte. The frilly blouses were never highly popular with Canadian teenagers, but a variation on the same elaborate theme, with fewer frills and smaller sleeves, known as a sissy blouse, did score with our young set and promises to become a standard item like blue jeans or sloppy joes.

Before a style can reach the stature of a fad, and therefore a must, teenagers want the assurance that "everyone is wearing it." This would seem to pose an insoluble problem of chicken-and-egg proportions but what usually happens is that the five or six leaders in the school community will take the plunge, whether it be sissy blouses or blue jeans, and follow the U.S. style. From then on the fad is as secure as any fad can be, and that is pretty secure when you are dealing with teenagers because they buy for distance. They haven't got the money to switch their styles as frequently as adults and they change, as a group, slowly.

Some auto companies have recognized the influence of teenagers in choosing the family car, and have made a message to teenagers part of their appeal. Another company makes a special razor for young men starting to shave and a cheese firm offers a year's free telephone service as a prize in a jingle contest for the high-school age group.

On a local level the pitch to youngsters is more direct and insistent. Through advertisements and various promotional devices, notably by the record companies, a strong bid is made for their attention and their money. Of the 125,000 to 150,000 records sold each week in Canada, 60 per cent are bought by teenagers.

Teenagers include the price of at least one movie a week in their informal budgets and the movie-makers tailor a good part of their product to that audience. A movie like *Bernadine*, starring Pat Boone, which cost $1 million to make, will probably net $3 million to $4 million at the box office. Of this about $500,000 will come from Canadian tickets, sold mostly to teenagers.

Promoters pay little attention to fan clubs on the theory that they are phonies. There is one notable exception. Most of the teenage clubs in Canada show considerable duplication in their rosters, but the exception, the Liberace fan club, is solidly supported by a cadre of motherly grey-haired women, the kind who frequently wonder out loud what teenagers are coming to.

It would seem that they are coming to economic maturity a few years younger than they ever did before. And as far as where they're going, they've probably already gone—shopping.

IN **1998,** *there were 2.8 million Canadian teens, between the ages of 13 and 19, who spent an estimated $5.7 billion. But with 90s teens more market-savvy, marketers are now targeting the 2.4 million "tweens," the demographic group aged nine to 14, who represent $1.4 billion worth of spending power.*

JOHN CLARE *joined Maclean's in 1946 and was managing editor from 1949 to 1952, when he became editor of* Chatelaine. *A novelist and short story writer, Clare continued to contribute articles to* Maclean's *throughout the 1950s and 1960s while he was an editor at the* Star Weekly. *He died in Toronto in 1981 at age 81 after a series of strokes.*

Canada's Biggest Big Businessmen

by Peter C. Newman

OCTOBER 12, 1957

WITHIN THE PAST DOZEN YEARS, most Canadians have become acutely and happily aware that more money is circulating in Canada than ever before. At the same time they have become somewhat more vaguely aware that the men who command the largest portions of it are, for the most part, much harder to name and recognize than the Sir Herbert Holts, Sir Henry Pellatts and Sir William Van Hornes of an earlier age.

Blandly and almost without notice, our postwar prosperity has spawned a new hierarchy of big businessmen whose decisions help shape the economic existence and influence the working life of nearly all Canadians.

Canada's paper money and coinage stocked in banks, cash registers, wallets, purses and under mattresses totals $1,800 million. There are more than 100 individual Canadians who, as corporation directors, help to control, invest and distribute business assets that are valued at more than the total Canadian currency in circulation.

Who are these men at the country's economic summit? How can their influence be measured?

There is no definitive or final yardstick. But in an effort to find some pattern in the anatomy of Canadian financial power in this year 1957, *Maclean's* recently made a survey based on two rough-and-ready, if inexact, criteria: How many business directorships are held by our hundred busiest directors?

What are the total assets of the various companies which each of these men serves as a director?

A study based on such arbitrary terms cannot, of course, provide a complete or completely accurate index to the relative influence of individual businessmen. It cannot assess strength of personality which often outweighs statistics in the impact of any executive.

The standards chosen—number of directorships and reported assets of the firms involved—also inevitably eliminate the names of some very powerful Canadian businessmen, in spite of their obviously Himalayan stature at the country's economic summit. John David Eaton, for instance, does not appear on the list because the Eaton firm is a private concern and does not, like most other business complexes, publish financial statements. Nor is the immensely wealthy Garfield Weston included, because so many of his holdings are outside Canada.

In spite of these reservations, some of the main features of Big Business '57 do emerge from the *Maclean's* survey of directors. Among the most striking conclusions are these:

- Through their directorships, about 125 Canadian businessmen today exercise a decisive measure of policy control over almost half the country's material wealth, as represented in factories, banks, railroads, mines, oil wells and other resources.

- Economic decisions often come from little-known figures whose names even businessmen only vaguely recognize. The Canadian who sits on the most boards of directors, for instance, is R.A. Jodrey, an obscure apple farmer who lives in Hantsport, N.S.

- The director whose board seats represent the greatest sum of assets is Charles Dunning, a farmer-politician who retired from public life nearly 20 years ago. He now serves as a director of industrial installations with a greater value than the $10 billion in bills and coins printed for the Bank of Canada and stamped out by the Royal Canadian Mint since their establishment.

- The centre of gravity of Canadian business power is slowly shifting from Montreal to Toronto. But of the 100 most active Canadian company directors, 44 are still Montrealers. Twenty-eight live in Toronto. Vancouver, Canada's third-largest city, has only seven representatives on the list.

• In spite of the $11.5 billion U.S. investment in Canadian resources, Americans make up a relatively insignificant contingent in the roll of leading Canadian directors.

• French-Canadian names are surprisingly rare. Little of Quebec's industry is controlled by French-speaking businessmen.

Those who live and work in the rarified atmosphere of Canada's economic summit are as various in their beginnings and their characteristics as, say, an equivalent number of schoolteachers or hockey stars. A few common denominators of habit and background recur without being universal. These include graduation from a Canadian private school (not necessarily followed by a university degree), membership in about a dozen private clubs, and an absence of personal ostentation. Few Canadian businessmen are active openly in politics. Many have developed avid non-business interests and personal hobbies.

"The world of the economic elite," says Professor John Porter, a Carleton University sociologist who has studied the characteristics of Canadian business leadership, "appears as a complex network of small groupings interlocked by a high degree of cross membership. Throughout the network runs a thin, but nonetheless perceptible, thread of kinship."

Canada's 15 most important universities have 80 prominent businessmen on their boards of governors. Fifteen of the University of Toronto's 26-member governing board are corporation directors. The Stratford Shakespearean Festival has eight leading businessmen on its 25-member board of governors.

Directors have the power to move factories without moving employees, they can hatch new company towns or, as one B.C. court case confirmed, sell the company's entire assets. "Being a director," says Frank M. Covert, a Halifax lawyer who is a member of 21 boards, "is a continuous education by virtue of association and the process of seeing how different people tackle the same or similar problems."

Multiple directorships, of course, multiply any director's power. Whether this is good or bad for the country at large and for business at large has long been a point of debate. "As long as the need for competent board members exceeds the supply, the situation of interlocking directorates will exist," says Peter N. Thomson, a director of Nesbitt, Thomson, one of Canada's largest investment houses. "However, I do not believe that such directorates in any way hinder competitive enterprise."

R.C. Berkinshaw, president of the Goodyear Rubber and Tire Company and a director of 11 other corporations, insists that "it does not necessarily imply that businesses are tied together just because some of their directors' names are the same."

Others disagree. C.A. Ashley, a University of Toronto commerce professor who has studied the anatomy of Canadian business leadership, recently concluded, "A comparatively small group of directors, who are constantly meeting with others of the group, and who, almost necessarily, develop some community of interest, if not a common outlook, constitute the real economic elite of Canada."

Interlocking directorships have long been a favorite target of the CCF, and David Lewis, national chairman of the party, claims that the growing concentration of corporate wealth has resulted in a virtual economic dictatorship by a privileged few. "A relatively small number of men," he says, "have almost complete control over our economic life. They have the power to decide if production will be expanded or contracted, if prices will be raised or lowered. Their decisions affect the welfare of thousands of people, but they do not have to answer to anybody."

Another recurrent debate concerns the real power exerted by American businessmen in Canada. Americans control nearly half of our industrial wealth, but hold only 15 per cent of the directorships in our dominant corporations. The only two Americans who appear high on the list of the 100 busiest Canadian directors are L.J. Belnap, an electrical engineer who heads Consolidated Paper Corporation and is a director of 13 other companies, and Ray Powell, senior vice-president of Aluminium Limited, who is on 10 other boards. Both are Canadian citizens.

Automobile manufacturing, the Canadian industry most commonly associated with American influence, is almost completely controlled by U.S. parent companies, but nearly all its management is Canadian. Only two senior executives of Chrysler Corporation of Canada were born in the United States, and one of them has lived here since he was four. All the department heads and executives of General Motors of Canada are Canadians. Of the 14 members of Ford of Canada's administrative committee, only two are Americans. Of course, the extent to which these non-U.S. directors take their voting instructions from the United States varies with each firm, but usually the extent is considerable.

Although they make up more than one-third of the country's population, the representation of French Canadians among Canada's nationally influential corporation directors is limited to Alphonse Raymond, a Montreal food manufacturer, Wilfred Gagnon, president of Dow Brewery, Raymond Dupuis, head of his family's Montreal department store, the presidents of the two French-Canadian banks, half a dozen lawyers, and the little-known Joseph Simard.

This is partially explained by Quebec's educational system, which, until recently, did not stress either economics or science. But nearly all the Quebec universities now have commerce courses and the next generation of important Canadian company directors is expected to include a sharply increased contingent of French Canadians.

Probably Quebec's most influential businessman today is Joseph Simard, who runs a private duchy at Sorel, Que., where he owns a forest of industrial installations, strewn around the junction of the Richelieu and St. Lawrence Rivers. He is a director of 23 firms whose assets aggregate well over $1 billion. His companies sell church pews, warships (he built the RCN's icebreaker *Labrador*), TV cabinets, rocket launchers, garbage trucks, gasoline-station signs, railroad cars and hosiery worth more than $30 million a year. He also runs Canada's largest privately owned tanker fleet, a 104-ship towing and dredging flotilla, and a 52-acre naval gunshop, which is one of the world's largest private armament works.

One recent transaction revealed the scope of Simard's international interests. In 1953, he sent a tug to Seattle to bring home the 700-ton, four-masted schooner *Fantome*, which he acquired by paying her overdue docking charges. The *Fantome* had been abandoned in Seattle by A.E. Guinness, the Irish brewing millionaire, at the outbreak of the Second World War. She is one of the most luxurious vessels ever built, requiring a crew of 40. There are only eight passenger cabins. The ship has a built-in fresh-milk dispenser—a deck locker to accommodate a sea-going cow.

Simard bought the 30-year-old yacht because he wanted to put her two auxiliary engines into one of his tugboats. But a personal inspection persuaded him to wait for a customer. Last year, Aristotle Socrates Onassis, the Greek shipping czar, saw the ship and immediately bought it for many times Simard's investment, as a wedding present for Prince Rainier and Grace Kelly.

Simard is almost totally unknown outside his own circle of intimates. Whenever Montreal reporters renew their requests for interviews too vigorously, he goes fishing in Labrador.

In spite of the scarcity of French-Canadian names on the roster of Canada's busiest directors, this country's brightest financial constellation is still centred in Montreal, where most of the fortunes dating back to pioneer Canadian railroad, mining and industrial ventures originated. Toronto's Bay Street, however, is gradually threatening to eclipse Montreal's more sedate St. James Street.

The greatest concentrator of business power in Canada is Argus Corporation, a Toronto-based empire of ownership whose stock interests control companies employing more than 60,000, with annual gross sales of $1.3 billion. Argus consists of a stenographer-lined corridor in a downtown Toronto office building, where a staff of 15 looks after the company's only asset: $75 million worth of shares in six of Canada's most important corporations—Dominion Stores, Massey-Harris-Ferguson, Canadian Breweries, B.C. Forest Products, Dominion Tar and Chemical, and St. Lawrence Corporation.

By being the largest single shareholder in these firms (ranging from 13.1 per cent in Canadian Breweries to 22.4 per cent in St. Lawrence Corp.), Argus can place enough of its directors on their boards to control policy. The $75 million stock investment of Argus thus rules assets worth more than $777 million.

Four Argus executives—E.P. Taylor, Col. W.E. Phillips, M.W. McCutcheon and John A. McDougald—have seats behind more than 100 boardroom tables. Their individual totals of assets directed aggregate to $19,054 million—

enough to wipe out Canada's national debt. These men do not own Argus, but by holding 40 per cent of its 1,370,272 common shares, they can and do regulate its investment activities.

Taylor recently has been spending more and more of his time directing the development of the 4,000 acres of sandy ocean frontage he bought on New Providence, the tiny island capital of the Bahamas. He is building rows of ocean-side mansions and a luxurious new golf club. Taylor's main hobby and recreation is horse racing. His stables employ 100 men, have a financial turnover of $800,000 a year and in 1956 produced 75 winners for $235,000 in purses.

After he graduated as a mechanical engineer from McGill in 1922, Taylor organized Red Line Taxis Limited, one of the earliest and still one of the largest Ottawa taxi fleets. Using his father's Brading's Brewery as the first link, he eventually daisy-chained 23 Ontario, Quebec, Manitoba, Saskatchewan, Alberta, B.C. and U.S. beer companies into Canadian Breweries Limited, one of the world's biggest brewing organizations. With his partners and associates, Taylor has been widening the scope for his financial dexterity by super-mergers of food, lumber and chemical firms. His Argus-dominated control structure has become a sort of maypole, with corporate ribbons reaching into nearly every Canadian industry.

Although he is usually portrayed as the prototype of Canadian big businessmen, Taylor's name is seldom brought up when Canadian economists play their favorite parlor game of guessing who is Canada's richest man.

John David Eaton, who owns nearly all the stock in his family's retailing empire, is a leading candidate, but the company's private books permit little informed guessing. Probably the man most frequently mentioned is Samuel Bronfman, the head of the giant Distillers Corporation-Seagrams Limited. This Montreal company and its U.S. subsidiaries sell more than $2 million worth of liquor a day.

The Bronfman family owns Seagram stock worth nearly $100 million, through a private holding company called Seco Investments Limited. This portfolio alone brings in a dividend income of more than $4 million a year.

Bronfman is also a director of large petroleum companies and a bedding firm, but he does not sit on the boards of any Canadian banks or major industrial corporations. His job as head of the Seagram complex pays him what is probably Canada's highest salary. Because his companies do so much business in the United States, they have to submit detailed reports to the American Securities and Exchange Commission, which include executive salaries. The SEC lists Bronfman's 1956 pay cheque at $351,042, ranking close behind the salary of Henry Ford II, president of the Ford Motor Company, which is the world's third largest corporation.

Allan Bronfman, a Seagram vice-president, is thought to be Canada's second-highest-salaried executive, with 1956 wages of $200,521. The presidential salaries of major Canadian corporations range up from $40,000.

Garfield Weston at his Cannes home in the south of France, 1957.

The SEC statements show that J.R. White, the head of Imperial Oil, receives $81,666 and that Henry F. Wingate, president of International Nickel, gets $155,050.

Many companies grant their chief executives extra compensation by giving them options on treasury shares below market values. Most firms also have special executive pension plans. This can be important. Sir George Bury, for instance, who retired as a CPR vice-president in 1919, is now 91, but still enjoys his daily visit to the Vancouver Club. In the past 38 years he has collected well over $500,000 in pension cheques.

Section 108 of the Canadian Companies Act allows directors to make bylaws "as to their own compensation." But most boards pay themselves modest fees. R.A. Jodrey, the Canadian with the greatest number of directorships, receives an average annual fee of $250 for each of his 56 boardroom seats.

Jodrey is an aloof, 67-year-old apple grower and pulp-mill operator who lives in austere seclusion at Hantsport, a dent in the rocky shoreline of Nova Scotia's economically ailing west coast. A blocky Baptist with cart-horse affinity for hard work, he spends 100 hours a month sitting on the boards of corporations whose $3.5 billion worth of assets extend from Newfoundland into South America. "The most important thing for successful operation," he says, "is good management. It is when management gets poor that control brings about a shake-up."

Jodrey is not listed in any Who's Who. He belongs to few clubs and no societies. During most evenings he slouches on his living-room divan, reading company balance sheets, accompanied by a constant replaying of his Stephen Foster record collection. The son of a Gaspereau Valley cabinetmaker, Jodrey left school at 13 to become an apple-picker. He established the Minas Basin Pulp & Paper Company in 1927 and now owns more than 300,000 acres of Nova Scotia timberland and two large power plants. More and more directorships were offered him in recognition of his sound business advice.

Of all the Canadian businessmen who established their own companies, none expanded their holdings faster than H.R. MacMillan, the dominant personality of MacMillan & Bloedel Limited, a Vancouver lumber complex which sells more than $3 million worth of wood products a week.

MacMillan's first profit was $300 from an ice-cream stand he set up for visiting farmers while he was a student at the Ontario Agricultural College in Guelph. In 1915, he resigned as B.C. chief forester and four years later, with one stenographer, he started a timber export business. By 1935 he was the world's largest charterer of merchant shipping and making so much profit selling other companies' timber that most of the firms decided to set up their own export departments. MacMillan immediately began buying up sawmills. They now cut up more than 500 million board feet of lumber a year.

Unlike MacMillan, most of the businessmen who have reached this country's economic summit attained their positions in companies already operating when they began their careers. Many simply took over the desks of their fathers, uncles or fathers-in-law. Charles L. Gundy, the president of Wood Gundy and Company, a leading Toronto investment house, inherited most of the 20 directorships in the companies financed by his father, including Canada Cement, Massey-Harris-Ferguson and Dominion Steel and Coal Corporation.

Their heredity did not save some sons from dreary years spent learning the business. G. Blair Gordon, the president of Dominion Textile and a director of 19 other companies, worked as a fitter's helper in one of his father's mills, in spite of his preference for playing polo. He still has a scar on his brow from an inkwell hurled at him by a striker at Montmorency Falls, Que., in 1938 during a stormy labor dispute. John David Eaton spent 12 years selling men's underwear and being moved through other departments before he was named to head Canada's largest retailing chain.

No Canadian has capitalized on an inheritance more spectacularly than Garfield Weston. When he took over George Weston Limited in 1924, his father's small bakery was earning $25,000 a year. Weston, who had spent his leaves as a First World War sapper poking around English biscuit manufacturing plants, began buying out Canadian biscuit makers and other food firms. The 57 companies he has since absorbed into George Weston Ltd. showed a 1956 net profit of nearly $5 million.

Since 1934, Weston has lived mostly in England, where his chain of bakeries has become the largest consumer of flour. But recently he has been satisfying his expansion impulses back on this side of the Atlantic. His ownership of Loblaws, added to his purchase, two years ago, of a controlling interest in the National Tea Company of Chicago, the fourth-largest U.S. supermarket chain, moved the annual food sales of his companies into the rarefied billion-dollars-plus bracket.

Few men possess the restless drive even to try empire-building on Weston's scale. The first step frequently is the transition from ambitious neophyte to company director and it takes place most commonly in the Toronto or Montreal law firms specializing in corporation problems. The lawyer sets the legal limits for most important company decisions. He often casts the deciding director's vote.

The most sought-after lawyer-director in Canada is J.S.D. Tory of Toronto. A doctor of law from Harvard and one of the most talented corporation lawyers on the continent, Tory now sits on 33 boards. His diminishing spare time is taken up with trying to improve the strain in his Aberdeen Angus and Guernsey cattle, on a 500-acre farm near King City, Ont.

The next most important directors' spawning grounds after the legal profession are the banks and investment houses. Canada's nine chartered banks—run by 246 directors—have assets aggregating $14 billion.

Until the early Thirties, bank directors were frequently named to the boards of corporations because of their bank connections. Now, the reverse is becoming common. The 97 directors of four of Canada's largest banks hold 905 important company directorships.

Canada had 36 banks at the turn of the century. The mergers that have reduced their number to nine have made the Canadian banking system one of the world's most concentrated. The United States, with roughly 10 times the population, has 1,500 times the number of banking institutions.

The Royal Bank, with assets of $3.6 billion, is not only Canada's richest bank, but the sixth largest in the world. James Muir, its president, is so conscientious about shareholder relations that when he was told a new shareholder was blind, he had earnings reports transcribed into Braille.

Muir's climb to the Royal's presidency is fairly typical. He left school at 15 to clerk in a cash cage. After 37 years in a dozen jobs at branches and in head office he moved into the bank's top job. Indeed, only two Canadian bank presidents—J.S. Proctor, of the Imperial, and J. Edouard Labelle, of the Provincial—have university degrees. A college education has not in the past been essential to leadership in Canadian business. Many Canadian directors have honorary doctorates. Fewer than half ever attended university lectures.

A notable exception is A.E. (Dal) Grauer, the president of B.C. Power Corporation, and a director of 13 other companies. Grauer enrolled in the University of British Columbia at 15, was a Rhodes Scholar at Oxford and later got a PhD in economics and political science from the University of California. He joined B.C. Power in 1939 after two years as head of the social-science department at the University of Toronto. He became president seven years later. He's one of scarcely more than a half dozen Canadian heads who refuse the aid of speech writers.

Almost one-third of Canada's 100 most influential company directors are private-school graduates—half of them from Upper Canada College in Toronto. "The idea here," says the Reverend C.W. Sowby, the principal of Upper Canada, "is not just to be good at a thing, but to be excellent."

Upper Canada College students are taught the value of money by being strictly budgeted to an allowance of between 75 cents and $1.25 a week. Most students have a head start in their careers over the average youngster through family connections, but their success is not limited to business. Of the 1,500 Upper Canada graduates who served in the Second World War, 26 became generals or the equivalent.

In spite of the success of such comparatively youthful Upper Canada boys as Colonel Eric Phillips, chairman of both Argus Corporation and Massey-Harris-Ferguson, the older generation of self-taught businessmen continues to hold the major share of important seats in Canadian corporation board rooms.

This group's patriarch is 72-year-old Charles Dunning, a quiet, pipe-smoking farmer-politician, who disappeared from the headlines in 1939 when he resigned from Parliament after a heart attack. Although he now commutes less frequently between his large Côte-des-Neiges home and his combination office-and-boardroom in Montreal's Sun Life Building, he still commands respect at the board meetings of corporations whose assets total close to $11 billion—that's what it costs Ottawa to run the country for two and a half years.

Dunning left school at 11 to run errands for a lawyer in his native

Leicestershire, England. At 14, he ruptured his heart valves in a swimming race and doctors certified him a permanent invalid. He emigrated to Canada at 17 and settled on a quarter section near Beaverdale, Sask., 25 miles beyond the end of steel, where he survived his first winter on $17 worth of supplies. When he was elected local delegate to the Saskatchewan Grain Growers' Association annual meeting, he earned his board at the Regina Hotel by stoking the furnace.

Dunning was appointed an association director, became interested in politics and 10 years later was premier of Saskatchewan. He went to Ottawa as an MP in 1926 and in three years, at 44, became Canada's youngest minister of finance. When the King government was defeated in 1930, Dunning became a "business doctor," reviving various Canadian companies. Through his resultant contacts, he was named a director of Consolidated Paper Corp., the Bank of Montreal, CPR and Ogilvie Flour Mills.

Dunning's activities in helping some of these corporations to absorb smaller firms personify the new approach to business growth. For some companies it has become far too slow and cumbersome to expand through a systematic building up of sales. It is much faster to buy out competitors.

Since 1900, more than 2,600 large Canadian companies worth about $4 billion have disappeared through mergers. Dominion Textile, Consolidated Mining and Smelting, Steel Company of Canada, and Canada Cement are some of the most productive results of the many corporate marriages. B.C. Packers is the amalgamation of 55 companies; Canadian Canners gulped 53 private canneries before it was itself swallowed by the California Packing Corporation last November.

The effect of this continuous corporate clustering has been to concentrate nearly half of Canada's industrial output in about 200 corporations. The investors who own the stock of these dominant companies have the right to fire or re-elect directors annually at will. "The power of the shareholders," said the late Russell D. Bell, who was head of Greenshields and Company, "serves as a check on the proper performance of duties by the directors in office."

This theoretically formidable economic force of the shareholder is seldom exercised, because most Canadian investors seem to agree that most

Canadian directors are successfully safeguarding their interests. Then, too, shareholder power remains largely latent, because few Canadians take the time to attend annual meetings. They prefer to elect directors by mail on one-slate proxy forms sent out by the existing board.

A dramatic exception is W.R. Sweeny, a Toronto investor who buys one share in companies that he suspects could be better managed. His holding allows him to attend the annual meeting, where he badgers directors with embarrassing questions. Originally a taxi driver in Elizabeth, N.J., "One Share Sweeny," as he's known on Bay Street, has capitalized so effectively on his remarkable investment instinct, that he recently bought a large downtown office building. "I look at things and sometimes I don't like them," says Sweeny. "Before I'm through they're corrected."

Sir James Dunn's death last year removed the last Canadian millionaire with large and lavish habits that once characterized his class. Dunn not only had his favorite barber flown in from Montreal to his summer estate at St. Andrews, N.B., but once also imported a Montreal veterinarian to clip his wife's poodle.

The pomp that once flavored big business is best preserved in about a dozen exclusive clubs discreetly located in Canada's main cities. They are extensions of the English club tradition—a second home for their members, where their privacy is as sacred as their shaving brushes. Membership is never restricted by written rules. Admittance committees act as a fine-mesh screen against those who are not wanted.

The most valued memberships are in the Halifax Club, the St. James's, Mount Stephen and Mount Royal in Montreal; the York, Toronto, and National clubs in Toronto; the Garrison in Quebec City; the Manitoba in Winnipeg; the Ranchmen's in Calgary; and the Vancouver Club.

The St. James's Club, founded 100 years ago by a group of Montreal businessmen fed up with waiters eavesdropping on their noonday chatter, is the most revered institution. The only concession to the gaming instinct of its members is a little-used billiard room. Much more popular are the over-stuffed fauteuils in the club's library, which prop up a daily stream of gently rumbling after-dinner dozers.

Clubmanship being a curious business of exclusion, those on the outside who can't get in simply set up a grander club. That's how Montreal's Mount Stephen Club began on Drummond Street during the late 1920s. Its four-inch-thick front door is adorned with a knob and hinges plated in twenty-two-carat gold.

The very rich and social Mount Royal Club on Sherbrooke Street offers silver toothpick containers with each ashtray. The Mount Royal's greatest crisis occurred at a bridge tournament in 1931 when Sir Herbert Holt socked a dull partner on the jaw. The game continued without explanation or apology.

Holt built up the greatest corporate kingdom in Canadian economic history. He sat on the boards of 235 corporations and once boasted that he wasn't a director of any firm in which he didn't have a large personal investment.

No Canadian businessman today wields economic decision-making powers equal to Holt's, but a large share of Canada's productive assets remain under the effective command of a relatively small group of directors.

The *Maclean's* study of Canada's economic summit showed no evidence that these men form any kind of monolithic compact, manipulating the country's destiny to their own ends. They do form a fairly small group. But it's divided into platoons which compete with Olympic-game vigor.

"Regardless of where the control of Canadian business rests today," says H.J. Carmichael, a St. Catharines, Ont., industrialist who sits on the boards of 15 major corporations, "there has never been a time in the history of our country when business has been more competitive."

PETER C. NEWMAN, *who joined* Maclean's *in 1956, was editor of the magazine from 1971 to 1982. Since then, he has contributed a weekly column until June, 1999, besides writing 20 books, including his trilogy on* The Canadian Establishment. *He lives in Hopkins Landing, B.C.*

Part Three

Profiles in Fame

MACLEAN'S

OCTOBER 1 1951 CANADA'S NATIONAL MAGAZINE 15 CENTS

Inside:

THE ROYAL COUPLE IN COLOR
BY KARSH

Six Exclusive Articles

10 PAGES OF ROYAL PHOTOS

MACLEAN'S

JUNE 1 1952 CANADA'S NATIONAL MAGAZINE 15 CENTS

The Queen's Dresses are his Secret

The Strike that Terrified all Canada
A MACLEAN'S FLASHBACK

St. John's, Newfoundland:
Oldest Boomtown in North America

MACLEAN'S

MARCH 17 1956 CANADA'S NATIONAL MAGAZINE 15 CENTS

A FULL-COLOR ALBUM
OF

Hidden
Canadian
paintings

Secrets of life and death
By Dr. Hans Selye

NEW SURPRISES TV HAS IN STORE FOR YOU

MACLEAN'S

OCTOBER 13 1956 CANADA'S NATIONAL MAGAZINE 15 CENTS

Harvest completed

Sidney Smith,

Canada's

new spokesman

BY BLAIR FRASER

COVER BY PETER WHALLEY

Our malignant god: publicity—by Lionel Shapiro

HOW THOUSANDS OF HOUSEWIVES ARE GOING BACK TO WORK

MACLEAN'S

NOVEMBER 9 1957 CANADA'S NATIONAL MAGAZINE 15 CENTS

Why the West will win the Grey Cup

BY JOHN KERNS

COVER: At Frobisher Bay, by James Hill

The spinster who lectures on love and childbirth

ROBERT THOMAS ALLEN DOESN'T WANT THE FIVE-DAY WEEK

MACLEAN'S

NOVEMBER 23 1957 CANADA'S NATIONAL MAGAZINE 15 CENTS

Mental illness:

hidden foe

of

New Canadians

How Paul Anka crashed Tin Pan Alley at fifteen

DAVIE FULTON: THE SECOND MOST POWERFUL TORY

MACLEAN'S

JANUARY 4 1958 CANADA'S NATIONAL MAGAZINE 15 CENTS

COVER: JOHN LITTLE The Quebec City-to-Levis ferry

A NEW PLAN TO KEEP PENSIONS FROM SHRINKING

Tyrone Guthrie's own story of Stratford

"The Grey Cup is an over-rated circus"

MACLEAN'S

NOVEMBER 21 1959 CANADA'S NATIONAL MAGAZINE 15 CENTS

COVER BY WILLIAM WINTER   Teen-age dance

Ellen Fairclough Goes to Ottawa

by Eva-Lis Wuorio

AUGUST 1, 1950

ONE DAY IN JUNE, I went to Montreal to meet Ellen Fairclough, of Hamilton, a successful public accountant, mother of an 18-year-old son, and wife of Gordon Fairclough, who owns a printing firm. She was in Montreal attending an IODE conference, but there was a new road opening before her, and I wanted to see her take her first steps along it.

In another day she would take her seat in the House of Commons as the only woman member of parliament. She would be the sixth Canadian woman to put MP after her name. I wondered how a new member—especially a woman—goes about preparing for the position.

What really happens to people when they represent people? Does it make a person feel differently? About her home? Or her family? How, most particularly, does a busy woman pick up a new way of life, an important one at that, representing all of us.

I met Ellen Fairclough in a long bright room in the Ritz-Carlton Hotel. I knew she had held down four jobs well: a public accountant with her own firm; a member of the Hamilton Board of Control and deputy mayor; a housewife; a mother to her pianist-son Howard. Besides these pursuits, she'd found time to be active as a vice-president of the Ontario chapter of the IODE; the immediate past chairman of No. 4 district of the Zonta Club, a women's service organization; a secretary of the Dominion Council of the United Empire Loyalists' Association; and secretary-treasurer of the Canadian Wholesale Grocers' Association.

The woman who opened the door wore a full-flowing pastel silk house-coat. Her husband had had it made for her at Christmas, she said. She carried herself well, which added a dignity to the prettiness of her coloring; clear pink-and-white skin, upswept grey hair, sparkling brown eyes and a smile that is accustomed to come quickly and therefore has molded her expression. Slim, quick moving, quick talking, she was back at the desk by the window while still saying "how d'you do."

"I thought I was going to win right through," she said. "You can feel the swing of it, you know." (She has run successfully since 1945 for the Hamilton

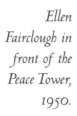

Ellen Fairclough in front of the Peace Tower, 1950.

City Council.) "The people were with me. Even with the Liberal papers, the worst thing they found to say about me was, 'The city of Hamilton needs you. Do not take a federal seat.'"

No, she didn't feel particularly excited or scared at going to Ottawa: "I've been at this sort of thing a long time now."

"Have you got any speeches planned yet?" I asked her.

"No. Cass Casselman, who's our party whip, told me—he's been an old family friend for a long time—that I might not even make a speech at all this session. He said just to sit and watch until I familiarized myself with all the proceedings. Of course, if anything particularly in my line comes up, I'll speak."

She had come to Montreal to attend the 50th annual meeting of the IODE. Her entrance into the convention lounges at the Mount Royal Hotel was a signal for many greetings. Obviously, she was well-known. Obviously, also, her long-time lodge sisters were not going to make more of a fuss about her because of her new status. And no less either. The IODE has been a close part of Ellen Fairclough's life since she left school.

Before the morning session was over we went out into the warm sunshine again. "It'll be my husband's birthday by the end of the week," she said. "I saw some sport shirts down the street."

In a men's shop near Dominion Square, she picked out a tan and a green-grey sport shirt and rather gay ties to match. "He likes to wear this sort of thing at home, now that the weather's warm," Mrs. Fairclough said. "He was my first beau. We met at a church society when I was about 16. I think we went together for about 10 years before we got married, so that he was almost part of the family long before the event. When I had to work late, he'd take my sister Mary to a movie or a dance."

She called the clerk and changed the ties to a slightly more conservative coloring and had the purchases mailed to her Hamilton office.

After lunch at the Mount Royal, Mrs. F.P. McCurdy, national president of the IODE, begged Mrs. Fairclough to make a quick trip to the convention hall, in spite of the fact that her Ottawa train was leaving soon, to be introduced to the other delegates. The ballroom was packed now as the members gathered to hear the new MP. With the ease of an old campaigner, Ellen

Fairclough organized the words of her impromptu speech like a regiment of soldiers and marched them out steadily, ending with ". . . with conscientious work and the help of your prayers I shall try to serve the women of this country to the best of my ability." Applause.

For the train she changed into a tan suit and hat. There was a private car tagged on to the Montreal-Ottawa train for the Governor-General and Lady Alexander, who were returning from inspecting Rimouski fire damage.

Mrs. Fairclough and I had seats in a chair car, and, as the verdant countryside slipped by, she talked about her son, Howard. "I think it's a very strange thing in our schools that sports get all the praise and the arts none," she said. "The school hero is the one who can throw the ball the farthest, not the one who plays a Beethoven sonata the best. Yet, quite possibly, it's those latter boys who'll be the famous alumni in years to come."

Howard Fairclough, a student at Westdale High, has won the Junior League Musical Scholarship for Ontario and is now studying the organ. "I think he got his musical gifts from my side of the family. All of us have always sung in church choirs and my sister plays the organ in the United Church."

At this point pretty Libby Lawrence, lady-in-waiting to Lady Alexander, came along with an invitation to us from their Excellencies to have tea in their car. For the first time I saw Ellen Fairclough somewhat nonplussed. "What'll I do now?" she demanded. "I'm allergic to tea!"

The private car is a pale-green light-rose room with chintz-covered chairs, a desk, magazine racks, and a tea table over which Lady Alexander presided. "I'll have water," said Mrs. Fairclough, MP.

"Anything in it?" Lord Alexander asked. "That seems awfully dispirited." Mrs. Fairclough said no.

"I left school when I was 16," she told their Excellencies, "but I couldn't get a job anywhere until I lied about my age and said I was 18. Now I don't know how old I am without counting on my fingers." She was born in Hamilton in 1905.

At the Ottawa station, their Excellencies waved a friendly hand of farewell. There was no one at the station to meet her. Mrs. Fairclough had made her own hotel reservation at the Chateau Laurier. There was no message of welcome or greeting for her at the desk. She went up to her room, saying, "Casselman, the party whip, told me not to make any appointments until I'd heard from him. I'll have to wait until he calls me."

Her room, her new Ottawa home, was on the second floor in the short end of the U of the hotel, looking out over the roofs of the main floor toward the tree tops of the Canal Park, but mainly showing only rows of windows of the wings. She did not intend searching for an apartment. "With the hours I must keep, without a housekeeper, it would be entirely too much bother," she explained. Then she added, "For a single member, I think it costs less here. And if I have any time I can catch up on my reading—historical novels and biography and whodunits on trains—and I can knit socks for Howard when I'm reading."

Over dinner in the Chateau Grill, the Finnish Minister to Canada, Urbo Toivola, came to give her the courtly bow of a diplomat and remark, "This then is the end of your private life, Madame Fairclough?"

Said Ellen, "Want to bet?"

That night, on the eve of her entry to the House of Commons, Arza Clair Casselman, K.C., MP for Grenville-Dundas, a Conservative whip since 1936, and the Hon. Earl Rowe, MP for Dufferin-Simcoe, Casselman's father-in-law and one of the top Conservatives, came to bid her welcome. They told her they'd found her a better seat than is usually afforded new members; instead of the back row she would have a desk in the second row, gallantly vacated for her by Frank Lennard, MP for Wentworth. Lennard would take a back seat. Also, by virtue of being a woman, she would get an office to herself in the crowded Parliament Buildings.

I had breakfast in the Chateau cafeteria with the Faircloughs the next morning, husband Gordon, a stocky quiet man, and son, Howard, a slim dark boy. Howard was excited, Gordon jovial but calm, Ellen quite normal in a dark dress with a jacket top, a perky hat. "I wouldn't be here today," Ellen Fairclough said, "if it wasn't for Gordon and Howard. They've helped me with all my campaigns. If they weren't interested and pleased about everything I do, I don't suppose I'd keep on doing these things."

"We knew mother would win," Howard said. "All my friends were working for her."

The signing-in ceremony, demanded of each new MP, was to be held at 11 a.m. I suggested they might prefer to be alone to discuss their family problems. "There aren't any," Ellen laughed. "I have a good housekeeper, and Gordon and Howard are quite accustomed to looking after themselves. Also, I'll be seeing them every weekend. Hamilton isn't so far."

Howard, the only excited Fairclough, twisted his fingers and said he wished there were a piano. There was, in a long barren ballroom, down the hall. Ellen sat in a straightbacked chair and listened to her son play through boogie woogie, the fast-fingered "Fire Dance," to singing sonatas of gentle melodies. And then, the chimes from the tower on Parliament Hill. "We must go," Ellen Fairclough said in her crisp way and got up while Howard was still playing.

Casselman telephoned. The signing-in would be at 2 p.m. After lunch, a couple of photographers turned up. In the buildings there were more of them. George Hees, of Toronto, who had just won another by-election for the Tories, his wife and daughter, joined George Drew and the Faircloughs.

In the oak-paneled Speaker's office, the two new MPs gave their oath and signed the illuminated book that had been signed by all the members of the House of Commons. Then the photographers came in again.

Casselman hurried the party to the green chamber. "It's nearly three. Come here, Ellen, and I'll show you what you must do."

In the empty House of Commons she walked between the leader of her party and her friend, Frank Lennard, toward the Speaker's dais. "Now," said Drew, "after I've introduced you, the Speaker will say, 'Let the honorable member take her seat,' and you'll go up this aisle, and all the way back and over to here."

"We must clear out, it's nearly 3 p.m.," Casselman said.

Half an hour later, with the House in session, I saw Ellen Fairclough enter again, holding lightly to the arms of George Drew and Frank Lennard. The Leader of the Opposition addressed the Speaker of the House. "Mr. Speaker, I have the honor to present to you Ellen Fairclough, member for the electoral district of Hamilton West, who has taken the oath and signed the roll and now claims the right to take her seat."

The spectators in the nearly full galleries leaned forward with curiosity, all but Gordon and Howard Fairclough in the members' gallery. They appeared frozen, but their eyes never left Ellen Fairclough. They watched her go even farther from the familiar things the three of them had known. With slight hesitation she sought and found her seat in the second row of Conservative benches. Gordon's wife, Howard's mother, was now in the Canadian House of Commons.

Several members of her own party slipped for a moment into the empty seat next to her, shook her hand in welcome. A Liberal Party wag, "Kissing George" Cruickshank, MP for Fraser Valley, crossed the green-carpeted aisle separating the Government from the Opposition and kissed her soundly on the cheek.

And then, after a decorous moment, Prime Minister Louis St. Laurent came across to shake the hand of his newest opponent. At that moment Ellen Fairclough looked up at the gallery opposite her. Though her smile broke out for her husband and her son she had to dab away a quick tear. A new life had begun.

On June 21, 1957, **ELLEN FAIRCLOUGH,** *then 52, became Canada's first female federal cabinet minister when John Diefenbaker named her Secretary of State. She later held two other portfolios before losing her seat in the 1963 election. She then returned to the business world as a senior executive with a trust company, chairman of Hamilton Hydro and, later, treasurer of the Zonta International women's group. A winner of numerous Canadian and international humanitarian awards, Fairclough still lives in Hamilton.*

EVA-LIS WUORIO *was assignments editor for* Maclean's *from October, 1947 to April, 1951 when the Finnish-born writer returned to Europe, where she wrote short stories, novels and children's books.*

Emily Carr, The Genius We Laughed At

by
J.K. Nesbitt

JANUARY 1, 1951

SHE WAS A STOCKY THICKSET woman, and when she walked the streets of Victoria's James Bay district, a rabble of dogs and cats at her heels, a monkey or a white rat on her shoulder and pushing a baby buggy full of groceries, the neighbors used to nudge each other and say: "There goes Emily Carr. She paints and she writes, and she's queer."

Almost until her death she remained unrecognized as one of Canada's great artists and writers. How were the housewives of James Bay to know that the *Times* of London would call this strange woman "a distinguished writer and a distinctive painter," that the *New York Times* would praise her "brisk and sensitive originality," that Dr. Max Stern, of Montreal's Dominion Gallery, would call her "the outstanding Canadian painter"?

Victoria looked on Emily Carr as an eccentric old maid, such a failure at writing and painting that she had to keep a boarding house and raise dogs for sale. In 1943, two years before her death, hardly anyone bought her canvases. Today, the paintings she valued at $35 and $50 sell for $250 and $350. One great swirling forest scene which she marked $125 is valued at $1,000.

About 400 of her paintings hang today in Canadian art galleries. Her work has been shown at London's Tate Gallery and in New York, Washington, San Francisco and Philadelphia. She destroyed 200 canvases because they were crowding her home. She often crumpled them and stuffed them in garbage cans. She burned some of her work because she didn't like it.

Sometimes she was so disgusted with a painting that she wouldn't sign it until years later. She never wanted to make money from her work. She once placed a price on a picture and when a buyer offered much more Emily snapped: "I've told you the price; you do not have to take it."

She made little from her paintings, but her books were more successful. The journals in which she scribbled blossomed into the award-winning *Klee Wyck*, sketches of her visits to the Indians; *The Book of Small*, impressions of her childhood and early-day Victoria; *The House of All Sorts*, the story of her boarders. Her autobiography, *Growing Pains*, was published after her death. Ten thousand copies of her books have been sold in Canada and more are being prepared from her journals.

She died at 73 after years of declining health with no awareness of the contribution she had made to Canadian art and letters.

She had tremendous drive, this odd woman. No one ever knew what was behind it. She often referred to a mysterious love that tortured and tormented her. Not long before her 1945 death, she said that she'd just had a letter from a man who had loved her 40 years before and who still loved her. Was this the secret of the frustration that lay inside her?

In her boarding house years, her lodgers were terrified of her sharp unruly tongue and stinging sarcasms. Many became her friends but they never could understand her—or her rages. Once a boarder insisted on hanging his socks to dry from his bedroom window. Miss Carr was not pleased. She was watering the garden with her monkey Wu on her shoulder. Just then the owner of the socks walked in the gate. "Those socks!" It was a shriek. "You take them away—or take yourself away from my house. I won't have, I won't have, I told you I won't have it, or you."

She shook her fist in the man's face and his glasses fell and shattered. Wu, chattering wildly, fled to the back garden. Then Emily turned the hose on the boarder and he fled, dripping. Next day he moved, muttering that Emily Carr was a mad woman and should be locked up instead of trying to paint and write.

Perhaps it was because Emily Carr was one of them that Victorians scoffed at her. They wanted her to be reserved and ladylike as became a daughter of one of the city's first families. She was born in Victoria on Dec. 13, 1871, of

English parents. Her father was a prosperous importer, a solid citizen of business and social standing. Her mother was gentle and delicate and Emily loved her dearly, for the mother understood this child who was so different from her other children, rebellious, dreamy, easily hurt, easily able to hurt. Emily grew up with four sisters and a brother.

Emily wrote that a snowstorm raged in Victoria when she was born and that it went into her being with the first flicker of life, never lulled in all the years, and that always she was fighting it. They called her Milly and she was a troublesome child. She tore her clothes climbing fences and trees. She talked to the cows and got dirty in the barn. She was saucy. There was much scolding from older sisters whom she humiliated in public. Milly created friction all her life. Her moods changed rapidly from nice to nasty.

She was called pretty as a young woman. The violets she wore at her throat accented the distant dreamy look that came to her eyes and turned them smoky purple in the midst of the most down-to-earth talk. Even in her later years she retained some of her early beauty. Her hands were delicate and at the same time strong. Her feet were small and graceful, surprising in a woman of squarish build. Her eyebrows, heavy and arched, gave her an Oriental look.

Her mother died when she was 12; her father two years later. With the money they left her, she went alone to San Francisco to study art. Later, in 1900 and again in 1910, she went to Europe and studied in London and Paris. She never mentioned her teachers, except Henry Gibbs in Paris.

On her first visit to England she suffered long periods of depression. She wrote that a suitor followed her to London and implored her to return to Canada to marry him. She refused. Her work, she said, was more important.

No one has been able to explain the "love" she mentions in her writings. She wrote that she found love more than half pain, that her love went where it wasn't wanted, that a great love was offered but she couldn't respond and so couldn't accept. But she was never specific. All her life she was terribly lonely. It wasn't company she wanted. She craved a kinship with another soul. She must have had such a kinship somewhere and once having tasted it, she could do with nothing less.

In her first English trip, she suffered a nervous breakdown and spent

18 months in a sanatorium, often praying she would die. She left England without goodbyes to friends. On her return to Canada she sold newspaper cartoons and taught art in Victoria. As an art teacher she was short with children, crushingly sarcastic if they copied instead of creating. Work, work, work—create, create, create, no matter what—that was her way. "Don't talk about it," she would say abruptly. "Chit-chat never accomplished anything."

On her second trip abroad, in 1910, she studied and learned a good deal. Back from Europe, she tried teaching in Vancouver. Vancouver's social set and the art crowd scoffed at her, because she wouldn't conform. She never conformed. Only recently a Victorian looked at a charcoal sketch she had done of her father before she was 14. "Now that's fine," he said. "If Emily Carr had stuck with that kind of painting instead of painting the junk she did, I'd admire her."

But Emily was never satisfied with mere photographic art. She wanted to paint what she felt, and she did. Her sweeping canvases of the woods, vast and changing as she saw them, make her known today. In the forest she saw movement all around her. Trees danced for Emily Carr and so she made them

Emily Carr with her pets in her Victoria garden.

dance in her paintings. Gangling treetops were ballet dancers bowing to Nature. To her nothing in Nature was ever still. Her forest paintings show the British Columbia woods lush and terrifying in their loneliness, tumbled, gigantic and chaotic.

Once she tried to start an art gallery in Victoria but she got no support. In 1913, she said she was through with painting. She would be a landlady. There was a rasping laugh in her throat when she said it, but she built a boarding house in Victoria. She bred English sheepdogs to bring in a few more dollars.

After her landlady days she lived by herself and she did a staggering number of canvases. In her final years she went to her sister Alice's nearby house where the two had separate apartments. Emily was so determined to remain independent that she placed a sign on the gate: "For Miss Alice Carr take the path to the right. For Miss Emily Carr take the gravel path to the left."

As the nature she loved was impatient, she too was impatient. When she wanted a picture frame she tore a picket from her garden fence and made one. She could make a lampshade from an oil can. She drove nails like a carpenter. She hauled pebbles from the beach for her studio yard. She buried her dead dogs herself, trundling them to the beach by wheelbarrow.

She called animals her creatures and she said they were more loyal than humans. Each night she recited "This little pig went to market" to her monkey Wu and she sang lullabies until Wu fell asleep in her arms.

Her sister Alice recalls Emily's animals. She says: "I'll never forget that awful winter when Milly was in hospital and I had to go to her house each day and look after a monkey, parrot, five dogs, chickens, canaries, chipmunks, squirrels and a white rat. Oooh—that white rat! Milly let the thing crawl around her neck and lick her throat. How could she?"

Orthodox Victoria never approved of this walking riddle of a woman whose spirit was often violent, whose words flowed hot and uncontrolled, who splashed paint until it glowed with life. Many said Emily was bitter because Victoria wouldn't accept her paintings. It was not that. She didn't like being rebuffed, but she had a sense of humor that made her laugh at those who said her paintings were queer and looked like children's blobs. "I paint what I see the only way I see it in the only way I know," she would snap. "I don't care what people think. I know lots of people hate my work. I can't help that. I'm trying to express something I feel, to satisfy myself."

Often she found relief in lonely Indian villages, sketching totem poles. She traveled by dugout canoe, smelly gasboat, horseback—a dog always with her. She made friends with the Indians. They called her "the laughing one." She understood them and they her. When they grunted she grunted back. Words weren't necessary. She was devoted to a drunken, heartbroken Indian woman named Sophie, who had lost all her many children. Sophie and Emily cried for hours together on the small graves. Emily painted Sophie's picture. It remained at the head of Emily's bed for the remainder of her life.

Her boarders walked on eggshells, but it was interesting too. Besides, Emily could cook. Curried sausage was her specialty. One of the boarders Emily didn't argue with was a young Englishman, Philip Amsden. She gave him her devotion and it was returned. There were 30 years between them but Amsden says that in her company he was never aware of it. Emily mothered him. His presence comforted her. Yet when he became engaged and asked if he could bring his fiancée to meet her, she snapped: "Certainly not! I don't care to meet her."

After a turbulent day washing dishes, making beds, stoking the furnace, fixing leaky pipes, nursing sick dogs and cooking stews, Emily climbed the narrow stairs to her attic studio and painted, or went to bed to scribble in her journals. She said if it wasn't for her daubings all the pieces that made her would fly apart and she could never put them together again.

Restless as the woods and clouds that she painted, Emily Carr went through her landlady days hating them. She was convinced she was through as an artist. She painted only to find refuge from the lumps of emptiness that knotted her life.

And she scribbled. She never told anyone she wanted to write a book. She said she scribbled to amuse herself. Once she visited a friend, carrying a large canvas bag. The friend imagined it contained knitting. Years later Emily confessed that her scribblings were in the bag but her courage failed when it came to reading them. Her spelling was atrocious and she had no idea of punctuation. But in 1941 she won the Governor General's Award with her first book, *Klee Wyck*.

Her writing was successful with the public before her painting. Recognition first came for her canvases in 1927. Suddenly, to her astonishment, the Group of Seven—noted eastern Canadian artists—discovered her. They were amazed at the magnitude of her work, its originality. They encouraged her. The group's interest gave her new life. She was not old after all—just 56.

The Group of Seven invited her to Toronto and she made three short trips there, excited as a college girl. She returned to Victoria to start the paintings that brought her acclaim in death. With her new confidence she said Canadian painters must no longer pay attention to Old World art. "We are through with the old sentimental ditties; we are through with the old sentimental canvases. It is no sin if you do not like creative art, but you do not have to ridicule it. Just ignore it. It's better to be a street sweeper, a charwoman or a boarding house keeper than to starve one's soul."

As she saw her books begin to sell and her paintings gain in notice, Emily willed the money from her work to set up scholarships to encourage B.C. art. Her estate was probated at $24,000 but today it is worth much more. She was plagued most of her life by poor health. Heart disease crippled her in later years but she was never angered by this. When she felt unwell she hummed a ditty: "I'm not very long for this world, my white wings will soon be unfurled. Old Peter will say, hoo-rip and hoo-ray, for Millie is coming today."

Growing weaker with the years, she had increasing surges of creation. She stole away from her doctor and her sister into the woods to paint and so exhausted herself she had to take to bed. In 1941, nearing 70, she lived by herself in the forest and did 15 giant canvases in a week. The movement she saw in nature was more stupendous than ever, and stupendously she portrayed it. In 1942 she did her last canvas, "The Clearing," which is the frontispiece of *Growing Pains*.

She bought an old trailer in those last years. A taxi hauled her to the woods and left her with her monkey and chipmunks, a white rat, a dog, and a copy of Walt Whitman's poems. She painted all day, wrote into the dawn. She cooked sparse meals on a camp fire and slept little. She knew there was not much time.

Not long before her death she was staying with her friend Ira Dilworth and his mother in Vancouver. One morning she announced: "I must go home today and go into the forest again. The forest still has something to say to me, and I must be there to hear."

Her doctor warned her not to go and her sister and friends added their arguments too. But Emily went back to the forest to put on canvas those startling, vivid sweeps of swirling movement. Defiantly, she said: "I don't want to trickle out. I want to pour until the pail is empty—the last going out in a gush, not in drops."

Interest in **EMILY CARR** *and her work has grown steadily, in Canada and around the world. In the late Fifties, her paintings could still be bought at the Hudson's Bay store in Victoria for $25 to $50; in the early Seventies, works could be found for under $1,000, but they now routinely sell in the tens of thousands of dollars. One painting, "In a Circle" (oil on canvas of a tree), sold in Toronto for $270,000 in 1987.*

JAMES NESBITT *was a longtime reporter and columnist for the* Victoria Times *and* Victoria Times-Colonist. *He died of a heart attack at age 74 in Victoria in 1982.*

Meet Mike Pearson

by
Blair Fraser

APRIL 15, 1951

SIX YEARS AGO, LESTER BOWLES PEARSON, O.B.E., M.A., LL.D., was promoted from Envoy Extraordinary and Minister-Plenipotentiary to be Canadian Ambassador to the United States. He was one of the first career diplomats to head an important mission. J. Hugh Campbell, CPR public relations chief who was then on loan to the government in Washington, thought this was an occasion for a Grade A press conference with all the trimmings.

Half an hour before the appointed time the photographers arrived and took charge. Anyone who happened along was conscripted to move chairs, set up lights, carry cameras. Finally everything was ready. The crew chief said, "Bring on your ambassador. Where is he?" Campbell pointed to a stocky boyish fellow in a rumpled suit who was lugging in a coil of cable for the Klieg lights. "That's him," he said. Mike Pearson grinned, dusted off his hands, sat down at the big desk, and the press conference began.

Three years in the Cabinet as Secretary of State for External Affairs haven't changed him in this respect. They've aged him a bit and tired him a good deal—when Parliament is in session, Pearson's working day averages 15 hours instead of the 11 or 12 he used to put in. They have also made him famous. Two newspaper polls last Christmas named him Canada's Man of the Year, and he's now rated the likeliest Liberal to succeed Prime Minister St. Laurent. His work last December on the three-man cease-fire commission of the United Nations, trying to find a peaceful settlement in Korea, brought him publicity and floods of mail from all over the world. Pearson continues to behave like the most ordinary of average citizens.

One Sunday last month, a reporter and a photographer called at the Pearson home in Ottawa to take some living room shots. Unluckily they came exactly on time. Had they arrived half an hour early they'd have got a much better picture—the Secretary of State for External Affairs was out shoveling the snow off his roof.

In San Francisco, at the United Nations founding conference in 1945, a women's-page reporter said to him, "Oh, Mr. Pearson, what is it you've got that other diplomats haven't got?" Pearson said, "I think I may be the only diplomat here who has ever been paid money for playing baseball."

Those are typical Mike Pearson stories, and there are hundreds of them—mostly true, but adding up to a misleading impression. They imply that all you need to be an ace diplomat is a big smile, a bow tie and a talent for games. Pearson has all these things, but there's more to him than that. "Mike is a very complicated character," said a close associate. "The first thing you find out, working with him, is that he's not the simple barefoot boy that people think him." He has, for example, the good diplomat's gift for appraising situations. In the year that followed Munich, most of his departmental superiors accepted the Chamberlain Government's view that there would be no war with Nazi Germany. Pearson didn't believe it. He was then secretary of Canada House in London, and he kept writing long personal letters to Ottawa arguing that war was imminent.

In the summer of 1939 he came back to Canada for three months' home leave. He spent July with his family at a summer cottage near Winnipeg, but as the days went on he felt increasingly restless. Then he saw in the newspapers that Hitler had "raised the question of Poland."

"This is it," Pearson said to his wife. "This means war."

He took the next train back to Ottawa, where he found everything calm and peaceful—nobody at all excited. Prime Minister King heard he was in town and asked him out to tea at Kingsmere, where King spent an hour or two explaining why Pearson was all wrong—there wasn't going to be any war. Chamberlain was certain of that.

Pearson decided he'd better get back to London. Canada House was short-handed and he could imagine what would happen there when war did break out. He went to Dr. O.D. Skelton, Under-Secretary for External Affairs, and asked for an immediate return to duty. "You've still got two months' leave coming to you," Skelton said, "but if you insist on going back that's up to you."

Pearson said, "I not only want to go back, I want to fly. If I go by ship I'm afraid I'll be too late." Flying to England is commonplace today, but in 1939 it was sensational—no Canadian government servant had ever flown the ocean in the line of duty. However, Skelton agreed. Pearson phoned New York and persuaded a friend at Pan American Airways to drop one steward to get him aboard a fully loaded plane that night. Then he got another friend to fly him to Montreal to catch the connecting plane for New York. Flying over, Pearson noticed with interest that most of his fellow passengers were German and Polish reserve officers, called home. He got to London just five days before Hitler invaded Poland.

Another of Pearson's unboyish qualities is an enormous capacity for work. Normally he gets up about 8 a.m. and is on his way to the office by 8:30 a.m. Occasionally he walks the mile or so from his house in Sandy Hill to the East Block; more often he drives his own car, then has a messenger take it home later in the morning. In either case he is usually the first to arrive. He finishes between 11 p.m. and midnight. If the House is in session he spends most evenings in the office. If not, he goes home to dinner about 7 p.m. with a briefcase full of dispatches.

Pearson's days haven't much pattern but they all begin the same way. First he reads the morning papers—*Ottawa Citizen* and Toronto *Globe and Mail.* (He breakfasts with the *Montreal Gazette.*) Pearson goes through a newspaper very fast but he doesn't miss much; in all his years of weekly press conferences I don't remember anybody referring to a press report Pearson hadn't read. He covers front page, editorial page, sports pages in that order, then scans the inside. After the newspapers, the morning telegrams. One of his associates showed me a typical day's batch—18 documents running to 42 legal-size pages.

If he has time Pearson then deals with his mail. He has a fair flow of official correspondence but he also gets a good many letters from private citizens. All letters marked "Personal" come to his desk, and any others his staff thinks might interest him. Some are obviously from cranks and crackpots, but many are from ordinary folk who are worried about the international situation. Pearson takes these seriously. He has strong views about the public's right to be informed about foreign policy (that's why he makes so many speeches) and he answers as many private letters as he can. Often he will dictate a reply several pages long. He dictates fast and smoothly, shifting from one topic to another without pause or effort, but he seldom gets through the morning's accumulation before it's time for his first appointment. This is usually a brief conference with his special assistant, Douglas Le Pan, or with Under-Secretary Arnold Heeney, or both. Anyone in charge of a division where things are happening is likely to be called in too.

At staff conferences Pearson is a good listener and a rapid reader of

External Affairs Minister Lester Pearson in his Parliament Hill office.

complicated memoranda. One External Affairs man said: "Mike used to scare the daylights out of me, he'd sign things so quickly. I'd bring in something that seemed to call for very careful thought and Mike would approve it in about 45 seconds. Then I noticed that this only happens in nine cases out of ten. The tenth case, the one he holds up, is the only one in the whole batch that might have got us into trouble."

Occasionally he might spend most of the day in External Affairs conferences; as a rule he can't. Cabinet and its various committees take a good deal of his time. Most of the 26 ambassadors, ministers and Commonwealth high commissioners in Ottawa have frequent occasion to see him. Almost anyone home from a Canadian mission abroad reports to Pearson in person. Reporters also pester him a good deal. It's the price of his unique popularity with the press that we all feel entitled to ring him up at any hour of day or night.

Pearson's relations with the Press Gallery are unusual. It's not just because most of us call him Mike—half a dozen other cabinet ministers are on first-name terms with any reporters who know them at all. His weekly press conferences are invariably well attended but they seldom produce much news. Pearson gives away no state secrets. One of the few things that makes him really angry is a "leak" of information. What he will do, though, is tell you his own opinion with extraordinary frankness. Quite often he puts his official life in reporters' hands with a clarifying, but grossly indiscreet, interpretation of the known facts. So far, he says, nobody has let him down.

Maybe that's one reason we all like him—he trusts us. But a more important reason is simply his astonishing gift for making friends. You meet Mike Pearson two or three times and you begin to think of him as an old pal. Apparently he has some of this effect even on the enemy. At a recent UN Assembly meeting, Soviet Foreign Commissar Andrei Vishinsky said, "I always listen with great attention to the Canadian delegate (Pearson) because he often says what others think but are afraid to say."

Certainly his greatest single qualification for diplomacy is this knack for getting on with other people. Pearson says he inherited it from his parents—his father, a saintly and devout Methodist minister who never outgrew his skill and delight in games; his mother, now 84 and nearly blind but still, her son says, "getting more out of life than anybody I know."

Whatever he inherited, he undoubtedly owes a lot to his upbringing as a minister's son in half a dozen Ontario towns. Pearson's official biography says he was born in Toronto, which is not technically correct—his birthplace is Newtonbrook, five miles outside the city limits. He was born on April 23, 1897, second son of the Rev. Edwin Pearson. From then until 1913, when young Lester entered the University of Toronto, the Pearsons moved five or six times to parsonages in North Toronto, Aurora, Chatham, Peterborough, Hamilton. For most youngsters the experience of moving to a new school is unnerving; Lester Pearson enjoyed it. "My younger brother used to hate the idea of leaving his old friends," he said recently. "I always thought of making new friends."

He was well endowed for it, a good student who was also a good athlete. Pearson can't remember learning to play hockey or to throw a ball; his earliest recollections are of doing both in the back yard with his father and older brother. He first played football in Hamilton's "Ninety-Pound League." He had won his letter at Toronto University by the middle of his sophomore year, when he left college to enlist.

Pearson wrote his second-year examinations in an army camp in the spring of 1915. Overseas service (first in Salonika, then as a Royal Flying Corps pilot until he crashed and was invalided home) gave him credit for another college year. He was able to graduate with a B.A. in the spring of 1920 and went to Chicago to work for a meat-packing firm in which an uncle held a high position. Two years there (starting as a laborer in the stockyards, working up to an office job in the fertilizer division) convinced him of two things: he didn't want to stay in business; he did want a real college education. He came back to Toronto, got a Massey Foundation scholarship and went to Oxford.

Arnold Heeney, now Pearson's right-hand man as Under-Secretary for External Affairs, went to the same Oxford college the year after Pearson came down. He still remembers being asked "How's Mike Pearson?" and the look of incredulous contempt when he admitted he'd never heard the name before. Pearson had been president of the amalgamated athletic clubs of St. John's College, star of Oxford's champion hockey team; in all respects a famous man. Anybody who didn't know Mike Pearson was obviously not a Canadian at all.

Meanwhile, Pearson had come back to the University of Toronto as a lecturer in history under the great George M. Wrong (whose son Hume has been Pearson's colleague in External Affairs for 23 years). He's remembered as a surprisingly good teacher who looked and acted like an undergraduate—lived at his old fraternity house, went to student parties, gave no sign of having either a care or a serious thought. His fellow lecturers, who were also young bachelors, noticed with some indignation that Pearson had the job of assigning senior history students to their respective seminars, and that all the prettiest girls happened to be assigned to Mr. Pearson. Within two years he was married to one of them—Maryon Elspeth Moody of Winnipeg.

In the summer of 1928, the Pearsons went to Ottawa to work in the Archives. Mike was preparing a book on the United Empire Loyalists (he still has his notes, hopes to finish it some day). He had lately been promoted to assistant professor and he was also coaching both football and hockey, so that altogether he had a pretty good income for a young history teacher. Nevertheless he decided before the summer was out to write the examinations for External Affairs. He came out at the top of the list and entered the department as a first secretary at $3,600 a year.

It was soon evident that Pearson had found his vocation. He came in under a Mackenzie King government; he got on equally well under R.B. Bennett. By 1934 he had attended four international conferences, two as Canada's representative, in addition to doing an important job at the Ottawa Conference of 1932. For his work as secretary of the Stevens Commission on Price Spreads in 1934-1935, Bennett got him an OBE and a special bonus of $1,000 (duly voted in External Affairs estimates).

The Stevens Commission job showed his skill in more ways than one. When the final report was being drafted, and circulated chapter by chapter among commission members, each secret installment turned up next day on the front page of the *Toronto Star*. Bennett was furious. Pearson, whose friends in the Press Gallery were already numerous, was worried lest he be suspected of what really was a grave breach of secrecy. One day a friend of his noticed a messenger leaving a brown envelope in the pocket of the *Star* man's overcoat. The reporter phoned Pearson: "I think I've located your leak." But they still didn't know who had sent it.

When the next chapter was completed the same thing happened, but this time Pearson's friend took the envelope out of the overcoat pocket and hid it under his blotter. Then Pearson telephoned every member of the commission; there had been an error in transcription, he said, and all copies were recalled for correction. Within an hour all but one were on Pearson's desk. He telephoned the delinquent: "Would you mind sending it along, sir? The Prime Minister is particularly anxious to have them all in today."

"I'm looking for it," the member replied. "Can't seem to lay hands on it. I think I may have sent it home by mistake."

"I'll have an RCMP constable call for it there, sir," said Pearson.

"No, no, don't do that. Leave it to me—I'll find it all right."

Another hour went by; then the conspirators slipped the envelope back into the *Star* man's pocket. Within 10 minutes the missing copy arrived in Pearson's office. He told the whole story to the Prime Minister. Bennett never forgave the offender, but his opinion of Mike Pearson went higher.

That summer Pearson was posted to Canada House, London, and his career from then on is well known. Back to Ottawa in 1941 as assistant under-secretary; to Washington in 1942 as minister-counselor, then minister, finally ambassador; Ottawa again in 1946 as permanent head of the Department of External Affairs. Then, in 1948, the great decision to enter the cabinet, and the hazards of party politics.

Pearson felt he had no choice. "A civil servant can only go so far in determining policy," he told a friend at the time. "When the essential decisions are made you're not even in the room." Pearson thought the next two or three years would be crucial; Louis St. Laurent, whom he trusted implicitly, was leaving External Affairs to become Prime Minister and no one knew who would succeed him if Pearson turned down the External Affairs portfolio. Pearson took it.

He was badly scared at the prospect of a by-election campaign, but to his astonishment he found he rather enjoyed it. It was another field for his aptitude in making friends. Also he had his usual good luck. Once he was on a campaign trip in Blind River, Ont. He found the populace greatly agitated because they couldn't get Hydro service; it was a provincial matter, of course, but Pearson agreed to meet a delegation at lunch and talk about it.

That morning he got a telephone call from Robert Saunders, chairman of the Ontario Hydro Electric Commission, who was anxious to talk to him about diversions of water at Niagara.

"I'm up at Blind River," Pearson told him.

"I'll fly up there to talk to you," Saunders said.

"Fine," said Pearson.

As the local delegation filed in, their MP was able to say, "You wanted to talk about Hydro, and here I've got the chairman of the Hydro Commission to lunch with us."

He likes being an MP, too, likes hearing people's problems and trying to straighten them out. He hasn't much time for it though; it's nearly a year since he has visited his riding. The fact is, he hasn't much time for anything these days, except work. This means a great distortion of his character and natural inclinations. Pearson is a-family man, for one thing. He used to like nothing better than playing with his two children when they were small. In the last 10 years, he's had little chance even to talk to them—for long stretches he was in England or in Washington while his son (now 23) and daughter (now 21) were in boarding schools in Canada.

Also Pearson is fond of a good time. He's never been a playboy in the ordinary sense—even after 23 years of diplomatic cocktail parties he can't tell the difference between rye and Scotch whisky, and he hates staying up late at night. But he does like going to shows and going to ball games.

Pearson was never offered Happy Chandler's job as U.S. Baseball Commissioner, in spite of sports-page rumor stories to that effect. If he had been, he would not, of course, have taken it, but he admits he would have been tempted. "Imagine, $65,000 a year for going to ball games! Florida every year for spring training! What a life!" Pearson did, however, make some money from his favorite sport—for a short time he was an infielder for a semi-pro team in Guelph, Ont.

Tennis is the only game he still plays (except for a spot of golf occasionally) and he likes that. Pearson at 54 is still in pretty good shape, and he has learned to use his head instead of dashing all over the court. He used to get a lot of pleasure out of music too. As a child he took piano lessons for about a year and he still surprises people once in a while by playing.

Finally, he has a keen appreciation of pure unadulterated loafing. One good way to spend Sunday, in Pearson's opinion, is not to get dressed at all—lie around all day in dressing gown and slippers, listening to the radio and falling asleep in a chair.

These are unexpected qualities in a man whose distinction in a very hard-working department is sheer industry. His aides admit they can't keep up with him. Pearson gets tired, but he doesn't stop. Stamina is the first thing his staff mentions. The second is good temper. "No matter what the flap may be," one of his subordinates said, "we always know the minister hasn't blown up, and won't blow up."

Both these virtues are made possible by Pearson's ability to relax at a moment's notice. He can fall asleep in a chair for 20 minutes and wake up fresh enough for another long siege of work. He never worries about decisions, past or future; he can always go to sleep at night. (Except on trains, oddly enough.) To a rare degree he has what psychologists call "security"—self-confidence without vanity.

It's hard to get Pearson's staff to admit he has any faults at all. If pressed, they'll concede a few: He isn't a good administrator. Pearson's interest is in policy, not organization. When he was under-secretary work tended to clog up among the few he knew and trusted most; others might be chafing for something to do. Also, in spite of his own talent for human relations, he isn't particularly good at putting the right men to work together.

He dislikes being wrong. If other people make mistakes Pearson doesn't fuss about it, though he always wants to know exactly whose mistake it was. But he does quite a bit of wriggling before he will admit that he made a mistake himself.

Also a doubtful point is his ability as a speaker. With a small intimate audience Pearson is superb—nobody in Canada has a quicker wit, a more engaging manner, a greater ease or fluency in delivery. In a big hall with a big audience he is less effective; his voice is light and rather high-pitched and the effort of getting it across to the back row impairs his easy informal style.

Finally, political confrères complain that he has little interest in or knowledge of domestic problems—no great lack in a minister of external affairs, but fatal in a prime minister. Colleagues keep urging him to take some other portfolio for a while, learn more about what makes Canada tick (and learn how it feels to have to choose among a set of unpopular alternatives). So far Pearson has ignored this advice.

This is a proof of his sincerity when he says, as he does to friends, that he has no wish to be prime minister. Men close to Pearson believe he really has no ambition beyond his present job. But they know, and Pearson must know, that he might have no real choice. He could serve quite happily under some prime ministers (notably Doug Abbott, the other leading contender for the succession). But Abbott doesn't want the job either; he'd rather get out of politics altogether. There are other possible successors to St. Laurent under whom Pearson wouldn't want to work. He might again, as he did in 1948, have to go into a new field or risk having his life work frustrated.

Under those circumstances Pearson would probably run for the leadership, and he'd have an excellent chance of getting it.

LESTER PEARSON *continued as External Affairs Minister until 1957, the year he won the Nobel Peace Prize for his efforts in defusing the Suez Crisis. The Liberals lost the June, 1957, general election and in January, 1958, Pearson won the party leadership to replace St. Laurent, who had retired. Later that year, John Diefenbaker's historic landslide decimated the Liberals, but Pearson rebuilt the party and in 1963 led it to a minority government. He won another minority in 1965. Pearson retired in 1968 and died in 1972 of cancer at age 75.*

BLAIR FRASER, *who drowned in an Ontario canoeing accident at 59 in May, 1968, was Ottawa editor at Maclean's from 1943 to 1960, and then again in the later 1960s. He edited the magazine from 1960 to 1962.*

The First Fuller Brush Man

by
Ian Sclanders

November 15, 1951

FORTY-SIX YEARS AGO, a rawboned youth from a Nova Scotia farm who was seeking his fortune in Boston wrecked a streetcar, forgot to currycomb a rich widow's horse, and left an important parcel at the wrong address. After these misadventures had cost him his first three jobs, he decided to be his own boss so nobody else could fire him. He installed a $15 machine in his married sister's basement and became a manufacturer. This was the beginning of a success story, for his name was Alfred Carl Fuller. His product was brushes.

Today, at 66, Fuller sits at the top of the brush heap, benignly supervising the operations of his international organization. His ledgers, when he glances at them, reveal an exceedingly satisfactory annual turnover of $38 million worth of brushes, brooms, mops (wet and dry) and other prosaic household items. And his best-known contribution to the North American scene, the Fuller Brush Man, is solidly established as the prototype of the brash and indomitable door-to-door salesman. The 6,600 Fuller Brush Men in the United States and the 1,200 in Canada ring six doorbells a second, eight hours a day, and if you live in an average community one of them will call at your home at least twice in the next 12 months.

With tenacious courage and smiles that are invincible to corns, bunions, fallen arches and insults, they lug their 21-pound sample cases through every city, town, village and hamlet between the Atlantic and the

Pacific, the Mexican border and the Arctic circle. They approach imposing mansions and unpainted shacks with the same friendly persistence and the same have-a-free-brush technique. Many carry dog biscuits as a free gift offer for hostile mastiffs. They have been known to help housewives plant flowers, paint walls, bathe babies. They have extinguished fires and assisted the stork, and one of them saved an infant's life by whacking it on the bottom until it disgorged the coin that was strangling it. Another chased a fox from a chicken coop.

In Pennsylvania, a Fuller Brush Man sold mops to two traffic cops who stopped him for speeding. In Texas, one was arrested for violating a bylaw. At the courthouse he paid a fine of $2.50, pointed out that the floors were dirty, and convinced authorities that they should invest $15 in brooms, mops and scrubbing brushes. But the gold medal for persuasiveness is claimed by the Fuller Brush Man who popped up at Hyde Park, N.Y., in the late 1930s and got a $13 order from President Franklin D. Roosevelt.

Fuller, who started it all, muffed an opportunity to duplicate the accomplishment of selling brushes to the chief executive of the United States. He had to interview President Harry Truman on behalf of the Connecticut Manufacturers' Association. As he emerged from the White House reporters button-holed him to ask whether he had sold Truman any brushes. "No, darn it," he smiled. "I forgot my sample case."

Fuller, referred to as "Dad" by a total of 16,000 people who produce and market his wares, has few of the attributes you would expect to find in the creator of the Fuller Brush Man. Most of us think of a supersalesman as a gay, devil-may-care, rock-ribbed extrovert who laughs, drinks and smokes too much, wears flashy clothes, splurges when he has money, and has an endless store of jokes, mostly on the smutty side.

In contrast with this image "Dad" Fuller is quiet, solemn, dignified, mild-mannered. He chuckles, but is never jackknifed by uncontrollable laughter. He looks guilty, like a youngster caught doing something he shouldn't do, if he slowly sips a single glass of beer or one small Scotch drowned in water. He doesn't smoke, even his sport clothes are conservative in color and cut, and when he hears a joke it goes in one ear and out the other. There are hundreds of gags about his salesmen but Fuller pays scant attention to them. Perhaps one of the reasons is because of his preoccupation with religion and metaphysics—for a quarter of a century he has been a Christian Scientist and most of his reading is Christian Science literature. Another reason is that the jokes strike him as not being true to life. There is one, for instance, about a boy who answered a Fuller Brush Man's knock. "Mom's out," he said, "and Pop can't see you because he has a sore back." The Fuller Brush Man: "Tell your father I don't want to wrestle him. I just want to sell him a new mop."

Fuller's reaction to this is that the salesman might have tried to sell the lad's old man a shaving brush, but that if he wanted to sell a mop he would have waited until Mom was home, mops being bought by housewives, not their husbands. In short, Fuller regards the sale of brushes as a serious matter. He admits that the gags have had a certain publicity value and have tended to diminish consumer resistance to the door-to-door huckster.

Six foot one and broad-shouldered, Fuller weighs 215 pounds. His nose and ears are generously proportioned, he has a close-cropped grey mustache, and his brown eyes are sharp but kindly under bushy black brows. His bald head and his face—definitely a pleasant face—are bronzed by the sun, for he is a chronic golfer who dislikes hats. He speaks hesitantly, in a low voice, and when his breezy and articulate wife, Primrose, is with him it is she who keeps the conversation flowing. It is also "Prim" who dispenses the liquid refreshments when the Fullers have guests.

Fuller is an ardent champion of the simple way of life. It is characteristic of him that although the company's two airplanes are always at his disposal, and he has a Cadillac, a Packard and a Buick, his favorite vehicle is a bicycle. The Fullers have a 14-room residence at Hartford, Conn., where Dad has his head office and his principal factory, but from spring to fall they stay at the Nova Scotia coastal town of Yarmouth with Prim's mother, Mrs. Charles Pelton, who has a big wooden house next to the Central United Church Tabernacle and across the street from the Yarmouth Public Library.

Dad is rated as a multimillionaire but he mows Mrs. Pelton's lawn himself. He is pleased when his wife or his mother-in-law (who is a judge's widow) sends him to the butcher shop for a couple of pounds of lamb chops or to the drugstore for a tube of toothpaste because this is an excuse for hopping on his trusty bike and wheeling through the crooked streets. Sometimes he likes to revisit the old farmhouse where he was born, at tiny Welsford, 150 miles from Yarmouth, in Nova Scotia's apple-growing Annapolis Valley. He sleeps there in the same room in which he slept as a boy, on the same lumpy mattress, because he is a sentimentalist.

It was on the family farm that the world's most famous huckster laid the foundation for his success—although he didn't realize it then. There are Maritimers who can put haywire to more uses than you can count, from fixing wagons to catching fish, and Fuller's brother Dwight was one of them. If he needed a gun cleaner Dwight would twist strips of rag between two strands of haywire, and if he wanted a brush he would substitute hog bristles for the rag. From Dwight, Alfred learned the rudiments of brushmaking.

By watching itinerant peddlers display their merchandise to his mother,

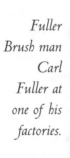

Fuller Brush man Carl Fuller at one of his factories.

and trying to fathom why some were quickly dismissed while others not only sold goods but were treated to tea and doughnuts, he learned the ABC of selling. His rural upbringing also gave him strong muscles, a deep and abiding faith in God, and the old-fashioned virtues of thrift, industry and honesty.

Last June, Hartford's Trinity College awarded an honorary master of arts degree to "Dad" Fuller, but his formal education was all gained in the one-room school at Welsford and ended in the seventh grade. His schoolmates say he had a tendency to gaze at the window rather than at the blackboard, and that he was too much of a daydreamer to distinguish himself as a scholar.

As the 11th of 12 children of Mr. and Mrs. Leander Fuller, and the second youngest of eight sons, he knew his chances of inheriting his father's farm were not worth worrying about. When he was 18, he bundled up his belongings, donned his blue serge Sunday suit, and bought a one-way ticket on the steamboat that plied from Yarmouth to Boston. His brother Harvey was a motorman on the Boston Elevated Railway and Alfred applied for similar work. He managed to pass for 21—the minimum age for B.E.L. employment—and was hired as a conductor. "It was a pretty good job for a country lad," he says. "It paid $12 a week and you had an opportunity to meet people."

In spite of this it bored him after 18 months, and he aspired to be a motorman like Harvey. He decided to do a bit of unauthorized practicing, his idea being that if he taught himself to pilot a tram he could surprise his boss and win a promotion. Impulsively he climbed into a car and tried to move it out of the carbarns. He lost control and it raced through the yards, jumped the track, and was badly damaged. So Fuller was fired.

Jobs were scarce in those times, especially if your former employer refused to recommend you. After Fuller had worn the soles of his shoes thin, searching in vain for a job that was comparable to the one he had lost, he went to see a wealthy widow, a Mrs. Ball, who had advertised for a gardener and handyman for her suburban estate. She engaged him at a niggardly wage and treated him like a slave. One of his many daily duties was the curry-combing of her white horse. He happened to overlook this once and the Widow Ball returned from her afternoon canter in a towering rage. The horse was shedding, her black velvet costume was matted with white hair and Fuller was fired again.

Driving a delivery wagon came next. "I was unsuited for it and had no particular interest in it," he says. He probably left more parcels at wrong addresses than anybody else in Boston's history. Among them was a very important parcel for a very important person—and Fuller rejoined the unemployed.

While all this had been happening, his brother Dwight—the one who made brushes back on the farm—had arrived in Boston and opened a small brushmaking shop. He had subsequently developed tuberculosis, sold out, and gone to the west for the sake of his health. Alfred knew Dwight's successor and in 1905 entered a deal by which he was to buy brushes from him and attempt to sell them at a profit.

The tall bashful awkward youth from Nova Scotia, who had thus far failed at whatever he had tried, soon discovered he had a flair for selling. The first time he ventured forth with his sample case, he made a sale on his second call. The same day he sold a brush without knowing what it was for. "I knew it was a radiator brush," he relates, "but I didn't know what a radiator was because I hadn't lived in a steam-heated house. I just said, 'Now this is our radiator brush.' The woman grabbed it and started brushing between the flanges of a radiator. In that way I found out the purpose of the brush."

He earned more money selling brushes than he had ever earned before. Within a year he had saved $375. He invested $15 of this in a hand-operated wire-twisting device and $65 in wire, bristles and wooden handles, and went into the manufacturing as well as the retailing end of the brush business. His sister, Mrs. Walter Gleason, let him use her basement as a workshop.

"Dad" Fuller cranked out bath, clothes, hand and floor brushes by night and peddled them by day. When Bostonians seemed to have all the brushes they required at the moment, he took a train to other places. One of them was Hartford, which impressed him as being a fine city. Late in 1906 he moved to Hartford, rented a shed for $11 a month, and formed the Capitol Brush Company. Six years later he was surprised to learn that there was another and older Capital Brush Company; he renamed his own concern, which has since been the Fuller Brush Company.

Fuller kept meticulous account of his expenditures and still has records which show that his disbursements in March, 1907, included 10 cents for stamps, 20 cents for a wrench, and 60 cents for express charges. At one stage he doubted whether his enterprise could survive. That was in October, 1908, when his balance in the City Bank of Hartford dropped to $72.79.

He weathered the crisis and by July, 1909, his balance had increased to $523.76. Meanwhile he had married and he had hired a $6-a-week helper, Philip Colturi, who is now one of his executives. With Colturi as an assistant he could turn out brushes faster than he could peddle them himself. He was soon recruiting salesmen in New York, New England and Pennsylvania. By 1910 he had 25 men in the field, six in his factory.

To expand, he needed more salesmen and they were hard to find. He solved the problem by inserting a $10 advertisement in *Everybody's*, then a magazine of national circulation in the United States. Within a week he had 45 enquiries from men interested in selling brushes and within a month he had hundreds. There was so much mail to be answered that he engaged a secretary, Ruby Perkins. Like Colturi, she's still with him and is now assistant-treasurer of the company.

According to Fuller it was the $10 magazine ad that transformed his small organization into a big one. In 1911 his sales force numbered 100. In 1913 he set up his company with a capitalization of $50,000 and elected himself president, treasurer and a director.

"Dad," who is fond of remarking that he started his own business "because I felt it would be nice to exert a measure of control over the duration of my employment," now has 2,700 permanent employees. These are his factory workers and members of his office staff at Hartford, Albany, N.Y., and Hamilton, Ont., and salaried field managers scattered throughout this continent. His Hamilton plant, built in 1921 to make brushes for Canada, has 350 on the payroll.

Besides his 2,700 employees, Dad has his 7,800 Fuller Brush Men, and 4,500 Fuller Brush Girls. The Fuller Brush Men and the Fuller Brush Girls are not employees but independent dealers—"just as independent," he says, "as the storekeeper on Main Street."

They establish credit with the company, buy from it wholesale, and sell retail to the public. The average markup on their 135 items of merchandise is 33⅓ per cent. The toughest part of their job is persuading housewives to let them come in and display their wares. Fuller himself, early in his career, found that a free gift was an effective door opener. The gift the Fuller Brush Man presents to you if he's inside your house—but not unless he's inside—is a vegetable brush. It is known among the initiated as the Handy and costs the salesman three cents.

In addition to originating the Handy, Fuller originated the "big five" method of selling. This consists of: 1, naming the brush; 2, explaining how it is used; 3, telling what it's made of; 4, stating the price; 5, telling why it is worth that much.

Cartoons to the contrary, the Fuller Brush man is seldom if ever greeted with outstretched arms by a beautiful siren who wears nothing but a transparent negligee and an enticing smile. Dogs are his worst occupational hazard and he is bitten once every four years. According to "Dad" Fuller, a Fuller Brush Man should earn $80 a week if he has a fair-to-middling personality and plenty of endurance. But he has to have the right kind of temperament or he can't stick at it.

The Fuller Brush Company, mostly owned by "Dad" and other members of his family, not only makes the brushes marketed by Fuller Brush Men, but industrial brushes of all kinds—such as brushes for machines that polish apples and machines that scrub sausage skins. It also produces 90 per cent of the brushes for all vacuum cleaners manufactured in North America and special brushes (weapon cleaners) for the armed forces. In recent years "Dad" Fuller has relied more and more on his two sons, Howard, 38, and Avard, 34. Howard, educated at Harvard and Duke, is both an aviation enthusiast and a yachtsman. Unlike his father, he smokes, drinks more than one Scotch at a sitting and doesn't go to church. Like his father, he takes his work seriously—so much so that he invented a complicated brushmaking machine—and is married to a girl from Nova Scotia, the former Dora Baker of Yarmouth. They have a son and two daughters. Tall bespectacled Howard is now president of the company, "Dad" having promoted himself to the less exacting post of chairman of the board. Avard Fuller, now vice-president in charge of sales, is married, has a boy and a girl, and is keen about model railroads.

Howard, Avard and the other advisers of kindly "Dad" Fuller say it's hard to prevent him from "giving his shirt away." His Hartford plant, set among broad green lawns, could be mistaken for an ultramodern high school, and his labor relations are such that he has yet to have a strike. Employees at Hartford can buy a meat-and-potato meal for half what it would cost them at a restaurant run for profit. And, thanks to "Dad," they have a 22-acre park with a nine-hole golf course, baseball diamonds, outdoor grills and picnic tables, and a clubhouse complete with bar.

Alfred Fuller is so openly generous with what he has that the *Hartford Times* commented editorially: "Indeed, when Hartford views the civic and philanthropic activities of Mr. Fuller, it might well conclude that it could scarcely do without him." In his native Nova Scotia he is equally esteemed. "Old Al," declares a lifelong friend at the sleepy village of Welsford, "has certainly brushed his way from rags to riches—but he's still the same nice guy."

ALFRED FULLER *died in December, 1973, at age 88. Primrose died in October, 1997, at 94, and donated their Yarmouth, N.S., home to the Yarmouth Historical Society, which maintains it as a museum. Earlier, in 1968, Fuller sold his company to Consolidated Foods, now Sara Lee Corp. The Fuller division still manufactures more than 2,000 mostly household items, which are sold the old-fashioned way, door to door.*

IAN SCLANDERS *wrote more than 200 articles for* Maclean's *from 1933 until he died in March, 1966, at age 56, of a heart attack while on assignment in Fredericton.*

Jerry Bull, Boy Rocket Scientist

by Fred
Bodsworth

MARCH 1, 1953

WHEN FOUR SCIENTISTS FROM Canada's Defense Research
Board visited Washington in March, 1951, Canadian liaison officials held a
cocktail party to introduce them to U.S. experts engaged in similar research.
An American scientist's wife, bored with the highly technical discussions,
sized up a spectacularly youthful-looking member of the Canadian party and
settled down beside him for a less scholarly conversation. After a few minutes
the woman's husband joined them and introduced the Canadian as "Dr. Bull."

The woman stared at the Canadian. "*Dr.* Bull!" she exclaimed. "You can't
be a scientist too? You're only a baby!"

Dr. Gerald Vincent Bull's boyish face would pass him off in any after-
four soda-fountain crowd as just another high-school student, but he has
already won a spot in the upper echelon of Canada's defense scientists. Jerry
Bull—he is 24 and doesn't look that—is DRB's chief aerodynamicist at its
Canadian Armament Research and Development Establishment (CARDE for
short, pronounced "cardy") near Valcartier, north of Quebec City. He ranks
among Canada's leading experts in supersonic aerodynamics—the science
newer and more baffling than atomic science which is studying the problem
of shock waves and resistance produced when flight speeds approach the
velocity of sound.

His job at CARDE is one of several hush-hush assignments out of which
Canada hopes to develop its own version of a guided missile which, together

with British and U.S. models, may in a few years crowd conventional piloted warplanes into obsolescence and bring push-button warfare and even space travel only a step away. The project is a vast and highly organized effort on which scores of scientists at CARDE and at other undisclosed points are working. On the team are electronic experts, rocket-propulsion engineers, explosives experts, aerodynamicists and physicists.

Jerry Bull's contribution is the missile's aerodynamic design, the first of many problems to be solved. Bull has to give "the bird," as the missile is known, a body, wings and control fins which will provide stability and precise manoeuvrability at speeds faster than that of a rifle bullet. Its design will have to overcome the shock waves of explosive force which bar the transition zone between subsonic and supersonic speeds. And, buffeted by these shock waves, it will still have to possess instantaneous response to its steering fins, for, even at the relatively slow missile speed of 1,000 miles an hour, a time lag of one second in steering response could mean that it would be a quarter of a mile off course.

The guided missile will decide the balance of air power within the next decade or two. Aircraft speeds and performance have continued to improve but pilots have remained flesh and blood, and the time is rapidly approaching when human pilots will no longer be able to react fast enough to control supersonic planes. "Before planes are improved much more we'll have to eliminate the pilot," says Bull. "And when you've done that you have a guided missile."

A guided missile is simply a bomb with stubby wings that flies itself and can be controlled by radar from the ground or from a nearby mother plane. When perfected, guided missiles will be launched from one plane against another, from air to ground, from ground to air or from ship to shore. If the target tries evasive tactics, the missile will change course and trail its target like a bloodhound. It will drop unerringly on ground targets without warning, moving so fast that it leaves even its own sound behind.

Since the days of the German V-2, the Model T of guided missiles which might have won the war for the Nazis had they had it a year earlier, many experimental missiles have been tested by Britain and the United States. They have ranged from the size of an artillery shell to that of a large bomber, from

500 pounds in weight to 50,000 pounds. Their speed has varied from 600 to 3,000 miles an hour, their range from one to 5,000 miles. The United States is said to have a long-range missile, now nearing perfection, easily capable of flying from North America to targets in Europe. According to a current U.S. army joke, missile firers are warned to duck when a long-range "bird" takes off to save themselves from being hit in the back of the head in case the missile circles the globe.

The importance of what Jerry Bull is doing is attested to by the frequency of the red ink Top Secret stamps which mark many of the documents on his desk and by the heavy padlocks which guard his filing cabinet. People who meet him for the first time sometimes find it hard to disassociate young Dr. Bull from the bizarre, miraculous world of space cadets and breakfast-food death rays in which so many young men, not much younger than he, are dreaming of the scientific future. Actually Bull was a model-aircraft fanatic as a boy but he was able to take his Buck Rogers or leave it alone. Originally he thought vaguely of becoming a poet, and poetry remains his most absorbing interest, next to aerodynamics.

Jerry Bull working in the aerophysics lab at the University of Toronto, 1950.

In his modest third-floor boarding house room, a stone's throw from where General Wolfe died, his personal library is a strange mixture of equation-filled textbooks and poetry anthologies. After a busy day of plotting air-flow graphs he frequently relaxes by wandering alone across the Plains of Abraham and reconstructing the 1759 battle which was the great turning point in Canadian history. Then he crawls into bed with a book of poems. His favorite is a volume of Longfellow in which "The Day Is Done" has been turned up so often that the book opens automatically at that point:

And the night shall be filled with music,
And the cares that infest the day,
Shall fold their tents, like the Arabs,
And as silently steal away.

One feature of the battle for Quebec which fascinates him is the fact that on its eve, Wolfe led his army flotilla upstream reciting Gray's "Elegy in a Country Churchyard." "He was a good judge of poetry," Bull comments. Wolfe is described as a rather odd and cultured personality who was difficult to understand intimately. Bull, a kindred type, would have understood him.

Bull is good-looking, of medium height and weight (five feet eight and 150 pounds), with wavy almost-black hair and rather large compelling eyes. He talks vivaciously about his hobbies and expertly about hockey, but when the conversation swings around to himself he hedges skilfully and modestly. "If you have to write anything about the guided missile, get this straight—it's a big job and what I'm doing is just a tiny part of it."

Dr. Irvine I. Glass, a University of Toronto classmate, said of him: "He's the easiest guy to get along with that I know. He gets you embroiled in terrific arguments sometimes, but just when you're starting to get mad he winds it up somehow so that you go away liking him more than ever."

Bull was born March 9, 1928, at North Bay, Ont., the second youngest of a family of 10 children—three girls and seven boys. His father, George L.T. Bull, KC, had the reputation of being one of the best criminal lawyers in Canada. His mother, Gertrude LaBrosse, was born in North Bay, daughter of one of the north's original prospectors. When Jerry was three, the family moved to Toronto where the father quickly established a busy law practice. But his mother died unexpectedly a few months later and his father decided to retire. The father and nine children (one of Jerry's sisters was now married) moved to the old family homestead near Trenton, east of Toronto, and an aunt, Miss Laura Bull, who was a retired nurse, became Jerry's second mother.

When Jerry was six his father, who died three years ago, remarried and returned to Toronto to practice law again. Jerry and three brothers were taken in by a married sister who lived at Sharbot Lake, north of Kingston. When he was nine Jerry spent a summer vacation with an aunt and uncle, Mr. and Mrs. Philip LaBrosse, on a 68-acre orchard, two miles east of Kingston. He fell in love with the old orchard—a love he still wistfully proclaims.

The insecurity of his childhood had left him shy and nervous. He wanted to remain with his aunt and uncle, but he was afraid to say so. On the last day, when the return for school could not be postponed any longer, Mr. and Mrs. LaBrosse drove him back to Sharbot Lake. When they arrived they discovered that nine-year-old Jerry had brought an empty suitcase—his clothes were still back in the farmhouse by the orchard. He had to go back to Kingston. Aunt Edith LaBrosse became his fourth and final mother. "I have no recollection of my real mother," Jerry says, "but no boy ever had finer parents than I had in Aunt Edith and Uncle Phil." And no parents are prouder of a son than Mr. and Mrs. LaBrosse are of Jerry Bull.

The LaBrosses had arranged to spend that winter in Florida. Uncle Phil took Jerry to Regiopolis College, a Jesuit resident school for boys in Kingston, where, as an undersized lad of nine, he encountered a problem that has dogged him ever since. The headmaster looked him over sternly. "How old?" "Nine." "Sorry, the laddie's too young." But the headmaster agreed to admit Jerry on the understanding he be removed as soon as the LaBrosses returned. Two months later Uncle Phil called in again to pick up Jerry. The headmaster's attitude had changed: "He's a fine boy, that. An excellent student. It's very bad, changing schools in midterm. Jerry should stay here." So Jerry spent six years at Regiopolis.

That first year with the LaBrosses, still believing in Santa Claus, he had his first real Christmas. He had had few toys in his life before. He was introduced to aerodynamics by a couple of balsa-wood model-plane building kits. The delicate adjustments of wing angles and balance required to make a model fly fascinated him. After that he made model planes, flew them and wrecked them as fast as he could induce his aunt and uncle to supply him with kits. Later he abandoned the prefabricated kits and designed his own. "He was always building planes," recalls Mrs. LaBrosse. "When I went shopping he insisted in coming along to make sure I bought the breakfast cereal with the plane designs on the box. It didn't matter whether it was eaten or not."

Periodically, and admittedly with less success, he tried creating poetry instead of planes. Most of his poems seemed to be about the old orchard. He is thankful today that none of them were preserved.

In 1942 the LaBrosses moved to Toronto. Jerry liked Regiopolis so well that the next year he returned and completed his senior matriculation there. He was only 16, but he thought his school days had ended. That summer of 1944, he went to work—back in the old Kingston orchard for its new owner. But in Toronto his aunt and uncle were discussing other plans. Early in September, LaBrosse wrote to Jerry. Would he like to be a doctor? Jerry wrote back immediately. He didn't want to be a doctor, but the University of Toronto was opening a new four-year course in aeronautical engineering, and this he *was* interested in. If his aunt and uncle would support him for another two years, he was sure he could finance the last two by working summers.

LaBrosse went to arrange for Jerry's enrollment. The problem of age reared its head again. "It's too difficult a course for a 16-year-old to start," he was told. LaBrosse argued. The professor agreed to have a look at the boy. Jerry came to Toronto, the professor talked with him for a few minutes and accepted him as the youngest member of the course. Four years later he graduated as a bachelor of applied science in aeronautical engineering, and took a drafting job with A.V. Roe aircraft company near Toronto.

During his four years of study, aircraft development had slowed almost to a stop because of the sonic barrier problem. Supersonics was a new and unknown field that had been only briefly touched by Jerry in his aeronautical engineering. The riddle of the shock wave was an intriguing challenge to him. But at A.V. Roe there was no opportunity for him to work on supersonics.

At this time, 1948, the Institute of Aerophysics for research and teaching in supersonic aerodynamics was being established under Dr. Gordon N. Patterson at the University of Toronto. The institute was sponsored and largely financed by the government's Defense Research Board. Little actual teaching could be done, for supersonics was then so unexplored that students had to work on individual research projects and teach themselves. Accepted students were handed research assignments by DRB, were paid an honorarium of $2,000 a year and became more or less DRB employees. Their research work and theses then entitled them to MA and PhD degrees. DRB started the institute on its way with a grant of $350,000.

Jerry resigned from A.V. Roe and applied for enrollment in the institute. His youth almost barred him again. Most applicants were much older students, many of them married veterans with overseas service. Bull, 20 but looking younger, appeared almost a child in comparison. Fifteen other aeronautical engineering graduates of the previous year had applied. Bull, the youngest, was the only one of this group accepted.

Bull began the most exhausting period of his life, and three years later left the Institute of Aerophysics 15 pounds lighter, on the verge of a nervous breakdown, and one of the youngest PhDs the University of Toronto has ever turned out. He threw himself completely into supersonics research, worked nights, weekends, at times around the clock. "He knows no hours," Patterson says. "The average chap working with him a month would have to sleep three days afterward to catch up the sleep lost."

Bull's first task was to team up with Doug Henshaw, another student, on the designing of the institute's first small supersonic wind tunnel. After several months Bull and Henshaw were ready late one night to assemble their tunnel. It was to be about seven feet long. They discovered there wasn't room enough in their tiny quarters at the University of Toronto. Bull decided there was no time to redesign the tunnel to fit the space, for they had to get moving on their research—the space had to be redesigned to fit the tunnel. And the tunnel would fit in one position if a 10-inch hole were knocked out of a partition so that one large valve could protrude into Dr. Patterson's office. Patterson arrived next morning to discover his desk crowded into another corner and the wind-tunnel valve sticking through the wall where his desk had been.

Bull and Henshaw soon afterward had to start work on a larger wind tunnel. The air storage chamber, a metal tank about six feet high and three feet in diameter, was being produced by an outside firm to their specifications. Late one afternoon, the tank was delivered and Bull and Henshaw brought it up to their quarters on the elevator. They discovered the firm had not followed specifications exactly and the tank was about one inch too wide to go through the door. Bull wouldn't consider waiting for another tank. They quietly left the tank outside in the hall, then that night returned and tore the door frame out to get the tank inside. Next day there were official enquiries about why the door frame at Room 36 was split and slightly askew. It had to be replaced. "I don't know whether Dr. Patterson ever noticed that our tank was bigger than the door," Bull says. "If he did he never mentioned it."

Later Bull and Henshaw found it necessary—with Patterson's reluctant consent—to make further adjustments. Next morning Patterson arrived, found that a partition had been entirely removed and that his office had practically disappeared. He had to climb over the top of the wind tunnel to reach his desk. His lips pressed thin in resignation, he climbed across it and went to work. After that Bull and Henshaw were frequently sitting on the edge of Patterson's desk as they worked with the wind tunnel. Periodically, as he tried to concentrate on desk work, Patterson was almost lifted from his chair by the ear-rending screech of a blast of air shooting at two or three times the speed of sound through the wind tunnel four or five feet away.

One morning late in the spring of 1949, when Jerry Bull was rushing work for his MA thesis, Patterson reached his mutilated office, climbed over the wind tunnel, pulled out his chair, sat down and thought he must have landed on a pin cushion. He leaped up and discovered the chair seat covered with splintered glass. Bull and Henshaw had got the wind tunnel working too well the night before, had pushed it up to three times the speed of sound and exploded the big four-foot-long observation windows in the side of the tunnel. Pulverized glass had covered everything and Patterson was finding glass chips among his books and papers for months afterward.

Patterson had been campaigning for new quarters for some time. The glass shower was the last straw. "I think he was getting fed up and I can't blame him,"

Bull says. A few months later the RCAF provided the Institute of Aerophysics with much larger quarters at Downsview Airport, north of Toronto.

Bull's first two supersonic wind tunnels were for preliminary study, out of which DRB hoped that the institute could develop a much larger tunnel for more advanced research. As soon as the institute acquired its larger quarters, work began at once on a huge $200,000 tunnel to be capable of producing air speeds up to seven times the velocity of sound (5,500 miles an hour). Patterson studied similar tunnels in the United States, few of which were as large as the one planned for Downsview. On his return, he and his research associate at the institute, Dr. Irvine I. Glass, got the big project organized. Bull's assignment was the design and perfection of the test section of the wind tunnel—the critical "nozzle" section where the highest air velocity had to be produced and where the actual testing of models was to take place.

The job took a year and a half. Late in the summer of 1950, the wind tunnel was nearing completion and plans were made for a formal opening of the Institute of Aerophysics, to be highlighted by a wind-tunnel demonstration on Sept. 26. It was to be a big affair. In addition to Canadian aeronautical and defense experts, officials were also to be present from Britain, the United States, Australia, New Zealand and South Africa. Air Marshal W.A. Curtis of the RCAF would be present to push the button and give the wind tunnel its first official test.

Patterson, Glass, Bull and the other students were working night and day to have the tunnel completed in time. At the same time Bull was also hard at work on his PhD thesis. "Jerry was working much too hard," his aunt recalls of this period. "On nights that he didn't stay at the institute he would come home, have dinner, go in his room to study and close the door at 7 p.m. At 11 or 12 when we were going to bed, we would knock on his door and tell him he should get some sleep. Through the crack under the door we'd see his light go out. Then in a little while it would come back on again. He would wait until we were in bed, then he'd get up again and continue studying."

On Sept. 23, three days before the big opening day, the wind tunnel was completed, everything tightened up and ready. That night they partially pumped out the big vacuum sphere and gave the wind tunnel a short test run.

No attempt was made to get a supersonic air velocity, but in this incomplete test everything appeared to be satisfactory.

Next day the floor was being painted and they couldn't get near the wind tunnel until late on the afternoon of Sept. 25, the final day. This time the vacuum sphere was completely pumped out and the starting button pushed for a full-scale test. The air screeched through. Everyone eyed the observation windows eagerly. But no shock wave appeared. The tunnel, designed to produce an air flow seven times the speed of sound, was falling short of even the speed of sound itself. Patterson and his students stared blankly at each other refusing to believe it. Could their year and a half of work and the expenditure of close to $200,000 have been based on miscalculations?

When they examined the packing which kept the wind-tunnel section of the apparatus airtight a ray of hope appeared. There were signs that it might be leaking. But to repack it would require the removal and replacement of some 400 nuts and bolts. There was no other way out. It had to be done. About 11 p.m. the tedious repacking task was completed. Examination of the packing material had proven that it was faulty. Patterson and his men felt certain now that the wind tunnel would live up to its specifications. They were exhausted and it would take an hour or two to pump out the vacuum sphere for another test. The inexhaustible Jerry Bull and a couple of machinists volunteered to stay and give the tunnel another test while the others went home to sleep.

The vacuum sphere was pumped out and, at about 1 a.m., Jerry pushed the button for another test. The whine of air inside rose to an ear-splitting shriek. A clearly discernible shock wave formed. The wind tunnel was functioning perfectly, pulling the air through it at a speed well in excess of the velocity of sound. Jerry and the machinists gleefully started pounding each other on the back.

But it was all over in a few seconds. There was an explosive crash, a couple of echoing thuds, the wind tunnel shook, and the whine of air rushing through it suddenly became silent. Bull knew what had happened. Inside were two 10-foot-long blocks of wood which gave the tunnel its interior contour. The desired hardwood hadn't been available in time and they had had to use softwood. Jerry knew without dismantling the tunnel that the intense suction of supersonic-flowing air had pulled the heads of the bolts through the wood and the blocks had ripped loose and shot like artillery shells against the vacuum sphere end of the tunnel.

To repair the damage meant removing and replacing those 400-odd nuts and bolts all over again. And now Jerry was alone except for two machinists. The dignitaries would be arriving for the grand opening in another 12 hours. They had just begun dismantling the tunnel for the second time that night when a door opened and Dean Kenneth F. Tupper, head of the university's engineering department, walked in. Tupper was driving home late alone, saw the lights of the institute still on, and dropped in. He was wearing a business suit, Bull and the machinists were in overalls. The dean threw off his coat, put on a smock and dug in. When someone had to crawl into the tunnel to loosen bolts from the inside, Tupper insisted on doing it himself. "It was the most tedious job I ever did," Bull says. "We'd never have been able to finish it if the dean hadn't worked like a galley slave to help us."

By 3:30 a.m. the wooden blocks were securely replaced, the tunnel fitted back together and ready for another test. No one felt like waiting for the sphere to be pumped out. The dean treated the boys to breakfast at an all-night restaurant and Bull went home for a couple of hours of sleep. He was back at 10 a.m. At 11 a.m., with only two hours to spare, the wind tunnel was put through another test. This time there was no mishap. It worked perfectly. Patterson and the students relaxed and waited for the VIPs to arrive.

That afternoon Air Marshal Curtis pushed the button for the tunnel's first official run. Nothing happened. Down near the front of the audience, Jerry Bull started trembling. Patterson, standing beside Air Marshal Curtis, reached behind him and gave the button a harder poke. The switch had merely failed to make contact. This time the wind tunnel started up with a piercing whine.

About this time the RCAF had decided that if we waited for a perfected U.K. or U.S. model, Canada would probably not be able to start producing missiles of its own for years, because the other nations would have to concentrate on their own home production before they could start teaching the production technique to anyone else. By creating our own guided missile from scratch, Canadian defense authorities hoped to have a missile especially designed for Canadian requirements much sooner. At the same time, the project, by encouraging young Canadian scientists to stay in Canada, would build up a team of Canadian experts experienced in missile production and handling, ready to swing into action the moment a guided missile is perfected.

The RCAF asked DRB to produce plans for a guided missile which could be turned over to industry for mass production. DRB appointed Gordon Watson to recruit the required scientists and organize the research team. As project engineer, Watson is responsible for co-ordinating the scattered research activities; as one of DRB's highest qualified electronics scientists he is also directing the development of the missile's intricate radar-controlled steering "brain." Watson's first move was to call in Gordon Patterson who, though a Canadian, is so widely recognized as a guided-missile authority that he has been appointed chairman of a U.S. Navy guided-missile consultant panel.

One of the first men Watson needed was a young aerodynamicist experienced in supersonics, hard-working and with flexible ideas that would enable him to co-operate closely with scientists working on other branches of the project. He had to be young simply because there are no aerodynamicists of the old school who have kept abreast of recent supersonics developments. Patterson recommended Jerry Bull.

At their first meeting Watson was sure Bull was too immature for a position that would, before long, require him to direct the work of scientists much older than himself. But, after a half-hour interview, Bull had the job of making Canada's guided missile fly. He went to CARDE, polishing up his PhD thesis on the train during the trip, and returned to the University of Toronto to receive his doctorate in May, 1951.

Since then, the story of what Jerry Bull has done is a top secret story hidden in the vaults and padlocked filing cabinets of CARDE. He has not remained at CARDE longer than a month at any one time because the need for consultation with British and U.S. scientists has taken him numerous times to Washington, Langley Field, Va., New York City, San Francisco and, for a month last fall, on a tour of research establishments in Britain.

Defense Research Board officials will say only that the boy who had no permanent home until he was nine "is doing an outstanding job for Canada." Two years ago Bull was offered double his starting CARDE salary to join a U.S.

government research project. He was told: "We don't know what you are earning now, but whatever it is we'll double it." But Jerry thinks Canada has been very kind to him and he stayed where he was.

Does he have any qualms about being employed in the creation of a weapon which, when fitted with an atomic bomb warhead, will be more fearsome than anything science has yet perfected? He is too deep a thinker not to have considered it. "What we are learning about supersonic aerodynamics can have many civilian applications," he states. "It can provide us with safer and faster air travel. It will help us to conquer space, man's last frontier. Some day, guided missiles may carry mail and express instead of a warhead, and a letter mailed in Vancouver could be in Halifax an hour later."

As for the guided missile itself . . . "War will never occur until a nation planning aggression thinks it can win. As long as the nations desiring peace can maintain better weapons than the nations desiring war there is a deterrent to aggression. Then they are not weapons of war, but weapons of peace."

GERALD BULL *spent a decade with the Department of National Defense, then joined McGill University in 1961 where he worked on a controversial "supergun" project financed by the Canadian and U.S. governments. The project was terminated in 1967 and Bull went into business for himself, becoming internationally known for his weapons designs. But his trade led him down shadowy paths: in 1980, he was convicted in the United States of selling weapons to South Africa and sentenced to a year in jail. Then, on March 22, 1990, at age 62, Israeli secret agents assassinated him in front of his Brussels home. At the time, he was working for Saddam Hussein's Iraq, developing a "supergun" that could deliver 52 kg shells up to 1,600 km.*

Glenn Gould, The Genius Who Doesn't Want to Play

by Gladys Shenner

APRIL 28, 1956

WHEN GLENN GOULD, a talented and temperamental young Toronto pianist, made his New York City debut in Town Hall a year ago last January, the critics were enthusiastic and Columbia Records was impressed enough to sign him to a three-year recording contract. But New York debuts are everyday events and Gould's modest triumph was virtually unnoticed by the general public in his own home town.

Exactly a year later, however, the release of his first recording, Bach's formidable Goldberg Variations, suddenly made Glenn Gould, at 23, a musical personality of international importance. Classical records are usually noteworthy because the artist is famous. This one record brought fame to a performer hitherto almost unknown. Until this year Gould had given only two concerts in the United States and had appeared in only a few Canadian cities. With his new recording, music critics suddenly showered him with superlatives. Newspapers even devoted editorials to him. Writers described Gould's eccentricities: his obsession with pills and nostrums of every kind, the elaborate hand-soaking rituals he indulges in to keep his fingers supple, his grotesque positions at the piano.

As a result of the recording, Gould has become one of the most sought-after performers in the concert world. Three weeks after the record's release he was solidly booked for the 1956-1957 concert season, which stretches from the fall to summer. He has engagements to tour Canada, the United States and Europe. He will appear with the eminent New York Philharmonic Orchestra next January and the august Berlin Philharmonic next spring. He's now accepting engagements for the year after next at $1,250 each, double his present fee. He has hit the musical scene with a volcanic impact. "New York is talking about Glenn Gould," a heading in the New York *Herald-Tribune* read. "The musical seas are swimming with pianists but few keyboard virtuosos in recent years have made as big a splash," the accompanying article said.

Gould, a mere youngster among concert pianists, won't accept instruction and dislikes practicing. Yet the Goldberg Variations is a work that takes most artists a lifetime to master. One of the most difficult pieces ever composed for the keyboard, it consists of thirty variations on the saraband, a slow dance popular in the 17th century. Bach composed it for the two-keyboard harpsichord. The pianist today must play much of it with one hand directly over the other, his fingers often interlocking. He must bring out two, three and even four intricate melodies at the same time. He needs stamina as well as skill, because it takes him 45 minutes to play the thirty variations.

Gould's recording of the Variations is one of two available. The other is by the Hungarian pianist, Joerg Demus. The Demus recording was made for Westminster, an English rival of Columbia, and came out with little fanfare. The Gould recording, on the other hand, has probably attracted more attention than any classical piece done in recent years by a relatively unknown performer. It prompted *Time* magazine to call Gould "one of the most talented young pianists to appear in years." The *New York Times* termed Gould "a young man with a future," and the *American Record Guide* pulled out all the stops: "In Glenn Gould we have not just a promising pianist but an artist who has arrived."

In Canada, the Gould recording sold 1,200 copies the first month, an unusual number for a work of such limited appeal. In the United States it is Columbia's best-selling new classical record and is currently outselling recordings of *The Pajama Game*, a popular musical. Even the erudite program notes on the Gould album, written by Gould himself, stirred attention. Their perception and originality brought Gould invitations to write for two musical publications, *High Fidelity* and *Musical Courier*.

There is a rich irony in all this, for Gould, a hypochondriac headed for phenomenal fame as a pianist, is actually not interested in a career at the keyboard. "The piano is a convenient way to make enough money so I can afford to compose," he says. "In 10 or 15 years I want to be known primarily as a composer, not a pianist."

After two and a half years, he has just completed his first major composition, a string quartet. One New York critic who heard it in rehearsal called it "the most significant work of its kind of the century." The quartet will be a feature of the Stratford Music Festival this summer and of a concert of contemporary music in New York's Town Hall next winter. Columbia plans to record it. A romantic one-movement work, the quartet takes 25 minutes to play, as long as most four-movement string quartets. Composing it, Gould worked an entire day over a single bar, neglecting the piano for weeks at a time.

Gould's attitude to his piano career is another of his eccentricities. For, at a time when prima donnas are not in fashion and the artist is supposed to act like the boy next door, Gould is, above everything else, an individual. He is far too thin for his five feet 11 inches and looks almost emaciated. His face is nearly gaunt. He dresses outlandishly, and even in the hottest weather he lopes down Toronto streets wearing galoshes, a heavy overcoat, a wool beret and two pairs of gloves. When he practices he wears a flowing striped dressing gown or a baggy blue sweater cut deep at the neckline and armholes.

Gould swallows pills indiscriminately. He makes a production of soaking his hands in water of increasing temperature before he sits at the piano. His posture at the piano made him the centre of a hot controversy in Winnipeg a few months ago, when he was a guest artist of the Winnipeg Symphony Orchestra. Newspapers devoted columns to letters about Gould's way of playing. Most pianists sit up straight, feet side by side in front of the pedals and hands and arms poised gracefully above the keyboard. Gould crouches over the keys, his shoulders high, his head pushed deep onto his chest, his legs crossed. His elbows and wrists hang below the keyboard and his lank blond hair falls over his forehead and often brushes the piano keys. At times he appears to be playing with his angular nose. He sits on a wooden folding chair that has a pink leather seat and legs that can be raised or lowered. As he plays he accompanies himself in a resonant bass voice and, if one hand happens to be idle, he uses it to conduct. He often keeps time by banging his foot on the pedal.

The mercurial Glenn Gould, 1956.

In Winnipeg, where the professional critics praised him unstintingly, there was as much discussion about these gesticulations as about the music itself. Ken Murphy, the *Free Press* critic, was deluged with letters. One concert-goer wrote that her enjoyment of Beethoven was "marred by the comically theatrical poses which resembled the agonies of the damned." The exhaustion Gould showed at the end of the piece, she said, "was due, no doubt, to his own physical exertions, not to Beethoven."

Gould has no intention of changing his piano crouch. "Sitting the way I do, I can get the exact sound I want. But this isn't something I would recommend for anyone else." Neither would most music teachers. Gould was practicing in the Steinway building in New York last year, when he was interrupted by a teacher working in the room next door. She thought that Gould was a student and asked him to play for her. "That's quite musical," she said. "But do you mind if I give you a little advice?"

Gould winced. He dislikes advice and never follows it.

"I have a lot of pupils like you who get odd notions about how to play the piano. But if you're ever going to amount to anything, you have to stop this nonsense. I'd certainly never let any of my pupils sit the way you do."

A side effect of all this is the noise he makes while he plays. When Gould recorded the Goldberg Variations, Columbia had to do innumerable retakes because the microphone kept picking up his voice as he sang along with the music, or his foot, as it beat out time. "Why don't you wear a surgical mask?" the recording director asked. Gould turned up with a gas mask. He didn't use it, however, and at several places in the finished recording faint sounds can be identified as the Gould voice or the Gould foot. "But it's done in very good taste," Gould says.

His hypochondria has come in for almost as much attention. Nervous, highly strung, Gould is terrified of illness. As a precaution he gulps hundreds of pills. He takes half a dozen different kinds of sedative to calm his nerves. He lines the squat bottles up in front of him, and then makes his choice. He is constantly experimenting with new types, taking away one bottle to replace it with another. At the first sniffle, he swallows antihistamines, which are cold preventatives, and terramycin, an antibiotic. Recently, at a reception after a concert in Ottawa, he was cornered by a stately gentleman who told him, at close quarters and at great length, how much he had enjoyed Gould's concert. "I'm so glad that my wife persuaded me to come," the man said. "I've had a fever all day, but it was worth getting out of bed to come and hear you." The horrified Gould rushed to the phone and ordered $20 worth of terramycin.

Gould gave up penicillin because it gave him a rash. He takes vitamin pills and stomach tablets to counteract nervous indigestion. He takes pills to stop sweating so his hands won't stick to the keys. He takes more pills to stimulate his blood circulation. He claims that practicing harms the circulation in his hands.

Gould is obsessed with his hands. He has them insured with Lloyd's of London for $25,000. When he practices he stops every hour to soak them for 10 minutes to take out the soreness and relax the muscles. He soaks them constantly the day of a concert and carries an electric kettle to concert halls and broadcasting studios to ensure his supply of hot water. "My hands are very thin," he says. "Just muscle, really. There's no great layer of fat, and the slightest tension or any exposure to cold or to air conditioning hurts them." He refuses to work in air-conditioned rooms, even in the hottest weather.

Last summer, when the temperature in Toronto soared into the 90s, Gould was called to a rehearsal in one of the CBC's air-conditioned studios. He arrived muffled to the ears. The collar of his overcoat was turned up and his wool beret was pulled down over his forehead. He wore his usual two pairs of gloves, the inner pair of wool with the fingers cut out, and the outer of suede lined with sheepskin. Under one arm he carried his folding chair and electric kettle, and under the other his brown-leather medicine kit crammed with pills and with tape for bruised fingers. While the other musicians sat around steaming, he boiled his kettle and soaked his hands and forearms. Then he asked to have the air conditioning turned off. The other musicians told him the janitor was gone for the day. "We had to lie," one said. "Glenn said it ruined his playing, but the heat was inhuman."

To Gould, all this is no fetish. "I worry more and more about my health," he says. "I'm not one of those hardy types who can go on no matter how I feel." He has often threatened to cancel a concert because he feels a cold coming on or because he has made himself sick worrying about the concert. So far, he has only threatened. He worries so much before a concert that he starts sedatives and sleeping pills at regular intervals three days before. "Lots of people think I'm a dope addict," he admits.

Gould is actually in good physical shape, according to his parents, Russell and Florence Gould, with whom he lives in a comfortable two-storey house in the east end of Toronto. They say all his ills are imaginary. "You fret yourself into a state," his mother chides him good-naturedly. His father, owner of a Toronto fur store, is fond of telling Glenn about Glenn's grandfather, founder of the store. The old man, a hypochondriac like Glenn, always carried a doctor's bag filled with medicines to work with him—and lived to be 87. "Use a little mental effort and you'd feel fine," Russell Gould tells his son.

To his other ills Gould adds inflammation of the tissues in his shoulder and hand muscles. "Listen," he says as he swings his arm. "Can you hear it crack?" He visits a Toronto chiropractor, Arthur Bennett, once a week. He stretches out, face down, on a narrow green-leather couch. "Ready, Glenn?" says Bennett, a short, nearly bald man in a white coat. At a grunt from the couch he begins to pummel and twist Gould's spine. He works his way up to the neck and twists it from left to right. He moves on to the arms, circles them back from the shoulder blades, over and over. Then he flips Gould's wrists around and rocks them in their joints. Bennett sits down to rest and Gould goes to an adjoining room to an electric-wave machine and gives himself a series of shocks. He believes this relaxes the muscles in his hands and arms. Then Bennett gives him ultrasonic treatments, high-frequency sound waves, also intended to relax his hand and arm muscles.

On tour Gould has a list of chiropractors in each city. When he played in Washington early last year, it was Sunday and Gould had to go as far as a town in Virginia to find a chiropractor to give him a treatment. Stories like this of course have made his eccentricities a legend. Gould claims he's merely controlling every factor that bears on his music. He practically rebuilt a piano to suit his technique. He sits half a foot lower than other pianists and says this position necessitates a special type of action from the piano keys. Gould thought that he had found this in a concert Steinway he saw in New York last spring. "I decided I couldn't play on anything else," he says, "and that I'd even take it on concert tours with me." He paid $6,000 for it. Over the protests of a number of New York pianists who had been using it for performances, he took it to Toronto. After practicing on it for a few weeks, he complained that the action of the piano keys was ruining his co-ordination. The keys were set a sixteenth of an inch too deep for him and slowed his finger work. He had pads put under the keys and the hammers sanded and brought closer to the strings. Then he replaced the Steinway's shiny black keys with a set 20 years old. The smooth white keys also bothered him—he likes a scratchy surface—so the manufacturers of the piano scoured the keys with abrasives, leaving them rough and dull.

"Do other musicians bother you as much as I do?" Gould asked Winston Fitzgerald, a Steinway executive.

"Can't say they do," Fitzgerald replied coldly.

Gould took the piano to several concerts in Ontario and Quebec where shipping costs ran to hundreds of dollars. In Sherbrooke, Que., the railway left the piano standing in its canvas cover in the rain for six hours. Exasperated, Gould shipped it back to New York for resale. He's now shopping for another piano.

Gould's insistence on perfection in a piano is reflected in the intensity of his playing. Music is almost a religious ritual to him. "A lot of people think being a musician is just like any other job," he says, "but it isn't."

He lives an isolated life. He gets up at noon and doesn't go to bed until three or four in the morning. He practices, composes, reads, studies and talks music all day. At three in the morning he is often at the piano. Gould's only hobby is reading and his literary tastes are just its esoteric as his musical tastes—heavy Russian and German prose and obscure poetry. He doesn't smoke: he says he has no time for vices. He suffers a curse familiar to other geniuses. He's always been too old for his years and has few friends, none of them his own age. His parents have become used to the fact he is different from other people and they surround him with warmth and understanding.

It was Florence Gould, a piano teacher before her marriage, who discovered her son's amazing talent. Glenn was three when she found he had perfect pitch. She started him on kindergarten music books the next year and taught him for seven years. When he was 11, Glenn won a scholarship to the Toronto Conservatory, where he studied with Alberto Guerrero. He has studied by himself since he was 19, an age at which even Paderewski worked under a teacher. "I couldn't teach him the way I did others," Guerrero says. "Glenn resented it if I told him, 'That's not right.' Even at 11 he had a perfectly good idea of his powers and he hasn't changed much."

For years Guerrero tried to tell Glenn how to play the opening phrase of Beethoven's Fourth Piano Concerto. The young boy merely gave him a frosty smile and continued to play it the way *he* wanted. "He won't take anyone's word for anything," Guerrero says. "And it's better this way, because he keeps his originality."

In many ways Glenn was not like a child at all. Rather like a wise little man. Offered candy, he would refuse. "Why should I eat something that's not good for me?" he would ask. He wasn't athletic and unless his mother reminded him to go out and play he would sit at the piano for hours, practicing and improvising. As a child, Gould also played the pipe organ and he gave his first organ recital in Toronto when he was 14. Although he no longer practices on the organ, he played it steadily from the time he was 10 until he was 16, and considers it one of the most important influences in his development. Now, whenever and wherever he comes across one, he stops to play it. In his teens, the piano and organ left little time for school and he attended only half days. He had private tuition to keep him abreast of his studies until he graduated from high school.

Studying and working alone, Gould became uncomfortable when he was with others and tended to stay away from them. He still does. He spends about six weeks each year in New York, but except for recording sessions he remains closeted with his piano in a two-room suite in a quiet apartment hotel. In the summers he secludes himself in the family cottage in Ontario's Muskoka district. He practices and composes, and except for the local store-keeper and postman and brief visits from his parents, he sees only his dog. In Toronto, he takes long walks along the shore of Lake Ontario, several miles from the Gould home. He gazes out at the water for hours. "I gather my inner resources from the outdoors," he says.

Recently, he thought that he was coming down with jaundice. "Nonsense," his doctor said. "You don't live dangerously enough." Jaundice can be caused by alcohol. Gould doesn't drink. He's careful about what food he eats and passes up fancy dishes for steaks, skim milk and plain biscuits.

His dedication to music has produced a crusading streak in Gould. He is determined to interest Canadians in modern music and has given Canadian premières to the works of the contemporary German composers, Schönberg, Webern and Berg. These works, based on dissonance, are often difficult for the uninitiated to listen to. After playing them Gould gives his audience a lecture on the work and its composer. Such concerts usually cost him money, since audiences are small and promoters hesitate to underwrite them.

Away from the piano he has a boyish charm sparked by an acid sense of humor. But he shoves all politeness and humility away from the keyboard. "I know that you're supposed to have reverence for years," he says. "But I have reverence only for capability. That's why I get into trouble."

Toronto musicians are still talking about his memorable clash two years ago with Alexander Schneider, a violinist of considerable repute and experience. Gould and Schneider were scheduled to make two appearances together in Toronto in July, 1954, one a television performance of chamber music and the other a joint concert recital. Trouble started with the TV rehearsals.

"Let's try that passage this way, dum dee dee da . . ." suggested Schneider.

"But you're putting the accent in the wrong place," Gould protested.

"I play with my heart, not my head," Schneider snapped angrily.

"I play it the way Beethoven wrote it," Gould said.

"But, of course," the violinist said. "I forgot that the great Gould communes with Beethoven regularly."

Gould kept stopping rehearsal to analyze the music. Schneider said that he didn't need it analyzed. "I've played this with Casals."

"I don't care who you've played it with," Gould said. "I want it done my way."

"How many times have you played this piece?" asked Schneider.

"Three."

The violinist was exasperated. "*I've* only been playing it for 25 years."

Gould has a phenomenal memory and never uses music when he performs. When performing chamber music, it is customary to play from the printed score. Gould refused, so in their first performance, TV viewers saw Schneider with music and Gould without. Schneider was further affronted when a camera closeup showed Gould bending over the piano with his eyes shut and conducting with his left hand.

Schneider said that he would never have considered performing with Gould if it were not for his great talent. This talent is so exceptional that Gould has achieved his fame by breaking all the rules set out for success. He practices only three hours a day, while most serious pianists practice at least six. He reluctantly doubles his practice time a few days before a concert. He won't practice scales although most pianists swear by them. "I'm not fond enough of the keyboard to spend my time on scales," Gould says. He plays Bach instead.

In the highly competitive concert world, where reputation and experience are counted in the number of concerts an artist gives, Gould has given fewer than 50 in the past five years. Ray Dudley, another Canadian pianist, gives as many as 60 concerts in a single season.

Gould has broken another rule most successfully by sticking to a limited repertoire. As he dislikes the vast field of 19th-century romantic music, his programs are rather esoteric. Composers like Chopin, Schumann and Liszt never appear on the Gould programs. Instead, he plays Renaissance music, austere 16th-century music which no one else plays on the piano. He specializes in Bach and Beethoven, plays a few works by Brahms, the odd one by Mendelssohn. He always plays some contemporary work.

Walter Homburger, Gould's manager, wants him to enlarge his repertoire. Gould insists he will continue to specialize. He is just as unsinkable in his attitude to the future. He was in no hurry to become famous. Now that he is, he is determined to continue to play only the music he likes, in whatever manner he likes. When he made his debut in Toronto in 1947 at the age of 15, Gould refused a concert tour of Canada and the United States which might have made him a child prodigy. "Look at all the pianists who play hundreds of concerts and finish there," he said then. "I'm not going to be like that."

His convictions have not harmed his career. Neither have his eccentricities. "They're not put on for anyone's benefit," he says. "But since they're there, they don't hurt."

GLENN GOULD *retired from the stage in 1964, announcing that "The concert is dead." From then on Gould focused on the technological possibilities of recorded music. Although he never attained success as a composer, his reputation as a performer continued to grow. His re-interpretation of the Goldberg Variations, one year before his 1982 death at age 50, by a stroke in his Toronto apartment, continues to dazzle the critics. Since he died, his stature among pianists has remained high and he has even become a cult figure: tourists come to Toronto to visit Gould sites, there are Gould conferences, and* Glenn Gould *is a twice-yearly magazine.*

Bill Shatner's
Adventures in Hollywood

by
Barbara Moon

OCTOBER 26, 1957

LAST APRIL, WILLIAM SHATNER, a 26-year-old actor from
Montreal, flew into Hollywood from New York City to do a half-hour TV
show. He had come a few days early because he wanted to make a routine
exploratory round of "the majors"—the five top film studios. The majors,
who regularly scout network TV for possible finds, already had Shatner's name
and face on file; but back in New York his agent had advised, "If they see you
in person, it makes a difference." The next morning his agent's Hollywood
representative began by showing Shatner to M-G-M out in Culver City.

They went straight to the office of Mel Balarino, M-G-M's casting director. Balarino looked Shatner over. What he saw was a splendid young bobcat of
a male, with a close cap of cinnamon hair, tufted eyebrows and white teeth
bared in a grin of undisciplined charm. Back on Canadian television the grin,
the charm and the look of rude young vigor had made Shatner one of CBC's few
matinee idols, with his own fan clubs. As an actor in radio, in Montreal and
Ottawa repertory, and at Stratford, the same attributes had consigned him to a
succession of romantic roles. He has played the light-tenor range from Prince
Charming in broadcast fairy tales to Lucentio, the pawky young lover in *The
Taming of the Shrew*. When he went to Hollywood he had already signed to do
Laertes, Ophelia's brother, in this season's *Hamlet* at the Stratford Festival.

Balarino, the casting director, said, "Come along with me." They walked
out and up a flight of stairs to the office of Pandro Berman, an independent

producer who has made a string of box-office successes for M-G-M. When Berman had surveyed Shatner in turn he said, "I would like him to be in our movie." "What is it?" Shatner asked politely, but Berman went right on: "Take him to meet Richard," he said.

So they went out and back down the stairs to the office of Richard Brooks, an independent writer-director who also works frequently for M-G-M. Brooks pointed his finger at Shatner as soon as they walked in the door. "That's the one," he said. "I want him." Thus, as it sometimes does happen in real life, Bill Shatner got discovered by Hollywood and won a lead in a big motion picture.

He's playing the part of Alexey, the wholesome one of the three brothers in a magniloquent Pandro Berman-M-G-M production of *The Brothers Karamazov*. Brooks, who is directing the picture, freehanded the scenario himself from Fyodor Dostoyevsky's psychological novel. Shatner is what is known as a "featured player," which means he gets secondary billing, his own dressing room and a junior star's salary. He is keeping the gross a secret but admits that during shooting he earns about $5,000 every three weeks. It took him a whole year, including a successful season in New York TV, to earn that much in 1956.

The senior stars in the show are bald-pated Yul Brynner, Old Vic actress Claire Bloom and Maria Schell, a winsome and spirited import from German films. *The Brothers Karamazov* is due for release early in 1958.

In the great Hollywood legend, being "discovered" signifies a consummation and a change of state, rather like "and so they were married" in the fairy tales. Latter-day footnotes insist that neither necessarily leads to living happily ever after, but the legend itself persists. Shatner, because he had read the footnotes, thought he knew exactly what to expect. He's had his eye on Hollywood almost since the moment, six years ago, when he suddenly decided he'd rather act than take over Admiration Clothes, the Montreal garment business his father had built up to bequeath to him. Shatner was a popular young buck on the McGill University campus at the time, but as soon as he'd pocketed his degree in economics he started to make his way in Canadian repertory, radio and television. At each of several subsequent crossroads he explored the one that led to the United States and the big time. Even two years ago, when he nearly signed an indifferent long-term contract with Twentieth Century-Fox, he thought of Hollywood as "the answer to all my dreams." Last year when he was co-winner of the Stratford Festival's Tyrone Guthrie scholarship he didn't use the swag, as others have, to study theatre in England or on the continent. Instead, he grubstaked himself to a try at New York TV and, just as he'd suspected it might, New York TV subtended the moment when Richard Brooks, out in Culver City, pointed his finger and said, "That's the one."

Someone in M-G-M's casting department had caught a TV drama in which Shatner starred and had suggested he might do for Alexey. When Shatner happened along in person soon afterward everyone could see at once that he had the qualifications. Or, as an M-G-M publicity girl put it recently, "He had the right face for Alexey. Besides, in the film he's sort of bracketed with Claire Bloom and she being English and Old Vic and Bill being Canadian and having done Shakespeare, it seemed suitable. You know?"

William Shatner in a 1950s Hollywood studio publicity photo.

M-G-M conceded him a rare non-exclusive contract whereby the studio has an option on his services for two pictures per year but leaves him free to work elsewhere in between. The weekend the deal was concluded, Shatner, in his own words, "went Hollywood," for two days. After a long-distance call to Stratford to say he wouldn't be coming after all, he went out and drank champagne cup, with gardenias floating therein, from a hollowed-out coconut with a two-foot straw. And he almost bought a house with two fireplaces, a pool, a barbecue pit and a glass-enclosed living room. His agent was hysterical. "Don't mortgage yourself to Hollywood!" he screamed, just in time. "Don't have to take roles you don't want, just to meet the next payment."

Shatner's only splurge on the strength of the contract has been an Austin-Healey sports car. A newsboy in Beverly Hills uses the same model to deliver the morning paper.

Shatner was told to report in a month, on June 3, for costume fittings. Shooting was due to start on June 10. He drove the Austin-Healey across the continent at the end of May with his bride of nine months, Gloria Rosenberg Shatner. He first met her in New York when he was acting in Tyrone Guthrie's production of *Tamburlaine the Great* and she was dancing in the Copacabana line. "The Copacabana," Gloria explains in her breathless young-girl voice, "is the one where they wear clothes." Gloria, 24, is a beautiful shy Toronto-born girl with wheat-colored hair, cheekbones, wide eyes and a wide soft month. Her stage name is Gloria Rand, but her career has been mostly dramatic academies, lonely rooms in girls' studio clubs, fruitless knocking on casting directors' doors and occasional tantalizing breaks that led nowhere. Any reviews she's had have been good. This season, after four years' trying, she'd finally got an assignment at Stratford—as the Player Queen in *Hamlet*—but resigned when Shatner did.

Shatner duly reported for his costume fittings, reread a paperback edition of *The Brothers Karamazov*, got his mimeographed copy of Brooks's scenario and, as he puts it, "had a quick steep in the role." He found his part was a fat one but, in Brooks's version, so relentlessly fresh-cheeked that he might have been back playing young fairy-tale princes or young friends to the hero. This time he was a young monk, but that was the only difference. He was not greatly surprised.

But a tiny disquietude was borne in on him. M-G-M was putting out no welcome mat for its new young find. No one from M-G-M's vast publicity department had got in touch with him. There had been only one press release that mentioned his name—a casting announcement for *The Brothers Karamazov*. It had said that the three brothers would be played by Yul Brynner, Richard Basehart and Richard Shatner.

The Shatners had been braced for the manifold perils of Hollywood processing; they had not been braced for its omission. Furthermore, no one had arranged for Shatner to meet his fellow cast members, nor had Brooks called. "I was hurt," says Shatner good-humoredly. At 7 a.m. on Monday, he presented himself at M-G-M, but no one at the casting entrance had been told to let him in. He tried three other entrances and then went back and convinced casting of his credentials. In the make-up department, he was coated with orange pancake and fitted with a monkish, brown skull cap of hair. A heavy dark-brown-felt monk's cassock is almost his only costume in the whole film.

Shatner didn't know about the studio limousine service, so he hiked to Studio 28, at the far end of the back lot. Here he knew what to expect: a cavernous gymnasium with a Technicolor set as bright as a ball park under a blaze of klieg lights; stagehands and technicians hustling around the shadowy perimeter like park officials under the grandstand. No one seemed to notice Shatner.

Somewhere in the gymnasium someone clapped his hands; a voice called, "On the set!" Shatner hurried to an opening between the flats and saw Brooks, in his denims. Brooks didn't see him. Brooks called out curtly, "Let's go. Rehearsals, everyone." Someone shoved Shatner along behind the flat to a door opening into the set, said "You're on, Mr. Shatner," and nudged him through. Summoning his opening lines, Shatner made his entrance. Not four feet in front of him was a bear. The bear snarled and lunged at him. There was a rattle of chains. A bottle dropped, spilling Coca-Cola on the floor. A man hit the bear on the snout with a length of lead pipe. Brooks said, "Well, move, Bill!" Shatner said, "May we try it again?"

Shatner says now, "That first day I felt as if I had two left feet." He subsequently found that the bear was local color for a Russian marketplace set, that the trainer customarily bribed him through his paces with Coke and used the pipe to disengage him from the bribe this side of satiety.

Just before lunch the first day, Brooks came over during a setting-up break and said "Meet your brother." This was Shatner's introduction to Yul Brynner. Brynner politely invited Shatner into his portable dressing room where they chatted for a few moments about sports cars and Tamburlaine. Brynner sometimes claims to be part Tartar. Shatner met the other stars one by one during the next few days as each turned up for his first scheduled scene. That first day at lunch break the set cleared quickly. Brynner went to his permanent dressing room where he has all his meals served. Brooks disappeared somewhere else. Shatner finally found his way to the bright noisy studio commissary and ate alone.

For his first three weeks as M-G-M's newest discovery, Shatner was broke. He found that in Hollywood, where a verbal agreement is binding, there had been no hurry about processing his contract. It was still in the hands of New York lawyers, so no pay was being put through for him. Normally an actor is paid weekly. Shatner and his wife dined on hamburgers at Smokey Joe's. In the evenings they piled into the Austin-Healey and prowled the spiral wooded streets of Bel-Air, listening to the crickets in the scented night air and peering wistfully in lighted windows.

By mid-July, though, they had money in their pockets and a secondhand Nash station wagon for Gloria to drive when Shatner was at work; they'd sailed to Catalina Island, driven to Tijuana for the bullfights and been to the races. At the studio, work was going well. Shatner, having combed the script for actors' chances, had announced triumphantly to Gloria, "I've found a couple of places where I can show zeal." Brooks had been heard to say, "Good boy," after a take. On the set Brooks proved to be a tense excitable director, given to sudden childish outbursts. He had stormed off the set because someone had borrowed the pencil he keeps on the table beside his canvas-back chair.

Shatner often ate lunch in the commissary with a minor player whom Gloria had known in New York. On the set he'd made friends with a stunt man who was teaching him how to fake a punch. Occasionally, in setting-up breaks, Brooks or Brynner would call him over to their group to chat. One day Shatner came back to the flat, stifling a huge grin and sporting a big-bowled pipe. Gloria noticed it immediately. "Yul Brynner gave it to me," said Shatner off-handedly. "I was complaining about breaking in mine and he went off to his dressing room and got this for me." He stroked the bowl. "Must be a $28 pipe," he said.

Gloria, who had met no movie stars since she got to Hollywood, had enrolled in a nearby ballet school and was in constant touch with her Hollywood agent. So far, though she'd read for a couple of parts, nothing had turned up. They had both begun watching their diets again: steak, fresh fruit, yogurt. While others in their apartment block lounged by the pool with gin drinks and suntan oil, Shatner would withdraw into a corner and skip an imaginary rope. Then he'd dive into the pool and later, when he'd straightarmed himself out, would report to Gloria, "Fifteen lengths that time. Best exercise there is." He had already ordered a toupee to camouflage a thinning spot in the cinnamon hair.

Nearly every free afternoon he and Gloria practiced their singing and voice projection. They picked passages from Shakespeare and read them aloud in five or six different styles. Sometimes they'd collaborate on a new play they're writing. One of Shatner's plays, *Dreams*, was produced by the CBC in the spring of 1956, before he and Gloria were married. They both had leads in it.

In short, Shatner has found nothing in Hollywood that he can't relate to his familiar routine as an actor or to the film world he's read about. He knew it would not be glamorous. He was not really surprised to find that it was nerve-racking, occasionally lonely, often uncertain. "This is just the big break, the first plateau," he says. "From here I could go forward or I could go back."

But Shatner had, one way or another, expected being discovered by Hollywood to make at least one difference: organized publicity. He knew all about the press agents, the impertinent questions, the stories planted in Louella Parsons's column, perhaps a false rumor or two. So far it hasn't been like that at all, and Shatner is mystified. "You'd think it would be good for the picture," he says in puzzlement. "I'm playing one of the three brothers and I'm an unknown in movies."

Midway through the shooting, this summer, the publicity girl that M-G-M Publicity Department says is assigned to Shatner didn't even know if he was married. When she learned he was she seemed disappointed. "It's easier to do publicity if they're single," she said. "Then we could pair him up with one of our starlets and do a layout . . . oh, maybe of them visiting Marineland."

She paused, obviously pursuing a train of thought. "I wonder what his build's like in bathing trunks," she said. A brown-felt monk's cassock is an unrevealing garment. "I just did a nice beefcake layout at the beach with one of our promising young actors. Beefcake, that's male cheesecake."

Why no publicity for Shatner so far? M-G-M feels it has enough on its hands promoting Claire Bloom, who is from England, and Maria Schell, who is from Austria. "It's a big prestige picture," said the publicity girl. "We've got to build up the stars: nobody knows them here. Besides, it's better for Bill. We can do a long build-up, like we did for Debbie Reynolds, you know? We did a long slow build-up for Debbie and now she's at the top she's staying there." After a minute she added carelessly, "Besides, we might publicize him now and then not pick up his option. That'd be a waste of time."

The publicity girl watched him walk away. "He's a nice boy. He should do well," she remarked briskly, "if he behaves himself." Her eyes narrowed. "I wonder," she said, "if he'd be willing to do beefcake?"

WILLIAM SHATNER *is, of course, best known for his role as Captain Kirk, captain of the* Enterprise *in the* Star Trek *movies, based on a TV series in which he also played Kirk. He has also directed both movies and TV shows, and is the author of a bestselling series of science fiction novels. He and Gloria divorced in 1969; Shatner now lives in Malibu with his third wife, Nerine Kidd.*

BARBARA MOON *was an assistant editor and staff writer at* Maclean's *from 1948 to 1952 and again from 1956 to 1964. Later a senior editor at* Saturday Night, *she now lives in Toronto.*

How Paul Anka Crashed Tin Pan Alley at Fifteen

by
Paul Gardner

JANUARY 4, 1958

AN OTTAWA HIGH-SCHOOL boy walked out of his Grade 10 class last April and left town to put his talent up for grabs on Tin Pan Alley, "because," as he said, "I figured I'd make it faster in the States." Paul Anka's foray to New York City was the same assault on fame and fortune almost every youngster builds his visions on, and it had as much chance of success as any of the other anonymous thousands that are actually carried out.

Four months later, on his 16th birthday, Anka wired his mother Camilia 16 camellias from Philadelphia. He was one of six top-featured artists in a touring rock 'n' roll group; he sings four songs once a night and occasionally twice a day and draws $1,000 a week. On the same night, *Variety*, the showbusiness newspaper, listed his recording of "Diana," a rock 'n' roll tune he says he wrote in 20 minutes, in 13th place in total sales on the continent. One week later, Anka himself was eighth in what the paper describes as Top Talent and Tunes.

The week after, Anka's rendition of his own song had slipped to ninth place; then it climbed to seventh, stayed there a week and jumped to second, high above competing numbers by such booming box-office names as Elvis Presley and Pat Boone.

The week "Diana" topped *Billboard*'s chart, Anka sang his tune on the Ed
Sullivan television show in New York. He made a second appearance as Sullivan's guest in November after singing on the Perry Como Show and on The
Big Record, which stars Patti Page. In the same month he played his home
town and at year's end took off on a British tour.

Anka draws in royalties of a cent for writing and about four cents for
singing on every record sold. Sales passed the million mark (more than
100,000 of them in Canada) in mid-September, three months after the tune

Paul Anka crooning at his Ottawa home, 1957.

hit the radio stations and record counters. "Diana" topped two million early in October, and was expected to go over three million by the end of 1957. Anka is also paid for every radio and television broadcast, though juke boxes pay nothing but the price of the record. Three more Anka songs have been recorded by other artists and he earns royalties from all of them. A new Anka recording of two Anka tunes, "Tell Me That You Love Me" and "I Love You, Baby," has been picked as a probable hit by all three entertainment trade papers. It had a quarter-of-a-million advance order from dealers—as much as some hits sell altogether.

The 1957 returns on his live and recorded singing and his song-writing are virtually certain to pile up to $100,000 when all the reports are in. Diana was released last June, which means he'll have earned that sum in about six months. He has a long-play album due for release early in 1958, which may be called Paul Sings Anka. He's had several movie nibbles—he'll make a screen test in February. By mid-June of 1958 he *could* match Elvis Presley's reported feat of earning $1 million in his first full year—if Anka's first full year is measured from his first major-label recording. More than a year ago he cut a record in California and it flopped. "They didn't promote it," Anka complains. "I made $1.82, clear!"

Anka's personal following has been pyramiding as fast as his bankroll. He now has about 50 registered fan clubs, with new ones springing up all the time. When he played in Atlanta recently, he was greeted by a large club he hadn't known existed. He gets thousands of letters from girls all over the United States and Canada, many asking for advice—"Should I let a boy kiss me on the first date?" Some of his fans add such subtleties as, "Got a steady? If not, I'm ready." He answers them all with cautious wisdom: "Keep calm and collected and all will go well."

The object of all this adulation is a short chubby youth with shiny jet-black hair and a light olive complexion. I met him for the first time in the Montreal Forum, where 23,000 rock 'n' roll fans assembled one Sunday afternoon for the touring show he is appearing in. His road manager, a pleasant but worried-looking young Ottawan named Bill McCadden, introduced us. There had been plane trouble and the group had arrived from Toronto (where they'd played to 10,000 people in Maple Leaf

Gardens) too late for rehearsal, so Don Everly, of the Everly Brothers, accompanied Anka in a run-through of one of his numbers. He was dressed in a scarlet sweater with a black sport shirt beneath, black slacks and white suede slippers. On stage he wore a dark suit with a white shirt whose collar points bulged out informally. "Do I look all right?" he asked anxiously just before going on.

When he's tired, as he was that day after three nights with very little sleep, Anka's face is flaccid and expressionless. But on stage later it lit up like a pyrotechnical display. He's five-foot-three, weighs 145 pounds, and knows it's too much. He followed three other acts. When emcee Harold Cromer announced, "Ottawa's Paul Anka," screams dinned through the Forum, accompanied by cheers, whistles, hand-claps and stamping. On bounced Anka, radiating personality and clapping with the audience. He sang a tune called "Happy Baby" to good applause, which grew deafening as he turned to his own "Don't Gamble With Love," in which he dropped his jumpy gestures for an occasional full-arm sweep.

His next number, a tune called "Gumdrop," brought out his wildest gestures. Dozens of photographers, all teenagers and mostly female, swarmed around in front of the stage. He had to say, "Thank you," four times to stop the applause. Then he held up his hands, said with a graceful gesture, "I dedicate this song to *you*," and lit into "I'm so young and you're so old, Diana."

The rafters rang, and it was 16 bars before any of the words were audible. He bounced through it twice, in a powerful voice, with the broken syllables (like a cracked phonograph record) that are the trade-mark of his rendition. Then he danced off the stage, waving his left hand like a flipper. After a minute or so of heavy applause, he took one bow and he was through working until the night show.

In the audience were his beaming father, Andy Anka, an Ottawa restaurant owner, his mother, his self-possessed 14-year-old sister Mariam, and his lively seven-year-old brother Andy Jr. His hometown cheering section included Diana Ayoub, a handsome Ottawa girl who last spring suggested that Paul write a song about her and to whom he dedicated his first hit. She was 18 in May, which explains its chivalrous opening lines. He says they're just "good friends;" Diana was his baby-sitter when he was 10 and she 13. One hundred and twenty other relatives, friends and fans from Ottawa were there in a bloc, besides many others who had come separately.

When Anka had rested for an hour or so we went to his hotel room. Soon afterward Diana, her girl friend Gayle Jabour (president and vice-president-secretary-treasurer, respectively, of Chapter 26 of the Paul Anka Fan Club of Ottawa) and a bevy of other teenagers burst into the room. Most of the girls kissed Paul, which caused him no chagrin.

Anka said, "I wanna sleep!" but no one paid any attention. The girls started talking about their fan clubs. Diana's had 293 members, but Anka said, "Aw, that's nothing. My sister Mariam has one for the Diamonds that has 420 members! Get crackin', kids, I need the support!" At this his mother, an attractive woman with large quizzical eyes, said, "Paul! Keep cool and collected, and they'll class you as a second Perry Como."

He suddenly collapsed and said sadly and wearily, "I'm going home! I want to have fun like I used to!" In the morning, he flew to Syracuse with the show.

It wasn't much more than a year since Anka had set out on his first long-distance crack at the showbusiness jackpot. Just before he turned 15 he wrote a rock 'n' roll song that he named "Blauwildesbestfontein"—the name of a South African city in John Buchan's novel *Prester John*, which had been required reading at school. To sell it he decided to try the Los Angeles music market, which he thought might be easier to crack than New York. At the same time the trip would give him a chance to visit his uncle, Maurice Anka, a tenor who sings in night clubs on the west coast. Paul sang at dances and parties and did a few turns himself at night clubs in Ottawa and Hull. When he had saved $150 he set off alone for California. He had just celebrated his 15th birthday.

His uncle had no connections among the recording companies so Anka leafed through the yellow pages, calling each company in turn to ask for a hearing. He was turned down through the Q's and was pretty discouraged when a company called RPM said he could come in and demonstrate his song next day. He did, with voice and piano, and they bought it. Before it was recorded the song needed more lyrics; Paul asked his uncle to write them. "I thought I'd cut him in," he says airily.

After he'd recorded his song and written his mother a letter describing "the GIRLS here," with sketches, he ushered for a month in a movie theatre at $30 a week to earn his return fare. That fall he sang "Blauwildesbestfontein" on Cross-Canada Hit Parade, his second television appearance. His first, on Pick the Stars, hadn't done anything for him, and so far "Blauwildesbestfontein" hadn't sold enough copies to pay for the recording session, so Anka went back to school. He enrolled in Grade 10 at Ottawa's Fisher Park High School, but by April he couldn't wait any longer to have a hit recorded—"I knew I had some in me."

He thought of making a demonstration disc, but even with a small orchestra, that would have cost $600. "So I thought I'd save my dad $500," he explains, "and go down and sell the song myself."

He went to New York cold, but ran into the Rover Boys, a Toronto quartet whom he'd met in Ottawa and taken home for coffee and sandwiches some months before. They made an appointment for him at ABC-Paramount, a comparatively new but strong record company. Anka kept the appointment but found the artists' and repertoire department closed. Next day he called for another appointment and met Don Costa, an arranger. Paul sat down at the piano and sang one of his songs, "Tell Me That You Love Me." Before he'd finished Costa said, "One moment." He called in the heads of the firm, and they listened to it and the three other songs Anka had with him: "Don't Gamble With Love," "Bells at My Wedding" and "That'll Be the Day." Then the company president called Paul's father in Ottawa to fly down and sign a contract. It was as simple as that, Anka says.

Since they'd decided to save "Tell Me That You Love Me," another "strong" number, for his second release, they needed one more tune for the reverse side of "Don't Gamble With Love." Anka hadn't even brought "Diana" with him, but he had it in his head—though he couldn't remember all the lyrics. So he sang "da da da" in the blank spots; the company okayed it and he sat up till 2 a.m. completing the song and indicating the arrangement. The next day he was still asleep at two in the afternoon; his recording appointment was at four. His phone rang: "Get over here and start cutting!" He did, with no rehearsal. And that's how a smash hit was born.

When he talks about composing Anka loses himself in his own words. "I can feel something *making* me write! It scares me sometimes, because I have a feeling it's something outside of me coming in and taking over. I have to sit down and write, and everything falls into place. Sometimes I change a note or a syllable later, but not much."

Although Anka would like to pick up the night-club career he started in Gloucester, Mass., when he was 10 (patrons tossed him coins totaling $35), his company won't let him. He agrees with them, though, on a second point: they want to ease him out of rock 'n' roll. He's had two ballads recorded already— "I Lost My Love," "written for 18 violins," and sung by 17-year-old Johnny Nash. A second, this one sung by himself, was released in December. It's called "You Are My Destiny"—with an "up-tempo" (polite for rock 'n' roll) number on the reverse side, though, "just to play safe."

Anka, by the way, likes Elvis Presley and buys his records, "but he doesn't *throw* me. He's smart, though. I'd like to congratulate him!" He also likes Pat Boone, but his three favorites are Frank Sinatra "to listen to," Sammy Davis Jr. "to watch," and Judy Garland—"both."

Anka has been a popular-music fan as long as he can remember, and his father and mother, who are both of Syrian origin, can remember his first "professional" performances. Some workmen were laying a sewer in front of the Anka house. Six-year-old Paul filled a bucket with water, floated a saucer on the surface and talked the men into tossing pennies. For every coin that stayed in the saucer he'd sing a song. Sometimes he'd make 30 cents a concert, including the mis-aimed pennies he didn't have to sing for. Even before that a neighbor, Harry Bradley, used to pay him 50 cents to entertain him and his family for the evening.

Three summers ago Paul was a soda jerk for a while in an Ottawa restaurant owned by a family friend, Phil Massad. Anka's mother had called Phil and said, "Please give Paul a job. I want a rest at home!" Massad says, "I could hardly get him to do anything except entertain the customers. Since we had no cover charge, that wasn't economic, so I had to let him go. He never resented it, though—still writes and asks after my kids." Later that same summer Anka and two school friends, Jerry and Ray Carrier, all barely into their teens, sang in a midway show at the Central Canada

Exhibition in Ottawa. They called themselves the Bobby-Soxers, and rehearsed at Anka's home. His mother says, "I got so sick of it I'd push them into the basement with their monotonous guitars and Mambo Rock! They drove me crazy!"

The night finally came when Anka won an amateur contest at the Fairmount Club. It was a big boost for the fired-up youngster: it meant a week's engagement at $75, and a chance to work with professionals. But even before this, he told me, he'd climb a ladder, get in a back window, sit in the balcony and watch the show at various clubs; he rarely got caught.

Alex Sherman, who owns six record bars in Ottawa, manages one in Montreal and promotes touring music shows, says that for several years Anka went in to see him about twice a week. "You be my manager!" the boy would say. "You'll make money on me!" Sherman groans, "I always threw him out, but now I'd love to have two per cent of him!"

I last talked with Paul Anka the night before he left for Tulsa, Okla., after a five-day layoff from the rock 'n' roll tour. We met at a quarter to one in the morning at his father's Ottawa restaurant. Anka told me that one of his ambitions was to have his own television show—The Paul Anka Show.

Why did he go to the United States for his success bid—no encouragement in Canada? "Well," he said, "I tried my songs on Canadian publishers with no results. The CBC did nothing to hold me back; but I could see no future here except very slowly. I figured I'd make it faster in the States."

It was hard to get him to talk of anyone else, but finally he said, "I'd like to build my parents a fine home, and send them away on a nice little trip. They need a good rest. And my grandmother, she's 82 and has shaking hands—what do you call it?—I want to send a doctor from the States here to see if anything can be done for her. I'm *going* to do that."

"Do you want to be a millionaire?"

"I never *thought* of that!" he said with obvious sincerity, and stopped munching potato chips for a minutes "Well, I'll take it if it comes, but I think it would be very uncomfortable. People on the street who used to nod to me look scared now. Today I went back to school and cleared out my locker—running shoes and stuff, there since April. I ran into a girl

I used to know pretty well. She just stared at me, and then she burst out crying! It kind of threw me. I don't think *I* act any different to people. I *hope* not!"

PAUL ANKA *has sold over 51 million records around the world, and written more than 800 songs, including My Way, Put Your Head on My Shoulder, She's a Lady, Having My Baby, and the theme for Johnny Carson's Tonight Show. Among his connections with Ottawa, Anka is a co-owner of the Ottawa Senators hockey team. He lives in Los Angeles with Anne Alison, whom he married in 1963; they have five children.*

Why Should Juliette Knock Them Dead?

by
Barbara Moon

APRIL 26, 1958

THIS IS NOT LIKELY TO go down as a vintage year for star vocalists on TV. Last fall the big U.S. networks ran up the flags for some westerns—and for almost a dozen spangly musical shows featuring a top singer apiece. But by this March it was safe to predict that only one girl singer, Dinah Shore, would last past June. *Variety*, the showbusiness paper, claimed the networks had lost between $50 million and $60 million on their miscalculation and called it "perhaps the major and most costly holocaust in TV annals." The mass audience, it seems, didn't like something about the shows.

It's hard to say just what. It couldn't be lack of a voice: opera star Patrice Munsel has a beautiful highly trained voice. It couldn't be lack of all-round talent: Canadian-born Gisele Mackenzie has perfect pitch, good legs, a violin she can play and excellent comedy timing. It couldn't be lack of friendliness: Rosemary Clooney has a wide Irish grin and a great desire to please. It couldn't be lack of gorgeous gowns: Dinah Shore frequently puts $1,500 worth of dress on her back for a show. It couldn't be lack of top guest stars, hit-parade tunes and hard work: Patti Page makes a point of all three on The Big Record.

That's why it's a paradox that the modest sleeper of this season's CBC-TV schedule is a girl singer. She calls herself simply Juliette, though she was christened Juliette Augustina Sysak and has been Juliette Cavazzi since her marriage almost ten years ago to musician Tony Cavazzi. At 30, she is a strapping platinum blonde with a radiant smile, a creamy contralto, glinting brown eyes, much warmth and a nice, newly won figure.

But Juliette's voice has never been trained; her legs are not memorable; she can't play a violin and won't attempt the simplest two-step, let alone a soft-shoe break with skimmer and cane; her show clothes are assembled by the CBC costume department and are of the "party-dress" description. Up until last fall she weighed in at over 150 pounds, which gave her, on TV, the homey solidity of a mail-order-catalogue model. She slimmed down to showgirl shape only when a doctor warned her her health was suffering.

Juliette's weekly 20-minute show—on the CBC network Saturday night right after the 11 o'clock news and just before the wrestling—has an unpretentious staple set, a skeleton script that provides bare continuity, no guest stars, a mere two supporting artists and only one hit-parade tune, if any. The rest are well-worn oldies. Yet on a single Saturday early this year a survey conducted by McDonald Research Limited showed that more than 95,000 households in Toronto alone were tuned to the Juliette show. It was outclassed by only two other Canadian shows in the entire viewing week: the NHL hockey game and the Saturday 11 p.m. news, which immediately precedes Juliette and marks the end of many people's viewing day.

Juliette's been on network TV since 1954 and has had her own show for two seasons; but this season, while U.S. song-stars plummet, Juliette's ratings are climbing steadily. The show is pulling in three times as much mail as last year—50 or 60 letters a week ranging in tone from favorable to rapturous. In spite of this strong showing the program has not been discovered with little cries of critical pleasure. Such TV critics as exist in Canada scarcely mention it and *Variety*, which customarily reviews each Canadian show at least once a season, hasn't mentioned it at all. In fact outside of the sponsors, Player's Cigarettes, only people seem to like the Juliette show.

Why?

According to one explanation it's sheer circumstance: Juliette happened to inherit the right time-slot. It was occupied previously by a variety program on which she was featured, the Billy O'Connor show. When the CBC decided to package Juliette singly she got the open spot. It starts well after one audience-survey firm, Elliott-Haynes Limited, stops bothering to rate the evening audience, and it never did much for O'Connor. But now the second-guessers are pointing out that people sit up late Saturday nights; that they don't bother switching the dial after the national news, which traditionally attracts a top audience; and that other channels have nothing to offer at that time anyway.

Another explanation suggests that people like Juliette out of sheer relief. Producer Sydney Wayne, who is comedian Johnny Wayne's kid brother, claims, "There was a definite need for a low-pressure show in the line-up. There's too much theatrical stuff on now—and too many tinsel shows." He adds, "Those U.S. musical shows, they're all tinsel." Wayne cuddles up his cameras to the participants to simulate intimacy; suppresses the decibel count to the point where trumpeter Bobby Gimby's most useful accessory is his mute; and never, never, never does rock 'n' roll. The height of frenzy on the show is for Juliette to travel forward the six paces that separate a medium close-up from a close-up, snapping her fingers in time to a slow-bounce tune.

But since the show's a bigger success than expected, those concerned are suddenly spotting the real, real reason. After consulting the magic formula in current chic among worried U.S. television experts, they see that what the show has is "audience identification." Audience identification, apparently, is what makes viewers more ready to get the word on refrigerators from Betty Furness than from the glamorous clotheshorses that used to prowl the TV kitchens. It's what prompted a New York City talent agency last year to send out an SOS for "believable-looking women in their thirties"; "no regional accent," the bulletin added. It has already proved a handy excuse, since other explanations fail, for Ed Sullivan's appeal. Now it's being used to account for the malaise of the musical shows: they got so showy the stars weren't folks anymore.

In the present case the term is used to suggest that Juliette makes everybody feel she might be their close personal friend—except women, who feel Juliette might be *them*. Juliette, in short, is folks.

To be folks a star must not be formidable in any particular, since too flawless a talent, wit, glamor, wardrobe or vocabulary, by contrast, threatens the viewer's self-esteem. Juliette just naturally makes none of these mistakes. Though continuity is prepared for the show, she merely wings it, converting the sense into her own words as she goes along. Her own words include "Hi," "honey," "fellas" and "c'mon." Her clothes flatter the audience by being festive, but don't alienate it by being out of reach. She issues firm instructions about them: "Not high style and not low-cut." For reward she gets many requests for the name of her dress shop and an occasional plea for cast-offs. She is also asked for the shade of her lipstick, for the make of her bra, for pictures and for advice.

When a doctor ordered her to lose weight last summer Juliette was honestly worried: she'd had pretty strong indications that the fans felt comfortable with her unashamed heft. Fortunately they went right on identifying like mad. A typical comment went, "You did not need to, to please your audience,

Juliette on the set of her popular CBC-TV show.

but I admire you so much." Indeed many, after one good look, were moved to reduce likewise and Juliette got so many requests for her diet that she had to get a form reply printed.

Occasionally a viewer identifies to the point of complete overlap: Juliette is regularly in receipt of letters from Canadian wives asking for signed photographs as gifts for their menfolk! One Ottawa woman, whose husband was in Egypt with the UN emergency force, confided by way of explanation that he had requested a pin-up for his tent; she was, it seems, unable to think of a pin-up more appropriate than Juliette.

In all this Juliette can be regarded as a rebuttal to at least one set of alarms about TV. For the first 10 years of television there was a lot of talk about TV's awful power to mold a vast audience. At the beginning of the second decade Juliette already presents a full-fledged example of the audience's power to mold TV. Seventeen years of bandstand, radio and TV singing have made her as sensitive as an electronic computer in registering the data of popular taste. To keep a constant check on the readings she still averages three weekly club dates before live audiences all year round.

The most requested songs, she reports flatly, are the old chestnuts from the first 20 years of the century: "Shine On, Harvest Moon"; "Poor Butterfly"; "Whispering"; "Roses of Picardy." Juliette never tires of singing them on her show.

People like songs they can sing along with. Juliette never picks up a new song until it's been on the hit parade for at least three weeks and then only if it has an easy, pretty tune. People don't like the songs connoisseurs of music like. Take Cole Porter: "A Cole Porter song's a waste of time," she says severely. "It's a throw-away. It's too *big* a number, too sophisticated."

Sophistication, she senses, can offend people. This January Juliette picked a mild torch song, "Mad About the Boy," for her program. It contains a line that goes, "Lord knows I'm not a school girl in the flurry of her first affair." Instinctively, in mid-passage, she changed it to "first *love* affair." "The other didn't sound nice," she explained afterward with a frown.

She senses equally well that people are *not* offended by pretty girls, God, Queen and country, mothers, marriage and ladylike behavior. Consequently Juliette lets her audience know that she's been happily married for almost 10 years to Cavazzi, a musician who is also her personal manager, and periodically introduces him to the viewers on the show. She is also noted for including a semi-religious song and a patriotic medley in most of her live shows. They are surefire.

She keeps herself carefully groomed at all times, including rehearsal, and she would rather smile while singing—at whatever slight cost to her tone— than grimace to get a note just right. "You've got to make a pleasant picture," she points out. She is dedicated to her viewers' tastes in music. A couple of years ago, when she was a TV beginner on the Billy O'Connor show, she was directed to put on a 10-gallon hat and hoke up a western number. She refused flatly and explicitly. "I won't make fun of music that 90 per cent of the people like," she said.

She was born in Winnipeg, the younger daughter of a Polish-Ukrainian railroad chef, and she spent her childhood on Worthington Street, an address distinguished only by the fact that some people named Durbin had lived there once who had a daughter named Deanna. "I think I was a homely child," Juliette says.

She has early memories of her older sister, Maya, drilling her in the words of popular songs, making her phrase them as though they were speech. She was five. Maya, who was 10, already had ambitions for both of them. Maya has since changed her name to Suzanne and has sung in nightclubs and on radio. In the midst of the Depression, the Sysaks moved to Vancouver, where Juliette discovered the Tomorrowland of the motion-picture palace and spent many Saturday afternoons watching Rita Hayworth and Betty Grable and Dorothy Lamour leading remote exciting lives in gorgeous costumes in gorgeous settings. Meanwhile, the two little girls sang in amateur shows and school bands and by the time Juliette was 13 she not only had a rapidly matur-ing figure but an already matured voice.

She was 13 when, in 1940, she entered a midnight amateur show at a local theatre. It was wartime and Juliette, even then sure in her instincts, sang "There'll Always Be an England." She brought down the house. When the clapping finally dwindled she consulted with Maya, backstage, and went on to sing "The Woodpecker Song" as an encore. Dal Richards, a local band leader, signed her on the spot. For the next two years she sang with Richards's

band at the Hotel Vancouver's regular dinner and supper dances. Since Hilde-
garde, the American chanteuse, was at the height of her fame the 13-year-old
copied her example and called herself simply "Juliette."

At 15 Juliette saw Rita Hayworth in *Strawberry Blonde* and got her own
brown hair dyed bright yellow. She has since bleached it to silver blonde. Juliette was already being billed as "Vancouver's singing sensation," and had her
own radio show. At 17 Juliette saw Dorothy Lamour in a movie and decided
to go glamorous: "She had a four-inch pompadour? I had a five-inch," she
recalls with guilty satisfaction. Even before that Juliette had joined comedian
Alan Young in Toronto for a season to sing on his Buckingham Cigarette
radio show. She was homesick and miserable and ate her way up to 180
pounds, which more than generously upholstered her five feet five inches. Back
in Vancouver during the next 10 years, she entertained at various Vancouver
night spots and assemblies; met Tony Cavazzi, a quiet, cricket-thin musician;
turned down a Hollywood contract; married Cavazzi; turned down a chance
to sing with Harry James's band; sang on radio; and stayed bulky.

In 1954 the Cavazzis moved to Toronto to tackle TV. During a guest
appearance on Holiday Ranch, Juliette was scouted by Billy O'Connor, the
leader of a small Toronto combo, and when his group got a spot on summer TV, O'Connor added Juliette as a singer. By the end of their second season together O'Connor and Juliette had clashed seriously enough to call it
quits. When the CBC decided to build a new little show around Juliette three
sponsors spoke for it: "Juliette's the easiest thing in the world to sell," comments Bob McGall, supervisor of CBC-TV variety. Player's Cigarettes won
out as sponsor.

The producer assigned to the show, Sydney Wayne, is a black-haired, tubby
young ex-stagehand who, in his spare time, composes highbrow music and takes
lessons in the European technique of acting that's inaccurately known on this
side of the Atlantic as The Method. He doesn't try to bootleg such tastes into
the studio, however. "Remember," he says coldly, "this is mass entertainment."
He further says, "We're not selling *oy veh*; we're selling pleasure."

Juliette is entirely content to help sell pleasure. "It's me," she says happily. "This show is me." It starts sharp at 11:10 on Saturday night, when the
band hits the signature tune, "Love and Marriage." The show's signature shot

is a full-blown rose lying across a sheet of music. Superimposed in a fluted script is the signature "Juliette." The signature was forged by a CBC artist; the rose is artificial; the music is a manuscript copy of a Prokofiev symphony picked because it looked suitably busy. The commercial announcer is Gil Christie, veteran of another audience-identification show, Tabloid. Christie portends Juliette each week with the same formula: "Now let's meet . . . and greet . . . your pet . . . Je-w-w-w-li-ette." He rocks on the first syllable as though getting his balance for the leap to the last.

Juliette appears, smiling, in a doorway up centre and descends some shallow steps while the band vamps an introduction to her first song. The stage set, which is supposed to represent her very own living room, has the glossy decor of a broadloom ad. The makeup of the show is as unvarying as the introduction. Juliette sings three and a half songs: the first is what she calls "a throw-away," some light catchy song like "When You're Smiling." She says "Hi there, everybody," with a big smile in her voice. Bobby Gimby and Roy Roberts enter camera range from either side and she links arms with both of them. The credits call them her "escorts" but she calls them "fellas" and says, "Hi there," adding a ripple of laughter to the big smile already noted in her voice.

Gimby, a youthful-looking man with narrow shoulders, spectacles and a perpetual look of innocent surprise, is an alumnus of The Happy Gang. He keeps his trumpet-playing small, to suit the show, and sings scat songs in a voice that's small with no effort. Roy Roberts, who looks like a retired hockey player gone a bit to fat, is this year's replacement for tenor George Murray, who has gone to Hollywood with his wife Shirley Harmer.

Juliette's second number is a bit bigger than the first, a ballad with an easy lilt, like "Catch a Falling Star," from the hit parade. Up in the control booth, Wayne produces athletically, twisting, jumping up, groaning out loud. "Dolly in closer," he yelps through the intercom. "Get rid of that cleavage. We're not selling sex; we're selling Juliette." When the camera dollies back Juliette sways forward from the waist in instinctive compensation. "That camera just seems human to me," she once said fiercely to an acquaintance. Then Juliette, Gimby and Roberts do a fast round robin of old tunes like "Bye, Bye Blackbird." Juliette sketches the words with her hands, fingers spread fastidiously as though her nail polish were still wet. The show closes with Juliette's big number, a standard like "Smoke Gets in Your Eyes," sung in a special set.

The whole thing's over in 20 minutes. She said recently, "Before you go on, your stomach's turning. But when you go out there the fear leaves you . . . the problems leave you . . . Then when it's all over your body's so limp you think you can't stand up."

Afterward she and Tony drive home in their last year's Olds 98 to their one-bedroom apartment in north Toronto where, on other nights of the week, she often sits and watches the big musical shows on the U.S. networks. "I get a kick out of Clooney. I watch her smile and I smile with her," she says. "Then I watch Dinah to see what she's wearing . . . and I love Patti Page. I love a mellow contralto sound." *She* has no trouble identifying with any of these stars. "A show I'd like to do," she mused recently, "is to emcee a large variety show." She pondered: "Do just three or four numbers myself . . . in a beautiful setting . . . in a gorgeous gown."

OUR PET, JULIETTE *continued on air until 1966, and was consistently one of the CBC's most popular shows. After it ended, Juliette did several TV specials and regular CBC-TV performances before retiring in 1984 to care for her husband, Tony, who died of Alzheimer's Disease in 1987. She now lives in Vancouver.*

How Wayne and Shuster Took New York

by Barbara Moon

JULY 19, 1958

WHEN JOHNNY WAYNE and Frank Shuster, Canada's only television comedians, went to New York City last month to substitute for Ed Sullivan as ringmasters of North America's best-known and longest-lived TV vaudeville show, it came as a fairly incredible climax to a fairly incredible few weeks.

Less than three months earlier, as all Canada knew, Sullivan had screened a film of one of the comedians' stylish TV spoofs and had promptly signed them to 26 appearances on his show in the ensuing 52 weeks. "Mark my words," he told them, "in six months you boys will be the hottest property on American TV." By the time Sullivan entrusted his entire Sunday night hour to Wayne and Shuster, the prediction no longer seemed far-fetched.

Indeed, it was well on its way to premature realization after the Canadians' first appearance with Sullivan. On his May 4 show, they did a parody of Julius Caesar, called Rinse the Blood off My Toga. Overnight everyone in U.S. show business knew about them, and about a line that had occurred several times in the script. Delivered by Toronto actress Sylvia Lennick, it went: "I told him. I said, 'Julie, *don't go!*'"

The critics called Wayne and Shuster's work "literate slapstick" and "civilized comedy." Their New York agent said, "Boy, it's like a brushfire." Several New York bars echoed a gag in their script by recaptioning the single martini a "martinus."

To reinforce the impact, Sullivan put his protégés on again the following Sunday, May 11, in a satire on the Scarlet Pimpernel called The Brown Pumpernickel. People began recognizing them on the streets and in restaurants. Strangers would say, "There go those crazy Canadians."

They'd already got a standing offer from a Las Vegas night club, a request from Random House for a book, and a feeler from a recording company. When Wayne wanted to see Say, Darling, a current Broadway play, while he was in New York, his agent wouldn't let him go: the request for tickets had been made so late in the day that only seats in the 20th row were available. "You're a star, baby," the agent explained patiently. "You gotta travel first class. You can't sit anywhere behind the eighth row."

They were not scheduled for the next two shows, but Sullivan decided to turn over the next show, the whole show on June 1, to the two Canadians to emcee. Sullivan needed the stand-ins because he was going to be absent in Europe lining up a future program.

On May 22, Wayne and Shuster did the last regular show of their 1957-1958 season on CBC-television. On May 26, they flew to New York to start preparations for the big assignment. It wasn't until June 13 that they knew definitely whether they'd ever work for CBC-TV again. On that day they became, by common consent, although the terms weren't announced, the highest-paid performers in Canadian television when they signed a CBC contract calling for five hour-long shows next fall and a sixth if their schedule with Sullivan leaves time for it. The CBC deal pleased them both for more than commercial reasons. Neither wants to move permanently to New York. Shuster won't even get a haircut there—he waits till he gets back to Toronto.

The June 1 Sullivan show was a triumph. A typically lyrical review appeared in Variety, the influential showbusiness weekly. It went, "Johnny Wayne and Frank Shuster are probably the freshest comedy team extant." Variety further reported that they'd be making 26 appearances in all and added, "If they do as well as they did on Sunday, it could probably be called the Wayne and Shuster show."

Everything that Sullivan and the CBS staff could do to ensure their success had been done. They got the star dressing room, heady praise, respectful attention, big money and the entire resources of Sullivan's well-oiled production machinery. Wayne and Shuster made their gratitude obvious. At the same time, they consistently acted as unofficial Canadian publicity agents. In a TV interview in Toronto they had insisted, "Canada is the big time. If you're good here you're good anywhere." In New York, they kept saying, "We like Canada."

In fact it was possible to see through the whole week in New York a quiet tug-of-war between the homefires and the lure of traveling abroad—first class. It started even before they arrived in New York. When Wayne phoned from Toronto to reserve rooms at Hampshire House, a posh residential hotel overlooking Central Park, the desk clerk asked courteously, "is that John Wayne, the movie star, or John Wayne, the television star?" Wayne, the swart, monkey-faced funnyman of the team, was assigned to the Empire Suite that Frank Sinatra occasionally occupies when he's on the east coast. Shuster, the sunny, soft-voiced straight man, was on the 15th floor. "You could learn to like this," he said.

The first day, they attended a preliminary production meeting at the CBS head offices on Madison Avenue. Sullivan's co-producer, Marlo Lewis, was in Europe till Thursday, so they were welcomed by John Wray, the director of the show. Wray, who is also a choreographer, is a gentle, nearly bald man with prominent light-blue eyes and a boyish smile. They discussed the line-up for the show. The other acts—seven of them—had been booked by Sullivan, some months in advance, some only the week before. They included a ballet troupe, a balancing act and five assorted singers ranging in genre from opera to rock 'n' roll.

In addition to emceeing the show, Wayne and Shuster were to contribute two "bits," the indiscriminate showbusiness term for anything less than a full performance. One was a song, "That's Television," that they'd pioneered on their Canadian show. Based on the errors, human and mechanical, that can sabotage a telecast, it was constantly to be interrupted by intricate patterns of contrived clumsiness on stage and on camera. The other bit, also a repeat, was penciled in as The $64,000 Squeal, a takeoff on The $64,000 Question. But five days earlier, on their final Canadian show, they'd introduced an off-beat baseball sketch in blank Shakespearean verse and Shuster, overriding Wayne's protests, insisted they try it on the American audience. "It's not as safe," he said, "but if it goes over it'll do more for us."

They spent the afternoon with the costume and casting departments and set designer Grover Cole. From the costume department they needed a complete set of baseball uniforms and accoutrements and sundry rig-outs for the TV song including a Valkyrie costume, size 44. From the set designer they needed a series of stage booby-traps and an authentic baseball dugout. The designer, an elegant young man who turned out never to have been inside a ball park, took himself off to Yankee Stadium to do research.

That night the comedians did some homework on ideas for opening and closing the show, and for introducing the other acts. "We didn't want to change the show," reports Shuster. "After all, we were just minding the shop for Ed. So we decided to do it the way he does: just introduce them and get off fast."

For the time being this was an academic decision: the acts weren't to show up for the first time until Sunday morning. On an ordinary Sullivan show most of the acts are singles—well rehearsed vaudeville or night-club routines. They go through their acts once in the forenoon on camera day, and only once more at a dress rehearsal in the afternoon, before a live audience. With two complex sketches, however, Wayne and Shuster were being given three days of rehearsal, plus an unprecedented camera rehearsal on Saturday. "Our stuff has a certain amount of production values," Wayne explains.

On Wednesday, rehearsals began in a big milk-processing plant on West 57th Street that CBS has converted into studios and staff offices. Wayne and Shuster had insisted that the authentic modal Elizabethan music written for the baseball sketch by their Toronto arranger, Johnny Dobson, be used on the show. The Ed Sullivan Show orchestra, under veteran Ray Bloch, wouldn't see the score till camera day, so a pianist accompanied the rehearsals.

Thursday morning, Marlo Lewis arrived back from Europe. Lewis, a big, heavily handsome ex-advertising man, with heavy-lidded eyes and a sunlamp tan, is Sullivan's co-producer and technical expert. He greeted the boys with an arm affectionately around each of their shoulders.

In Sullivan's absence, Lewis was responsible for the show, so over lunch in the cafeteria downstairs Wayne and Shuster checked their own plans with him. Over the din Wayne explained again, for Lewis's benefit, "We thought we'd follow the same format. We want to make it clear that we're just standing, as we say in Latin"—Wayne made a dewy-eyed *moue*—"in loco Sullivanis." Everyone at the table laughed.

"We've got a wonderful bit to introduce Jeanmaire," said Wayne. Jeanmaire is the prima ballerina of the Ballet de Paris, a French troupe that was to be featured on the show. Lewis nodded. He was already deep in the problem of timing the show.

"We've got a wonderful gag for the audience introduction," Wayne said after a minute. He explained: instead of introducing the usual celebrities in the audience they'd introduce a man named Julius Melnik, who'd been sitting in the audience every night for 10 years hoping to get on camera. He'd never been newsworthy enough before, but now he was, precisely because he'd been waiting for 10 years. "So the camera pans down," Wayne chortled, "only he's not there. Just an empty seat. But his wife's there. So we ask, where is he? So his wife says he just had to go outside for a minute. So we say, 'After 10 years he's not here when we're finally going to introduce him?' So his wife says, 'I told him. I said, Julie, *don't go!*' "

He paused, and then laughed to show he understood the impossibility of the gag: "We'd have to fly Sylvia down just for that one line." Lewis looked up. "I like it. It's funny. Do it."

Wayne said, "We've got a straightforward bit for the closing. It's sort of a friendly thing, very nice. You know, we're-the-only-country-that-won't-throw-rocks-at-your-embassy-so-c'mon-up."

Back in the rehearsal hall, Lewis watched a run-through of "That's Television," hugging himself the way Sullivan does. Wray, the director, asked if they'd like to do the baseball sketch now. In it, Wayne plays a catcher-in-a-batting-slump as though he were Hamlet, and Shuster plays the team manager as though he were Horatio. The script is an outrageous mixture of baseball lingo and Shakespearean borrowings.

Wayne said to Lewis, a bit anxiously, "This is a little different, but it's what we want to do." Lewis nodded and leaned forward to watch. He chuckled quietly all through it and sat smiling after they had finished.

Shuster said, "Johnny and I had a big argument about whether we'd do it."

"It's pretty risky," mused Lewis. "I love it myself," he added hastily.

Shuster said, "It's different. We wanted to be different."

Wayne broke in, "We tried it in Canada, you know."

"How did it go there?" asked Lewis.

Wayne said, "Swell. We had a lot of mail, a very good reaction." Lewis

*Johnny Wayne (left) and Frank Shuster clown around with
Ed Sullivan on his show, 1959.*

nodded several times, and then once decisively. When he got up to leave, a bit player called derisively, "Marlo, *don't go!*""

Friday morning, they rehearsed "That's Television" steadily for a couple of hours. Besides the comedians themselves there were 14 participants, each of whom had to come in precisely on cue to illustrate a single line of the song. A musical-comedy soprano had been hired solely to hit one top note and then burst into a coughing fit. She had a lusty voice and magnificently Wagnerian proportions, but when Wayne explained that he wanted a single Valkyrian ho-yo-to-ho, it turned out she'd never heard of Wagner. "I'll get a record and learn it, though," she promised.

Arthur Hiller, an ex-CBC producer who is now riding high in Hollywood, wandered into the rehearsal about noon on his way from Toronto to the west coast. Wayne and Shuster hailed him delightedly and introduced him to everyone as "a Canadian who's doing Big Things in Hollywood." Hiller and the comedians compared notes on the standard of U.S. technical production. Wayne said, "The difference is, in Toronto they have one guy trying to do five jobs; down here they've got five guys."

Hiller said, "Have you noticed how fast they can strike a set?"

Wayne said, "Well, you don't have to wait till the boys put down their copies of Proust . . ."

". . . and stroke their beards," finished Shuster. "A stagehand down here doesn't want to be something else. He just wants to be the best stagehand there is."

At rehearsal Saturday morning, the ample soprano, having contributed her single Wagnerian bar, came down into the dim house and settled herself in a front seat. "Those boys are so good," she said. "They flip me." Someone asked how she'd tracked down the cry of the Valkyrie. She rolled her eyes: "I tried all over, yesterday, to find a record," she said. "But I couldn't. Finally I found a girl friend and she knew it, so she spent last night teaching me. It's got a sort of scoop up to the top." She giggled, "Wait'll you see my costume. It's a gasser."

Shuster and Dobson, their music arranger, came down from the stage and sat in the row behind her. Shuster was still seeking reassurance about the baseball sketch. "My head will roll," he said. "I hadda argument with Johnny about whether we'd do another one . . . safe . . . but good. But *safe!*"

Brinkman, the stage manager, called, "Baseball sketch everyone," and Shuster climbed back on stage. "They had their own show in Canada, eh?" said the soprano. She reflected. "Would there be much work for a person my type in Canada?" she asked. A cameraman called to a six-year-old, obviously a relative, who was playing up the aisle toward the back of the house. "Watch *this* one, Gerry," he said.

The cameraman himself chuckled out loud all through the sketch. At the end he caught the soprano's eye and they nodded approvingly. The soprano glanced round at the circle of backstage people who'd gathered to watch. "If you're good around here," she said, "boy, you're *good.*" The cast went through the baseball sketch twice more. This time they were in costume, for the benefit of a photographer from *TV Guide.*

At two o'clock they were through. Wayne went to pick up his wife and three little boys, who had come by overnight train, to take them to the Bronx Zoo. Shuster went off with Dobson to see *Abner*, a musical comedy, and spent the evening quietly with relatives. His wife had house guests from New York and had to stay in Toronto.

Ed Sullivan called on Sunday morning, from the Savoy Hotel in London, to wish the boys good luck. They were at the theatre at 10:30 a.m., seeing the other acts in the show for the first time. There was Sallie Blair, a new young Negro discovery, who prowled through a torch song with glistening eyes and a voracious smile; Jimmie Rodgers, a young rock-'n'-roll record star with loose limbs and automatic rhythm; Edie Adams, the curvy blond wife of comedian Ernie Kovacs, who did a traditional ballad and then burst into a nightclub imitation of Marilyn Monroe; Mario Del Monaco, a beefy young Metropolitan tenor with well-manicured hands and a big voice; Doretta Morrow, a blond soprano from musical comedy; the Ballet de Paris troupe, and the Amin Brothers—the inevitable circus act for the benefit of the kiddies.

Wayne and Shuster rehearsed their two sketches for the first time with the full orchestra, under Ray Bloch, and many of the musicians laughed right out loud. The rest of the time the Canadians sat out in the house watching the stage.

Around noon, comedian Jack Leonard drifted in. A heavy man in sun-glasses with thick, furrowed features, he appears sporadically on the show and almost always drops around on camera day. He sat with the boys and greeted them: "Ah, the Jewish Mounted Police," in a penetrating voice. Wayne and Shuster doubled up with laughter. The Wagnerian soprano, resplendent in winged helmet and cuirass, clanked slowly up the aisle. "We got her from the Israeli tank corps," Wayne said to Leonard.

"Have you seen Sylvia?" Shuster asked. "I told her to come at one. She flew in this morning."

Sylvia Lennick came down the aisle, waved to everyone and sat down. "I've been in this business in Toronto for years," she said, "and nobody ever heard of me. I do one line on this show and suddenly I'm famous. They've got a drink at the Stage Door in Toronto now called the Big Julie."

The agents had begun to gather in the theatre for the afternoon dress rehearsal. They sat in the front rows, like cattle buyers at the corral fence, chatting quietly and watching the stage. A boy passed out matzoh-ball soup in cardboard containers and turkey-on-rye in waxed paper to the performers. The Amin Brothers were rehearsing on stage—one slim, swarthy Egyptian balancing a second slim, swarthy Egyptian on the balls of his feet, through a breathtaking series of pinwheel turns.

Dobson said, "These kids get flown in and knock their hearts out in rehearsal; then comes the show and Sullivan says, 'Okay, boys, knock it down to your best trick, make it 40 seconds.' " A cameraman broke in, "I'll say this for Sullivan, he can really pick out the fine points."

Wayne said, "We had a wonderful bit we were going to do. We were going to get this unicycle act and introduce it as the act Sullivan has had standing by for 10 years in case the show was short. Every week for 10 years he's flown them over from Italy just to stand by. So we were going to put them on at last. Only they've forgotten how to unicycle. They've spent the last 10 years just flying back and forth from Italy."

Shortly after 3 p.m., the balcony was opened to the public for rehearsal and began filling up. The pit, at the dress rehearsal, is reserved for people connected with the performers—agents and staff. Wray went to the control booth at the back to direct the show from there and, at 3:35 p.m., Lewis came on stage, greeted the audience, told them to watch their monitors during the "That's Television" number, introduced Wayne and Shuster and, brow knit, waved in applause fiercely from the balcony. The comedians ad-libbed a few warm-up gags and then started the show.

Wayne called out, "You better laugh at us, or we'll stone your embassy in Ottawa." The audience in the balcony, however, was fairly subdued until Jimmie Rodgers, the rock-'n'-roll star, was introduced. A crescendo of cheers and screams bounced down from the big dome.

"The balcony's filled with teenagers," said a CBS publicity man disgustedly. The show ran about eight minutes over time. While TV-emcee Bud Collyer, who was doing the live commercials in Sullivan's absence, rehearsed in a corner of the stage, Lewis, Wray, Wayne and Shuster went into a huddle in the boys' dressing room. They had been assigned to Sullivan's own dressing room on the second floor with Sullivan's own Coke machine in the corner.

Lewis decided to cut part of the ballet. Wayne and Shuster said both their sketches would be played faster on the show. "We'd rather pace it up than cut it," said Shuster. They had already speeded "That's Television" by, among other things, cutting out the soprano's ho-yo-to-ho. Now she simply mouthed the hard-won note and sputtered the cough.

By and by the boys slipped out to an automat for a quick coffee and some soup. When they came back they found their dinner jackets laid out, freshly pressed by the costume department. "In Canada, I wear it the way it comes from the suitcase," remarked Shuster. On their other appearances they had gone up to the make-up department on the seventh floor; this time the make-up man came to their dressing room.

At 7:30 p.m., the doors were opened to the theatre audience. Mrs. Wayne, with the three youngsters, was led to a seat in the front row. The house filled slowly. At 7:45 Shuster came down from the second floor to count the house from the wings. He thought it looked empty and mentioned it to Lewis. Lewis snorted. "There's a six-months' waiting list for tickets to this show," he said. "It'll be full by show time." The orchestra started tuning up.

Lewis was still making last-minute changes in the show. At five minutes to eight he told the boys he was switching the Metropolitan tenor with the musical comedy soprano. "Del Monaco's stronger than Doretta Morrow," he said. "We'll use him earlier." At three minutes to eight, Lewis came out on stage, welcomed the audience, asked for their applause, told them to look at the monitors during "That's Television," and introduced Wayne and Shuster. The Canadians came out and ad-libbed a few gags. "Don't be afraid to laugh out loud," said Wayne.

At eight o'clock the orchestra broke into the opening fanfare. The announcer's voice could be heard saying: ". . . the Ed Sullivan . . . Show!" The sponsor's billboard appeared on the monitors. In the second before their own faces would appear on the monitor and before an estimated audience of 40 million in the United States and Canada, Wayne glanced down into the audience at his wife and children. He and Shuster turned to each other and, solemnly, in the spotlight, shook hands.

At nine o'clock, Sullivan was on the phone from London to know how the show had gone. The house was still applauding and the stage was jammed with well-wishers and autograph seekers. The hour had gone so fast that Wayne and Shuster had had time for barely 20 seconds of hands-across-the-border at the end. Sylvia Lennick was limp; they hadn't got to her bit from the audience until 8:54. "I must have put on fresh lipstick 14 times in that 54 minutes," she said. A cameraman said, "Boy! The things that *really* went wrong on the "That's Television" bit! And the language on the intercom!"

Taking Sullivan's call in the wings, Wayne—his fist jammed in his free ear to keep out the noise—said it seemed to have gone all right.

WAYNE AND SHUSTER *made a record 67 appearances on The Ed Sullivan Show. Despite their popularity in the United States, they remained based in Toronto. Frank still lives there, but Johnny died of brain cancer at 72 in 1990. In three and a half decades of CBC-TV specials, the team became a Canadian institution.*

The Man Behind Jake and The Kid

by McKenzie Porter

SEPTEMBER 13, 1958

TOWARD THE END OF next year, CBC-TV will probably begin screening the adventures of *Jake and The Kid*, whom W.O. Mitchell has made two of the best-known figures in Canadian fiction. For 16 years stories of the homespun prairie philosopher Jake, and his sensitive 12-year-old pal The Kid, have appeared periodically in *Maclean's*. For five years before the introduction of Canadian TV, in 1954, they were the subjects of a popular weekly series of CBC radio sketches.

The delay in bringing *Jake and The Kid* to the television screen has been occasioned largely by Hollywood interests which engaged Mitchell in protracted and unsuccessful negotiations for the American TV rights. Now that plans for Hollywood production have collapsed, Canada's National Film Board is making 26 half-hour *Jake and The Kid* movies which CBC-TV intends to exhibit over two winter seasons of 13 weeks each beginning in the fall of 1959.

The gentle comedies are set in the mythical prairie village of Crocus. Around *Jake and The Kid* move many other prairie types such as Repeat Golightly, the gabby barber; Miss Henchbaw, the acerbic schoolmarm; Way Freight Brown, the droll station agent; and Old Man Gatenby, a septuagenarian who is addicted to love stories, food fads and vendettas. The tales reek of galluses, denims and long johns; of salt pork, chewing tobacco and linseed cake; of gophers, cowponies and combines; and of chinook winds swirling clouds of topsoil and faraway horizons. In the world of

Mitchell's imagination, city folk are a fleeting phenomenon, a mere haughty blur set in a ribbon of amber light as the CPR transcontinental goes hollering through the prairie night.

William Ormond Mitchell, a 44-year-old native of Weyburn, Sask., soaked up prairie atmosphere during the Depression, when he paid his way through the University of Manitoba by working as an itinerant laborer and door-to-door salesman. Later he earned his living as a schoolteacher and wrote fiction in his spare time. He was teaching part-time in High River, Alta., in 1947, when his first published novel, *Who Has Seen the Wind*, was acclaimed by critics as a masterly panorama of life on the prairie. The novel rolled up $14,000 in royalties and ever since Mitchell has lived by the pen alone.

Another of his novels, *The Alien*, a brooding study of a part-Indian schoolteacher caught between two worlds, won a *Maclean's* $5,000 Novel Award in 1953. Last winter one of the CBC's most-lauded TV dramas was Mitchell's *The Devil's Instrument*, a compassionate commentary on the stern morals of the western Hutterite sects.

The author lives with his tiny, dark, pretty wife Merna in a modern ranch-type bungalow at High River, a small foothills town 30 miles south of Calgary. They have three children, 14-year-old Ormond, 12-year-old Hugh, and three-year-old Willa, and own four saddle horses, a retriever and a poodle. Mitchell does most of his writing in a studio at the back of the house. Sitting here, against a background of shotguns, rifles and fishing rods, he looks at first glance more like an off-duty infantry officer than a man of letters. He carries his slight, erect frame on a springy stride. His short black hair, flecked with grey, and his firm, well-tanned features, are embellished with a fierce military mustache. The impression of soldierly phlegm is heightened by a stentorian voice, an aromatic pipe, and a taste for thick tweeds, knitted ties and Edwardian waistcoats.

But Mitchell's literary brilliance is betrayed by the big grey eyes he inherited from Scottish and Irish ancestors, eyes that are sometimes ablaze with his hatred of sophistication, sometimes abulge with his braying, galvanic mirth, and sometimes misted over by the drift of his creative reveries. When he is abstracted by fiction plots he slips over the edge of reality. A couple of years ago he held a ladder while Merna, who suffers badly from vertigo, climbed valiantly to the bungalow roof to do some shingling. The plan was that Mitchell would climb to another section of the roof, allay Merna's fear and share the labor. But as he was carrying the ladder around a corner of the house a plot began to simmer in his mind. He dropped the ladder to the grass, meandered away, and left his wife "frozen" to the roof for two hours.

If he is not brooding over plots, Mitchell is usually hunting for new character traits and fresh expressions. He spends hours shooting the breeze on the steps of the High River post office with farmers, ranchers, horsemen, cowboys, storekeepers, mechanics, Hutterites, Indians, Chinese cooks and passing bums. During these colloquies he's apt to take a notebook from his pocket and write down a bit of salty philosophy or folksy humor. Once an old cowboy, complaining of the drought, said to Mitchell: "It's enough to make a gopher's tail burn." In his next story Mitchell switched the expression to: "It's enough to give a gopher heartburn."

He writes by night, groaning and sweating as he gropes for words. John Drainie, the Toronto actor who played Jake in the radio series, learned one night how exhaustively Mitchell explores the vocabulary. Dining with the writer he was puzzled to see a jar of varnish on the table. Throughout the meal Mitchell sniffed at it periodically. At first Drainie was too polite to comment but eventually he exploded: "Bill! What in hell goes on?" Mitchell explained: "I've been trying for a week to find words to describe the smell of varnish. And I can't. And, dammit, it's driving me crazy!"

Although he writes tenderly, Mitchell reacts toughly to unreasonable criticism of his work. For years the CPR derived publicity from the fact that Mitchell set Crocus on that company's transcontinental track. Yet once, after a *Jake and The Kid* radio show, a CPR official rebuked the CBC for permitting Mitchell to ridicule, in the sardonic words of Way Freight Brown, the "wood notes wild" of the company's travel posters. From that day forth Mitchell set Crocus on the CNR line.

When Gordon Sinclair, the TV personality and columnist, suggested in the *Toronto Star* that Mitchell was "drying up," the author was stung to a quick revenge. He inserted into a *Jake and The Kid* radio sketch a character named St. Clair Jordon. In playing this part the Toronto actor Tommy Tweed imitated Sinclair's brassy voice. The story presented St. Clair Jordon as a prodigal son of Crocus who had made a great name as a war correspondent. Yet during a patronizing return to Crocus, St. Clair Jordon dismayed the inhabitants by proving too timid to stop a runaway horse.

On sight of Sinclair, Mitchell's face still turns to stone. But his enemies are few. Writers, actors, musicians and painters, east-bound or west-bound through Calgary, drop in at the Mitchells' High River home in a year-round cavalcade. They find multifarious other guests, such as Ronald Brown, a millionaire stockholder in Home Oil Ltd., W.G. Hardy, head of the department of classics at the University of Alberta, Vincent Stanley, a High River men's clothier, or Pete Dixon, an Indian chief, enjoying Mitchell's hospitality and entertainment. Peter Francis, who produced the *Jake and The Kid* radio series, has described Mitchell as "the sort of raconteur who soon has everybody rolling about the floor with laughter and pleading with him to stop." Mitchell acts out his stories with vigorous mugging, arm waving, mimicry,

W.O. Mitchell at work at his home in High River, Alta., 1948.

ventriloquism and even choreography. To give force to an element of surprise or climax he may suddenly execute a spectacular back-flip.

At a party two years ago, Mitchell did his imitation of the late Mackenzie King discussing family allowances with a French-Canadian habitant. Bruce Hutchison, the writer, laughed so much that he had to be revived. What revived him was the odor of the goose that Merna was serving for dinner. Mitchell feeds his guests like 18th-century squires. They eat massive helpings of deep-frozen wild fowl, venison and trout bagged by their host in a relentless exploitation of every hunting and fishing season.

On summer Sunday mornings, Mitchell breaks his usual routine by rising early. On his back patio he fries pisa-like towers of pancakes and then bawls, in a voice that scatters local chickens, "Come and get it!" Every neighbor within earshot knows he's welcome to breakfast. With Merna tending an enormous coffee pot, up to a score of guests will gather, feast, and then loll around until noon listening to Mitchell's inspired rantings.

As a family the Mitchells are amiably indifferent to time. There isn't a clock in the house. Mitchell claims he can guess the hour to within five minutes by the sun. But this talent is often dormant. A few years ago, when the Toronto author Marjorie Wilkins Campbell stayed overnight with the Mitchells, it was important that she should arise early to catch a morning train. Mitchell assured her she would be called. But in the morning Mitchell was oblivious to the sun. Mrs. Campbell awoke herself, with only a few minutes to spare before train time. She dressed hurriedly and crept out of the house, leaving the entire family slumbering blissfully. "You take the Mitchells as you find them," she says, "and you leave them with a mixture of love and awe."

For some years the Mitchells were as indifferent to city amenities as to time. After much goading by relatives, however, they installed indoor plumbing. When the equipment was ready for use Mitchell made the occasion ceremonial. He telephoned his mother-in-law, Mrs. S.N. Hirtle of Vancouver, and said, "You are now going to hear something that will do your dear heart good." He then pressed the lever, held out the receiver, and, at a distance of 500 miles, let Mrs. Hirtle listen to what she regarded as a long-overdue gurgle.

Throughout his life Mitchell has displayed an uncommon temperament.

He inherited artistic talents from his father, the late Ormond S. Mitchell, a prosperous Weyburn, Sask., druggist, who had raised his University of Toronto fees by reciting poems on concert platforms. Mitchell senior died when William Ormond, the second of four sons, was six. Mrs. O.S. Mitchell reared the family comfortably on her husband's estate. But she had her troubles. In infancy Mitchell developed a tubercular wrist and had to carry his arm in a brace. He acquired his secondary education at a boarding school in St. Petersburg, Fla., and so lost touch with Weyburn boys of his own age. Unable to participate in vacation sports at home, he took to wandering about the prairies alone. The solitude induced introspection and developed his imagination. Once he picked up a copy of *John O'London's Weekly*, an English literary review, liked it, took out a subscription, and developed writing ambitions. Even in his late teens, when his wrist had recovered and he had become a high diver and gymnast of repute, he still dreamed of an author's life.

While studying for an arts degree at the University of Manitoba, he wrote a novel about a man who turned into a goldfish and communicated his plight in the bowl by blowing Morse code bubbles. A publisher's letter of rejection advised Mitchell to shun the fanciful and stick to reality.

When Mitchell graduated, the Depression was at its deepest and he couldn't get a regular job. So rather than sponge on his mother he tramped all over the prairies working as a casual farm laborer. Riding the rods to a distant harvesting he fell in with a hobo who earned a few dollars by making egg-stands out of baling wire. Mitchell spent many weeks with the hobo, helping sell the stands from door to door. Out of this experience flowered about a dozen short stories which were rejected, says Mitchell, "because I over-idealized the life of the nomadic bum."

In 1934, Mitchell decided his talent was in need of European inspiration. Armed with a tiny legacy he set off to tour Britain and France on an old motor bike. He soon proved himself unable to cope with the complexities of densely populated areas. He tottered off a Greek cattle boat in London, green with the nausea that sprang from a trans-Atlantic diet of curry twice daily. Two hours after he landed, he was doped and robbed of half his cash "by a little old dockside landlady straight out of *Arsenic and Old Lace*." In Soissons, he collided with a streetcar. In Toulouse, he pitched his pup tent on a foggy night and awoke next morning to find himself reclining in the middle of a crowded suburban boulevard. After running out of funds and going without food for four days, he got a week's work riding behind contestants in the Tour de France bicycle race and throwing to the roadside crowds handbills advertising an athletic supporter. Next, he kept himself by doing a dangerous high-diving act at Biarritz. Before his mother sent him the fare home, he was reduced to helping a monkey pass the hat around for an Austrian organ grinder.

On his return to Canada, he started writing stories about Russian counts who made love to mysterious blondes in luxurious Riviera hotels, and about hunchbacked spies who skittered, dagger in hand, along the alleys of the Place Pigalle. He didn't sell a line, so he planned to seek inspiration in South America. In Seattle, he tried in vain to ship aboard a south-bound freighter as a deckhand. While there he took an extramural course in short-story writing at the University of Washington. "This taught me," says Mitchell, "that successful writers write about people and places they know."

Early in the war, when he was keeping himself in Calgary by selling oil rights, life insurance and radio-station ads, he harked back to his harvesting days and recalled an old homesteader whose hobby was "figurin'." With the stub of a pencil the homesteader passed his evenings working out how many cups of tea it would take to fill the south cowpasture slough, or how many grains of wheat would be required to lay an unbroken line of them from Regina to Saskatoon. Out of this congenial old gaffer Mitchell developed his first conception of the younger, and wiser, Jake. As a foil to Jake, Mitchell settled for The Kid, an approximate re-creation of his own boyhood personality. The resulting story, You Gotta Teeter, he sold to *Maclean's* in 1942.

That year he was also selling encyclopedias from door to door in Edmonton. While selling a set to the late Rev. S.N. Hirtle, a Baptist pastor, he made a date with Merna, the minister's daughter, and soon afterward married her. Seeking security, he started high-school teaching in Alberta, first at Castor, then at New Dayton and finally at High River. There he wrote more stories for *Maclean's*, limited his teaching to part-time substitute work, and finished *Who Has Seen the Wind?*

Published in 1948, this novel was described by the *New York Times Book Review* as "a piece of brilliantly sustained prose, a very beautiful, keen,

perceptive rendering of human beings engaged in the ordinary, almost mysteriously meaningful, drama of every day." With the $14,000 in royalties,
Mitchell built his bungalow. Then, turning against the prairies once more, he
accepted a job in Toronto as fiction editor of *Maclean's*.

The Toronto cost of living stunned him and he rebelled by buying
$6 suits at discount houses. In the office he wore what he called his smoking
jacket, a thick black garment made of horse-blanket material. Once he
turned up at work in running shoes, and on another occasion, through
absent-mindedness, appeared wearing one stout shoe and one bedroom
slipper. He was notorious for giving the most hopeless aspirants to literature
hours of encouragement and advice.

In 1949, 18 months after settling in Toronto, Mitchell sold *Jake and The
Kid* to the CBC. On receiving Jake's part in the weekly radio episodes, John
Drainie predicted accurately that the series would be successful. Drainie also
anticipated the danger of a boy actor's voice breaking before the show out-
ran its popularity, so the part of The Kid was played for five years by a
woman, Billy-Mae Richards, a Toronto violinist and housewife. In the early
days of radio's *Jake and The Kid*, Mitchell played a few bit parts himself, and
then quit because he decided that such participation was unfair to professional actors. After this, he returned to the mike only once—as the squeaky
voice of a gopher.

Meanwhile, Mitchell's two sons, affectionately known to their dad as
Ormie and Hughie, and to their dad's many friends as "those little hellions,"
were being transformed by the confinement of city life into wildcats. When
Mitchell entertained he had to shout above the racket of Ormie and Hughie
steeple-chasing over the chesterfield, chicken-dancing around the table, or
bashing out discords on the ancient piano. During one party, Mitchell persuaded the boys to go to bed by promising to tell them a story. Downstairs,
for more than an hour guests listened to Mitchell's distant droning. Then
there was a silence that was shattered by Ormie yelling for a glass of water. "I
thought you were in bed," cried Merna. "We can't get into bed," bawled
Ormie. "Dad's there, fast asleep."

For three years, Mitchell tried to come to grips with city life but was
forever thwarted by a hex. Once he dropped Merna at the Medical Arts

Building on Bloor Street. He said he would park the car and join her in the doctor's office. But before he parked, his mind began to dwell on a story and he "came to" in a strange part of the city. Two hours later he found his way back to the Medical Arts Building. By this time he'd forgotten the doctor's name and he began a vague search of the building. But Merna had seen the doctor and was hunting for her husband around the Bloor Street parking lots. Meanwhile, Bob Needham of the Toronto *Globe and Mail* was making his way toward the Mitchell home as a dinner guest. He told his taxi driver to move slowly along the street as he was not sure of the house. Then he saw a crowd, a fire engine and a dwelling in flames. Knowing of his hosts' vulnerability to disaster, Needham cried: "That's it. That must be the Mitchells'."

From firemen, Needham learned that Ormie and Hughie, fighting with wet towels in the bathroom, had shorted a faulty plug and set the place alight. About eight in the evening, Mitchell and Merna found each other and hurried home to the hungry Needham. As the power had been cut off, Merna lit candles and prepared a cold meal. Just as the party was sitting down to dine, in a dimly lit atmosphere of smoke, acrid smells and dripping water, the fire broke out again. A few weeks later, Ormie and Hughie escaped into the street naked. The neighbors got up a petition protesting against the Mitchells' way of life. The Mitchells' landlord asked them to move.

Merna realized now that in the city Mitchell was as unhappy as a wild pinto in a circus. Shortly afterwards, he realized himself that the prairies wanted him back, and were exercising over him an unbreakable spell. He resigned from *Maclean's*, recited a sparkling string of self-deprecatory anecdotes at his farewell party, and returned with his family to High River. At first the neighbors out there couldn't understand why the Mitchells were all "eatin' reglar." When Mitchell explained that he was a writer they said, "Yes. But what do you do for work?" After a time, however, the High Riverites realized that Mitchell works hard while they are sleeping. Now they are looking forward to Mitchell's latest novel, a yet-untitled work, about the battle between a prairie small-town newspaper editor and an inquisitive social scientist from the city.

Mrs. McCorquodale, the editor of *The High River Times*, says: "If snatches of High River conversation pop up in Bill's work there will be no sense of outrage or betrayal. The neighbors know that Bill has an honest liking for human beings without trappings or affectations and that when he brings them into his stories he is laughing not at them but with them."

The finest testimony to Mitchell's place in the hearts of Westerners was voiced a few years ago by the late Senator D.E. Riley, of High River, who, employing the understatement of frontier vernacular, said: "That Mitchell's a bit on the clever side. But he's a nice young fellow. He'll do to take along."

THE "YET-UNTITLED" *novel was* Roses Are Difficult Here, *which was not published until 1990. In total, he wrote eight novels and more than 300* Jake and the Kid *radio scripts. He won the annual Stephen Leacock Medal for Humour twice, and among his plays was the award-winning* Back to Beulah. *Mitchell died in Calgary of prostate cancer in 1998 at age 83, two months before Merna also died of cancer at 78.*

Bruce Hutchison Visits Zsa Zsa Gabor

by Bruce
Hutchison

MAY 23, 1959

HOW I GOT INTO THE clutches of Miss Zsa Zsa Gabor (pronounced Gabour to rhyme with amour) I can't rightly say. One thing led to another. This affair, let it be understood from the beginning, was innocent on both sides, highly intellectual and pure to the point of horror. But it didn't turn out as planned.

It had been planned as a scientific inquiry into a major North American phenomenon—an impartial analysis of Hollywood's primary commercial product, loosely called Sex Appeal, as pre-eminently represented by the Hungarian enchantress. It turned out instead to be a rather ghastly joke. The joke, of course, was on me. Miss Gabor saw to that with her unequaled experience and a cunning which I can only call diabolical. But I forgave her everything. She and her fellow practitioners are greatly misunderstood.

Having flown across the continent to interview a love goddess, I saw that a man had been sent on a boy's errand the moment I entered her mansion outside Los Angeles. I was too old for this grim kind of work and much too naïve. The mansion's owner (as I learned too late) had been trained from girlhood as an expert fencer and had kept herself in athletic training. Now she stood at her doorway alert, taut, *en garde*.

She was dressed for combat, armored in martial crimson from head to foot. The long, shapeless housecoat revealed nothing but a nimbus of argent hair, an exquisite face of glazed ceramic and two tiny hands. They gripped an invisible rapier. Armed with nothing more than a pencil, a notebook and a simple, rustic faith, I faced a deadly duel.

Not that Miss Gabor was impolite or inhospitable. She was charming, overpowering, delicious. She squeezed my hand warmly, dazzled me by a smile that would keep the St. Lawrence ice-free all winter, laughed gaily in a soft, metallic tinkle and expressed a deep admiration for my country, my profession and my mind. She didn't even complain, though I had arrived a full hour late after losing myself in a maze of disjointed roads. In short, she was obviously relieved to recognize me as a quaint, primitive type from the northern wilderness, an elderly sitting duck. For an international siren who had dismissed three rich husbands, was planning to acquire a fourth and had deliberately scandalized her nation of adoption year in and year out, the thing was too easy.

The duellist took one look at her victim, sheathed her weapon and offered me a drink. Wishing to keep my head clear for the work before me, I suggested coffee. That, she confessed, as she drew me into a bottomless chesterfield, would be difficult. She had just hired a new maid and "in Hollywood, you know, a new maid is equal to a nervous breakdown." However, coffee soon appeared from nowhere in a splendid silver pot. Miss Gabor's tiny hand lifted the pot and, in a delicate, stylized gesture, as if she were doing it on the stage, filled my cup. Two lumps of sugar and a special smile were added "for such a sweet gentleman."

This ritual gave me a chance to look around the magnificent room filled with *objets d'art*, priceless bric-a-brac, an amorous French poodle, two minute, yapping Yorkshire terriers and Miss Gabor's palace guard. Taking no chances, she had stationed her press agent, a dour, protective person, in the background lest my questions prove difficult. She had summoned her personal autobiographer, Mr. Gerold Frank, a brilliant and likeable man, for intellectual support, I suppose. She had also provided a photographer, who crawled all over the floor exploding flash bulbs. This defense in depth, as she must have realized at once, was quite unnecessary. When the photographer asked me to move closer to her on the chesterfield she patted my hand in reassurance. I was harmless.

It had been agreed in advance with the press agent that the purpose of my mission would not be crudely stated in this chaste home. The phrase "sex appeal" would not rear its ugly head. Miss Gabor, as I had been warned, rarely gave interviews. Her personal life (though explored in the papers every day) was sacred and her real interests, I gathered, were in higher things like acting and painting. Still, if I would keep the conversation on that lofty level she would see me. I promised her now that I would abide by these rules. She nodded approval as I repeated the agreement with comic solemnity. You might have thought that we were assembled to negotiate nothing less than world peace.

Avoiding the forbidden word sex, I asked Miss Gabor to explain the

Zsa Zsa Gabor entertains Bruce Hutchison at her Hollywood mansion, 1959.

mysteries of glamour, a more dignified word for the commercial product which is discussed and sold in Hollywood the way an economist discusses the national income or a broker sells shares of United States Steel. While Miss Gabor was considering the question, I took the opportunity to observe the subject of the investigation more closely. She was not the person I had expected to see.

What, you may ask, had I expected? Again, I can't rightly say. Perhaps a dumb, hot blonde with seductive perfume and rehearsed answers from an old script; or possibly a blue angel like the early Dietrich in fluffy garters; or maybe a Theda Bara in metal brassiere as remembered from my panting youth. In any case, I expected something ludicrous, the material of a little harmless parody and, with luck, even a morsel of information. The Love Goddess, contemporary version, was nothing like that. For one thing, she didn't wear perfume or display her figure. For another, unlike most actresses, she was prettier in life than in motion pictures, much smarter and—despite her reputation—strangely chilling.

On the screen she might appear boisterous and ardent but in life Miss Gabor (though no one will believe it) made me think of a china figurine, or a doll of porcelain, skilfully articulated and wired for sound, or an old-fashioned miniature painted on a snuff box—a beautiful miniature, mind you, the work of a master, but painted and unreal. Her hair floated in a cumulus cloud shot with streaks of silvery light, but coldly dark at the roots. (If that platinum color was artificial an able metallurgist had done the job.) Her face was finely chiseled by nature and glazed by art in a flat, uniform buff color, except for the scarlet lips. The hazel eyes were darkly ringed with accurate draftsmanship. From their outer edges two coal-black lines had been penciled obliquely upward for at least three quarters of an inch and were worn candidly as a sailor wears tattoo marks. The general effect was wholly pleasing and artistic—just good, honest design intended to deceive no one.

Again no one will believe it, but the impact of this extraordinary person was coldly impersonal, as she no doubt desired. Other men no doubt have regarded her differently but I felt myself to be in the presence of a statue. The first siren of my acquaintance was as sexless as a knife and equally sharp.

Miss Gabor turned on me her luminous eyes and an air of puzzled inquiry almost believable.

"What is the question?" she asked.

"Glamour," I said, secretly trembling lest I should forget myself and use a more common word. "How do you explain glamour?" She knew what I meant all right but she needed time to think out an answer as phony as my question.

Glamour, she began, by way of evasive action, came from childhood training among the best people, from manners taught in a fashionable home, from the right school and the right clothes. These things she had been taught in Budapest, in Vienna and at a finishing school in Switzerland. "My mother and father," she explained, "instructed me what to wear, how to talk, how to enter a room—you know, everything a girl needs to know. That's glamour."

All this, of course, had nothing whatever to do with the question, as she was well aware. My expression must have indicated that I considered her remarks sheer nonsense and I could see that she was irritated. "If," she said defiantly, "a woman has a pretty face and a good figure and a million dollars, that's glamour enough for any man."

Miss Gabor persisted in equivocation by citing an example of spurious glamour. A certain famous actress (whose name I was forbidden to use but who certainly has the primary Hollywood product in abundance) was a friend of hers, a dear dear friend, and so beautiful that everyone gasped as she entered a room. "But when she opens her mouth," said Miss Gabor, "it's all ruined. She can't talk. She didn't go to the right school. The glamour—it just evaporates. Like that!"

"Garbo had it," she said irrelevantly, "and so had Harlow, and Dietrich, and Monroe and Liz Taylor."

"And you?" I ventured.

At that she shrugged modestly and repeated that she had been brought up well. I decided to infringe the formula and put the thing bluntly: "Why do men like you?" Another tinkle and a good show of girlish confusion as she replied: "I just don't know."

That statement probably had the advantage of being true. At any rate, our investigation was getting us nowhere. The love goddess, a perplexed oracle, perforce gave her answers in riddles. I went over it again, laboriously, clumsily, idiotically. Miss Gabor listened intently, a frown of deep reflection furrowing the lovely brow. The ceramic glaze took on a sharper glint. She deftly switched the subject from female to male glamour on which, I assume, she is a recognized authority. "There are 30 or 40 perfectly wonderful, beautiful men in Hollywood," she affirmed. "It makes you swoon just to look at them. But when they start to talk! Why, every last one of them only wants to buy a ranch and be a cowboy. If I had to spend a whole day with a man like that I'd blow my brains out for boredom. No, they haven't any glamour."

In England, though, things were a little better. Sometimes she had found the real thing there—"the young lord, perfectly dressed, perfectly mannered, with a castle in the country and race horses and, you understand, everything." Her face lighted up at these memories, but briefly. Alas, she sighed, these glamorous young nobles usually were yokels at heart, only interested in horses, hunting and crops. They soon bored her. Good heavens, how young men bored her! That, I inferred, was why she sometimes befriended but never married them. Hence the list of eligible candidates for Miss Gabor's tiny hand might appear to be extensive but was quite limited after all. A Turkish ambassador when she was 16, then the hotel tycoon, Conrad Hilton, then George Sanders, the actor and her "dream man"—these alone had qualified so far as husbands. But the engagement finger of her left hand reminded me that there would shortly be a fourth. That finger was freighted with the biggest diamond I had ever seen. To avoid exaggeration I must state that, contrary to general report, it was not as big as a hen's egg. It was only the size of a bantam's egg; that is, an unnaturally large, overgrown bantam.

The owner saw me gaping at this jewel. She caressed it fondly and raised one black eyebrow to acknowledge my astonishment, though in point of fact I was only wondering whether she could get her left glove on and how she managed to raise her arm under the weight of its cargo. (Her matching diamond earrings, half an inch in diameter, would have kept the average family in comfortable retirement.) The ring gave Miss Gabor another chance to dodge my questions. She forgot herself and violated the terms of reference to announce: "I'm engaged to a distinguished and wonderful gentleman. This is his ring. It's a blue diamond. Or perhaps you didn't notice?"

One might just as easily have ignored a searchlight in a dark sky. "Can you imagine it?" she demanded with a convincing expression of distaste. "Some people actually say I'm marrying this distinguished and wonderful gentleman just for his diamond!"

"Outrageous!" I said but didn't ask the gentleman's name. It lay outside the terms of reference. "Or they say," she went on, "that I'm marrying him for his fine house!" (A house equipped, I had been told, with an endless spiral pool enabling the residents to swim from room to room.) "What would I want with another house? Why would I ever give up this beautiful house that I love?"

"Ridiculous!" I heard my voice saying in a tone of disgust.

Some people, she added, were even suggesting that she give the diamond back to its donor in proof of her integrity. Wasn't that outrageous? I agreed that it was outrageous.

"Everything you see," she exclaimed, "I paid for myself. Everything. I am a working woman. You understand?" I said I understood and I did, too. A few trifling gifts of friendship from admirers surely did not breach her strict code. Some churlish fellow in Congress had lately enumerated the costly favors allegedly bestowed upon her by the son of a Caribbean statesman and had uttered certain harsh comments on her habits, but that critic could never have seen the working woman. Otherwise he would have realized the simple truth—Miss Gabor had just been born with a genius of human affection, a great big loving heart. Her friends, she assured me, understood her motives, but the American press didn't and scandalously misrepresented her. "Yesterday," she recalled, "my agent handed me a pile of newspaper clippings about so high (the tiny hands indicated the height of at least a foot) and they said Zsa Zsa is this, Zsa Zsa is that—nonsense! I read one or two items and threw the rest on the floor. I pay no attention to newspapers. I don't need them. They need me."

What, I repeated firmly, about glamour? Didn't it include the quality of intelligence? "Oh, yes," she agreed enthusiastically. "Intelligence, of course."

Just as I thought she was dodging again, this curious woman uttered a penetrating comment on American civilization. The United States, she said, was in no danger of communism because it was too close to the Communist system already. "How's that again?" I demanded, and not too politely.

Her riposte was calm and, I thought, very shrewd. The American system, she said, had provided all the high living standards and everything else that the Communists only promised to deliver. They were merely imitating American life. So why change it? No need, therefore, to fear the Communists in America.

Did she believe in democracy? She said she did, but I detected a notable lack of enthusiasm. On second thought, she loved the principle of aristocracy as she had known it in her Hungarian youth. It was only right that the most talented, educated and elegant people should have greater rewards than the others, wasn't it?

I saw that under the brittle ceramic glaze she had an impish sense of humor. She could laugh at herself and she wouldn't make a fool of me—not quite—if I kept my place. I began to like her.

Moreover, I began to sympathize with her life of grinding labor. Why, I asked, did she work so hard in movies, television and night clubs? "I have to,"

she said simply, "because I like to live well. I must make money. I have my house to keep, my furniture, my Renoirs—you know."

The fluttering hands swept the room of treasures, all paid for by her honorable toil. I muttered my appreciation and remembered, privately, that her toil included weekly television advice to ladies in favor of an electric razor for use in shaving their legs. No one could work harder than that. What would happen, I inquired, if she ever found herself poor? Poverty, she assured me gravely, had no terrors for her. "My parents gave me a good education. I could make a living in many ways, in any station of life—interior decorating, clothes designing—oh, many different things. For the last two weeks I've been skiing in an old sweater and a pair of slacks and I was perfectly happy."

The newspapers, she repeated, never could understand her. Besides, "I'm always saying the most awful things when I shouldn't and the papers pick them up. I don't know why I do it."

For once a faint pink of embarrassment oozed across the buff glaze. Possibly to hide her confusion she picked up one of the two revolting Yorkshire terriers, a ball of fluff called Mr. Magoo, and pressed him to her bosom, kissed his nose and asked me if he were not beautiful. I detested the beast on sight and said he was the most beautiful dog I had ever encountered. Its twin barked jealously. They were useful stage properties.

She picked up a photograph in a silver frame. It showed a handsome woman in her late fifties, I estimated. This, she said, was her mother, the truly beautiful member of the family, whose three daughters owed all their beauty and charm to her. I saw no resemblance and declared that the two generations were practically identical.

The mother owned a jewelry business in New York City, Miss Gabor informed me, and was about to remarry, an event which delighted the daughter. The parents, I also learned, had christened Miss Gabor "Sari" after her godmother, the great Hungarian actress, Sari Fedak, but the child found it impossible to pronounce that name so instead called herself Zsa Zsa. Then she showed me a photograph of her father, a stout, soldierly figure, who was divorced from the mother but had the daughter's doting affection. Finally she produced a photograph of her own daughter, a sprightly girl of 12, whose father is Conrad Hilton. As was doubtless expected of me, I said it was impossible to believe that Miss Gabor had a daughter of this advanced age. She slapped my hand to acknowledge the false compliment and admitted archly that she could have a child much older.

Of course I wanted to ask her own age but my courage didn't go that far. The official biography handed to me by the press agent noted, in a masterpiece of ambiguity, that she had been born "on February 6." I would place that date at something just short of 40 years ago. Yet at the distance of a few feet Miss Gabor might be taken for under 30. It was only when we sat down again and resumed the weary duel that I observed at close range the minute lines, thinner than cobwebs, at the corners of her eyes where the glaze had begun to crack, invisible to any camera. The discovery that even love goddesses are not immortal depressed me. To tell the truth, this whole affair had depressed me hideously, though not as much, I dare say, as it had depressed Miss Gabor, but her sportsmanship and professional code maintained the farce to the end. While it had produced by way of information exactly nothing, at least the primary product had never been mentioned by name. In Hollywood that must have been a record of some sort.

As I rose at dusk to take my leave Miss Gabor pressed my hand again and raised a black eyebrow in a look of understanding. She was telling me that I hadn't been as silly as I appeared. "This," she asserted, "has been the most intelligent interview of my whole life!" I would have been insulted if I had thought that she expected me to believe her.

At the door the glaze was shattered momentarily by a last tinkle of sardonic laughter to reveal a flash of the Me behind the Zsa Zsa. "When you write your piece," she giggled, "I won't mind if you pull my leg—just a leetle."

That invitation was kindly meant but somewhat late. She had been pulling mine for the last two hours. And feeling suddenly decrepit, I staggered away from the potent distillation of champagne, quick silver and Sheffield steel—no, platinum. As I looked back through the huge picture window I saw a relaxed duelist in the only natural, unstudied act of the afternoon. She was crouching beside her stone fireplace; the housewife's tiny, practical hands were lighting a fire. The glaze had dissolved into an honest smile of satisfaction after a good day's work.

Alas, her moment of relaxation was to be fleeting. Just as I completed this report the newspapers carried a shattering postscript from New York: "Zsa Zsa Gabor says her scheduled marriage to Hal Hayes, wealthy building contractor, is all off because she is not madly in love." The duelist's rapier had struck again, unerringly at the heart. That news further depressed me. Miss Gabor's diamond will never look so well on any other hand.

Zsa Zsa Gabor now lives in Germany and Beverly Hills, Calif., with her eighth husband, Prince Frederic von Anhalt. She has also been romantically linked with Sean Connery, Richard Burton and Rafael Trujillo, Sr., the former playboy dictator of the Dominican Republic. Her latest movie appearance was in 1996, in A Very Brady Sequel.

Bruce Hutchison, one of Canada's most respected journalists and public commentators, won three National Newspaper Awards and wrote numerous books. A frequent contributor to Maclean's, *he died in Victoria in 1992 at age 91.*

Part Four

Making News

The Secret Life of Mackenzie King, Spiritualist

by
Blair Fraser

DECEMBER 15, 1951

For 25 years, Canada's famous Prime Minister was a practicing spiritualist. He believed that, through mediums, he had communicated with his mother, Franklin D. Roosevelt and even his dog Pat, after they had died. Here, for the first time, is revealed the best-kept secret of Mr. King's amazing career.

ONE WET SATURDAY AFTERNOON in October, 1948, William Lyon Mackenzie King lay ill at the Dorchester Hotel in Park Lane. His visitors were few and uniquely eminent. King George VI, Winston Churchill, Prime Minister Nehru of India—so the London press was keeping a close watch on the hotel lobby. Reporters were amazed when two plainly dressed women came in, asked for Mr. King's suite and were shown up immediately. The two women did not reappear. They were ushered out by a side door (they couldn't understand why at the time) and the reporters never did find out who they were—Geraldine Cummins, well-known medium and author of many books on spiritualism, and her friend and collaborator Beatrice Gibbes.

That was as close as any outsider ever came, in Mackenzie King's lifetime, to the best-kept secret of his career—the fact that the Prime Minister of

Canada had been for more than 25 years a convinced and practicing spiritualist. Actually the word is somewhat ambiguous. Mr. King was not a member
of the Spiritualist Church and spiritualism was not a religion to him: he
remained to the end of his days a good Presbyterian. But he did believe in the
life after death, not as a matter of faith but as a proven fact. He did believe
it possible to communicate with the departed, and that he himself had talked
beyond the grave many times with his mother, his brother and sister, and such
friends as Franklin D. Roosevelt and Sir Wilfrid Laurier. He did repeatedly
attend seances and have sittings with mediums in London and elsewhere.

To his real intimates he made no secret of these beliefs. Some of them
joined him many times in sessions with the ouija board at Ottawa. They knew
from his own lips what comfort he got from his "communion with the dead."
Members of his personal staff knew it too—in some cases Mr. King didn't
know they knew, but they all did. Everybody kept the secret, for an obvious
reason: If the facts were publicly known, people might have thought the
affairs of Canada were being conducted on advice from the spirit world.

Indeed, Mr. King had not been dead a fortnight before a statement to
that effect was published in the spiritualist weekly, *Psychic News*. His old
friend, the late Duchess of Hamilton, in an interview said Mr. King had
always sought spirit guidance in affairs of state. This was untrue—on Mr.
King's own testimony and on the evidence of those who knew him best. He
sought contact with his dead mother and brother and friends not to consult
them, but simply to talk to them.

Mrs. Helen Hughes, a pleasant Glasgow housewife who is one of the
best-known of present-day mediums and who sat with Mr. King often over a
period of many years, explained it to me over a cup of tea in the Psychic College, Edinburgh: "It was as if he had his mother living over here in Britain—
what would any son do, if he came here on business? He'd look her up; he'd
want to see her and talk to her. He didn't want her advice about public affairs,
for he knew more about them than she did. He wanted to know how she was,
whom she had with her. He wanted to talk to her about family matters."

Mrs. Hughes cannot recall a single instance, in all her sittings with Mr.
King, when there was any mention of public affairs. The only exception, if
you can call it an exception, was the question of Mr. King's own retirement

from public life. "He was warned," she said. "At least three years before he died, his mother told him he was doing too much, his heart wouldn't stand it. He took her advice in the end, but not soon enough."

Perhaps one reason he delayed was that he got opposite advice from President Roosevelt. He asked F.D.R.'s counsel at a sitting with Miss Cummins; the answer came back, "Don't retire, stay on the job. Your country needs you there."

After Mr. King had gone back to Canada, Miss Cummins got another message; the President had changed his mind. He now thought Mr. King's health too precarious for the load he was carrying, and urged him to retire at once. Miss Cummins passed the word along to Ottawa. (Perhaps I'd better say at this point that I myself am not a spiritualist and do not believe in these alleged communications from the next world. For the sake of brevity and

Mackenzie King with a portrait of his beloved mother at Laurier House,
where King lived from 1923 until his death in 1950.

clarity, I haven't bothered to use words like "alleged" and "purported" in every other sentence. Whether or not you or I believe these messages were real, the point is that Mackenzie King did believe it.)

At a later sitting with Miss Cummins he got a message from F.D.R. which did concern public affairs. The President told Mr. King to watch Asia—that's where the war danger lay. The Berlin airlift which was a focus of attention then was a side issue, a Soviet bluff. There was no mention of Korea by name, but F.D.R. did say he thought there'd be war in the Far East within two years. Miss Cummins recalls that the Prime Minister "seemed puzzled and a little shaken by this part of the communication. He said he made it a rule to ignore advice thus given, and trusted solely to his own and his advisers' judgment."

What he wanted from a medium, and what he normally got, was intimate converse with his own family. Like so many others, Mackenzie King became interested in spiritualism because he was a lonely and a sorely bereaved man. The mother to whom he was and remained devoted; his beloved brother Macdougall King, the doctor; his favorite sister Isabel—all had died in a few years. His bereavement was sharpened by the thought that he had not been at his mother's death bed. At her insistence he had gone back to his 1917 election campaign in North York, leaving her mortally ill; she was dead when he returned. Mr. King never quite forgave himself for this.

He was introduced to spiritualism by the late Marchioness of Aberdeen, who was herself a believer. Lady Aberdeen told him of Mrs. Etta Wriedt, an American "direct-voice" medium who acquired great fame in her day. It was Mrs. Wriedt who received in 1911 the gold watch bequeathed by Queen Victoria to "the most deserving medium" of the time. The Queen had intended the watch for her Highland gillie John Brown, a medium through whom she believed she could talk to her beloved Prince Albert. Mrs. Wriedt in her turn got the watch after having shown, to the satisfaction of British editor W.T. Stead, that she had received a communication from the spirit of Queen Victoria in July, 1911. Mrs. Wriedt decided before her own death that the Queen's watch ought to go back to England. She entrusted it to Mr. King, who took it there on his next visit and gave it to the London Spiritualist Alliance. There, mounted on a blue velvet cushion, it is still on display.

All that came later. In the early 1920s, Mr. King was convinced of the genuineness of Mrs. Wriedt's gift by the experience of a friend of his. The wife of a Liberal senator, now dead, had lost her father, and the father's will couldn't be found. After futile search she consulted Mrs. Wriedt. The medium told her it was in a chest of drawers in a house in France. She looked, and there it was. That's the story as Mr. King used to tell it.

Mrs. Wriedt used a silver trumpet from which, at her seances, the voice of the departed would proceed. An old friend of Mr. King recalled: "She'd put the trumpet in the middle of the circle and it would roll around and stop in front of the person about to receive a message. I remember the thing rolling up to me and giving me quite a rap on the shin. The voice that came out did sound very like a person I knew who had died. However, I was a bit shaken when she got hold of somebody who was supposed to be French. That trumpet spoke very bad French."

Apparently that didn't shake Mr. King, whose own French was rudimentary anyway. He became more and more interested in spiritualism as the years went by. For the last 20 years of his life he found time, on every trip to Britain, for sittings with various mediums.

Mrs. Helen Hughes remembers the first she ever had with him, in the early 1930s: "I had no idea who he was. They don't tell us, you know. All I knew was, a gentleman would be coming for a sitting at 10:30 in the morning. He just came in and sat down without saying anything.

"One of the voices I heard was a man who said he was his brother. Mr. King wanted to be told something about him, and it came through that he was a doctor. After a while I got the name, Mac. He said a lot about the family—he'd say: 'Do you remember, Willie, when we were children, do you remember so-and-so?' After it was over, Mr. King said, 'I know that was my brother. He spoke of things nobody else knew, nobody but the two of us.'"

Through Mrs. Hughes and the late Hester Dowden, another medium of considerable fame, Mr. King got in touch not only with the human members of his family but also with his beloved Irish terrier, Pat. Mrs. Hughes once reported to him: "Your sister is here, and she has a beautiful dog with her. The dog doesn't seem to have been very long over there (i.e., very long dead)." Mr. King was greatly impressed and told Mrs. Hughes a story he had told to many friends in Ottawa. The night before Pat died, Mr. King's watch fell off his bedside table "for no apparent reason"—he found it in the morning, face down on the floor, with the hands stopped at 20 minutes past four. "I am not psychic," Mr. King said, "but I knew then, as if a voice were speaking to me, that Pat would die before another 24 hours went by." Sure enough, that night Pat got out of his basket with a last effort, climbed up on his master's bed, and died there. Mr. King looked at his watch—it was 20 past four.

Mrs. Hughes's method, as a medium, is what they call "clairaudience"— she hears voices and reports what they say to the client. Sometimes, though not always, she can see faces and bodily forms. Sometimes she is in a trance, sometimes fully conscious, but in either case the message comes through in her own Scottish voice. Mrs. Wriedt was a "direct-voice" medium through whom the deceased could speak directly in his or her own early accent.

Hester Dowden and Miss Cummins got their communications by "automatic writing." Mrs. Dowden used to be fully conscious and made comments of her own, sometimes rather facetious and irreverent, on the messages coming through. Miss Cummins goes into a trance, she says, and loses consciousness completely before her hand begins to move across the page. She sits down and "goes into the silence," shading her closed eyes with her left hand; after a while her "control," an ancient Greek named Astor, announces his presence and begins to send messages from other departed spirits. Miss Cummins writes all this down in a rapid script with all the words run together, no spaces, and in handwriting that varies markedly as different "communicators" speak.

Mr. King's habit was to take the written messages off the foolscap pad, sheet by sheet as they were completed, and to keep the originals himself. He would send back copies to the mediums, often with comments of his own on the "evidential" material they contained. Of one message from President Roosevelt, reporting that F.D.R. had met Mr. King's mother, the Prime Minister said: "The phrases he used, the characterization, were exactly what I'd have expected from Franklin Roosevelt if he'd met my mother in life."

These spirit messages, the originals as well as the copies, are still extant in Ottawa and in London, but even now they are treated as closely secret.

None of the people associated with Mr. King's spiritualist activities will talk freely or willingly about him. Had it not been for an initial breach of silence just after Mr. King's death, they'd be even less willing to talk. Most of King's contacts with mediums in Britain were made through Miss Mercy Phillimore, secretary of the London Spiritualist Alliance. Miss Phillimore won't discuss Mr. King's interest in spiritualism, won't reveal to whom she sent him or when or where. But she will talk, very strongly and indignantly, about that unfortunate statement in *Psychic News* that he "always sought spirit guidance in affairs of state."

"Mr. King was an investigator," she said. "He did accept the spirit hypothesis and he had the courage to say so, but he never ceased to be critical in appraising evidence. He was a highly intelligent man with shrewd judgment, and to say he consulted mediums for advice in statecraft is preposterous. It is also outrageous, an insult to his memory."

Actually Mr. King seems to have behaved, in his psychic experiments, with all the caution and circumspection he displayed in other things. The London Spiritualist Alliance, founded under its present name in 1881, is one of the oldest organizations of its kind. It is regarded in spiritualist circles as a pretty careful investigator of mediums' claims, and it also has a reputation for secrecy. Ordinarily, I was told, the mediums didn't know who Mr. King was. Miss Cummins recalls that at her first meeting with him she thought he was a clergyman from New York City. She says she was so ignorant of Canada that she thought the capital city was Montreal, yet the messages on that first day included such relatively obscure names as W.S. Fielding, who was Mr. King's rival for the Liberal leadership 32 years ago, and Sir Oliver Mowat, a Premier of Ontario in Sir John A. Macdonald's time.

Mrs. Helen Hughes says she had been giving him sittings over a period of four years, sometimes two in a single week, before she knew his name. She learned his identity for the first time in 1937, at a party given by the Duchess of Hamilton at the London Spiritualist Alliance headquarters in Queensberry Place, South Kensington. One of the guests at that party was a Scotsman named J.J. MacIndoe, and it was he who first revealed that Mackenzie King was a spiritualist. He wrote a letter to the *Psychic News* just after Mr. King's death; the letter was published, and *Psychic News* promptly sent a reporter to interview the Duchess of Hamilton for more details. Both stories were widely reprinted in Canada.

With the secret thus broken, Miss Cummins wrote an appendix to the autobiographical book she was preparing, published this year under the title *Unseen Adventures*. It comprised a partial report of the two sittings she had with Mr. King in 1947 and 1948. Private and personal communications were deleted, but she did reveal that he had got messages from his family and from President Roosevelt. She sent proofs of the appendix to a friend in Ottawa who showed them to Mackenzie King's executors. One of them, Duncan MacTavish of Ottawa, was flying to England the next day on other business. Leonard W. Brockington, of Toronto, was already in London. Together they called to urge Miss Cummins and her publishers to suppress the story. Reluctantly, and at considerable cost and inconvenience, they agreed to cut out Mr. King's name and a number of identifying details, including the name of President Roosevelt.

In the book as published, the appendix is entitled Reminiscences of a British Commonwealth Statesman. Mr. King appears as S.M.; F.D.R. as X.Y.Z. Miss Cummins was rather taken aback when I turned up at Miss Gibbes's small house in Chelsea, already able from previous information to identify these pseudonymous characters and fill in a number of the deleted details. She is still worried lest she be accused of breaking faith in consenting to see me at all. In general, though, people who knew of Mr. King's beliefs are glad the story is coming out.

All spiritualists, the believers and the researchers alike, have an interest in letting the facts be known. They feel that if a man as eminent, as astute, as famous for realistic judgments as Mackenzie King was convinced their conclusions were genuine, they have a right to his testimony before the world. While he lived, his secret was kept with absolute fidelity, but they see no point in secrecy now. Moreover they are absolutely convinced that Mr. King himself would agree with them. He told several people here, in the later years of his life, that it was his firm intention to publish a full account of his psychic experiments and beliefs in the memoirs he then hoped to write. He hadn't quite decided whether this chapter would be published during his lifetime or withheld until after his death, but publish it he would, sooner or later.

He wanted to communicate his own unshakeable faith in the life after death. "People who don't believe in survival," he once said to Mrs. Helen Hughes, "haven't yet begun to live."

Therefore they feel that whatever Mr. King's executors may desire, his own wishes are served by publication of the facts. From the little I knew of Mr. King I think they're right. If Mr. King's belief has turned out to be true, and if he is indeed looking over my shoulder from some astral sphere, I don't think he'll mind.

Intrepid, The Biggest Private Eye of All

by McKenzie Porter

DECEMBER 1, 1952

The most secret of all cloak-and-dagger operations of the Second World War was directed by a mysterious millionaire from Winnipeg named William Stephenson. Here, for the first time, is the story of the man who pulled the strings which spiked Hitler's guns in the western hemisphere.

THIS IS ABOUT A MYSTERIOUS middle-aged Canadian millionaire who during the Second World War became the mastermind of British intelligence throughout the Americas. His New York City headquarters staff of more than 1,000 hand-picked Canadian men and women spoke of his doorkeeper as "Peter," of his secretary as "Gabriel" and of him as "God." Only a handful of them knew him by sight. Today his name is unfamiliar to the ordinary citizen, but he is known to the world's foremost industrialists, bankers and statesmen as Sir William Stephenson. He was knighted for his war services by King George VI and awarded the U.S. Medal For Merit, its highest civilian decoration, by President Truman.

After winning the MC, DSC and Croix de Guerre in the 1914-1918 war, Stephenson built up a fortune with capital derived from royalties on an ingenious can opener he found in a German prison camp. By the middle Thirties,

his financial interests were world wide and he was in a unique position for gar-
nering industrial intelligence. He provided Winston Churchill with ammunition for oracular speeches on the growing might of Hitler during the days of
Baldwin's blindness and Chamberlain's timidity.

In 1940, Churchill sent him to New York to command all his government's secret-service operations in the western hemisphere. Stephenson
directed an organization called British Security Co-ordination from an office
in Rockefeller Center on Fifth Avenue. The staff was mainly Canadian
because Canadians had a special facility for getting on with Americans and
could be recruited nearer at hand. Under Sir William's leadership BSC trained
hundreds of Canadian and American parachutists for jumps into occupied
Europe; caused the sinking of many enemy submarines by decoding their
radio signals and pinpointing their position at sea; delayed Hitler's attack on
Russia by six weeks with a few calculated indiscretions; neutralized a vast
German sabotage ring in the Latin American republics; contributed to the
smashing of dummy companies operated in various parts of the world by the
German industrial cartel of I.G. Farben; helped to sustain American faith in
British victory during the dark days between Dunkirk and Pearl Harbor; and
ruined the reputation in the United States of the Vichy French with a dossier
so full of boudoir gleanings that President Roosevelt described it as "the best
bedtime story I have ever read."

When a treacherous British seaman offered to sell the German consul in
New York news of convoy movements it was BSC that produced evidence
which led to his execution. When Sir Henry Tizard took British scientific
secrets to Washington and found himself in the company of two men he took
for FBI agents, BSC discovered they were Nazi spies. When Noel Coward, the
renowned British author-actor-composer, was bitterly criticized in the House
of Commons for being out of England in her hour of peril, he was doing
highly secret work for BSC.

Stephenson, who crossed the Atlantic 43 times during the war, had a
habit of turning up at the scene of any crisis. By chance he was in Ottawa on
the night that Igor Gouzenko, stalked by superiors who were determined to
bump him off, fled the Russian Embassy and pleaded for political asylum in
Canada. Frenzied with fear, Gouzenko watched the Department of External

Affairs hesitate on account of the immense diplomatic and political conse-quences involved. Insiders think it was Stephenson who urged that Gouzenko be given shelter, and thus opened the dam gates to that flood of bizarre information which led to the spy trials of 1946, and the subsequent arrest of the atom-bomb traitor Alan Nunn May.

In addition to his secret work during the war, Stephenson played the clas-sic Canadian political role of hinge between London and Washington. Through him most of the facilities of the centuries-old British Secret Service were made available to the United States. At the end of war, J. Edgar Hoover, Chief of the U.S. Federal Bureau of Investigation, wrote Stephenson a letter of gratitude for the tips he had received from the United Kingdom on mat-ters of internal security and General William J. Donovan, head of the U.S. Office of Strategic Services, said: "Bill Stephenson taught us all we ever knew about foreign intelligence." In intelligence circles during the war, Donovan and Stephenson were popularly known, respectively, as Big Bill and Little Bill. Ernest Cuneo, who was wartime liaison officer between Stephenson's BSC and Donovan's OSS, and is today president of the North American Newspaper Alliance, says, "Stephenson is the only man who enjoyed the unqualified con-fidence of both Churchill and Roosevelt."

Robert E. Sherwood, deputy director of the U.S. Office of War Infor-mation, frequently consulted Stephenson on how Churchill might react to certain passages in speeches he was writing for Roosevelt. When, in 1946, President Truman awarded Stephenson the Medal For Merit, this coveted honor went, for the first time in history, to a non-American.

William Samuel Stephenson was born near Winnipeg 56 years ago. Between the wars he spent most of his time in England where he owned a Tudor farm on the Thames at Marlow and a town house in New Cavendish Street, one of the most aristocratic quarters of London's West End. After the war he retired for several years to Jamaica. Today he lives with his American wife in a penthouse with a fabulous view atop one of the most expensive blocks in New York.

On Wall Street, Threadneedle Street, Bay Street and St. James Street, Stephenson today is known for talents and sentiments far removed from the orbit of the cloak and dagger. For six months this year he was chairman of the Newfoundland and Labrador Corporation, a crown company formed to bring new industries to the 10th province. In that time he cajoled enough new investors to Newfoundland to keep Premier Joseph Smallwood busy for the next three years. "The idea," Stephenson said, "is to provide an extra bottle of milk for the kids."

Stephenson is the originator and mainspring of World Commerce, a British-Canadian-American company at 25 Broad Street, New York, which, by barter agreements and dollar guarantees, is trying to get around the currency restrictions now choking world trade. Recently the *Christian Science Monitor* quoted an Italian businessman as saying: "If there were a hundred World Commerces there would be no need for the Marshall Plan."

Stephenson is a slight erect figure with the springy walk of a lightweight boxer and there is a faint hint of the ring in his rugged countenance. He has a ruddy complexion, crisp grey hair and a mouth that slips easily into a wry grin. His eyes, so dark it is impossible to determine their precise color at three feet, have great impact. They bear steadily on the visitor, not in any unfriendly way but in a mood that seems to shade back and forth from whimsical observation through speculation to vigilance. It takes a strong personality to hold his gaze. Charles Vining, recently retired president of the Newsprint Association of Canada and a wartime lieutenant of Stephenson's, says: "I would hate to be in the same room thinking of something I didn't want him to know."

Many stories are told of Stephenson's powers of perception. During the war a Canadian secretary who had pricked her forefinger and covered it with a tiny square of plaster entered his office. Without looking up from his desk Stephenson said, "What have you been trying to do? Kill yourself?" The pace at which he reads is also legendary. "I've watched him reading a novel," says a close friend, T.G. Drew-Brook, a Toronto stockbroker, "and he reminds you of a man riffling through an index for a reference."

One girl on his wartime staff handed him several sheets of closely typed manuscript. He flicked the pages, grunted and handed it back. "Surely," she said, "you can't have read it properly?" He gave her a succinct résumé of its contents, reciting several passages verbatim. Although he is reticent, Stephenson, a hearty drinker of dry Martinis, is gregarious at heart. Among his many friends are Louis St. Laurent, Brooke Claxton, Dana Wilgress (former

Canadian high commissioner in London), the Aga Khan, Henry R. Luce (editor-in-chief of Time Inc.,) and the British newspaper barons Kemsley, Camrose, Rothermere and Beaverbrook. He also plays host to scores of obscure people he has met and liked during his travels.

Stephenson rises each morning at five. Every day he takes a long walk. He is a crack shot with a pistol and loves hunting and fishing. He has shot tiger and black panther in central India and Kashmir. Today he hunts and fishes in Prince Edward Island, one of his favorite resorts. He reads a lot and collects books, curios and paintings. Lady Stephenson is a quiet gracious woman, the former Mary French Simmons, of Springfield, Tenn., whom he met on an Atlantic liner in 1924 and married soon afterward. Friends say they are a devoted couple. They have no children.

In spite of his multitude of associates in high places, Stephenson rarely gets into print. Throughout the war he was never mentioned by the press of either Britain or the United States. His personal clippings for 30 years would not cover four sheets of foolscap. He dislikes talking himself and is adept at making others garrulous. He never speaks to writers of his early life or of his wartime experiences. Most of BSC's chronicles still remain under Top Secret labels in the archives of Ottawa, London and Washington. Even so, from a wide variety of sources in Europe and America, it has been possible to piece together a picture of Stephenson's extraordinary career.

He was born in Point Douglas, just outside Winnipeg, in 1896. His father owned a lumber yard and, as a boy, Stephenson liked to tinker around with the machinery. When the First World War began, he was 18 and still at Argyle High School, Winnipeg. He was excellent at mathematics, manual training and boxing. He went straight from school into the Royal Canadian Engineers and was commissioned before his 19th birthday. Within a year he had won the Military Cross in France. Later he was gassed, and he spent his convalescence learning to fly. He transferred to a Royal Flying Corps squadron in which the Toronto stockbroker Drew-Brook was serving. "When he arrived I was orderly officer," says Drew-Brook. "I reported to the CO that he looked so sick I didn't think he would be much good. He was an unspectacular pilot until he got badly shot up. Then he was ready to take on the entire German air force."

Stephenson shot down 20 planes in six weeks. One of his victims was Lothar von Richthofen, brother of the famous Baron von Richthofen. Early in 1918, he went to the aid of a French two-seater aircraft which was engaged by five Germans. In the whirling dogfight the French gunner failed to distinguish him from the foe and disabled his machine with a burst of fire. Stephenson bailed out over German territory and was captured. The contrite French gave him the Croix de Guerre with Palm.

Behind barbed wire in Holzminden, Germany, he excelled at the daily contest to see who could steal most from the guards. Among Stephenson's loot was a can opener, so cunningly designed he began to brood over it. Because of wartime difficulties it had been patented only in Germany, Austria and Turkey. When Stephenson escaped some weeks later he took the can opener to England and patented an improvement of it in every country in the world.

After the war he spent a year or so in Winnipeg. But soon royalties from the can opener netted him enough money to return to England and try his own hand at inventing. During the Twenties, he developed and financed a device which enabled the London *Daily Mail* to transmit the first publishable photograph from one point to another. The 28-year-old tycoon then revealed himself as a prophet when he told excited reporters: "In a few years everybody will have moving pictures in their own homes radiated from a central point. It is simply a matter of speeding up the wire-photo principle about 25 times."

Before he was 30, he had made $1 million and married Mary Simmons, who was wealthy in her own right. The early Thirties saw him in control of a score of companies. He was Sound City Films, which produced more than 50 per cent of British movies; he was General Aircraft Ltd., which created the twin-engine low-wing Monospar and won Britain's classic King's Cup in 1934; he was Earl's Court Ltd., which built the world's biggest stadium and exhibition hall in the London suburb of that name; he was the Pressed Steel Company Ltd., which made 90 per cent of British car bodies for such firms as Morris, Humber, Hillman and Austin; he was Catalina Ltd., one of the first manufacturers of plastics in the United Kingdom.

In the middle Thirties he was operating on five continents and in touch with the biggest banking houses on earth. He was already telling his associates that democratic capitalism could be saved only by developing backward areas and raising standards of living. With the Aga Khan he financed new schemes in the Middle East and India. He traveled widely and was entertained by ambassadors, prime ministers and industrialists. In the diplomatic salons of Europe he stood quietly in a corner, smiling in his characteristic wry way, inclining his head, encouraging people to talk . . . talk . . . talk. Then he took his leave politely. As he fitted together the jigsaw of information, he saw the pattern of impending war.

Stanley Baldwin brushed off Stephenson's warnings. But the Foreign Office listened to his stories of the secret factories that were spewing out new arms for the Reich. For several years before the war he made trips to Germany at his own expense, ostensibly on business. His access to the balance sheets of foreign companies enabled him to form an accurate idea of what happened to the raw materials that Germany was piping in.

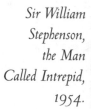

Sir William Stephenson, the Man Called Intrepid, 1954.

In 1936, Stephenson gave Churchill proof that Germany was spending the equal of $4,000 million a year on guns, tanks and submarines. All through Chamberlain's appeasing term, Stephenson is said to have supplied Churchill with facts and figures which gave punch to the great orator's speeches and set mighty forces stirring behind the tranquil façade of England. In late 1939, after the outbreak of hostilities, Stephenson was in Helsinki when Russia invaded Finland. No details of the trip may be given. Associates say, however, that Stephenson carried out one of the most delicate missions of the war "at great personal risk."

When Churchill became Prime Minister in 1940 and sought a man to co-ordinate British counter-espionage, anti-sabotage, economic warfare, political warfare and secret intelligence in North and South America, he thought of the astute and well-informed Canadian, Stephenson. Just before the fall of France, Stephenson reached New York and set up an organization which was to become the eyes, ears and nose on this side of the Atlantic of such secret cadres as PID (Political Intelligence Department), Political Warfare Executive (Ministry of Information), MI5 (War Office), Naval Intelligence (the Admiralty), Special Branch (Scotland Yard), Special Operations Executive (Ministry of Economic Warfare) and Security Executive (Ministry of Transport).

The scope of his responsibilities demanded specialists in many fields. Because he knew Canadians would get on well with Americans he turned to his own country. He recruited scientists, industrialists, economists, geologists, farmers, stockbrokers, schoolmasters, newspapermen, policemen and many other types from all over Canada. The military personnel ranged from admiral, general and air marshal down to the lowest noncommissioned ranks. BSC, as it became known, was in touch with British intelligence agents from the Arctic to the Antarctic. Before the war was over the headquarters staff in New York exceeded 3,000.

Stephenson reached the United States at a time when Dunkirk, the blitz and the U-boats had shaken American confidence in the Commonwealth's ability to pull through alone. He told Roosevelt: "The arsenals of Britain are empty. But she will win out. The British do not kneel easily."

One of his first jobs was to offset the propagandist influences of pro-Nazi groups financed from Berlin, and this he did by disseminating Britain's point of view in circles extending from the theatre to embassies. In an old farmhouse near Toronto, he had BSC train secret agents for operations behind the German lines. Hundreds of Canadians, most of them of Central European origin, volunteered for courses in parachute jumping, weapon training, unarmed combat, knife play, use of explosives, lock picking, shadowing techniques, ciphers and radio communications. Final exercises were held in central Toronto. Operating as if in hostile territory, the trainees had to find themselves shelter, set up a secret radio and begin gathering and broadcasting information. Many of them were picked up by Canadian counter-espionage forces, quietly released when BSC explained the true role, and taken back for further schooling. The majority dropped into Central Europe and provided the Allies with useful information. Many were never heard of again.

Stephenson's Ontario school tutored FBI men and other Americans who became the foundation of Donovan's OSS. It also drilled in anti-sabotage tactics many British and trusted foreign executives of industrial plants in South America. The Latin American republics were the scene of tortuous undercover struggles between Stephenson's men and German agents. Oil, tin, bauxite, antimony, mica, balsa wood, rubber, sisal, copper, quinine and many other raw materials coveted by both sides brought clandestine economic warfare to its zenith there. Stephenson's policy was to unearth the German agents, prove them guilty of breaking the laws of the country in which they were operating and get the South American governments to take action against them.

Americans who served in a liaison capacity cite one case from BSC's record which is typical of its highly co-ordinated work. In 1942, a series of radio signals emanating from a man who signed himself Apfel were intercepted by BSC monitors in Chile. There were references to many German names including Hirth, Braun and Gersten and a mention of the need for more funds to start work in the northern republics. British agents in South America were alerted and were able to learn that Hirth, Braun and Gersten were members of a sabotage ring and the mysterious Apfel was their chief.

Information on Apfel was difficult to get. BSC followed many false leads. Commercial, industrial and diplomatic contacts were questioned discreetly over and again; enquiries extended to Peru, Uruguay, Argentina and Brazil. Finally a BSC informant in a German bank in Argentina reported that Apfel was the nickname of a man named Von Appen who was head of the Hamburg Amerika Line in Valparaiso. Later the same informant saw a German sea captain by the name of Lange remove what looked like seven large tubes from a strong box held by Von Appen in a German bank in Buenos Aires.

Stephenson's agents got hold of the "tubes," which were sabotage devices. This led to the arrest of Von Appen by Chilean police. He confessed nothing, but was restricted in his movements to a small village. Chilean surveillance, however, was not very effective. In 1945 a Chilean ship blew up. Evidence pointed to Von Appen again. Under rigorous cross-examination he confirmed BSC's suspicions: he had been assigned to destroy South American installations of value to the Allies, including the Cubatao power station which supplied electricity to the Brazilian cities of Santos and San Paulo.

There were simpler and more colorful operations. Before the United States entered the war the British were anxious to immobilize about 20 German and Italian ships which were preparing to sail from the Mexican ports of Tampico and Vera Cruz. No British vessels were available to intercept them. A Stephenson aide mentioned this to the U.S. Navy. As the enemy ships moved into the Atlantic by night, U.S. warships suddenly turned searchlights on them. Two of the German ships were immediately scuttled by their crews. The rest fled back into Mexican ports, where they remained until the end of the war. Thus, without a shot being fired or a breach of neutrality committed, the United States won a naval battle for Britain.

In May, 1941, the government of Bolivia was pro-British. But its military attaché in Berlin, Major Elias Belmonte, was fanatically pro-Nazi. BSC learned that Belmonte, with Nazi aid, was planning to establish a Hitlerian regime in Bolivia. It was important to confront the Bolivian government with proof of this conspiracy. A British secret agent in Portugal reported that plans for the *coup* were in possession of a German courier who was bound by air for Bolivia. His first port of call would be Recife, in Brazil. BSC agents in Brazil were ordered to intercept the courier and steal the plans.

For three weeks the airport at Recife was watched, but BSC had no luck. On June 18, 1941, a woman who had been planted as secretary to a German agent named Fritz Fenthol, in Rio, informed BSC that her boss was leaving for Buenos Aires and thence for Bolivia with an envelope addressed to the German minister in La Paz. In Buenos Aires, Fenthol called at a German bank. In the elevator a BSC man picked his pocket. The documents proved to be the detailed plans by which Belmonte hoped to stage his revolt and seize power. They were presented to the Bolivian government. Belmonte was arrested. The Bolivian minister to Berlin was withdrawn. The German minister in La Paz was kicked out. And Bolivian raw materials continued to flow smoothly to the British.

One of BSC's cases was that of George Thomas Armstrong. Armstrong served as fifth engineer in a British merchantman. He had several convictions against him in the United Kingdom for petty thefts. He saw in the war nothing more than a chance to make some easy money. He thought it would be a good idea to sell the Germans news of convoy movements. He bluntly approached German agents in Lisbon. They suspected he was a counter-espionage agent and would have nothing to do with him.

Armstrong failed to take into account the fact that on every British merchant ship, and in many foreign ones, there was a man working under the title of Observer, whose duty was to keep his eyes and ears open on the lower deck. The Observer did not miss Armstrong's visit to the Germans. When the ship docked the next time in New York the Observer reported, as was customary, to BSC. BSC watched Armstrong visit the German consul in New York. The consul was not so careful as his Lisbon compatriots. He bought some information from Armstrong. Evidence of the deal was procured by BSC. No attempt was made to apprehend Armstrong on American territory. When he stepped off his ship in England, however, he was arrested. On July 9, 1941, he was hanged in Wandsworth Jail, London, the first British traitor of the war to be executed.

Germany was desperate for industrial diamonds and, deprived of legitimate sources by the British blockade, Nazi agents built up a huge smuggling ring. Sailors and passengers in neutral ships made small fortunes by getting diamonds through British naval control ports in the bowls of pipes, false heels, cigarettes, chewing gum, balls of wool, needles, walking sticks with trick ferrules, and many more crafty places. Most of the smuggled diamonds came from South America and reached Germany via Portugal. It proved impossible to choke the pipe line at the receiving end in Lisbon, so transmitting points in Uruguay were tackled. Inspectors W. Rudkin and Ivor Reece, of Scotland Yard, were sent to Uruguay to work in co-ordination with Stephenson's outfit. The traffic was choked in a few months. Toward the end of the war British agents in Germany reported many factories were working at half capacity because of the diamond famine.

The spider's web extending from Stephenson's BSC headquarters in Rockefeller Center to a legion of scattered undercover men had at its core the most efficient communications system in the world. A Canadian electronics expert, whose name cannot be given, designed equipment which coded and decoded messages in seconds, thereby saving hours of human effort. BSC business in code made up more than 50 per cent of the traffic on the normal trans-Atlantic cables and kept a secret transmitter in Canada operating at full capacity day and night.

In 1943, a German submarine surfaced off the coast of Uruguay. It broke radio silence for a few seconds to report its position in code. The message was picked up by a BSC radio monitor on the coast. It was transmitted to New York. It went through the decoding machine and was passed on to the Admiralty. The Admiralty informed a Royal Navy task force at sea. Only three minutes elapsed between the submarine's first broadcast and the receipt of the signal by the RN destroyers. Within half an hour the submarine was sunk with depth charges.

Stephenson's opposition was not lacking in skill and daring. Early in the war Sir Henry Tizard arrived in the United States with a carload of British secrets in nuclear fission, radar, proximity fuses and penicillin. It was Stephenson's responsibility to protect him. When Tizard reported to Stephenson that two FBI men were already looking after him Stephenson made enquiries. The supposed FBI men were German spies.

Stephenson personally directed operations which led to the exposure of espionage by Vichy French diplomats who functioned in the United States until Pearl Harbor. The U.S. relations with Vichy were useful because, in Churchill's words, they opened "a window" on occupied France. But the pro-Nazi activities of Vichy officials in the United States gave Britain many misgivings. Until de Gaulle, for example, seized the French islands of St. Pierre and Miquelon, off the south coast of Newfoundland, they fed a radio station in these colonies with propaganda designed to breach British-Canadian-American accord.

Stephenson's staff produced photostatic copies of letters, receipts, memoranda and other incriminating documents. Among those implicated was Gaston Henri-Haye, Vichy ambassador to the United States. The French appetite for gallantry was exploited to the full. Mistresses of many Vichy officials reported confidences to BSC. The dossier, relished by Roosevelt as "bedtime reading," did much to destroy the illusion of Vichy as a pitiful but honorable government striving to preserve the remnants of a glorious civilization.

Stephenson also helped to expose the chain of companies operated throughout the world by the German trust I.G. Farben. BSC agents in the employ of these firms in the United States photographed instructions from the Reich that goods they manufactured must be labeled "Made In Germany" and exported to South America to give industrialists the impression that, in spite of the war, Hitler was in "business as usual." Confronted with Stephenson's evidence, the U.S. Custodian of Alien Property seized $1,500 million worth of German assets.

One of the best examples of British-American co-operation before Pearl Harbor took place in Yugoslavia. At the end of January, 1941, Yugoslavia, Britain's remaining hope in the Balkans, nervously wavered toward the Axis by signing a pact of amity with Hungary, one of the junior partners. Prince Paul, the Regent, refused to receive Anthony Eden. In Yugoslav air force headquarters in Belgrade, however, there was a man named General Richard Simovic whose office was the secret centre of opposition to the pro-Axis government policy and to German ambitions. Stephenson suggested that it would be a good idea for the United States to send an emissary to Simovic.

General William J. Donovan, later commander of OSS, was chosen. Donovan would have exceeded the President's constitutional authority had he committed the United States to helping Simovic. But, at a social function, Donovan let drop a few calculated indiscretions, suggested by Stephenson, which electrified Simovic into action. The indiscretions convinced Simovic that the United States was now 100 per cent behind Britain and that therefore Britain could not lose.

On March 27 Simovic seized power. Young King Peter escaped from regency custody down a rain pipe. Prince Paul was banished. British flags flew everywhere. People danced in the streets. The German minister was publicly insulted. The *Führer* was astonished and infuriated. On April 6 he invaded Yugoslavia after a crushing air raid on Belgrade. Simovic's forces were overwhelmed, but the diversion delayed the German drive into Russia by six weeks, which may have had a decisive effect on the Wehrmacht's plan to take Moscow before snowfall.

Stephenson's role in high-level negotiations between Churchill and Roosevelt is well defined by Ernest Cuneo, of NANA. "He always knew," says Cuneo, "what neither of them could ever give. Therefore the other never asked. He cut out the customary diplomatic rigmarole whereby one statesman says to another: 'If I asked you this in public what would you say?' "

Throughout the war Stephenson was at his desk 20 hours a day, seven days a week. His staff wondered when he slept. Friends say his tremendous demonstration of endurance aged and exhausted him. At two o'clock one morning, during the New York dim-out, the senior BSC staff on the midnight-to-eight shift saw him flit from the office and were thankful he proposed getting some rest. At 3:45 a.m., he telephoned from his room in Dorset House, a hotel across the way, to say that a chink of light was showing under one of the office blinds. At five he was back, shaved, changed, spruced up, ready for the next day's work.

Stephenson was immensely proud of his Canadian female staff. He took a personal interest in making sure they all got decent quarters in Manhattan. One of his instructions to them was that they should never give anyone the impression they were in secret work. For the protection of BSC most of the girls voluntarily lived limited social lives. Throughout the war only two girls were guilty of indiscretions. Overawed by the importance of their work these two began to cultivate an air of intrigue. When this was spotted they were sent home.

One of the most important members of the staff was an elderly Scottish woman named Esther Stewart Drummond Richardson. As head of the coding department she had the reputation of a slave driver. When she became fatally ill in New York shortly after the war, Stephenson sat up all night at her bedside during her last hours of life.

On D-Day, Stephenson flew as a rear gunner in a bomber over the invasion coast. He was annoyed because he encountered no German aircraft to shoot at. But he found some consolation in the fact that the huge armada below, about to close the ring around Hitler, owed much of its force to his own efforts.

For a time after the war, according to a close friend, nothing seemed important to him. From 1946 to early 1951 he lived in semi-retirement in a beautiful home in Montego Bay, Jamaica. He ate like a bird and lost his once-famous palate for vintage French wine. The primitive dwellings of the natives touched his pity. He surprised many famous guests by inviting them to accompany him on a visit to a neighbor who turned out to be a mulatto farmer with whom he chatted for hours. He sometimes hired 200 natives to come and sing to his friends and every Christmas he threw a party for between 400 and 500. He built his native neighbors a fine new church.

Gradually he recovered his interest in business. He took new industries to Jamaica and Newfoundland. John Pepper, vice-president of World Commerce, one of the companies Stephenson originated, says: "He is a great Canadian and has done more than any other man in the world markets to bring Canada's enormous potential to the notice of international investors." His postwar activities have extended behind the iron curtain. A typical transaction of World Commerce took place last year in the Balkans. Yugoslavia and Bulgaria were short of dollars and short of medicine. Each country, however, had about $300,000 worth of paprika on their farms. World Commerce exchanged a year's supply of penicillin and sulfa for the paprika, which they then sold on other markets. World Commerce works on a commission basis but sometimes it foregoes a profit if it feels it can help an impoverished or backward country by giving it the facilities of its international connections.

Because Stephenson was resident in a British colony when he was offered the title of Knight Bachelor, he was able to accept without embarrassing the

Canadian Government. Most of his Canadian friends were delighted and many thought he ought to have received a peerage.

Stephenson, however, is more proud of a comment written against his own name in green Churchillian ink, on a list of candidates for honors which was submitted to George VI. It read: "This one is dear to my heart."

SIR WILLIAM STEPHENSON'S *reputation grew to mythical propor-tions in the 1960s and 1970s, in part because of biographies such as* The Quiet Canadian *(1962) and* A Man Called Intrepid *(1976). Predictably, more recent works have taken a more contrarian view. He died in Bermuda in 1989, at the age of 93; his death was preceded by Mary's in 1978.*

A Secret Rendezvous with Igor Gouzenko

by Blair Fraser

SEPTEMBER 1, 1953

Maclean's Ottawa editor meets the Russian Embassy clerk who broke a spy ring and has since hidden out under assumed names that only the RCMP knows. While keeping one jump ahead of Kremlin vengeance he has written a novel that may bolster his sagging fortunes.

NOT MORE THAN A DOZEN people know where Igor Gouzenko lives, or under what name, and I am not one of them. Neither are his publishers, J.M. Dent and Sons (Canada) Ltd., of Toronto. To communicate with Gouzenko they write in care of the Royal Canadian Mounted Police, Ottawa, who deliver his mail to him by courier. Ever since September, 1945, when the then-Russian cipher clerk laid before the RCMP 109 secret Soviet documents which exposed a Communist spy ring in Canada, Gouzenko has been hiding—as he will be for the rest of his life. The Soviet secret police have a long arm, and no man living has so grievously affronted them as Igor Gouzenko.

They don't know it, but he is about to affront them again, this time by exposing not what the Kremlin is trying to do in this country but what it is actually doing at home. Gouzenko has written a 300,000-word novel of life inside Soviet Russia. It is probably the only creative work extant which tells what the USSR is like to its own citizens. No one inside Russia could write such a book and survive. No one else has yet escaped who has had the necessary literary talent. If the book is as successful as Gouzenko's publishers hope, he will swing up to another high point in a roller-coaster career. Eight years ago, he was a nobody, an obscure little cipher clerk in the Soviet Embassy who lived with his wife in a small flat in Ottawa. Seven years ago, he was world-famous—the man who exposed the Russian espionage system. Six years ago, he was rich, having got a small fortune for publication and film rights to a ghost-written book that bore his name. By now he is more than half forgotten and the small fortune a good deal more than half spent.

But the Soviet secret police have not forgotten him. Igor Gouzenko, who broke out of a prisonlike existence in the Russian foreign service to become a citizen of a free country, is not and cannot be as free as his fellow Canadian citizens. He has lived in six different dwellings during the eight years under at least two false names. His own children do not know their real name and probably never will. Because of the children he cannot now change his identity again. They are 10 and eight, too old to be told without explanation (as they were told a few years ago) that they and Daddy and Mummy all had a new name now. "We don't like our old name," their father told them.

Each of Gouzenko's new identities was chosen with great care. He was supplied with a new country of origin to explain his still heavy foreign accent. In each case it had to be a country from which few immigrants have come to Canada and none at all to the district where Gouzenko was to live. He received not only all the necessary papers—passport, birth certificates for himself and his wife and children—but also a skilfully concocted biography which he memorized. All its details correspond with Gouzenko's present age, skills, aptitudes and general situation.

Those who know they are meeting Igor Gouzenko are not, of course, told any of his new names. When they are introduced to him, as I was in Toronto a few weeks ago, they meet a Mr. Brown. Mr. Brown was waiting for us at the home of C.J. Eustace of the Dent publishing firm, but I didn't know that when I set out. My appointment was with Eustace at his Bloor Street office. Gouzenko came alone from the home of a friend with whom he was staying, and whom Eustace didn't know. None of us could have traced him once he stepped outside Eustace's door.

I shook hands with a short stocky fair-haired man who, in spite of a receding hairline, looked rather younger than his 34 years. He wore a light grey suit of ultramodern cut—wide padded shoulders, long jacket—which accentuated his short square build. Though he apparently lives a sedentary life he looks like a man in good physical shape.

On the floor beside him was a suitcase full of large brown-paper packages. These turned out to be the manuscript of the new book, *The Fall of a Titan*—a novel of modern Soviet Russia which runs to more than 1,100 manuscript pages. Gouzenko has been working on it for four years. He had brought with him great chunks of the original manuscript, written in Russian longhand on foolscap pages; also various drafts of the translation done by his old friend, Special Constable Mervyn Black of the RCMP. When the introductions were over, "Mr. Brown" went back to what he had been doing when we came in—squatting on his heels in a well-lighted spot to display some of his wife's paintings. One that he particularly liked was a bright red maple overhanging a quiet brook. I suggested we might use it as an illustration for this article, but Gouzenko shook his head. Too risky, he said. The scene was commonplace enough but several dozen people would be able to recognize it as a corner of a certain pasture in rural Canada.

Did he paint too? I asked. "I paint in my spare time. I like to paint portraits of my RCMP guards; they have plenty of time to pose for me. Maybe some time it'll be possible to have an exhibition of these portraits. Incidentally, my neighbors don't know I can paint. I keep this secret—it is an identifying clue." (Gouzenko studied architecture in Moscow before he got his wartime job as cipher clerk.)

He showed me a loose-leaf sketchbook full of portraits done in pencil. I didn't know any of the subjects, but the drawing looked good. One was of Inspector Herbert Spanton, who had been in charge of his security in the early days; Gouzenko tore it out, autographed it, and gave it to me as a souvenir. Speaking of guards (he still has one most of the time, posing as chauffeur or handyman), what kind of life had he led during his eight years of qualified freedom? Gouzenko shrugged. A good life; he was used to its restrictions and didn't mind them. As the conversation went on it appeared that his brief career as a Canadian had been even more remarkable and unusual than most people supposed.

When the Gouzenkos fled from their Somerset Street apartment in Ottawa on Sept. 5, 1945, they were quite destitute. Neither had anything but the clothes they stood in, and to complicate matters Anna Gouzenko was pregnant and rapidly outgrew her one dress. Those were the days of acute shortages when a man had to be a war veteran to be sure of getting a new suit of clothes. The RCMP had to concoct an elaborate story about a veteran whose house had burned down and left him practically naked in order to buy complete new outfits for Gouzenko and his wife.

At first they lived in complete charge of the government and the RCMP; first at a Mountie's summer cottage and later in military camps. That was when Gouzenko was the star witness in the spy trials which resulted in the conviction of 11 men and women and finally alerted the West to the huge and menacing proportions of Russia's "attack from within." But long before the trials were completed, Gouzenko passed from dire poverty to comparative wealth. By April, 1947, he had completed the last of a series of transactions through which his book, *This Was My Choice*, brought him a total of almost $150,000.

Cosmopolitan magazine paid him $50,000 for serial rights. Twentieth Century-Fox paid $75,000 for the movie rights. The book itself paid fairly well in royalties. Gouzenko was rich beyond the wildest dreams of a Russian cipher clerk. The man who in his first days in Ottawa had gone out and bought five pounds of grapes—"much much more than we could eat"— because he had never before been able to buy all the grapes he wanted, now found himself able to buy anything he wanted, absolutely anything.

Gouzenko didn't say so, but from the rather wistful way he spoke about his new book and the money it might earn, I gathered that he has spent most if not all of his small fortune in the past six years. He still lives in a beautiful house and drives a better-than-average car but he no longer talks like a man with no financial worries.

What did he do with this sudden windfall of wealth? "My first impulse was to give everybody presents. I was happy. I didn't realize how much $150,000 was but I knew it was a lot. I myself never had any toys when I was a child. Some children had, even in Russia, but we were poor even by Soviet standards. My mother was a teacher and teachers get very low pay. At one time we lived in a single room with seven other people. So first I bought lots of toys for the children, every kind. That first Christmas after we got the money the house was filled up with them. I bought a record player, the very best, and lots and lots of records. One I bought, what they called a limited edition, only a few copies were ever made. It cost $25. I remember how horrified our RCMP guard was at such a price for an album of records. Then I bought a nice house in the country. I don't like cities. Anyway, Canadian

Igor Gouzenko, in a classic shot, holds his Governor General's award-winning novel, Fall of a Titan, *1954.*

cities are not very big, and in Canada the country has almost everything the city has to offer and a lot more besides. We have owned three different houses now, always in the country. We bought a car at the same time as we bought the house."

What sort of car? An ordinary cheap one, or an expensive make? "It was a little above average price. I thought it was safer," Gouzenko began. Then he stopped and grinned, evidently realizing that he was talking nonsense. "I guess it is mostly I like big cars. You can always find a good excuse for doing what you want. We have changed cars several times, the more changes the better. When we bought our second house four years ago and changed our name and everything, the RCMP were very clever at getting us new license plates."

At this point we all went in to lunch and the conversation became general. Among other things we talked about the trial and execution of the Rosenbergs, the man and wife in the United States who had given atomic secrets to Soviet Russia. I asked Gouzenko what he thought of the case. To my surprise he was very much against the Rosenberg trial, thought it had been very badly handled. What alarmed him was not the verdict of guilty or even the sentence of death but the fact that some of the evidence was not made public. "Once you start convicting people on secret evidence where will it end? What's to stop them from shooting anybody at all and putting it down to security reasons? A democracy must not use the methods of a dictatorship, just as a dictatorship cannot use the methods of a democracy. Soviet Russia is finding that out right now in the satellite countries. They try to give a little freedom, a little relaxation of tyranny, and what happens? Riots and rebellions break out. Dictatorships cannot afford freedom.

"But democracies can't afford not to have it—all the protections of law are for everybody. When things happen like the Rosenberg trial they are too hard to explain to outsiders. For one thing the Rosenberg trial might discourage people like myself who might be willing to help you by coming over to your side. They look at things like taking evidence in secret and they naturally wonder what is the difference between a free democracy and a dictatorship."

After lunch I asked Gouzenko whether he himself still lived in fear of discovery and revenge, or whether he now felt safe. "In the beginning we were very suspicious of everything and everybody. Fear has big eyes, you know. At the very first we were afraid the Canadian government might give us back to the Russians—they didn't seem to know what to do with us. My wife was quite calm even then, though. She is a remarkable woman—she ought to have been a man. Nowadays we don't feel frightened. The best rule is, always be on the alert but don't get panicky when danger threatens."

Didn't they ever get into unexpected situations? Suppose, for example, some neighbor had a guest who really came from the country Gouzenko now pretends to have come from and suppose the neighbor asked the Gouzenkos over to tea? "All I can say is, fortunately that has never happened."

But if they felt so safe now why had they moved so often? Why had they bought three different houses in six years? "No special reason. We didn't feel in any particular danger. Partly it was just to have a better house, better location. Also, on the general principle that it's better not to stay too long in one place. The real danger is always the thing you don't see. People will notice something and you won't even know it. So—we moved. If I could afford it I would move even oftener."

Gouzenko said he hadn't lost money on his various houses. He always sold them for a bit more than he paid, but as he talked I began to get a picture of what had happened to the $150,000. He mentioned buying a farm which he still owns, "which brings in some profit but not much;" he gave no indication of any other investment of any kind. Evidently he had lived on his capital at a pretty high rate.

What did he do for vacations? Travel at all? "We have traveled around quite a bit in Canada. The longest trip was a motor tour to Niagara Falls, the whole family. I do not go to the United States. There might be some mix-up about my documents, or I might have my picture taken. I am very careful about pictures—you are the first man who has seen snapshots of my house and my wife and children. About crossing the U.S. border, I feel 'Don't ask for trouble.' The feeling that I can go if I want to is enough. Maybe if I were forbidden I might fight like hell to go—I am also quite stubborn at times."

How did he spend his time after the first book was published and the money rolled in? "No special routine. I can force myself to work very hard and long when I want to, but then I wanted to relax. I would get up at nine or 10 o'clock. You can say I was sometimes very lazy. I might play some records or help my wife in the garden or maybe go to a movie. Then I would jot down ideas for the book. I was already intending to write as my life work. I would also read the papers, Canadian papers mostly but for a time I also read the Moscow newspaper *Pravda* very carefully.

"It is quite surprising what you find in *Pravda* from time to time. One of the most horrible stories in my book came right out of *Pravda*, except that I watered it down. I didn't think Canadian readers would believe the things *Pravda* described. *Pravda* told about workers in a chemical explosive plant and how the fumes made them ill. It told how workers lay there in a fever for days, unable to move, and nobody paid any attention. They put these things in *Pravda* to make the workers in ordinary plants think at least they are not as badly off as that. It makes them more content with their own working conditions."

We began to talk about the book, which was what Gouzenko had wanted to talk about in the first place. He is pinning tremendous hopes on it. "I worked on it four years. The first book, *This Was My Choice*, I wrote in only four months. Six hundred manuscript pages in Russian—I didn't pay any attention to style or anything like that. At the top of a page I would put some topic, and then I would write the page on that topic. Mervyn Black (an RCMP officer born in Russia of Scottish parents) translated it for me—it's a wonder he didn't ruin his eyesight trying to read my writing. I used to write it lying on my stomach under a tree. Everybody else would go swimming; I would force myself to stay behind and work."

Actually what Gouzenko wrote was the factual material for the book, a sheaf of memoranda. *This Was My Choice* was ghost-written. It is a third-rate piece of work. Even though I knew Gouzenko hadn't written the first one, I expected his new book to be of similar quality. On the day of our interview, 500 pages of the final draft had been typed. I took them with me to read overnight, making an appointment for the following morning at the same place, same time.

As we drove downtown, Margaret Blackstock, who has edited the Gouzenko novel for Dent's, said, "When you make an appointment with Mr. Brown he never keeps it. He never comes at the time you set, he comes either earlier or later and often he changes the place." So I was not surprised when she telephoned later to say Mr. Brown couldn't come in the morning, but we'd spend the evening together at a different place.

The postponement gave me time to read all the 500 pages of manuscript. To my astonishment it turned out to be an excellent piece of work. In the ghost-written *This Was My Choice*, real characters including Gouzenko himself look and sound like wooden puppets. In *The Fall of a Titan*, imaginary characters (and some real ones too, but in imagined situations) have the very breath and warmth of life. It is the story of the last years of Maxim Gorky, the great Russian novelist who died three years after his return to the Soviet Union in 1933. Gorky was later said to have been murdered by his doctors and many people were executed for this crime in the purge trials of 1937. Gouzenko examines the mystery of Gorky's life and of his death—why such a man could have been an advocate and defender of the Stalinist regime; how and why he came to change his mind and fall silent; how and why he had to be killed in the end by the Soviet secret police. But though Gorky's life and death provide the core and central theme for the novel, Gouzenko's stage is broad and his cast of characters large. Three or four whole families are represented, as well as a dozen or more minor characters.

When I finally met "Mr. Brown" the following evening and we went off to dinner together with his editor, the talk was again of the book—how it had been written, what it tried to portray, which characters were real and which imaginary. This time there was no element of ghost-writing. Gouzenko had read every line of every draft of the translations and sent back voluminous corrections of his own.

In the course of a leisurely dinner, though, we talked of many things. Canadian politics, for one. "I don't take a very active part in politics, except of course to vote," said Gouzenko, who has been a Canadian citizen since September, 1948. "I do think we should have stronger Opposition. Opposition should be strong and vigilant. I have seen the one-party system at first hand and this makes me think no party should have too big a majority. Keep government answerable for every step. Press, also, must be absolutely free and fearless. Must not be afraid to print bad things about government."

I asked what he thought of the economic system in Canada, and of course he said he liked it. Gouzenko is a free-enterprise man: "People in Russia are kept working under the most horrible conditions by the fear of punishment or exile to concentration camps. Here in Canada much better results are achieved by competition—and all this without fear or pain. Without competition there can only be concentration camps."

This was the attitude I'd expected, but I was surprised by his opinion of advertising. Despite his contempt for the radio soap opera and similar extreme cases, Gouzenko thinks advertising is "undoubtedly one of the greatest inventions of modern society. It keeps people abreast of the times and teaches them how to improve their lives. Things which were before mostly available only to city people are now known and available to farmers, thanks to advertising. The purpose and effect of advertising overshadows any faults that result from it by bad taste or the dishonesty of some people."

Both Gouzenko's children are now in school, and the elder has attended school in two different districts. I asked Gouzenko what he thought of Canadian education and how it compared with the Russian. His answer astonished me: "I am most impressed by the discipline in Canadian schools. They are so quiet. In Russia the schoolroom is as noisy as a bear garden. Here the children are so polite to their parents and teachers. It is amazing.

"I think this is self-discipline; not from any particular training but because life is so much easier here. In Russia children are first of all hungry—that makes them nervous and irritable. Then there is always a feeling of strain. Maybe the father is in danger of arrest or in trouble at his work—serious trouble, not trivial as it would be here. These things are all reflected in the behavior of the children."

Did Canadian children have more fun than Russian children? "Play is about the same. There is more emphasis on games here, not so much on military training. In Russia the military games start young and are very realistic. In army play, the children even peel potatoes as a punishment."

Didn't he have any criticism of Canadian schools? "No, not serious criticism. My children like school. In the lower grades where they are I can see no serious faults. In the higher grades, what I have seen of them, I have the impression the teaching of some subjects is somewhat limited in outlook and perhaps even old-fashioned. Languages, for instance. In Soviet schools we learn English, German and French from the fourth grade. During the war it was useful to thousands of Russians to have even the limited knowledge of German that we got in school. In Canadian schools they teach Latin. That seems to me old-fashioned and of limited use."

One question I put with great curiosity: Had he acquired any religious beliefs or affiliation since he came to Canada? And if so, after a childhood under an atheistic regime, what impression did Canadian churches make on him? "My children go to Sunday school like other children," Gouzenko said. "As for me, my neighbors go as often as I do—which is to say, not much. This does not seem very important.

"The first time I went to church it was very hard for me to grasp. I went quite often in the first years, though, and finally found some interest in it. Basically it must be good. It is preaching love—in Russia the basic thing that is taught is class hatred. It is better to preach love, preach what is good even if we do not always do what is good when we grow up. Better at least than to preach what is bad."

All through these two long conversations nobody had called Gouzenko by name. We spoke of him and to him as "Mr. Brown." As we parted on that second evening, I said: "Well, good-by. It's a pleasure to have met you, Mr. Gouzenko."

He looked up with an odd expression, startled and also wistful. "It is a long time since I have heard anyone call me by my name," he said.

We shook hands, and I left.

FALL OF A TITAN *won the 1954 Governor General's Award. Igor Gouzenko wrote several later novels, but none were published. He lived in hiding until his death, reportedly of a heart attack, in 1982, near Toronto, at age 63. In his occasional public appearances, he always wore a pillowcase over his head—it became his trademark—and none of his eight children learned their parents' identity until their teens. His widow, Svetlana, is said to be alive and living in Mississaugua, Ont.*

My Twelve Hours as a Madman

by
Sidney Katz

OCTOBER 1, 1953

Here is the minute-by-minute report of a *Maclean's* editor who swallowed an experimental drug that turned him into a raving schizophrenic: what he saw, what he felt, what he said and did—fully documented by tape recordings, photographs, scientific witnesses and his own tormented memories that still haunt him.

ON THE MORNING OF Thursday, June 18, 1953, I swallowed a drug which, for 12 unforgettable hours, turned me into a madman. For 12 hours I inhabited a nightmare world in which I experienced the torments of hell and the ecstasies of heaven.

I will never be able to describe fully what happened to me during my excursion into madness. There are no words in the English language designed to convey the sensations I felt or the visions, illusions, hallucinations, colors, patterns and dimensions which my disordered mind revealed.

I saw the faces of familiar friends turn into fleshless skulls and the heads of menacing witches, pigs and weasels. The gaily patterned carpet at my feet was transformed into a fabulous heaving mass of living matter, part vegetable, part animal. An ordinary sketch of a woman's head and shoulders suddenly sprang to life. She moved her head from side to side, eyeing me critically, changing back and forth from woman into man. Her hair and her neckpiece became the nest of a thousand famished serpents who leaped out to devour me. The texture of my skin changed several times. After handling a painted card I could feel my body suffocating for want of air because my skin had turned to enamel. As I patted a black dog, my arm grew heavy and sprouted a thick coat of glossy black fur.

I was repeatedly held in the grip of a terrifying hallucination in which I could feel and see my body convulse and shrink until all that remained was a hard sickly stone located in the left side of my abdomen, surrounded by a greenish-yellow vapor which poured across the floor of the room.

Time lost all meaning. Hours were telescoped into minutes; seconds stretched into hours. The room I was in changed with every breath I drew. Mysterious flashes of multicolored light came and went. The dimensions of the room, elasticlike, stretched and shrank. Pictures, chairs, curtains and lamps flew endlessly about, like planets in their orbits. My senses of feeling, smelling and hearing ran amuck. It was as though someone had rooted out the nerve nets in my brain, which control the senses, then joined them together again without thought of their proper placings.

But my hours of madness were not all filled with horror and frenzy. At times I beheld visions of dazzling beauty—visions so rapturous, so unearthly, that no artist will ever paint them. I lived in a paradise where the sky was a mass of jewels set in a background of shimmering aquamarine blue; where the clouds were apricot-colored; where the air was filled with liquid golden arrows, glittering fountains of iridescent bubbles, filigree lace of pearl and silver, sheaths of rainbow light—all constantly changing in color, design, texture and dimension so that each scene was more lovely than the one which preceded it.

Two weeks have now passed since I spent a half day as a madman. (I was so frightened and bewildered by the experience that it is only now that I am able to sit down and write a complete account of what happened to me. Even now, as I relive the nightmare from this safe distance, I grow tense and my body is bathed in perspiration.)

I VOLUNTEERED TO BECOME a temporary madman in the interests of medical research into the problem of mental illness. This is one phase of research where some of the guinea pigs have to be human beings. For animals can't describe their sensations.

The drug I took was LSD—lysergic acid diethylamide—an alkaloid of ergot, the poisonous rust that sometimes grows on rye. Two years ago when bread made of infected rye flour was sold in a French village many of the inhabitants died of poisoning or went stark raving mad. The mental condition produced by this drug—developed by a Swiss chemist—closely resembles acute schizophrenia, the most prevalent and the most serious form of mental disease in Canada. About half the patients in our mental hospitals suffer from some form of this terrible mental torture. In spite of the fact that psychiatrists identified schizophrenia (sometimes known as dementia praecox or "split personality") 50 years ago, our information about it is still scanty. We do know that the victim lives in a disordered world of his own, suffering from hallucinations and delusions. His thinking, mood and behavior are affected. Schizophrenics sometimes commit suicide and murder in response to false beliefs which overpower them.

By artificially creating a condition like schizophrenia in a normal person—as was done in my case—researchers hope to find the answers to a number of hitherto baffling questions. The psychiatrist wants to know: What does a schizophrenic feel? What does he see? What does he think? How does he think? How can he best be approached by a therapist? These answers are not easy to obtain from the chronic psychotic who has little or no insight and is usually uncommunicative. The biochemist seeks information which may finally lead to a cure for schizophrenia: What toxic substance is found in the psychotic which is absent in the body of the normal person? If this substance can be identified, then it is conceivable that a chemical agent can be created to counteract it, very much as penicillin and Aureomycin can kill certain kinds of infection. This could theoretically lead to the cure of half our mental patients.

The bizarre experiment in which I was involved was part of a research project being conducted by the Saskatchewan Schizophrenia Research group, with funds provided by the Department of National Health and Welfare, Ottawa. So far 19 volunteers have taken the drug. Eighteen of them are members of the nursing and medical staffs of mental hospitals. So far as I am aware, I am the only outsider to have taken the drug.

The results of the experiments are now being carefully studied and analyzed. No experimental drugs can ever be given to mental patients. For to further weaken their slender hold on reality would probably rule out all possibility of a cure at some future time.

I stepped into the Stygian world of schizophrenia from the officers' lounge in the Saskatchewan Hospital in Weyburn. It is a comfortable, homey living room, furnished with a soft rug, chesterfield, easy chairs, end tables, lamps and oil paintings. Preparations for the experiment had begun early on the morning of Thursday, June 18. Psychologist Ben Stefaniuk gave me a Rorschach test to measure my emotional stability. In this test, you view a series of ink blots and describe what you see in them. I passed with flying colors. This precaution is always taken; the LSD drug might have lasting effects on an emotionally unstable person.

Several preparations were made to help me recall later what I had experienced. A tape recorder stood on the table in front of me. It was to operate for four hours—the period of my most severe derangement. On either side of me were Stefaniuk and Dr. Humphry Osmond, clinical director of the Weyburn hospital. They were to interview me constantly, eliciting what I was feeling, seeing and thinking. Also present were Charles Jillings, a staff psychologist of the hospital, and Elaine Cumming, a sociologist, who carefully recorded the movement of people in and out of the room and my reactions to them. Mike Kesterton, a photographer, constantly shot pictures in color and black-and-white film both for *Maclean's* and for the project's records. This was the first LSD experiment in Saskatchewan to be recorded photographically. Throughout my psychosis various doctors were quietly ushered into the room to make observations and ask me questions.

Osmond and Stefaniuk were to be my main links with the world of reality. During the brief flashes of lucidity they were to try and help me ward off the devastating feelings of despair and fear which were to overtake me. They constantly reminded me—not always successfully—that I was Sidney Katz, a *Maclean's* editor; that I was in a hospital in Weyburn; that I had taken a drug which produced a condition like schizophrenia; that the effects would wear off before the day was over.

Past experience has shown that LSD produces such an overwhelming emotional and intellectual upheaval in the individual that the experiment must be very rigidly controlled. At no time was I left alone. Once, in a Swiss mental hospital, a practical joker sneaked a few grains of LSD into a staff nurse's coffee. The frantic girl, apparently driven to believe that she had become schizophrenic, leaped to her death from the hospital rooftop.

What follows below is a detailed description of what happened to me after I took the drug. I pieced this account together from my own vivid but distorted recollections, aided by the tape recording, Mike Kesterton's photographs, sociologist Cumming's notebooks and from later interviews with other observers who were present.

10:45 A.M. I was handed half a glass of water containing 200 one-millionths of a gram of LSD by Dr. Osmond. This amount of the drug could comfortably sit on the head of a pin. I drank it. The liquid had no taste or smell.

There were no immediate effects. The talk in the room centred about Kesterton and his cameras and equipment. Beside me on the arm of my chair was my black leather notebook in which I had hoped to record much of the experiment. At 11:02, I wrote: "My co-ordination is not so good." At 11:03: "Slight nausea." At 11:06, in a sprawling hand, "[Dr.] John Smythies enters the room." That was to be the end of my legible writing for that day.

11:07 A.M. I felt mysterious waves coming up from my stomach, traveling up my neck, through my head and then going up and around it. I experienced a growing sense of unreality. I explained, "It's a bit like getting drunk; you see things all right but you're aware that you've drunk too much and you're going to feel like heck the next day."

I suddenly became apprehensive and suspicious. I carefully examined the faces of the people in the room, feeling that possibly they were trying to do me harm. I tried to read their glances for some clue as to what giant conspiracy they were engaged in. I could hear Dr. Osmond talking clearly but his words were an unintelligible jumble. Now the waves coming up from my stomach multiplied. They seemed to run through my entire body, leave me, and continue to circulate in the air immediately around me.

11:10 A.M. Everything in the room was now becoming blurred and distorted. My eyes rested on Dr. John Clancy, a handsome dark Irishman in his mid-30s, who was sitting opposite me some 15 feet away, his chin resting on his right hand. As I looked at him, I became acutely conscious of his breathing as if I were a superelectronic stethoscope. With each breath he took, he started to change. First, the flesh from his face fell away and his head became a cadaverous caricature in frightening two-tone of blue and white. A fine, fuzzy white beard started to sprout on his chin. Compulsively, I breathed in unison with him. Now, with every inhalation and exhalation the hand which rested on his chin began to swell like a beach ball being inflated by an air pump. The hand quickly assumed the features of a hideous, purplish cloven hoof.

11:12 A.M. I reported, "Everything is becoming more unreal and bizarre." Stefaniuk asked, "Can you describe it?" As a reply, I looked at the back of my hands. My sight became microscopic. I could clearly discern every crease, pore and blemish on my skin. Each exuded its own pale light and seemed to have a life of its own. A small nicotine stain on the side of one of my fingers contained no fewer than 20 shades of color ranging from bright yellow to deep, dark brown. Suddenly, my left hand started shrinking so I hurriedly looked at the right one which was growing. It became so large that I found it difficult to hold up so I put it down.

11:14 A.M. Asked how I felt, I replied, "I'm restless, perspiring and nauseated." No sooner had I said this than I broke in, "Oh God! Look at Ben's (Stefaniuk) face!" Stefaniuk's face had grown about a third larger than its usual size. Its surface had become broad and angular, overlaid with diamond-shaped patterns. He looked like a cross between a foxlike creature and a Neanderthal man. Close diagonal parallel lines of blue light moved across his white coat. Engrossed, I was reluctant in answering his questions about what I was seeing. When he persisted, he seemed to grow more evil and cruel. The lines on his face hardened and the light grew from blue to angry purple.

I again held out my hands and experienced for the first time a terrifying hallucination that was to recur time and time again during the hours that lay ahead. Again, I could make out every mark and crease on the backs of my fingers and hands. Again, they exuded light and had a life of their own. But now the markings took a more definite form: they were short, juicy wormlike creatures that writhed and wriggled vigorously. Soon I was conscious that my hands and body were vibrating as a prelude to a shrinking process. As I watched, my fingers grew shorter and telescoped into my hand, my hand telescoped into my arm. Suddenly, I was outside of myself looking down from above. My arms were now mere stumps as if they had been amputated near the shoulder. My legs were now shrinking and withering and my skin was coarse and scaly. I felt the pressure of space closing in on me from above, forcing my head—which was now double its normal size—out of shape. I fought against this awesome, macabre transformation by trying to stretch my arms and legs but found that I was powerless. Ultimately, all that was left of me was a hard, sickly, nauseous stone located in the lower left side of my abdomen, surrounded by a greeny-yellowish vapor which poured across the floor. Never in my lifetime had I felt so ill, so frightened and so depressed all at the same time.

A minute later my body was whole again. The observers were questioning me as to what had happened. The horror was too fresh to discuss. Lights were flashing over the rug, and with each flash the designs changed. I concentrated on one of the larger designs. It appeared to be the top of some fantastic jungle flower. As I watched, it became infused with life until it was part plant, part animal. The same thing was happening to the smaller designs, until the whole scene reminded me of the floor of a tropical jungle. It was not an unpleasant sight. I felt the thrill of an explorer whose eyes are the first to behold some miracle of nature in some far-off corner of the world.

I looked at my hands and again I could feel the vibrations and contractions which preceded the hallucination that I was shrinking. I struggled against it by vigorously stretching out my arms and legs. I succeeded. "See," I said jubilantly, "I got them back again."

Now Osmond was testing the responses of a schizophrenic to a psychiatrist. "Suppose I were to say to you, that none of these hallucinations were happening; that it was all your imagination . . . how would you feel?" I hesitated. I knew that I couldn't convey the torment I was enduring. Finally, I blurted out desperately, "I'd tell you to go to hell!" He repeated the question. "It wouldn't establish any contact," I said. "I told you my problem is one of being dragged away to something terrible." My fear heightened as I spoke. "Give me your hand," I pleaded. "I want help . . . I want a hand." I grabbed Osmond's hand. The effect was one of amazing comfort. My fear greatly subsided and the room came into focus. But a few seconds later I was plunged again into the abyss of madness.

Stefaniuk began presenting me with simple problems to test the reasoning capacity of a schizophrenic. "I give you a 10-gallon pail and a seven-gallon pail and I want you to bring back three gallons of water," he said. "How would you do it?" I tried desperately to get the answer but I was unable to concentrate for more than a second at a time. "I've worked that problem out a hundred times but I can't do it now," I said. Stefaniuk asked me why. "That's the point," I said helplessly. "I can't and I don't know why I can't."

Sidney Katz took on many challenging assignments during his 15 years at Maclean's *but perhaps none more so than his terrifying experiences with LSD.*

11:28 A.M. The awareness that I was incapable of even simple reasoning threw me into a panic. I felt alone and helpless. I looked desperately around the room. I again asked Osmond for his hand. "I regard you all as my friends," I said, trying to reassure myself that this was so. "Physical contact is very important . . . something to hang on to . . . it's like a vortex . . . something unknown keeps pulling me in."

Somebody suggested that it was not all frightening—that I was capable of seeing beautiful things. I passed my hand across my face at arm's length in arclike fashion and a miracle took place. With that simple motion, I created a masterpiece of such surpassing beauty that I immediately forgot my sickness and my fear.

As my hand passed through the air, I noticed that I had 10 fingers instead of five. Each finger left in its path of movement a soft streak of light, at the end of which were delicate, polychromatic transparent bubbles. I concentrated on the streaks of "afterglow." To the accompaniment of a gentle crackling sound, they shimmered and broadened out into subtle shades of gold, silver, yellow, blue and red until they formed a mass of light from floor to ceiling. I turned to the bubbles. As I watched, they kept multiplying until I beheld a glittering, sparkling iridescent fountain, seeded with thousands of small, perfectly formed liquid-gold arrows. Compared to this, all colors I had previously seen were pallid.

I had become a great creative artist with a single sweep of my arm. I felt a proprietary interest in my vision and I was reluctant to share it with others. "You are seeing images," Stefaniuk was now repeating. "Images of what?"

I would only reply: "They keep multiplying . . . keep building up . . . they're uncontrollable," and then lapse into an absorbed silence.

I now entered a different state. Most of the time I was completely absorbed in my hallucinations and illusions. But by talking sharply to me several times or clutching my hand, Stefaniuk or Osmond could give me a flash of semi-lucidity during which I would be vaguely aware of the room and the people in it. At one point I said to Stefaniuk, "I'm clear now." But a few seconds later when I looked across at Clare Blake, the hospital recreational director who had just entered the room, he had the unmistakable face of a large pig. I could make out the smallest detail of his pinkish snout.

11:39 A.M. Osmond produced a glass of water and said, "Look into this and tell me what you see." I cautiously peered in. At first it looked like an ordinary glass of water with one of Osmond's fingers visible at the bottom. But as I watched, his finger grew whitish and fleshy and specks of black, brown and maroon appeared. These specks multiplied rapidly and gradually began to elongate. Then they became a swirling mass and began edging up the side of the glass. The mouth of the glass seemed to open up and become large enough to contain me. The swirling mass became a fast-moving vortex which seemed to hypnotize me and beckon me. Now the mouth of the glass was an enormous chasm; the murky vortex was swirling around at a breakneck speed, exuding magnetic rays which slowly but surely were sucking me in. I was petrified. I felt as cold as a block of ice. I resisted and struggled against the fatal pull. Just at the instant when the battle seemed lost, I succeeded in turning my face away from the glass. The vortex immediately lost its hold on me. Osmond was talking to me. "You haven't told us what you saw," he said. I ignored his question. I pleaded with him instead. "You've got to keep me away from that thing."

What would have happened to me had I kept looking into the glass of water? What if the macabre invisible forces had succeeded in plunging me into the black labyrinth? Would the distress have been great enough to cause permanent madness? Would the shock have been strong enough to cause my heart to stop beating? These are questions I will never be able to answer. As a matter of fact, several of the other LSD volunteers share my reactions to the glass of water.

I sat silently. I was miserable and despondent. My mind was so saturated with snatches of imagery that I couldn't describe any of it coherently. For the first time in my life I learned the real meaning of the word "dependency." I explained, "The only thing that matters to me now is that you are my friends and that I trust you." I was completely dependent on those around me to give me reassurance that I was not damned to the eternal hell of insanity. Had this reassurance not been forthcoming during my semi-lucid intervals or had I been left alone for even a minute to the mercies of my hallucinations, I am convinced that I would have perished from grief.

11:50 A.M. I was offered a drink of water. I took a sip and it tasted sour.

The thought crossed my mind that perhaps an attempt was being made to poison me so I refused to drink any more.

As I turned to talk to Osmond I caught a glimpse of the beige net curtains on the window behind me, covered with the sun's rays and blowing in the breeze. This touched off a constantly moving and changing arabesque of vines and leaves, executed in the finest filigree of some astral material which was colored lemon, saffron, orange and gold. It was a scene of great beauty and tranquility.

Stefaniuk asked me about my mood. "It's mostly one of depression," I replied. "I've got to keep hanging on." He asked if I was afraid something would happen. "It's just the terrible feeling I have," I replied. How could I explain that I was perched on the edge of an abyss of horror, and that every second I feared being toppled into it, doomed to an eternal life of indescribable pain and wretchedness?

12 noon. I was asked if I was hungry but the very idea of eating revulsed me. Osmond told me to lie down on the chesterfield and told me that he was going to place a towel over my eyes. "You are in for a pleasant surprise," he said. The contact of the soft toweling on my eyes transported me to a world a billion miles away. It was as though I was lying on my back in some fabulous oriental mosque looking into the very gates of heaven. At the very top of my vision was a soft, holy glimmering light. I had complete 360 degree vision and all around me were Gothic arches and domes, and doors opening into doors. The predominant colors were gold, silver and pearl. I could make out row upon row of tiny oriental empresses, clad in pearl-studded robes, their faces a study in peaceful bliss. All the parts of this vision constantly moved, now flowing together, now apart, now interlacing to form ever-changing designs.

12:20 P.M. I found that I was hypersensitive to sound, light and smell. Ordinarily I enjoy smoking, but now I couldn't bear to have the people around me smoking. The slightest sound in the room—the whirring and clicking of the tape recorder, a cup being set down on a table—were transformed into other sounds by my disordered brain. I heard melodies so dulcet and airy that they could only have been played by orchestras of fairies or leprechauns. Listening, my troubles seemed to disappear and I had a pleasant floating feeling.

Osmond asked me how long I had been under the drug. I couldn't answer. Too much had happened. Sometimes the time seemed to stand still; at other times it raced by. Actually, less than two hours had elapsed since the beginning of the experiment.

12:30 P.M. I suddenly leaped from my chair and rushed to the open window which overlooked the hospital's front lawn. "I hear music," I shouted, "I hear music." (Later, I discovered that the "music" was the hammering of carpenters, working on a new nurses' residence a hundred yards to my left.) I looked out and beheld a panorama of infinite beauty. The sky glittered like a pale azure crystal; embedded in it were yellow-apricot colored clouds. On my right was a vast expanse of vineyards, on which bloomed flowers which sparkled like prisms caught in the sunlight. Groups of gaily dressed men and women sat on patches of bottle-green grass having a picnic. There were no limits to my vision. I could see clearly to the horizon and then beyond. The mile-long gravel road to the town of Weyburn stretched ahead like an endless broad highway of translucent yellow glass.

I turned my gaze leftward and suddenly became aware of approaching music and the shouts of a crowd. A procession was beginning to go by. "It's like Bastille Day and the Fourth of July," I exclaimed. There were brass bands, bands of drums and pipes, bands of tambourines. I could discern the bandsmen in the distance marching by, clad in bright satins of orange, green, red and yellow. Then came marching columns of jesters, clowns, red-coated soldiers, archers in green, sailors in light blue, mounted knights with colored plumes in their headgear, turbaned Sikhs with glistening skin, ornate floats, candy-striped circus vans, ambling elephants and giraffes, Beefeaters in their Elizabethan garb, as well as contingents of other marchers whom I could not identify then and never will. They all marched, danced and skipped on their way, finally disappearing on the left. It was a million times more colorful and exciting than the Coronation procession.

12:40 P.M. Back in my seat in the room again, I was excited and elated. But a few minutes later I was again fearful. I looked up at an oil painting on the wall of a violin on a table set against a background of dark velvet drapes. The violin became swollen and moved up and down, and the drapes began to move ominously as though some grisly monster, now held captive, were about to spring to his freedom and devour me. I told Stefaniuk that I felt ill and uncomfortable. "I will suggest that you feel good," he said. Again I was put lying down on the chesterfield with the towel over my eyes. Again, I was lying on my back in the fabulous oriental mosque looking into the gates of heaven. The now familiar procession of dainty empresses in their pearl-studded robes continued just where they had left off the last time. Stefaniuk was now repeating to me, "Do you see the golden chair?" I looked carefully and a beautifully carved golden chair with a raspberry-colored tapestry seat-covering appeared. Soon dozens of similar chairs radiated out from it. "On that chair you see a beautiful woman with long golden hair, dressed in a Cellophane costume," Stefaniuk continued. "Can you see her, Sid? Can you see her?"

As he started talking about the beautiful girl with the golden hair, an amazing thing happened. The texture of my vision changed from hard materials of predominantly gold and pearl to soft, feminine materials that one associates with the boudoir—delicate pastels of shimmering silk, satin and velvet. At the same time, the fragrance of a never-to-be-manufactured perfume filled the air. But I never did see the girl with the long golden hair clad in Cellophane.

Now Stefaniuk handed me one of the cards of the Rorschach test—a card nine by five inches covered with black and colored ink spots. "Tell me what you see," he said. "We want to know why schizophrenics won't co-operate with us in Rorschach tests." I looked at the colored blots and could see that they had turned into thick enamel. Now the entire card was made of thick enamel. I felt a strange sensation in my left hand which held the card— the skin grew tight and hard. I looked down at my hand to find that the skin was now a flesh-enamel type of substance, hard, brittle and airtight. I could feel the enamel coating creeping up from my hands to my arms and down my body. Soon, I felt that I was suffocating. I quickly handed the card back to Stefaniuk and the sensation left me. I hadn't offered any explanation. "Schizophrenics won't co-operate in a Rorschach test and you won't either," Stefaniuk was saying.

1:15 P.M. Bonnie, an amiable black mongrel dog, was led to my side. "Pat her," Osmond told me. Apart from the animal's head and body alternately shrinking and elongating, there was nothing extraordinary about her. As I patted her on the head with my left hand, a strong dog odor assailed my nostrils. A few seconds later my hand and arm grew hot and heavy. I looked down at it and the skin darkened and rapidly turned into a glossy, black thick coat of hair, exactly the same as the dog's. Was I now to turn into an animal? I quickly pulled my hand away and a few seconds later cautiously peeked at it. The thick coat of hair had vanished as quickly as it had come.

1:33 P.M. The effect of the drug was beginning to wear off. Now began an eerie period, which was to last almost two hours, during which I lived alternately in two distinct worlds—the world of reality and the world of madness. I became aware that for a few seconds at a time, everything was crystal clear and normal—the room about me, my hands, the faces of my friends. But even as I rejoiced I would hear a whirring sound in my ears, the clear outlines of my surroundings would melt away, and again I would be in the nightmare realm.

Elaine Cumming, the sociologist, was now sitting beside me, her head bent over. "Is my hair coarse?" she asked. Even as she spoke it became coarse and prickly to my touch. Clouds of black, purple and brown seemed to be pressing down on me from above. The skin on her face was erupting and heaving until it became eczematous and scaly. "Is my hair coarse?" she asked again. Now her eyes became sunken, her nose long and droopy, her hair matted and disheveled. She looked like a sorceress, a harridan—a weird sister from a fairy tale by Grimm come suddenly to life to haunt me. "Is my hair coarse?" she asked. Now she was leering at me. I examined her, with considerable disquietude, then removed my hand from her hair and turned away from her. A few seconds later the witch had become Elaine Cumming.

2:30 P.M. The periods of lucidity were now becoming more frequent and lasting a little longer—perhaps 10 or 20 seconds. This gave me time to perceive clearly the difference between sanity and insanity. I was thrown into a state of panic. What if I were never to recover? What if I were doomed to spend the rest of my life, torn between the two worlds? But before I could consider the matter for long, I would be back again in the world of madness where the furniture flew around and the walls swayed.

In my next period of clarity I appealed to Osmond and Stefaniuk for reassurance. Osmond told me, "I've taken the drug, so has Stefaniuk, so have several other doctors and staff members. They've all come out of it. So will you." But I remained unconvinced. A few minutes later, Stefaniuk urged me to keep describing what I saw. I couldn't. I had no stomach for it. I was too stricken with fear. In the condition I was in, I would have to be kept in a mental hospital. I thought of my wife and two little boys. Who would care for them? Had I been fair to them in taking the drug?

Stefaniuk was persistent. "It's important for the experiment that you continue to report everything you feel and see. I know you want to get out of it but we want more material from you." I looked at my hands despondently and began, "My hands get bigger and smaller . . . When I keep looking, every mark comes to life . . . I see different colors in my skin and that suggests a lot of different things . . ." A few minutes later Stefaniuk again posed the problem of how you measure off three gallons of water with a 10-gallon pail. This time I could work it out.

3 P.M. The hallucinations ceased. I found myself slumped on the chesterfield, perspiring, my shirt unbuttoned, and every inch of my body utterly exhausted. I could now feel the gentle prairie breeze from the window playing across my face. I looked out and saw the warm, blue sky and the friendly sun. It was all very reassuring.

The acute stages of my madness had lasted for over four hours. But my ordeal was not yet over. There are many gradations of mental illness, short of experiencing hallucinations, which are very distressing. I was to learn something about them during the next eight hours.

I entered a brief period of grandiosity and expansiveness. My spirits soared. The hallucinations had vanished but I was still capable of seeing illusions, i.e. distortions of an existing object. I discovered this when I was asked to come to the river's edge and look down. The sunlight was playing on the ripples of the water's surface, throwing off reflections. I concentrated on a single ripple and soon the rays of reflected light began to wriggle significantly, then multiply, spread out and interlace. I became so engrossed by the illusion that I momentarily lost consciousness of my surroundings. My sense of distance completely left me and I felt myself being drawn toward the water.

I repeated the experiment a little later standing on a dam, watching tons of water plunging into a gorge 30 feet below. I didn't feel like destroying myself, but again I felt myself being sucked into the water. I hurried away to a safer spot, perspiring and sick at my stomach. Could this have been the irresistible impulse which mysteriously leads some schizophrenics to commit suicide?

5:30 P.M. I was now in the hospital canteen. I was jumpy and on edge. Osmond explained that my body was suffering from shock as it emerged from the drug and prescribed a heavy sugar diet. In the next few hours I was to consume seven chocolate bars, two packages of Life Savers, six Cokes, and two large pieces of cake coated with a heavy icing. It didn't result in nausea and soothed me somewhat.

Osmond and Stefaniuk now left me briefly and I retired to my quarters with Mike Kesterton who was to take care of me. I now entered a mood of depression and apprehension. I felt alone and desolate. I was totally incapable of any emotion.

7:30 P.M. My apprehension reached the point where it was almost intolerable. My whole being was ridden by a powerful fear that something horrible was about to happen. It occupied all my attention; it prevented me from thinking about anything else or enjoying anything else. During my stay in hospital I had met a few patients who were in that condition perpetually. They had no hallucinations, no illusions—only a persistent anxiety which totally crippled them. I asked myself, "In the absence of more dramatic symptoms, how could they convincingly explain to an outsider the true extent of their suffering?"

I found it impossible to stay still. I was restless and I wanted to be outside and moving. Kesterton and I were joined by Chuck Jillings and Al Hauser of the hospital staff and we walked through the hospital grounds. A flight of birds rising from a grove of trees appeared strange and alarmed me. We stopped to watch a ball game. My attention was attracted by a woman leaning against a fence with a dead child over her shoulder. I approached her cautiously. I was relieved to learn that it was only an illusion caused by her arm and a colored windbreaker resting on the fence beside her.

9:30 P.M. We walked five miles or so before it grew dark. Back in my quarters with Kesterton, I was still apprehensive. I found that I derived some comfort from doing familiar things—taking a shower, drying myself with a soft towel, rinsing out a pair of socks. Later, I was lying in bed in my pyjamas when Kesterton casually announced that he might wander down to the dining room for a cup of coffee. This threw me into a panic. I didn't want to be left alone and I didn't have the strength to get dressed and join him. I breathed easier when he announced that he had changed his mind and would stay.

At 10 o'clock I was lying in bed with the lights turned off, Kesterton in a cot beside me. I tossed for two or three hours, unable and unwilling to go to sleep. Whenever I closed my eyes I would see an endless technicolor procession of bizarre and outlandish masklike faces, grinning and jeering at me. I could escape only by opening my eyes and looking through the transom at the bright light in the hall or at the clear outline of the window, framed against the clear night prairie sky.

I was in a dilemma. Dr. Osmond had given me two capsules of sodium amytal which he said would put me to sleep. But, after my LSD experience, I was reluctant to put any more drugs into my body. And even if I did take the sedative and fall asleep, what guarantee did I have that the masklike faces would not still be there? And if they were, would I be able to escape from them by rousing myself?

By one o'clock in the morning I was so exhausted physically and mentally that I no longer had the energy to continue debating with myself. With my last drop of strength, I reached for the capsules on the bureau beside me and swallowed them.

I awoke next morning at nine o'clock from a deep dreamless sleep. The events of the preceeding day came rushing back to me. I looked cautiously about the room. My clothes were neatly laid out on the chair; my wallet, keys, pen and cigarettes were on the bureau. Outside the sky was blue and the sun was shining. I was happy and relieved to find that everything was nice and normal. The only visible effect of the LSD experience on me was a hangover, but it was no more painful than the morning-after-the-night-before variety.

I was starving. I showered, dressed in clean clothes, picked up Mike Kesterton and grabbed a cab into Weyburn. I walked along the street looking at the passing people and glancing at the store windows, rejoicing that I was back again in the land of the living. We went to a restaurant where I demolished large quantities of orange juice, eggs, toast and coffee. Food never tasted better. I thought of my wife and my children and went to a store to buy them some gifts.

My thoughts now turned to the patients in the mental hospital. I was fortunate. I had endured the torments of hell for only 12 hours and now I was free. But how about them? Many of them have been mentally ill for five, 10 and even 15 years. How long did a single tortured hour appear to be to them? A day? A month? A year? An eternity?

I returned to the hospital and walked through the wards alone. In the past, I have spent many, many hours in mental hospitals both as a student psychiatric social worker and as an observer. But on this day, I saw everything through different eyes. A tall and gaunt schizophrenic patient came up to me, grasped my hand for a few seconds, and then without uttering a word stole away. I recalled how desperately I had clutched at Osmond's hand. What endless vortex was this man fleeing from? A blond youth in his late twenties stood trancelike, staring at a shadow on the wall, an ecstatic smile frozen on his face. How many millions of miles away was he?

I left Weyburn with a sense of urgency. Half of all our hospital beds are filled with mental patients. Half of these again suffer from schizophrenia. We don't yet know the cause of this disease but there is good reason to suspect that it is due to an error in body chemistry. A few specks of a drug changed me, a normal person, into a madman. Is it, therefore, not entirely possible that the schizophrenic is a person whose body constantly manufactures minute particles of a similarly poisonous substance?

If this should be the case science can only hope to identify and counteract it when the funds available for research are in the millions, not in the thousands as at present. We should insist that our best doctors, technicians and laboratories be immediately sent to rescue the schizophrenic from his endless hell. No goal can be more urgent or more humane. I know.

SCHIZOPHRENIA *remains a debilitating disease that eludes a cure. An estimated 300,000 Canadians will be diagnosed with the disease at some point in their lives. The direct cost of treating the disease is estimated at $2.3 billion annually, plus $2 billion in indirect costs.*

Afterword

ELVIS PRESLEY ON ED SULLIVAN. Jean Beliveau at the Colisée. Brush cuts and white bucks. Ah, the Fifties. In Canada, they were simpler times, days of post-war peace and prosperity—even if, for many teens, they were decidedly unexciting. It's almost as if the protective cocoon of the Fifties served as an incubator for the trends of the wild and woolly Sixties. *Maclean's* was there, as true as maple syrup and seemingly as dependable as Percy Saltzman, CBC's chalk-flipping weatherman. The articles from *Maclean's* in this volume capture the spirit of that era which, while less boisterous than those to come, pointed the country in some promising directions.

The 36 articles in the book were selected and edited by Michael Benedict, Editorial Director (New Ventures), who has launched two other *Maclean's* collections: *Canada At War* (1997) and *Canada On Ice: 50 Years of Great Hockey* (1998). In the Fifties, *Maclean's* was *the* place where magazine writers wanted to work. For most of the decade, the legendary Ralph Allen presided over a talented stable, including Pierre Berton, Blair Fraser, Peter C. Newman, Sidney Katz and Barbara Moon, along with regular contributors June Callwood and Trent Frayne. Their work graces this collection, bridging the gap to a time that may be almost a half century away, but to some of us seems like only yesterday.

ROBERT LEWIS
EDITOR-IN-CHIEF

Photo Credits